The makers of public policy

The makers of public policy:

AMERICAN POWER GROUPS AND THEIR IDEOLOGIES

R. Joseph Monsen, Jr.
ASSOCIATE PROFESSOR, COLLEGE OF BUSINESS ADMINISTRATION
UNIVERSITY OF WASHINGTON, SEATTLE, WASHINGTON

Mark W. Cannon
CHAIRMAN, DEPARTMENT OF POLITICAL SCIENCE
BRIGHAM YOUNG UNIVERSITY, PROVO, UTAH

McGraw-Hill Book Company

NEW YORK   ST. LOUIS   SAN FRANCISCO

TORONTO   LONDON   SYDNEY

[1965]

The makers of public policy

preface

Americans are living in a new age—an age in which almost all decisions of individuals, groups, and businesses are affected by government. From the time when, as an infant, he is issued a social security number when his grandparents deposit money in a bank for him, until his retirement when he receives his social security pension, government policy determines or regulates much of a man's life. A law tells him at what age he may accept employment; when he must undergo compulsory military training; and when he enters business, government prescribes many of the decisions he can make. With this inexorable trend toward greater government influence over our society and economy, we are constantly plagued by the questions *"How* is public policy determined, and *who* really makes it?"

Agreement is widespread that our farm policy, for instance, has been an irrational and costly failure, yet when laymen or students ask, "Who is responsible for such a program?" and "How was it allowed to develop?", the answer is too often shrugged off as simply "politics." This, of course, begs the question and leaves it more unanswered than before. Today American society is so complex that general issues have many facets combining political, social, and economic elements. It is not possible to describe a problem or its solution as solely political or economic. Too often scholars ignore the major issues of our day for the study of neater, but unfortunately less significant, problems.

As Edward S. Mason emphasized in a presidential address to the American Economic Association, the widespread ignorance of the influence of interest groups and their ideologies on public policy often handicaps reasoned policy formulation.[1] Yet to what book could an interested indi-

[1] Edward S. Mason, "Interests, Ideologies, Stability and Growth," *American Economic Review,* 53 (March, 1963), 1–17.

vidual turn to find the official goals and ideologies of the major groups which make American public policy? It was this lacuna which motivated the authors to make this study.

Although the growing impact of government policy is recognized, the manner in which it is made and the men who dominate its formulation are often obscure to the general public. Even many successful businessmen fail to realize the cardinal role government now plays in their decision making. United States Steel's Roger Blough was publicly chagrined and embarrassed when he was forced to rescind a price increase as a result of presidential opposition in 1962. Such incidents illustrate that the successful executive must understand the environment of business (in all its public connotations) if he is to function effectively. Hence a main focus of business schools must be increasingly upon the making of public policy. Realization of the need for understanding is seemingly coming more slowly to businessmen and business schools than to other groups. In an attempt to shed greater light on the making of public policy, this book outlines briefly the goals and ideologies of the major national policy-making groups.

The focus here is largely upon public policy at the national level— with the notable exception of the public school teachers, who thus far have directed most of their attention to state and local levels. The limitations of space necessarily impose some constraints upon what topics can be handled. Thus foreign policy is generally given less consideration in order to concentrate more fully upon domestic policy. Likewise, the major power groups considered here are largely occupational groups which are dominant forces shaping our domestic public policy. While in some cases it is possible to break the ideological groups presented here down further, the decision of the authors has been to use the largest ideological groupings possible that are meaningful in issues of public policy to simplify and highlight major ideological and policy conflicts at the national level. It is recognized that each occupational group has deviant minorities, and such divisions are explained in the pertinent chapters. However, the emphasis is on the dominant ideological themes of the groups which battle in the political arena. Where minority positions are influential in policy making, they are treated in some detail. This decision has made it possible, we believe, to concentrate attention on the major national power groups and their ideologies in such a way as to avoid the confusion to the reader that a substantially larger number of categories would entail.

Although most public policy issues in the press are discussed in what are really ideological terms of one group or another, it is not always easy to identify immediately which group is espousing a particular argument. Thus this study succinctly attempts to present, for the first time in a single volume, the *ideologies* of these major groups which largely determine public policy in America. It is hoped that this compilation may prove both interesting and useful; for, heretofore, the official positions and ideologies of the groups have been scattered in numerous pamphlets, articles, and books. The conflicts and parallels of goals and ideologies between the various major groups of our society stand out much more clearly when presented in this concise form. Then it becomes easier to recognize the arguments and propaganda presented by the groups in their struggles to influence and control public policy.

It is hoped that this book will be interesting to general readers, to students and teachers, and to participants in the political struggle. The ever-widening interest in the national power struggle and policy making enables this book to be helpful in particular classes in political science, economics, business, sociology, history, and education. In addition to filling a lacuna which exists in these disciplines, particularly regarding the ideologies of the most powerful American economic groupings, this book offers three general hopes: first, that greater awareness may be gained about which groups dominate our legislative process and how they operate in the making of public policy; second, that by succinctly stating the positions and ideologies of the various major power groups in one volume it will be easier correctly to ascribe to a particular group the propaganda and arguments popularly heard regarding major domestic issues; third, that such information can raise discussions of public policy to a more rational and informed level in this country.

This book was initiated by the senior author, an economist, out of interest generated by his previous study of American economic ideologies, *Modern American Capitalism: Ideologies and Issues*.[2] In order, however, to make possible a broad and realistic approach to public policy making, the book is necessarily interdisciplinary. The coauthor is a political scientist who has had considerable personal experience in congressional politics on both House and Senate staffs.

Help in the writing of this book, which covers a diverse array of groups, is gratefully acknowledged. Valuable comments were received from Theodore J. Krepps, Emeritus Professor of Business Economics, Stanford University; Sumner Marcus, Chairman, Department of Business and Its Environment, University of Washington; Paul Y. Hammond, The RAND Corporation; Robert S. Jordon, Assistant to the President, George Washington University; Stephen Horn, Legislative Assistant to Senator Thomas Kuchel; Robert J. Huckshorn, Associate Director of the National Center for Education in Politics; Paul Tillet, Assistant Director of the Eagleton Institute of Politics; Cornelius P. Cotter, Chairman, Political Science Department, University of Wichita; Phillip S. Wilder, Jr., Wabash College; John H. Kessel, University of Washington, Political Science Department; Pierre

[2] R. Joseph Monsen, Jr., *Modern American Capitalism: Ideologies and Issues* (Boston: Houghton Mifflin Company, 1963).

Carasso, New York City; and at Brigham Young University David K. Hart, Louis C. Midgely, and Karl N. Snow, political scientists; James T. Duke and William G. Dyer, sociologists; Stephen L. Alley, Chairman, Education Department; Ralph Smith, Graduate Education Department.

Far more than the usual absolution from responsibility is proffered to these scholars. A number of them have only seen portions of the book dealing with their specialities. However, their helpful comments are all gratefully acknowledged.

The authors also wish to recognize the considerable help of those who aided in preparing materials pertinent to the specific chapters. Thanks particularly go to Thomas S. Carlson, Peter G. Prina, Floyd LaMond Tullis, David H. Thomas, B. Wilford Daynes, Lennis M. Knighton, Perrin Walker, Doran Hunter, Graham Dodd, Clifford G. Edmunds, Kenneth Godfry, Jean Fletcher, and Frederick W. Crook.

In summary, this book attempts to cut across economic, political, and sociological disciplines in pursuit of answers to our central questions: "Who makes public policy, and what are their goals and ideologies?"

R. Joseph Monsen, Jr.
Mark W. Cannon

Contents

Preface   v

CHAPTER 1: INTRODUCTION   1

THE DEFINITION AND ROLE OF GROUPS   5
WHAT DETERMINES GROUP POWER   10
GROUPS ARE CONTROLLED BY MINORITIES   17
IDEOLOGIES AND GOALS   19
THE PURPOSE OF THE BOOK   22

formal power groups

CHAPTER 2: BUSINESS   24

INTRODUCTION   24
BUSINESS IDEOLOGY   26
THE CLASSICAL BUSINESS IDEOLOGY (NAM)   28
THE SMALL BUSINESS IDEOLOGY   43
THE MANAGERIAL IDEOLOGY (CED)   46
A CASE STUDY OF BUSINESS IN POLITICS   56
CONCLUDING SUMMARY   60

CHAPTER 3: LABOR   64

INTRODUCTION   64
THE IDEOLOGY OF LABOR (AFL–CIO)   74
A CASE STUDY OF UNION LOBBYING   86
CONCLUDING SUMMARY   93

CHAPTER 4: AGRICULTURE   96

INTRODUCTION   96
THE POWER GROUPS OF AGRICULTURE AND THEIR IDEOLOGIES   101
The Farmers Union (The Farmers Educational and Cooperative Union)   102
The National Grange (The National Grange—Order of the Patrons of
    Husbandry)   108
The Farm Bureau (The American Farm Bureau Federation)   114
FUTURE FARM POLICY   121
THE CASE OF A LOOPHOLE   125
CONCLUDING SUMMARY   128

CHAPTER 5: NEGROES 133

INTRODUCTION   133
IDEOLOGY   135
DISTINCTIVE CHARACTERISTICS OF NEGRO GROUPS   141
THE WHITE REACTION   146
THE CASE OF THE MARCH ON WASHINGTON   147
CONCLUDING SUMMARY   148

CHAPTER 6: PUBLIC SCHOOL TEACHERS 150

INTRODUCTION   150
CHARACTERISTICS OF THE NATIONAL TEACHERS' ORGANIZATIONS   154
Ideologies of the AFT and the NEA Compared and Contrasted   160
THE CASE OF LABOR'S AMERICAN FEDERATION OF TEACHERS IN
    NEW YORK CITY   171
CONCLUDING SUMMARY   175

informal power groups

CHAPTER 7: INTELLECTUALS 177

INTRODUCTION   177
CONSENSUS AMONG INTELLECTUALS   180
INFLUENCE OF INTELLECTUALS   184
CAUSES OF INTELLECTUALS' LEFT-OF-CENTER IDEOLOGY   191
THE IDEOLOGY OF THE AMERICAN INTELLECTUALS   194
THE CASE OF THE REPUBLICANS COURTING THE INTELLECTUALS   208
CONCLUDING SUMMARY   218

CHAPTER 8: THE CIVIL BUREAUCRACY 222

INTRODUCTION   222
STRATEGIC POSITION OF CIVIL BUREAUCRACIES   228
IDEOLOGY OF THE CIVIL BUREAUCRACY   236
INHERENT CHARACTERISTICS OF BUREAUCRACY AND SOCIETY'S DEMAND FOR
    EFFICIENCY   239
CHANGING VIEW OF THE ROLE OF GOVERNMENT   241
THE CASE OF THE FOREIGN SERVICE ACT OF 1946   247
CONCLUDING SUMMARY   254

CHAPTER 9: THE MILITARY BUREAUCRACY 258

INTRODUCTION   258
THE GROWTH OF MILITARY POWER   264
THE MILITARY'S USE OF ORGANIZATIONS, PUBLIC RELATIONS, AND POLITICS   270
CIVIL–MILITARY RELATIONS   282
MILITARY IDEOLOGY   291
THE CASE OF THE HEBERT PROBE   298
CONCLUDING SUMMARY   305

conclusion

CHAPTER 10: THE DANGERS OF SUCCESS: CONSEQUENCES OF FULLY IMPLEMENTING EACH IDEOLOGY 308

CHAPTER 11: HOW AMERICAN DEMOCRACY REALLY WORKS 317

THE SOCIAL FUNCTION OF GROUPS AND IDEOLOGIES   329
POLITICIANS AND PARTIES   331
CODA   334

Appendix   337
Index   343

I
introduction

The makers of public policy—and their goals and ideologies—are strangely
unidentified to the American public. Government decision making is not
simply the congressional voting process that many suppose. A knowledge
of the major occupational groups in our economy and the ideologies which
rationalize and guide their actions dramatically reveals the key factors influencing the inner process of public policy making in this country.

In America, as in most of the world, power rests ultimately and increasingly with the national government. How our laws and regulations,
which compose what we call public policy, are made is of critical importance to all of us who are subject to those laws. The social structure of the
United States is composed of numerous independent status power pyra-
mids—based largely upon occupation. The major exception is the Negroes.
However, dissatisfaction with low occupational status is a significant part
of their power drive.

While every individual could be classified on some sort of scale as to
political, economic, or social power, today power to affect public policy
rests mainly upon an individual's relationship to a major group or organization. Single individuals in this country, unless affiliated with some power
group, seldom influence the course of government.

The major formally organized groups within business and the professions, labor, agriculture, and public school teaching, and the major
informally organized groups such as the intellectuals, the civil and military
bureaucracies (the latter allied with veterans organizations) compose, with
the Negroes, the major makers of public policy. All except the Negroes
and the veterans are occupational groups.

Religion, which once could have been easily classified as a major power factor, no longer ranks as a basic determinant of general public policy, outside of certain regional areas in this country. Even the Catholics, for instance, have considerably less impact on public policy today than is usually thought. As time and conditions change, so do the groups who wield power within societies.

Occupation has become the major tie that binds people together into common economic interest groups. It is through these organized groups that influence is exerted on Congress. The force of tradition and family no longer dominates our mode of thinking or even our style of life. Each generation is now expected to find its place, its goals, and even its consumption patterns in relation to the peer group—usually occupational—with which it identifies. Hence, the major occupational power groups in this country are held together not only by economic interest but also by common ideologies and styles of consumption.

That economic differences in America produce the "most common and durable" political factions was noted long ago by James Madison in the tenth *Federalist* paper. An understanding of the most powerful economic factions of our modern society, with respect to both their economic aims and their ideological expressions, helps explain our little-understood but vitally important public policy-making process. The system of American government is one in which many groups struggle to control or influence government so that laws and actions will favor their own interests. A knowledge of the most powerful and influential groups in our society opens the door to understanding the making of our public policy. Earl Latham describes this group combat as follows:

What may be called public policy is actually the equilibrium reached in the group struggle at any given moment, and it represents a balance which the contending factions or groups constantly strive to weigh in their favor. . . . The legislature referees the group struggle, ratifies the victories of the successful coalitions, and records the terms of the surrenders, compromises, and conquests in the form of statutes.[1]

The political role of groups was recognized as early as Plato and Aristotle five centuries before Christ. In the Renaissance, Machiavelli followed Aristotle's lead and made group conflict the foundation of his "equilibrium politics, the basis of both stability and liberty."[2] Other pioneering leaders in the area of group theory included Montesquieu, Burke, Marx, and de Tocqueville. Arthur Bentley, in his book *The Process of Govern-*

[1] Earl Latham, "The Group Basis of Politics: Notes for a Theory," in Heinz Eulau, Samuel J. Eldersveld, and Morris Janowitz (eds.), *Political Behavior* (New York: The Free Press of Glencoe, 1956), p. 239.

[2] W. G. Carleton, "Political Science and the Group Process," *The South Atlantic Quarterly,* 54 (third quarter, 1955), 340.

ment, written in 1908, suggested a completely new American perspective for the study of politics and attempted, with the so-called school of "analytical pluralists," to investigate the process and consequences of groups' political roles.[3] A few such analysts are Pendleton Herring, E. E. Schattschneider, David Truman, and Earl Latham.[4]

While this book draws attention to the policy-making role of the dominant economic groups, it also recognizes that legislators are more than reflections of the principal groups which helped to elect them. It is true that legislators are dependent upon key groups for their election, and there is considerable implicit "buying" and "selling" of reciprocal support in the political marketplace. This inevitable bargaining process in a representative government runs counter to one sentiment in our national character—that public officials should stand uncompromisingly for what is "right" regardless of the consequences. The fact that public officials rarely adopt such a pose, but rather are negotiators and compromisers, has contributed to a degradation of their character in American humor.

Two centuries ago, for example, Adam Smith described the politician as an "insidious and crafty animal."[5] In one of Mark Twain's cynical comments he asserted that "there is no distinct native American criminal class except in Congress."[6] Wendell Phillips said that "politicians are like the bones of a horse's foreshoulder—not a straight one in it."[7]

While such amusing statements may suggest a distaste for politics, they even more significantly suggest a common failure to appreciate the functions fulfilled by the political process.

Stated very simply, in any society there are both positive and negative demands on government.[8] These demands are not likely to have much political impact if expressed by only a few citizens. To carry weight individuals must represent, or be represented by, significant groups of people who can exercise political power. As McClosky and Dahlgren phrased it: "The primary group is an essential bridge between the individual and the 'great society.' "[9] Thus interests come to be articulated largely by collec-

---

[3] For an analysis see, for example, Leo Weinstein, "The Group Approach: Arthur F. Bentley," in Herbert J. Storing (ed.), *Essays on the Scientific Study of Politics* (New York: Holt, Rinehart and Winston, Inc., 1962), pp. 151–224.

[4] See particularly David B. Truman, *The Governmental Process* (New York: Alfred A. Knopf, Inc., 1951).

[5] Speech of Dr. Joseph F. Menez at Notre Dame University on "Politics as a Vocation," *Congressional Record,* 86th Congress, 2d Session (February 15, 1960), A124445.

[6] *Ibid.*

[7] *Ibid.*

[8] A prominent theoretical analysis of political systems is found in the Introduction of Gabriel A. Almond and James S. Coleman, *The Politics of the Developing Areas* (Princeton, N.J.: Princeton University Press, 1960), pp. 3–64.

[9] Herbert McClosky and Harold E. Dahlgren, "Primary Group Influence in Party Loyalty," *American Political Science Review,* 53, 3 (September, 1959), 757.

tions of like-minded people. By contrast, there would be chaos if there were no groups through which individuals could obtain political expression. Peak associations which are composed of many lesser associations are generally more influential in the policy-making process than are the multiplicity of smaller groups.

The diversity of interests of various segments must be aggregated and reconciled into the making of public policy. This function is carried out partly by peak groups and partly by politicians and parties. When the political process is viewed in this light, it is clear that negotiating and inducing compromise among the competing demands of major power groups is a necessary function rather than a regrettable evil. As Edmund Burke observed: "All government . . . is founded on compromise and barter."[10]

The interaction between the politician and the power groups of his constituency allows room for substantial creative activity on the part of the politician as he combines personal values and concepts with the mix of power group positions in formulating his own stands. Thus he may have wide latitude in choosing his own positions from his personal reasoning in issues which are not basic to the power groups and the political party which he must accommodate. If he feels strongly on a specific issue, even though his stand is clearly opposed by his party and significant power groups in his constituency, he may still succeed in his deviation provided he is able to accommodate these groups in other important matters.

The skill of the politician determines his latitude in taking deviant positions. If he is out of harmony with some key groups, he may even be able to form a new majority coalition of groups with which he is in greater harmony. In extreme cases politicians have even changed parties, as Senator Wayne Morse did. It must also be kept in mind that all groups have dissident and shifting minorities. In fact, "The larger the group, the more likely it is that it will be made up of people with different interests and with a wide range of intensity with respect to their interests."[11] This means that "legislators and administrators if they have the courage need not be bludgeoned by the representatives of many special interest groups . . . but may be left free to work out programs that reflect more nearly the general interests."[12] Generally, however, politicians who succeed in being elected have a natural affinity toward the interests of, and often long membership in, the dominant groups and parties of their constituencies.[13]

[10] Menez.

[11] Lewis A. Froman, Jr., *People and Politics: An Analysis of the American Political System* (Englewood Cliffs, N.J.: Prentice-Hall, Inc., 1962), p. 35.

[12] V. O. Key, Jr., *Politics, Parties, and Pressure Groups* (New York: Thomas Y. Crowell Company, 1947), p. 615.

[13] See Lewis A. Froman, Jr., "Inter-party Constituency Differences and Congressional Voting Behavior," *American Political Science Review*, 62 (March, 1963), 57–61.

When a public official is out of harmony, he is often replaced. This happened to such a well-known Congressman as Brooks Hays (D, Arkansas). In the face of strong pro-segregationist sentiment, he remained moderate and was dismissed.

National legislative leadership may give such prominence to a legislator that it strengthens his independence from local interests. However, the defeat at the polls of Senate Majority Leader Ernest McFarland (D, Arizona) in 1952 and Senate Majority Whip Earle Clements (D, Kentucky) in 1956 shows that even with national fame and position, politicians are more secure when they satisfy local power groups.

Our emphasis on the importance of groups in policy making recognizes a creative role of political leaders in which their intelligence, reason, and conscience are intermingled with group pressures.[14] The politician's role in the process of compromise does not suggest low character and integrity. James Farley stated that he had "found more truth telling" and "sincerity" among politicians than among any other group with whom he had associated.[15] Leonard Hall similarly insisted that "a politician's greatest asset is his word. If his word isn't good, he doesn't last long."[16]

The emphasis on the major power groups is not intended to suggest that might makes right.[17] Each individual must judge policy outcomes by his personal set of values. But the group emphasis does provide the most realistic method of viewing the formation of government policy.

THE DEFINITION AND ROLE OF GROUPS

The term "group" denotes one of the outstanding political uncertainties. Its range of definitions is vast, varying between the very general and the notably specific. Philip Monypenny defines a group as "a system of force whose state at any given time is an index of policies being pursued by government."[18] Each political scholar shades his definition to fit his particular disciplinary specialty. David Truman suggests a group to be "a pattern of interaction between individuals."[19] Following the lead of the above-men-

14 See Peter Odegard, "The Group Basis of Politics: A New Name for an Ancient Myth," *Western Political Quarterly*, 11 (September, 1958), 689.

15 Menez.

16 *Ibid.*

17 For illustrations of legislators who displayed courage in opposing intensely felt views of dominant interest see John F. Kennedy, *Profiles in Courage* (New York: Harper & Row, Publishers, Incorporated, 1961).

18 Philip Monypenny, "Political Science, and the Study of Groups," *Western Political Quarterly*, 7 (June, 1954), 190.

19 W. J. M. Mackenzie, "Pressure Groups: The 'Conceptual Framework,'" *Political Studies*, 3 (1955), 253.

tioned scholars, the authors have taken the liberty of defining the term to comprehend both the generalities and the specifics of this study. *Groups, as the term is used here, are essentially composed of individuals bound together in varying degrees by either common interests, goals, attitudes, beliefs, or interactions.*

Even though an individual in our society may belong to numerous groups, he generally feels closely identified with only a few. Much of the membership of national power groups, therefore, is made up of passive or indifferent members. Overlapping membership may put an individual under cross pressure which sometimes reduces the intensity of his commitment on a particular stand. In such cases he will adhere to the group which has the greatest command of his loyalties.

All groups could generally be considered "power groups" since they "concentrate human wit, energy and muscle power for the achievement of perceived purposes."[20] Power groups, as considered by the authors, refer to the aggregations which influence legislation and public policy and other matters. These vary considerably in influence. Certain "veto" groups[21] may carry great weight on a single issue, such as the American Medical Association, which defeated more powerful groups, such as labor, in preventing the enactment of government health insurance laws.

Other amalgamations, such as the AFL-CIO, are involved in most of the major economic issues. The most puissant groups, therefore, are those which influence policy over a wide spectrum. The power nexus in the United States today is in the hands of perhaps a dozen of these major groups whose potency rests on their constant ability to influence lawmakers on a large number of issues. These groups include those with a minimum of formal organization, such as the intellectual community, as well as those which are highly organized, such as the chambers of commerce.

Groups arise out of needs which can be fulfilled better socially than individually. A major impulse toward organization is *self-expression,* whether politically, religiously, socially, philanthropically, athletically, or otherwise. The other major impulse toward organization is *security,* particularly economic.[22] The success of a group, therefore, depends upon its ability to satisfy its members' needs for self-expression and security.

As a society increases in size and economic complexity, associations proliferate. Thus, although de Tocqueville was surprised at the number of associations he observed in America more than a century ago, the number which existed then was small compared with the number today. This pro-

---

[20] Latham in Eulau et al., p. 235.

[21] See David Riesman, *The Lonely Crowd* (New Haven, Conn.: Yale University Press, 1950), pp. 242–248.

[22] W. Lloyd Warner, *American Life* (Chicago: The University of Chicago Press, 1962), p. 31.

liferation of groups has occurred because the country's growing urban and industrial complexity multiplies the specific needs which can be served by groups. Greater leisure and wealth provide the time and money required for group activity, and the increased size of economic and political units magnifies the need of the individual to belong to associations. Wilson suggests that though these groups have always satisfied basic needs they have not always been taken into account by American political thought.[23]

There is a correlation between industrialization and the growing role of the government in the economy. This is illustrated quantitatively by the fact that in substantially underdeveloped countries government tends to spend 10 per cent of the gross national product, whereas in highly industrialized nations the government sector tends to be 30 per cent.[24] In addition to this relative growth of government expenditures, there is also an increase in governmental intervention in the economy, as exemplified by the United States since the 1930s.

Thus no one escapes the power and impact of government rules and regulations today. The economic well-being and even the survival (e.g., antitrust laws) of existing groups depend upon their success in winning government protection and favors and in preventing damage by government, such as that caused by heavy taxation. The result is that we have more than 6,000 trade associations[25] in this country whose growing focus of activities is legislative and executive lobbying. This figure does not begin to count the component units of these associations, such as individual corporations, which also lobby. These organizations recognize that the degree to which legislative, administrative, and judicial outcomes benefit or damage them depends upon their success in the political coliseum. As a result of the shift from a market to a mixed economy with considerable political intervention, corporate executives recognize that they cannot be concerned with production and marketing problems only. They must also be alert to governmental reaction to their decisions. This was dramatically illustrated in early 1962 when President Kennedy successfully insisted, by coercive threats, that the steel companies rescind their announced price increases.

Even such idealistically oriented groups as public school teachers are becoming more politically militant because they view this device as the necessary means of obtaining adequate school budgets in the face of rising competition for public funds.

Although numerous associations functioned more than a century ago,

[23] Francis G. Wilson, "Public Opinion: Theory for Tomorrow," *Journal of Politics,* 16, 4 (November, 1954), p. 615.

[24] Karl W. Deutsch, "Social Mobilization and Political Development," *American Political Science Review,* 55 (September, 1961), 493.

[25] *The World Book Encyclopedia* (Chicago: Field Enterprises, 1963), vol. 14, p. 282.

the American ethos at that time was based upon the intellectual heritage of John Locke and Adam Smith.[26] Individualism was emphasized, and the units of economic and political society were viewed as rational atomistic individuals. In this atmosphere tightly knit groups were viewed with suspicion and hostility, and violence erupted against such cohesive groups as the Masons, Catholics, and Mormons.[27] In contemporary America, by contrast, in the age of industrial giantism, cohesive organization is not only tolerated but recognized as an administrative necessity.

Individuals belong to numerous occupational, educational, social, fraternal, religious, and veterans groups. Fortunately, there are many overlapping memberships which tend to lessen some of the harshness of group combat.

While membership in several associations may put an individual under political cross pressures, his occupational association, affecting his pocketbook, will usually dominate. Additionally, the economic associations normally have more power than the other groups in the political system. Although the Catholics are credited with stopping Federal aid to education, Catholic pressure simply supplemented other economic and ideological pressures. In reality, the opposition of the chambers of commerce is probably more potent than Catholic resistance to Federal aid to education.

Another example occurred where members of societies for the prevention of cruelty to animals worked to obtain humane slaughter laws. This group sometimes wrote more letters and made more numerous personal visits to congressmen than any other interest group. However, because of meat-packer resistance, it took years before even a weak compromise law could be enacted in 1958. This law authorized the Secretary of Agriculture to study speedy and humanitarian methods of slaughtering animals. However, in practice it failed to change the existing procedures to any appreciable degree.

It can be concluded that in our modern technological society the stakes of political victory are becoming increasingly important and are fought for by groups which are becoming increasingly politicized. While, as we have mentioned, all groups can exercise a degree of influence on certain issues, the peak economic groups appear largely to control the policy-making process.

Because of the growing recognition that if you are going to clean the Augean stables you may have to get into the mire, increasingly more groups and individuals are becoming involved in politics, even though they

[26] See Louis Hartz, *The Liberal Tradition in America* (New York: Harcourt, Brace & World, Inc., 1955).

[27] Mark W. Cannon, "The Crusades against the Masons, Catholics and Mormons: Separate Waves of a Common Current," *Brigham Young University Studies*, 3 (winter, 1961), 23–40.

are often repelled by some of the things they see. Groups are also increasingly aware that no major political outcome is neutral. It will always benefit some groups at the expense of others. The degree to which lobbying (influencing legislation) is carried on by private groups is suggested by the fact that an examination several years ago estimated that lobbying expenditures exceed $20 million a year.[28]

There is a reason why these well-organized macrogroups play a greater role in American politics than in those of some other countries. The reason is the diffuseness and lack of central control and discipline in our party system.

The centrifugal tendencies of American political arrangements encourage the organization of interest groups to influence government activities. Every agency tends to have a constituency in roughly the same way a senator or representative has, except that it is likely to be defined not in terms of congressional districts or states but rather in terms of functionally-oriented groups that are nation-wide or regional in scope.[29]

What is the relationship between these interest groups and the parties?

In some situations, particularly in one-party states, it almost appears that the political party is merely a formal structure through which the factional groups arising in the social structure struggle to control government. Where the party organization is lively and vigorous, it can deal with group interests autonomously from an independent basis of strength.

The interest group, of course, concerns itself with the nomination or election of candidates favorable to its policy demands; its propaganda publicity, and financial support may be given to either or both parties for promoting its views. Individually, its leaders and members may join and acquire high office in party organizations, but the more usual relationships between party and interest groups are those of personal access.[30]

Rossiter contends:

This tendency for interest groups to align themselves with one or the other of the major parties is a growing one, for more and more groups have found it less and less possible to remain neutral toward parties that are becoming more and more national in outlook and support. Once the process of partisan alignment has been set in motion, it propels itself along at a quickening pace. The sharpening commitment of many powerful unions to the Democratic party has forced many powerful trade associations to adopt a posture of only thinly veiled Republican partisanship.[31]

28 Avery Leiserson, *Parties and Politics* (New York: Alfred A. Knopf, Inc., 1958), pp. 235–236.

29 Marver H. Bernstein, *The Job of the Federal Executive* (Washington, D.C.: The Brookings Institution, 1958), p. 128.

30 Leiserson, pp. 78, 234.

31 Clinton Rossiter, *Parties and Politics in America* (Ithaca, N.Y.: Cornell University Press, 1960), p. 23.

WHAT DETERMINES GROUP POWER

Power is the ability to influence people through persuasion and compulsion.[32] The power of a group in forging public policy is determined by the effective use of its wealth, numbers, leadership, organization, and on other factors contributing to its access to and control of strategic positions in the Congress and the executive offices.

Wealth has long been recognized as a key to political power. One of the motivations to obtain wealth is the desire for social and political power. Some of the uses of wealth by a powerful group are recruiting adherents, building an organization, publicizing policies, employing skilled lobbyists, and contributing to the campaigns of friendly candidates.

The mere holding of wealth, however, does not guarantee political results. In the first place, the owners must be willing to use their wealth in politics. Second, the expenditures must be effective. Third, other factors such as numbers, organization and leadership, and strategic position must be allied with wealth in order to be victorious. Thus abundant wealth was insufficient to advance Averell Harriman's desire for the Democratic presidential nomination in 1952. Yet wealth, effectively utilized and allied with other factors, was a key ingredient in John F. Kennedy's winning the nomination and presidency in 1960.

The impulse to nationalize industry in foreign countries stems partly from the desire to wrest political power from present owners. Yet some disillusioned Marxists have abandoned socialism because they have concluded that when there is a monopoly of economic power, the group which controls the state is even more likely to abuse power than when property is scattered among private owners whose organizations are thereby empowered to check each other's abuses. For example, Max Eastman observed:

It is no accident that "complete collectivization" in Russia, instead of setting the workers and peasants free, set free the hands of a complete tyrant. It seems obvious to me now—though I have been slow, I must say, in coming to the conclusion—that the institution of private property, the dispersion of power and importance that goes with it, has been a main factor in producing a limited amount of free-and-equalness which Marx hoped to render infinite by abolishing this institution. Strangely enough, Marx himself, as an historian, was the first to see this. He is the one who informed us, looking backward, that the evolution of private capitalism with its free market had been a precondition for the evolution of all our democratic freedoms. It never occurred to him, looking

[32] See Bertram M. Gross, *The Legislative Struggle: A Study in Social Combat* (New York: McGraw-Hill Book Company, 1953), pp. 142–150.

forward—with Owen's dream in his eyes—that if this was so, those other freedoms might disappear with the abolition of the free market.[33]

Numbers are also a key to power. In international politics, for example, Communist Chinese leaders appear to believe that in the event of conflict their superior manpower could outweigh superior industrial and technological power. Domestically, union leaders often try to marshall their membership to help defeat conservative solons at the polls. "It is by a show of numbers in one form or another that elections are won, Supreme Court decisions made and bills enacted."[34] Numbers provide the raw materials for organization and leadership and can supply wealth through dues. Sometimes numbers provide near monopolies of certain skills or services. Electricians unions and the American Medical Association are examples.

Leadership is another key to power. Groups with great potential power, such as the "undisciplined battalions" of agrarian voters between 1780 and 1800, must often wait for a skillful leader, such as Thomas Jefferson, before they can become effective.

Powerful leaders must have a variety of skills. They must gauge their members' potential unity and use ideals and symbols (ideology) to inspire enthusiasm and loyalty. They must define objectives, choose weapons, develop public relations and intelligence services, nurture every source of power, build alliances, and negotiate the final compromises. Leadership results from such personal qualities as persuasiveness, vitality and endurance, decisiveness, intellectual capacity, and responsibility. Research shows that leaders interact more with lay members than lay members do with each other.[35]

Leaders often develop cohesive and thorough organizations which are more powerful than larger but unorganized wealth or numbers. The Communist and "Castroite" take-overs in Russia, China, and Cuba and the Nazi take-over in Germany all illustrate this on a grand scale.

In order for a group's power to be converted into public policy, the group must have access to lawmakers, particularly those who hold strategic positions such as committee chairmen, congressional and bloc leaders, and the President. Degrees of access vary from only the chance to be heard to virtual assurance of favorable action on requests.

Access to legislators is influenced by both formal structural factors

[33] Max Eastman, "Socialism and Freedom: A Criticism of Sidney Hook," in Sidney Hook, *Political Power and Personal Freedom* (New York: Criterion Books, 1959), p. 361.

[34] James Bryce, *The American Commonwealth,* 3d ed. rev. (New York: The Macmillan Company, 1908), vol. 2, p. 9.

[35] Jane Warters, *Group Guidance* (New York: McGraw-Hill Book Company, 1960), p. 28.

and informal factors.[36] Illustrative of the formal structural factors is the geographic location of a group in relation to the electoral system. For example, economic enterprises which are scattered among many sparsely populated states, such as silver mining and sugar beet production, have significant access because of the bargaining power of the major bloc of senators whom they can influence. Were it not for the equal allotment of two senators to each state, large or small, the power of various agricultural and mineral groups would be vastly diminished. Another structural factor which also improved the access of agricultural groups to power was the drawing of congressional district lines by state legislatures.

In 1962, according to a *Congressional Quarterly* analysis, rural areas held twenty-seven more seats in the House of Representatives than their population warranted.[37] This restricted the access of burgeoning suburban areas which, according to population, should have had twenty more seats than they did. Central cities were underrepresented by seven seats.

A structural factor negatively affecting access to the Presidency, which greatly influences legislation, is the electoral college. The winner-take-all system, wherein all the electors of a state rate as a unit, places much more importance on the urban areas than do the House or Senate electoral systems. A presidential candidate whose programs appeared hostile to urban interests could not win the populous states, without whose support a victory in the electoral college would be highly improbable. For example, during this century only one President, Harry S Truman in 1948, was elected without winning New York. Thus Senator Estes Kefauver of Tennessee argued in 1963 for a change in the electoral college, contending that it overrepresented the giant metropolitan areas of the East.

The result of electoral systems which give greater rural access to the Congress and greater urban access to the Presidency is a rural-urban split in both parties. Thus there is both a liberal, urban-oriented presidential party and a conservative, rural-oriented congressional party within both the Democratic and Republican parties.[38]

To illustrate the difference between the two parties, most immigrant groups and Northern Negroes reside in the major urban areas. Consequently, the urban-oriented presidential candidates of both parties are more likely to espouse liberalized immigration and strong civil rights legislation, whereas Congress often restrains such legislation because of its greater rural, native American, and Southern orientation.

[36] See David B. Truman, "The Dynamics of Access in the Legislative Process," in John C. Wahlke and Heinz Eulau, *Legislative Behavior* (New York: The Free Press of Glencoe, 1959), pp. 150–164. This is taken from Truman, *The Governmental Process.*

[37] *Congressional Quarterly* (February 2, 1962), 153.

[38] For a development of this thesis see James MacGregor Burns, *The Deadlock of Democracy: Four-party Politics in America* (Englewood Cliffs, N.J.: Prentice-Hall, Inc., 1963).

The relation of structure to access is also illustrated by the seniority system for selecting committee chairmen, who often dominate their committees as feudal lords controlled their fiefdoms. The seniority system aids groups located in one-party states, notably the Democratic South. It is more than coincidence that four of the six crops designated as "basic" for farm price supports were grown below the Mason-Dixon line. These were peanuts, cotton, rice, and tobacco.

Among the informal determinants of access, the politician's constant need for both technical and political information is important. Many political careers have foundered on mistakes made in ignorance of the full implications of a policy. For example, a freshman congressman who voted in 1959 to terminate appropriations for a missile was unaware that the ram-jet engine for the missile was produced in his own state. He subsequently lost a bid to become a United States senator from that state, perhaps partly because he showed less awareness of such implications than his more experienced opponent. Consequently, groups which supply authentic and vital information to a politician will also have access to him for their needs.

Another informal determinant of access is the set of attitudes, relationships, and affiliations which a public official brings with him to office. Thus, a congressman who was a former director of the American National Association of Junior Colleges became a spokesman for this group even though they were not a major power factor in his state. More than one-third of the members of Congress generally belong to the American Legion, which assures support for the Legion's proposals from many of these members.

Of lesser importance is the "social lobby"—the entertaining of legislators in the hope that a feeling of obligation will be created toward the host group or individuals. Congressmen often must choose from among several banquet or cocktail party invitations for a particular evening while they are in the capital.

Another factor affecting access to legislative power is the internal set of relationships within the legislature. The arrangement of subgroups and cliques and the unwritten system of obligations and privileges affect the access of a group to a legislative body.

Finally, the role of office (i.e., the prescribed behavior for a person occupying a particular status) affects access. The "rules of the game" call upon a legislator "to avoid open partiality to the contested claims of a small minority; he must at least appear to be solicitous for the vocal needs of his constituents, but he is expected in some measure to look beyond his constituency . . . he must support the political and civil freedoms involved in a fair trial, in petition, in speech, press, and assembly."[39]

Knowing when a financial transaction is a legitimate campaign contri-

39 Truman in Wahlke and Eulau, p. 160.

bution and when it is a bribe is also part of the sometimes ambiguous role of a congressman. For example, a bill to free natural gas in part from public regulation was lost a few years ago because a senator announced that he had been offered a bribe. The natural gas lobby never regained the influence it previously held. Yet in different circumstances, including different personalities, a legislator might not have felt that his role prevented him from silently accepting such a contribution.

Thus, in addition to the basic ingredients of power, such as effective wealth, size, organization, and leadership, other factors also affect a group's access to legislative power. These factors could be referred to as its net influence. They are primarily the governmental structure as it aids and handicaps various groups, the legislators' personal group affiliations and identifications, the legislators' relationships with each other, and their identifications with legislative subgroupings and their legislative roles.

The manner in which a legislator fills his role affects his relationships with his colleagues, which in turn affect his influence together with the groups he represents. The United States Senate, for example, has the atmosphere of a very exclusive club where permanent influence requires behavior within senatorial norms. To illustrate this fact, Senator Joseph McCarthy was an extremely powerful Senator until December, 1954. At that time the Senate voted 67 to 22 to condemn him for abusing a Senate subcommittee and acting "contrary to senatorial traditions." Following the decision that Senator McCarthy had violated his senatorial role, his influence in the Senate was closed by

. . . a door, quite unseen, but quite heavy. . . . He might well remain a great power to a substantial minority in his own party and elsewhere. But in the Institution [Senate] he was a power no longer.

For again the Senate has its ways, and one of these was illustrated in the post-condemnation days. Again and again when McCarthy rose to speak there was in the chamber that rarest of all demonstrations, a demonstration of conscious disorder and inattention.[40]

To consider another example, Senator Hubert Humphrey had little influence during his early years in the Senate because he was remembered for his brashness in opposing party leaders by successfully demanding a strong civil rights platform plank at the 1948 Democratic National Convention. This move precipitated the formation of the Southern Dixiecrat party.[41] However, as Senator Humphrey became less hurried and adopted more senatorial habits and moods, he enjoyed an ascent to grace, becoming majority whip and then receiving his party's nod for the vice presidency.

Many of the factors which have been enumerated affect the success

[40] William S. White, *Citadel: The Story of the U.S. Senate* (New York: Harper & Row, Publishers, Incorporated, 1956), p. 133.

[41] *Ibid.*, p. 113.

with which a group lobbies. Considerable data about lobbying have been supplied by Lester Milbrath.[42] The relationship between the pressure group and the lobbyist is varied and not always clear. It runs the gamut between the highly oriented mass lobby group and the "lobbyist entrepreneur."[43] The mass organization is exemplified by a hierarchical structure with headquarters in Washington, and there is usually a strong tendency toward the establishment of an oligarchy within the organization. The entrepreneur is a one-man operator, and his operations are organized on a less formal basis.

In the area of policy making it is found that in the pressure groups which are mass-organized, such as the Farm Bureau, the making of policy is usually dominated by an executive committee consisting of the top elective officers of the organization.[44] Policy making becomes less structured and complicated in the trade association and the corporation lobby groups. In these smaller lobby groups the policy function often lies within the lobby group itself. Thus the roles in policy making vary according to the type of organization being studied.

The question is sometimes posed, "Where are lobbyists recruited?" In one recent study it was shown that legal and political skills were important. In a representative sample of 114 respondents, 28 had been employed in governmental service prior to becoming lobbyists, and 23 had had previous careers in law.

The study also indicated that there is a distinction between the political behavior of lobbyists as individuals and the political activities of the groups they represent.[45] Most lobbyists do not take any active part in partisan political activities. As one lobbyist put it: "I don't want to get labeled too heavily. I don't want to get the people in Congress to feeling that I am sticking my nose into their election activities."[46]

Contributing to political campaigns is the most widespread of the political activities reported by the lobbyist. However, there is a distinct difference among the groups in their methods of contributing. Labor organizations tend to make a great number of contributions, with the average size being quite small. Business lobbyists tend to favor fewer contributions, but the average size of the contribution is larger than that of the labor lobbyist. The farm groups are unlikely to make any contributions.[47]

The prime objective of the lobbyist is to gain access to the legislature or the executive branch. In Milbrath's study it was ascertained that in quantity and quality the majority of lobbying is done in the executive area, though the difference is not excessive. Lobbyists list several criteria as being important in keeping the channels of communication open.

[42] Lester W. Milbrath, *The Washington Lobbyists* (Chicago: Rand McNally & Company, 1963).

[43] *Ibid.*, pp. 34–36.

[44] *Ibid.*, p. 42.

[45] *Ibid.*, p. 87.

[46] *Ibid.*, p. 78.

[47] *Ibid.*, p. 82.

1. Officials are overburdened with information, so it is very important to make communications succinct and to the point.
2. The communication must be credible, and be backed with appropriate facts and research data.
3. The information must be reliable. The relationship between the lobbyist and the governmental decisions made, in order to last, must be based on trust.[48]

Many methods and techniques are used to bring success to the lobbyist in his objectives. The following appear to be basic and important.

1. Be pleasant and nonoffensive. Pleasantness is important in keeping the channels of communication open.
2. Convince the official that it is important for him to listen to you. This means that the official must be convinced that he has some stake in the information given. A demonstration of constituent interest is one method.
3. Be well prepared and well informed. Governmental officials expect lobbyists to be knowledgeable.
4. Be personally convinced. Something cannot be sold if the seller is not sure of his own product beforehand.
5. Use the soft sell. Do not try to push and get yourself into a position where compromise as an alternative is excluded.
6. Leave a short written summary of your case. A further reminder is usually appreciated by decision makers.[49]

Pressure group and lobbying activity has had, even by its verbal connotation, a bad reputation. Though undoubtedly some of the accusations made are valid, many of them can be classified in the realm of political folklore. One of the more prominent ones is that governmental decisions can be bought or stolen. Probably in a very few isolated cases this has been done, but in the majority of cases the mere fact that the decision-making process is divided and spread out between the branches of government makes it virtually impossible for this to happen. The factor of multiple participation by actors makes it very unlikely that this type of behavior could go on without detection.

Another accusation is that certain pressure groups control some of the decision makers. Though this is true in some cases, the factors of diversified regions and individual responsibility to the nation as a whole make it difficult for a decision maker to be captured by one group. Still another belief in the realm of political folklore is that the majority of lobbyists are former congressmen who are hired for the contacts they have. Milbrath's survey gives indications that this is not true. Many respondents felt that lobbyists' access could be reduced by their close identification with controversial groups or previous roles.

Contrary to popular belief, entertainment, parties, and gifts appear to have little influence on decision makers. Frequently the legislators are alienated by this type of activity because they are overburdened with it. In

[48] *Ibid.*, pp. 210–211.   [49] *Ibid.*, pp. 220–227.

addition, many lawmakers complain because they have too little time to spend with their families. The social lobby, then, does not really serve as more than a means of opening communication channels and maintaining them in some cases.

One of the problems with which the lobbyist is faced is his inability to assess accurately the strength of his opponents. Oftentimes groups or lobbyists will fail to act or will overreact owing to this inability. The result is sometimes a condition of stalemate or excessive combat. It is not unusual, therefore, to find the various participants within the lobby structure forming a "united front." These coalitions, however, are usually not stable, and once the original object is won or lost, the united front dissolves.

It is important to put the lobbyists and their activities in the proper context. Undoubtedly they serve a positive function as a buffer between the executive and legislative branches. They decrease the legislative dependence on the executive and help to keep officials aware of segments of public opinion.

GROUPS ARE CONTROLLED BY MINORITIES

Whether it is a student-body group on a college campus or the AFL-CIO, the majority of the membership of most groups is usually passive while the actual control and manipulation of the organizations are managed by relatively few individuals.

A number of writers, such as sociologist C. Wright Mills in *The Power Elite* (see Chapter 9), have argued that there are only a few men in America who hold real power. Those who hold such power do so, in almost every case, by virtue of their control over the mechanism of an organized group. In a real sense, then, the power holders (or perhaps more accurately, the manipulators of power) in America are a small but highly heterogeneous elite.

On a community level, the elites interact both socially and occupationally. Many of the community's important decisions are made in the environment of the "luncheon circuit" and the "athletic club."[50] The elites of the community tend to reside together in areas of the community isolated from the mass of community problems. Nationally, the interaction of elites is similar to that on a community level. Floyd Hunter, in his study *Top Leadership, U.S.A.,* concluded that the nation's leading occupational leaders personally knew one another better and interacted more than they did with lower-strata members of their own professions.[51] His research supported

50 Floyd Hunter, *Community Power Structure* (Chapel Hill: The University of North Carolina Press, 1953), p. 16.
51 Floyd Hunter, *Top Leadership, U.S.A.* (Chapel Hill: The University of North Carolina Press, 1959), pp. 223–224.

his discovery that informal "friendship, committee work, clubs and recreational associations, customer relations, and financial matters" were shared by the national leaders.[52]

For those who desire power, the chief way in our society to achieve it is to become one of the elite who effectively control a major group. There are, therefore, very real reasons for depicting modern America as "an organizational society." It is in these major organizations that the basis and control of power in America lies.

The reasons for minority control of groups start with the very existence of a formal organization with a standardized, habitual pattern of interaction and decision making. Virtually all large groups find that policy and decision making necessitate smaller, more workable groups than the entire group meeting in a body can provide. Thus, the development of smaller executive bodies to make policy decisions is a fact of organization. The larger the group and the more complex its activities, the more urgent it is to have leadership in decision making put into the hands of a few. This creates situations which make manipulation and continued control by active minorities possible and frequently easy.

A second factor which makes possible the control of groups by a clique is the development of managerial skills whereby those in office or those with experience in the working of the system can maintain effective leadership. Examples of this are found among union leadership, as well as the National Association of Manufacturers (NAM) and the American Medical Association (AMA), to name only a few. In these organizations long-term holders of various elective and appointive positions, as well as behind-the-scenes manipulators, maintain themselves frequently for years on end.

A third factor which makes possible the maintenance of minority control over a group is the use of finances. For instance, at one period in recent history over half of the NAM's funds were contributed by only 5 per cent of its company membership. In addition, larger firms in the East usually have held general control of the organization. It would seem quite logical that those contributing the largest share of an organization's expenses would have the loudest voice in its undertakings.

A fourth means by which minorities control group organizations is the ability to expend the time necessary for leadership duties. For example, it is almost always urban specialists who hold the majority of the key positions in the AMA. They are usually the wealthiest members and can arrange to take time off from their practices. In any group, particularly where officers are paid little or where the demands of time away from one's general occupation are great, it takes individuals who can afford both time and money to man such positions. This condition is frequently true with state chairmen of both the Democratic and Republican parties.

Although leadership is always relative to the situation, certain indi-

[52] *Ibid.*, p. 38.

viduals are gifted with leadership abilities which make them "natural" politicians. Which of these leaders gravitate to the administrative or political offices in any organization depends upon the group's "size, structure, organization, communication system, cohesiveness, personality content, values, and role concepts."[53] Given some of the other factors present to make possible their being able to devote themselves to such posts, a single individual or a small group of such men can dominate group organizations for years.

Actually, there are only a few members of most groups who desire administrative or political posts enough to campaign vigorously for them or maneuver diligently to maintain such posts, once elected. Throughout the existence of most associations there is only a small minority available upon which to draw. Even though evidence shows that "every increment of intelligence means wiser government . . . the crowd prefers to be ill-governed by people it can understand."[54]

Gratitude to established leaders is also a factor which permits leadership to be maintained over the years. If leadership is doing an adequate job, there is generally little incentive to try new individuals unless the position is highly lucrative or prestigious and thus attracts considerable competition. Even when such offices do seem highly attractive, the fear of defeat is strong enough to make contestants reluctant to try for positions unless they can feel reasonable assurance of winning. Therefore, minorities inevitably control and direct organizations and groups. This condition means that a small number of people manipulate great political power.

IDEOLOGIES AND GOALS

It would be helpful to define what is meant here by that most ambiguous term, ideology. Once again each expert in the field appears to have his own particular definition. Robert Dahl, for example, explains that an ideology is a set of integrated doctrines espoused by political leaders to "explain and justify their leadership in the system."[55] Andrew Hacker philosophically defines the term as "a rationalization for current or future political and social arrangements."[56] Karl Mannheim suggests that ideologies are "conscious disguises of the real nature of a situation, the true nature of which would not be in accord with his interests."[57]

53 Warters, p. 35.

54 Cecil A. Gibb, "Leadership," in Gardner Lindzey (ed.), *Handbook of Social Psychology,* vol. 2, p. 886, quoted in Warters, p. 28.

55 Robert A. Dahl, *Modern Political Analysis* (Englewood Cliffs, N.J.: Prentice-Hall, Inc., 1963), p. 20.

56 Andrew Hacker, *Political Theory: Philosophy, Ideology, Science* (New York: The Macmillan Company, 1961), p. 5.

57 Karl Mannheim, *Ideology and Utopia: An Introduction to the Sociology of Knowledge* (New York: Harvest Books, Harcourt, Brace & World, Inc., 1936), p. 55.

An ideology, as used here, is essentially a "set of ideas characteristic of a group . . . that relates certain of their supposed attributes [i.e., goals, principles, and objectives] to some more commonly esteemed values in such a way as to bestow honorific status upon them [their objectives] and their institutions and provide the basis for invidious comparisons against their competitors."[58]

The linkage between a group's goals, principles, and publicly esteemed values is frequently of an emotional nature. Daniel Bell argues that "the most important, latent function of ideology is to tap emotion."[59] This may well help account for the fact that ideological statements are rarely refutable or verifiable. The famous English economist Joan Robinson has argued that one of the hallmarks of an ideology is that it is not capable of being tested.[60] Further, Raymond Aron, the brilliant French economist and sociologist, takes the following position:

> Political ideologies always combine, more or less felicitously, factual propositions and value judgments. . . . They cannot be described as literally true or false, nor do they belong to the same category as taste and colour. The ultimate philosophy and the hierarchy of preferences invite discussion rather than proof or refutation; analyses of present facts, or prognostications about facts to come after, with the unfolding of history and the knowledge we acquire of it. Experience progressively modifies doctrinal constrictions.[61]

A group's ideology presents a more or less systematic and rigid dogma by which the group attempts to hold and develop the internal loyalty of its members while striving to preserve or transform its environment. Ideology, in this sense, is the conversion of ideas into social levers.[62] Ideology in this book will be used to refer to the group's whole body of dogma as well as specific parts of it. Thus, individual statements of the goals and principles of a group will be considered "ideological," as well as the statements attempting to link them with the widely held values in the society. In this sense, then, ideologies are composed of two segments, the factual statement of a group's position on issues, and the linkage statements which attempt to justify, rationalize, and convert by showing (often emotionally and sometimes illogically) that the group's policy position is in harmony with the society's commonly esteemed values.

[58] R. Joseph Monsen, Jr., *Modern American Capitalism: Ideologies and Issues* (Boston: Houghton Mifflin Company, 1963), p. 8.

[59] Daniel Bell, *The End of Ideology* (New York: The Free Press of Glencoe, 1960), p. 371.

[60] See Joan Robinson's discussion of the difference between science and ideology in *Economic Philosophy* (London: C. A. Watts & Co., Ltd., 1962), chap. 1.

[61] Raymond Aron, *The Opium of the Intellectuals* (New York: W. W. Norton & Company, Inc., 1962), p. 236.

[62] Bell, p. 370.

But not all statements of a group are necessarily "ideological." Ideological statements must be characteristic of the group and must be part of its defensive or offensive mechanism. The emphasis in this book on ideology inevitably dramatizes the conflict in American economic and political society. Yet it must also be recognized that the battles are fought in America within a much broader framework of common agreement than is the case in many countries, such as France.

Ideological statements are selected not to represent a picture of the world from the most realistic or objective point of view, but to present "a model designed to isolate certain salient features of actuality which the model builder, the Ideologist, regards as of crucial importance."[63] Thus, a group's ideology may represent a vision of reality that those outside the group find unacceptable. However, ideology is not developed for the purpose of realistic explanation, but rather as a tool to advance the position and goals of the group.

The first thing that the student should learn about ideologies and the groups who espouse them is that an attitude of independent objectivity is needed to determine "wherein lies the truth." If one expects to find the full truth of an apocalyptic vision in an economic interest group's ideology, he will probably become either disillusioned or a zealous "true believer." This study attempts to identify and examine the biases of our major economic interest groups and their ideologies. By seeing the many facets of public issues today, it is hoped that the ingredients and development of public policy can be made more understandable.

It should be pointed out that it is naïve to assume that a group's overt ideology outlines all its underlying goals. Nonetheless, a study of a group's public ideology and its economic interests is useful in determining what the general goals of the group are. The actual goals of the leadership elite of a group, however, are always much more difficult to determine; for the goals of the leadership may not be congruous with the goals of the majority of lay members. The group leadership tries first of all to effectuate its own policies. If the leadership feels strongly enough, it may even overrule goals set by the majority vote of the group on some issues. Hence, even when an ideology expresses the goals of a group as a whole, it may not always reflect the actual goals pursued by the leadership of the group who direct and control the mechanism of the organization. Recognizing these qualifications, it will be assumed that the goals of the group are a composite of the group's ideology and its economic interests.

In cases of a conflict, a group's immediate economic gain will generally override its apparent ideological commitment. The exceptions to this rule are usually found only where the leadership is in firm control and, at the

[63] Arthur Schlesinger, Jr., "The One against the Many," *The Saturday Review* (July 14, 1962), 10.

same time, is committed to an ideology to the degree that it feels impelled to use the mechanism of the organization to pursue personal ideological attachments over the group's economic interests. Undoubtedly, there are instances in which the group pursues a course which, owing to faulty reasoning, incompetence, misinformation, and other factors, results in goals that do not or cannot maximize its own interests.

The pursuing of economic goals is further complicated by the fact that short- and long-run maximization of economic interests are not always the same. It may well be that the larger the group, the more it will tend to favor short-range economic interests over more distant ones. It is generally the leaders of groups and nations who, frequently being better informed on a given issue, will tend to favor long-run interests. Leadership, however, is usually bounded in such cases by the need for political support, i.e., consent of the group. Thus, the less the leadership feels it needs the mass support of the group to maintain its position, the less it will support short-term over long-term considerations. This is seen in the extreme in Communist dictatorships, where consumption is generally restricted in favor of government investment in economic growth. A concluding chapter of this study deals with the major goals of the groups discussed here and the implications for the society and economy should any single group realize all its basic aims.

THE PURPOSE OF THE BOOK

This book identifies the major occupational power groups in our society, as well as other major power groups, as to their ideologies and the reasons why they hold them. Inferentially, their underlying goals are identified, and the mechanisms of bargaining and compromise in the day-to-day determination of economic and other aspects of public policy are also alluded to. The hope is that by shedding more light on those who dominate the legislative mechanism, the basic areas of agreement and conflict in our society can be more readily seen. With a broader general understanding of how public policy is actually made in our society, there is less danger of a monopoly over government power developing and less chance that legislation can be passed by a minority which flagrantly violates the general will.

In studying the expressed goals and ideologies of the groups, this work generally takes at face value the assertions and public statements of the groups themselves. It is recognized that there is occasional camouflage, and this is sometimes pointed out. The public expressions of the basic American power groups do offer the best available guidelines to the actual views and directions that each group desires to follow. Such data present a guide to the future of history.

To prevent abuse of power by major groups, a public understanding of who holds power and how power is used and to what ends is of crucial significance for the course of democracy in America. Economist John Kenneth Galbraith believes that large organized groups should be encouraged so that they can exercise countervailing power on one another. In order for policy makers to work toward what appear to them to be equitable power relationships, the present power of major groups must be spotlighted and understood. When the power mechanism is veiled, it is extremely difficult to develop a wide base of effective participation. Today in America, access to power is virtually impossible if individuals do not understand the makers and making of legislation and the channels through which power flows and operates in present-day society. Further, such knowledge has now become a prerequisite for successful union, agricultural, and business management.

With the increase in the government sphere of influence over economic decisions, the firm and other economic bodies in America today must know how to gain access to the legislative and policy channels of government if they expect to survive, compete, and be profitable. Both the traditional power to tax and the modern processes of regulation have the power to destroy and the power to benefit. Thus the future of economic groups and individual firms in America depends increasingly upon their ability to control and manipulate power at the seat of government.

2
business

INTRODUCTION

Business as a power group is involved in the making of public policy on three levels: national business groups, trade associations, and individual businesses. Since the last two act in behalf of the special interest of an individual firm or industry, our attention in this chapter will be focused primarily on the macro level—that of the national business groups who are involved generally in the broad scope of national public policy and who speak for business as a power group.

Before proceeding to a macro investigation, perhaps a few comments should be made about the micro level, or the individual business representative and the industry trade association. At the present time not even all large companies as yet have Washington representatives. Of the 200 largest corporations in this country, a Brookings Institution study reported that 130 maintain full-time Washington representatives.[1] Some of the other large firms and many smaller ones maintained Washington representatives on a part-time basis. These representatives serve one or a combination of three functions: to market their company's services or products to the government directly or indirectly; to handle the company's activities and relations with administrative and executive agencies; and to influence legislation. The representatives do not like to be regarded as lobbyists, and few

[1] P. W. Cherington and R. L. Gillen, *The Business Representative in Washington* (Washington: The Brookings Institution, 1962), p. 7.

24

are so registered. Most, however, are involved in activities frequently considered lobbying by most definitions.

The Brookings study found that business, particularly at the individual level, is beginning to realize that the continuing large governmental expenditures for defense and other purposes plus the continuing growth of regulation and control over business by government necessitate increased attention to the Washington scene. Furthermore, the increase in labor power and activity on Capitol Hill appears to be making businessmen feel increasingly compelled to devote more attention to the aspects of business-government relations. Yet individual companies seem to make few legislative program commitments and rely largely upon the activities of the NAM (National Association of Manufacturers) or the Chamber of Commerce or the CED (Committee for Economic Development). In fact, companies have preferred the anonymous political atmosphere with which these macro organizations have permitted them to operate.

The trade associations, likewise, have generally preferred to let the NAM, the United States Chamber of Commerce, or the CED carry the ball as far as national policy is concerned, while they have focused their attention on economic interests directly vital to their trade membership. This means that business, as far as most individual firms and industry-level associations are involved, has thought that its attention should be focused primarily on short-run economic problems directly affecting them. This policy—or perhaps *lack* of long-range policy—has probably been detrimental to their longer-range interests. "You must get active in politics if you want to stay active in business," said George M. Humphrey, Chairman of the National Steel Corporation.[2] It would appear that business may be gradually awakening to the modern challenge of the political arena and its economic consequences, even though the Brookings study indicates that individual firms have little knowledge as yet about how to proceed. In the era before us, there is little doubt that they will of necessity have to learn. The NAM particularly has been impressed with labor's mobilization of manpower to win elections so that congressmen and senators will be beholden to them and receptive to their legislative programs. The NAM is currently attempting to organize a plan for future elections. Medical groups, frequent allies of the NAM, have already started to mobilize themselves, their wives, and their friends.

The remainder of this chapter will discuss the macro level of the business power groups. As a national power group, business is oriented in several separate directions: the classical approach, followed largely by the NAM and the United States Chamber of Commerce; the small business approach, publicized to some extent by the National Federation of Inde-

[2] W. H. Baumer and D. G. Herzberg, *Politics Is Your Business* (New York: *The Dial Press, Inc.*, 1960), p. 19.

pendent Business; and the managerial approach, sponsored largely by the CED. Each of these subgroups of the national business power bloc has its own distinctive ideology which, while identical on many issues, is separated from the other by a deep cleavage in basic economic philosophy. It is necessary to examine each in turn to understand what their ideology is, why they hold it, and inferentially, what their major legislative policy goals appear to be.

Much of the following discussion will, therefore, be analytical, devoted to the reasons involved in the holding of their particular ideologies and political goals. A concluding section of the chapter takes up the problem of business power and public policy. A case is presented showing how business as a power group has operated on the political scene in Washington to influence a specific issue of public policy.

It is hoped that by approaching the problem of business power and public policy from viewpoints, ideology, and goals, a clear understanding can be gained about who and what forces are behind the making of policy in our present-day society. The problems involved in the determination of economic and public policy in this country are complex. The expansion of government control and regulation into traditional business decision-making areas is the most pressing issue that firms in America will face in this century.[3] Hence, the rationale, goals, and manipulative policies and techniques by which business attempts to face this problem are of critical importance to all who are concerned with the future of business in America.

BUSINESS IDEOLOGY

As already indicated, business in the United States today is divided into categories. One division has been called the classical business ideology and is disseminated primarily through the publications of the National Association of Manufacturers, Foundation for Economic Education, the Committee for Constitutional Government, the United States Chamber of Commerce, the American Enterprise Association, and the Americans for Constitutional Action, to name a few. This ideology essentially embraces what the economists refer to as classical economics—economics based upon the free competitive market with government playing a relatively small role. With a number of exceptions, this was the model under which the United States was popularly viewed as having functioned until the 1930s.

The small business ideology is perhaps most easily thought of as a

[3] J. J. Wuerthner, in *The Businessman's Guide to Practical Politics* (Chicago: Henry Regnery Company, 1959), states, "One of the broad political trends of the last several decades has been the increasing acceleration of government intervention in business and industry." P. 3.

subgroup of the classical ideology described above. While big (or bigger) business is well represented nationally by such groups as the NAM, the United States Chamber of Commerce, and the CED, small business is less well organized. A number of organizations representing the small business view have been in existence at one time or another, yet none have had a very long history. Perhaps The National Federation of Independent Business, founded in 1943, is today the largest and most vigorous of the small business pressure groups.

The essence of the small business ideology is the preindustrial agrarian spirit that flavors its highly emotional attacks against big government, big unions, and big business. (The attack against big business is its major difference from the classical ideology as espoused by the NAM.) While taking a position on most economic issues nearly identical to that of the classical ideology, small business ideology is presented in more strident and less rational tones, perhaps, than that of the NAM. This higher emotional overtone in the small business ideology may well be because the small business man feels greater anxiety and threat in our present industrial society than members of either the NAM or the CED.[4]

The other main business ideology is what has been called the managerial ideology of business, and it takes its name from the stress placed upon the role played by professional management in big business. The ideology is disseminated particularly through the Committee for Economic Development, which was organized in 1942, and it could be considered a reaction against the National Association of Manufacturers. It is a reaction in the sense that the CED attempts to change many of the basic ideas of traditional classical economics and to adapt them to what it considers modern business conditions. *Fortune* magazine has frequently been one of the major public expositors of this business creed. While it has much in common with the classical ideology, the managerial ideology has essentially "accepted the fact that government was big and was constantly growing bigger and that there was no returning to a simpler and happier past in this respect. It believed that the question was not *how much* government should do, but *what* it should do and once this was determined how it could be done most effectively."[5]

The groups sponsoring the classical business ideology generally agree on most issues, but there are exceptions, such as the issue of free trade. The greatest tension and disagreement within business circles comes between those who hold the classical creed based on classical economics (i.e.,

[4] See the work of John H. Bunzel, *The American Small Businessman* (New York, Alfred A. Knopf, Inc., 1962) and "Comparative Attitudes of Big Business and Small Business," *Western Political Quarterly,* 70, 1, March, 1955.

[5] Karl Schriftgiesser, *Business Comes of Age* (New York: Harper & Row, Publishers, Incorporated, 1960), p. 224.

as postulated by Adam Smith as far back as the eighteenth century) and those who accept the managerial ideology, which to a large extent accepts Keynesian economics (as first developed by J. M. Keynes in 1936) in its foundation and concepts. The small business ideology, on most economic issues, will not differ from the position of the classical creed. We shall look at these creeds separately to determine their basic ideologies and political goals.

THE CLASSICAL BUSINESS IDEOLOGY

The classical ideology is based upon the concept of private property in which demand and supply operate through the market to establish prices freely, and with rational economic men acting in their own best interests in an attempt to maximize profit. Competition is viewed as being an effective and generally sufficient preventive of abuse, and a regulator of the economy. "According to the ideology, 'progress' is built into the competitive system; it is an automatic result of the system functioning."[6] Essentially, classical economics has been taught in all the major economic textbooks in this country until recent decades.

The position of the NAM, as officially declared, is that the basic problems facing all economies—what should be produced, how should it be produced, and who should receive—are best solved and decided through voluntary adjustment of the free market rather than through government intervention. This view holds that prices in a free market are the most efficient and responsive mechanisms for allocating demand and supply. The free market, therefore, becomes the pillar upon which the economics of the classical creed is based. Although it holds that regulation should be largely accomplished by competition, this view nevertheless agrees that government does have the minor function of acting as a regulator to strengthen and "make more effective the regulation by competition."[7] It does not insist that there be no government regulation whatsoever. It does, however, demand that the *role of government* be limited simply to making the free market operate more efficiently.

The classical creed is summed up by the NAM as follows: "In a word, from the point of view of the public welfare, competition serves as a regulator and reducer of prices, as an incentive to improve production efficiency, as a guarantor that we shall get what we want, and as protector of

---

[6] Francis X. Sutton et al., *The American Business Creed* (Cambridge, Mass.: Harvard University Press, 1956), p. 172.

[7] National Association of Manufacturers, *The American Individual Enterprise System: Its Nature, Evolution, and Future* (New York: McGraw-Hill Book Company, 1946), vol. 1, p. 57.

the freedom of opportunity."[8] Those familiar with Adam Smith's *Wealth of Nations,* published in 1776, may find little difference between it and this argument.

Perhaps the major focus of the classical creed in business today concerns the encroachment of governmental decision making upon what is considered the rightful area of private business decision making. Government, then, and occasionally unions, are considered to be the two major nemeses that business faces.[9] The ideology of the classical creed today is directed largely, therefore, toward what it considers its two main threats— government and labor. In a booklet entitled *Industry Believes,* the NAM credo together with a summary of its position on various current political and economic topics is given. This booklet clearly outlines the basic theme of the NAM's ideology as the need to limit "big government" and established economic decision making based almost exclusively upon the free market mechanism.[10]

The principles of freedom of action recognize that individuals know their own wants best and human dignity requires that free men should not have their wants dictated by others. Freedom of action is based, therefore, on individual decisions and voluntary agreements and not on commands and obedience. It recognizes that the individual producer is best qualified to make sound decisions concerning his business problems, and that the aggregate of such decisions as tested in the free market results in wiser solutions to the economic problems of society than would decisions imposed by any outside agency.

Nevertheless, the government of law is necessary to guarantee freedom of action, to encourage individual initiative and to settle conflicts. It is an essential condition of freedom of action that the methods of competition must be peaceful and honest.[11]

From the above quotation, the classical creed argues that the basic function of government should be "primarily political rather than economic." It goes on to argue that:

The responsibilities of government do not encompass competition with its own citizens. Insofar as governmental activity invades the field of private enterprise of this country, it threatens the other elements—civil rights and civil liberties—inherent in our system of government.

Government competition with private enterprise is a major deterrent to the flow of job creating capital into private enterprise. It destroys private capital investment incentives and can only lead to state ownership of all enterprise.[12]

[8] *Ibid.,* vol. 1, p. 59.

[9] Government, as it is seen in the business creed, is inherently evil. It is always viewed negatively, as a restraint on the individual. Sutton, p. 186.

[10] For further information see Wuerthner, p. 4.

[11] National Association of Manufacturers, *Industry Believes* (New York, 1963), p. vi.

[12] *Ibid.,* p. 61.

In regard to *competition,* the NAM, while stating that small business units do and should continue to occupy an important place in the economy, nevertheless sees much that is desirable in the growth of business individually and in combination.

While advocating equitable laws against monopoly and restraint of trade, and their fair and effective enforcement, [nevertheless] industry submits that business size, whether achieved by growth, acquisition or merger, is not in itself a criterion of undue concentration or lack of competition.[13]

The individual seller must be permitted to meet price and other forms of competition, and to enter into such voluntary and mutually satisfactory arrangements with his distributors and dealers as will best promote the economical distribution of goods, without regulation or restriction by the federal or state governments.[14]

There seem to be two basic reasons for the advocacy of the classical ideology. First, the businessman may be convinced intellectually and pragmatically that the classical economic theory, which restricts the scope of government activity, is valid and "true." In this sense, the businessman accepting the classical economic theory becomes, in Eric Hoffer's words, a "true believer." Hence the logic of classical economic theory and the frustration of government taxation and regulation all combine to form strong—even if occasionally pragmatic—loyalties to the business creed labeled here as the classical ideology.

Second, the businessmen who espouse this creed feel essentially alienated from government. To them government represents a major threat to the profitability of their firms through taxation, regulation, and on occasion, outright competition. The annoyance and increased cost of government-demanded bookkeeping for tax and regulatory requirements, plus the decreasing area of industry's full decision-making responsibility, only increase and further inflame the issue of the government's role in our society. It is economic interests and psychological frustrations which cause certain businessmen to embrace an ideology that comes close to eliminating the present role of government in business affairs.

The reason why other businessmen reject this creed and follow the managerial ideology may be found in the possibility that there are different types of "businessmen"; that is, those professing the managerial ideology may be the professional manager types who are organization men in the sense that they regard their function as conciliators of opposing interest groups. Possibly there may exist different concepts of the role that members of the CED and NAM visualize for themselves; personality types may, as well, affect the type of ideology which the businessman accepts or rejects.

[13] National Association of Manufacturers, "Summary of *Industry Believes*" (New York, 1962), p. 10.
[14] *Ibid.*

For example, the more authoritarian and rigid personalities may be attracted to business ideology which is economically more rigid and precise and which would make them less regulated and less threatened by governmental restrictions and, hence, more powerful in their own right.

Labor

The classical creed of the NAM states that a sound and equitable national labor policy should provide a climate for and encourage good wages, good working conditions, and high productivity. This involves a protection of the individual rights of employees, including the right to bargain individually or collectively, free of compulsion or exploitation. It also includes protection giving employers the right to run their business on a competitive basis with no pressures to disclose confidential business information. Employees should be free to join or not to join a labor organization and to participate or to refrain from participating in organized activities, with compulsory union membership prohibited by law. The NAM would prohibit all forms of union activity designed to force individuals to join unions, including organizational picketing, forced recognition of a union, violence, coercion, boycotts, and all other kinds of compulsion. The NAM argues that labor unions and business should be equally subject to the laws for prevention of monopolies. This would require that the Sherman Antitrust Act be made to include specifically labor unions. "Graft and corruption are symptoms of the illness that besets the labor movement, not the cause of it. The cause is the enormous economic and political power now concentrated in the hands of the union leaders."[15] It further argues that the use of union funds for partisan political purposes should be prevented by statute.

The NAM also believes that the states should enact legislation to regulate and restrict strikes and boycotts and that no employer should be compelled by law to engage in joint collective bargaining on any basis. Finally, the classical creed contends that labor disputes should be settled with a minimum of government interference and that government seizure of plants and property in connection with labor disputes should be prohibited by law.

Thus the classical business groups regard government and labor as their two main opponents and feel considerably discriminated against in terms of power. Historically there is some justification for these feelings of the business community, for particularly in the last three decades there has been a tremendous surge in the legal, political, and economic power of unions which has necessarily curtailed and limited areas of business power. Barry Goldwater favors "a redress of the balance—to restore unions to

[15] Barry Goldwater, *The Conscience of a Conservative* (New York: Hillman Books, 1960), p. 42.

their proper role in a free society."[16] Further, government has increasingly expanded into areas of traditional business jurisdiction, and this has also had the effect of limiting business decision making. Business has apparently identified the Democratic party as largely responsible for these attacks on its decision making and power position. The majority of businessmen today adhering to this classical creed (outside the Deep South) are strongly Republican.[17]

It is obvious why the classical ideology stresses the threat of labor as next only to that of government. Organized labor represents decreased control over the firm's costs, workers, and areas of business discretion, and this loss of power probably accounts more for the feeling of business regarding labor than does the fear of decreased profits. John T. Dunlop has suggested that the position of the classical ideology regarding labor is essentially that of a slogan—or "initial demand made by one party in collective bargaining rather than a negotiated settlement or a realistic compromise. They are on a par with many resolutions for legislation passed at AFL-CIO conventions."[18]

Agriculture

The classical creed argues strongly that freedom of decision making must be restored to individual farmers and that the agricultural economy must be allowed to balance its products through the market by the forces of demand and supply. The Chamber of Commerce believes: "Wage, price, rent and other economic controls, direct or indirect, are unnecessary and harmful and should be avoided except when imminent external threat to the national security or actual hostilities indicate such controls are necessary."[19] Price supports and other types of farm subsidies therefore should be terminated. It does state, however, that the termination of such programs "should not be taken, however, without . . . advance notice so that farmers may adjust their operations to the conditions of a free market and the regulator of supply and demand . . . provision [should be made] for withholding from the market accumulated government stocks of farm commodities, except as disposal will not interfere with profitable marketing of current output."[20] The classical creed, through its main disseminator, the

---

[16] *Ibid.,* p. 49.

[17] For further information see Donald Matthews, *U.S. Senators and Their World* (Chapel Hill: The University of North Carolina Press, 1960), p. 36.

[18] John T. Dunlop, "Consensus, National Labor Policy," *Proceedings of the Annual Meeting of the Industrial Relations Research Association,* 1960, p. 10.

[19] Chamber of Commerce of the United States, *1963–1964 Policy Declarations* (Washington, D.C., 1963), p. 12.

[20] NAM, *Industry Believes,* p. 32.

NAM, has argued that the interference with the free market in agriculture has created the problem of both surpluses and gluts and resulted in a fantastic economic burden to the economy. "It should not, however, be an obligation of the federal government to guarantee the prosperity of any segment of the economy, including agriculture."[21] It might be noted that this is one of the major issues on which professional economists might generally agree with the NAM. A market-oriented farm policy would satisfy classical economic theory, save money, and decrease government power.

The Balanced Budget

One problem which is particularly disturbing to the classical creed is that of governmental deficit financing. The classical position is that the budget should be balanced at all times and that the scope and cost of government itself should be reduced. "A balanced budget, including provision for debt retirement, is imperative. To maintain a growing economy, balance should be achieved at the lowest expenditure level which will provide essential public services and the requirements of national security."[22]

In fact, the classical ideology opposes the federal spending of funds in almost any form. Unlike the managerial creed, the classical ideology opposes the spending of federal funds for countercyclical policy in times of recessions. Except for defense purposes, it opposes the use of subsidies for agricultural and educational purposes and, in most cases, grants-in-aid to state and local governments. "In recent years the federal government has continued and in many cases increased federal 'grants-in-aid' to the States in a number of areas in which the Constitution recognized the exclusive jurisdiction of the States," writes Senator Goldwater.[23] While stressing a balanced Federal budget, nevertheless, the creed does argue that "achieving budget balance should be [based] on economy in government and not on increased revenues."[24] Senator Goldwater reiterates, "The only way to curtail spending substantially is to eliminate the programs on which excess spending is consumed."[25]

The past prevalence of the classical emphasis on frugal government is illustrated by the fact that in 1932 Franklin D. Roosevelt campaigned for the Presidency with the promise of "cutting federal expenditures." The classical ideology has strong commitments on the issue of government spending and a balanced budget. Besides the obvious concern over taxation, which will be taken up next, government spending is a basic mechanism of government control and power. It is difficult to imagine new gov-

---

[21] Chamber of Commerce of the United States, p. 23.
[22] *Ibid.*, p. 41.
[23] Goldwater, p. 26.
[24] *Ibid.*, p. 2.
[25] *Ibid.*, p. 68.

ernmental agencies being created (regulatory or otherwise) without increased government spending to pay for them. This argument holds likewise no regard for the idea of an unbalanced budget, which implies both governmental expansion and the need for tax increases.

Classical economic theory holds that the national budget and government finances work on the same principles as an individual. Therefore, it is deemed morally wrong for the government to go on spending more than its revenue. The whole economic and power analysis is at this point buttressed also by an emotional, moral argument. In some cases, of course, where an individual firm stands to benefit directly from government spending, the firm is usually able to overlook its own ideology if a conflict is created between it and the benefit to be received.

Taxation

The Chamber of Commerce takes the stand that "we must recognize that 'the power to tax is the power to destroy.' "[26] The creed argues further that a reform of Federal taxes is urgently needed in order to supply adequate amounts of venture capital to maintain an expanding economy and produce an increasing number of jobs for an expanding labor supply.[27] It urges that both individual and corporate taxes should be sharply compressed. The classical ideology opposes the idea that fiscal policy should be used by the government as an instrument of money and credit control to advance "countercyclical policy." Restated, it is opposed to attempts by the Federal government to use money and controls to stimulate or repress the economy. It argues that only the Federal Reserve System should have the independent responsibility for regulating the supply of money and credit.

The fact that the classical ideology argues for a revamping downward of the tax structure is hardly surprising—in fact, it is difficult to find any group which would not like this. A basic difference is involved, however, over the concept of using taxes, not only for revenue, but also for countercyclical policy. To admit this concept is to accept Keynesian economics, a step the classical creed refuses to take. The acceptance or rejection of Keynesian economic theory is still the basic differentiating feature between the classical and managerial branches of the business creed.

Wage and Price Controls

Obviously the classical creed is opposed to any determination of wages and prices except through the marketplace. The NAM charges that governmental interference with the normal operation of economic forces only

[26] Chamber of Commerce of the United States, p. 42.
[27] For further information see *ibid.*, pp. 42–44.

reduces the area of competition and causes inflationary pressures. As would be expected from this line of reasoning, the classical creed argues that the increasing concentration of political and economic power in the Federal government is contradictory both to tradition and to constitutional provisions. It therefore argues that government should be stronger on the local than on the Federal level.

The classical creed opposes inflation and uses it as an ideological weapon against government spending. Inflation, according to this segment of business, is an evil induced by the government itself. The policy of the national Chamber of Commerce is: "There must be continuous and critical review of all government activities and spending authorizations, by Congress, the executive branch, and the people."[28] Price increases as such, as long as they can be passed on, present no particular economic problems for the firm. In fact, inflation can cause the firm to make money on its existing inventories. The threat of government controls over prices and wages is a very different matter, and businessmen holding to the classical creed understandably are bitter in their opposition to it. It may be argued that the classical ideology opposes inflation not only because it makes the value of money unstable, but also because business fears excessive wage demands from unions and more government controls.

Distribution of the Functional Shares of Income

As an ideological issue, concern over the relative size of individual incomes has received far less attention than distribution of income between the various groups in the economy. In other words, the percentage shares of profit, wages, etc., are generally scrutinized more closely than the range of personal income distribution, at least from an ideological standpoint. This greater interest in the functional shares of income is perhaps due to the ideological bias involving distinction between earned wages or salaries and unearned income, such as interest, dividends, or rent. Even in supposedly capitalistic countries, the bias against the type of income classified as "unearned" is evident in the tax structure; corporate dividends, for example, are taxed when earned by the corporation and again when paid out to the stockholders.

One of the most remarkable facts of economic life in America today is the relative change in distributed shares of national income. In 1900, employee compensation was about 55 per cent of the total, entrepreneurial income was about 24 per cent, corporate profit was almost 7 per cent, interest received was 5.5 per cent, and rent was about 9 per cent. Fifty years later, employee compensation had risen to 67 per cent, entrepreneurial income was less than 14 per cent, corporation profits (between 1949 and 1957) had increased to nearly 13 per cent, while interest was only 2.7

28 *Ibid.,* p. 41.

per cent or almost half of its previous figure, and returns from rent had decreased drastically to 3.4 per cent. Even before taxes, distributed shares of national income have changed remarkably in regard to "the unearned income."

With economic justification, the classical ideology argues that unless a fair rate of return can be made on capital, there will not be sufficient capital invested to furnish money for new firms and to expand existing ones. "Throughout the ideology runs the doctrine that higher productivity is the sole and sovereign remedy for all economic ills. This and this alone can relieve unemployment, stop inflation and raise real wages."[29] The general position of the classical creed would be that the marketplace should determine the relative distribution on a straight supply-and-demand basis, and that government should end such discriminatory taxing practices as progressive taxing and double taxation.

Unemployment

While in its recent policy statements the classical creed recognizes the existence and need of unemployment compensation, it nonetheless does so reservedly. It generally sees unemployment, depression, or recession as having been caused by the government's increasing intervention within the traditional market structure. The marketplace, according to this theory, is able to solve its own problems without either depressions or recessions of significance if the government does not interfere. Today this argument, however, is in direct opposition to the Keynesian theory of government, a view which has generally superseded the classical theory in economic circles today, and which calls for countercyclical deficit spending to offset depressions and recessions as well as for government manipulation of credit for the same purpose.

On the issue of unemployment, the classical ideology is at greatest odds with most of the other major power groups. It opposes any means whereby government power and interference in business are increased. Furthermore, classical business groups not only reject the Keynesian thesis that government can and should manipulate or cushion the movements of the business cycle, but also regard Keynesian economics and government countercyclical policy as a process of letting down the barriers against socialism.

Such protagonists of the classical ideology as *The Freeman* magazine, for example, denounce Keynesian economics as only a disguised form of socialism. Paradoxically, however, Lord Keynes was a multimillionaire who refused to join the British Labour (Socialist) party and viewed his policies as a means of eliminating depressions and thereby saving capitalism from revolution and communism.

[29] Sutton, p. 125.

Economic Growth

The classical business creed essentially argues that the necessary spur needed for economic growth in the United States today would be a drastic and immediate tax cut, which would in turn further the accumulation of capital and increase investment in business. A reduction in taxes is its main positive policy recommendation for increasing the economic growth rate. On the other hand the classical creed does not necessarily accept the need for an increase in the rate of economic growth in the United States. It regards the United States, in a sense, as "a miracle" of economic growth and development, and it feels that the United States can serve as a model for all other developing countries if the free market is operative and if government's role is restricted. The classical creed is often highly opposed to any government interference which attempts to increase the rate of economic growth.

Generally this position is held out of fear of the increasing role of government in the economy. If it is admitted that the United States economic growth rate is less than desirable, then the remedy may well take the form of government involvement, as some of the other groups demand. Yet the classical ideology contends that a return to the free market with less confiscatory taxes in the upper bracket would stimulate economic growth. By so doing, the classical ideology attempts to parry any drives for economic planning and government intervention, which might be argued as necessary for economic growth. Thus, the classical group is pitted against the intellectuals and labor, as will be seen later in Chapters 3 and 7, and against other groups who favor vigorous government action and economic planning to improve the performance of the economy.

International Trade

The classical creed, at least as posited by the Chamber of Commerce and other business groups, evidences considerable strain over the issue of international trade. "The United States should pursue a constructive and realistic tariff policy which seeks to encourage a high level of international trade and investment, while affording reasonable protection for United States industries and agriculture against destructive or unfair competition from abroad."[30]

Traditionally, the classical theory of economics, upon which the classical ideology is based, has long been an advocate of free trade. Yet certain of the business interests who control the major expositors of the creed have apparently never been fully converted on this particular issue. It is possible to find articles in *The Freeman* magazine arguing against United States

[30] Chamber of Commerce of the United States, p. 55.

action to lower tariffs and pursue a course toward freer trade. This fact is particularly interesting because the managerial ideology has consistently advocated freer trade. While this dichotomy might cause difficulty for some, the advocates of the classical ideology admit no problem over the issue. This, however, is not difficult to understand since the function of an ideology is to rationalize, explain, and justify particular ideas or actions. Inconsistency is no problem to ideologies unless it creates too great a strain upon the membership, and there are in reality few fully consistent ideologies, hence most groups do not point out the inconsistency in the ideology of others because of similar problems in their own. To the observer these inconsistencies are nevertheless important because they reveal general areas in which economic or other specific interests conflict directly with some other general part of the ideology.

In this instance, members of the NAM are apparently convinced that they have more to lose from freer trade than to gain from it—enough to reject the idea of free trade as preached by classical economists. On the other hand the fact that advocates of the managerial ideology approve of freer trade appears to indicate that their operations are efficient enough to allow them to sell more abroad than they would stand to lose through foreign imports. If such is the case and if the membership of the NAM represents more middle-sized firms than the CED, whose members tend to be the largest corporations, then it would appear that, based on these two assumptions, big business, as represented by professional management and the CED, is more efficient than middle-sized firms in this country. On the other hand, efficiency is not the only factor which makes a company an export company. Uniqueness of product and lack of foreign production centers also make companies competitive in international markets.

The American Medical Association

One currently dynamic group within the constellations of classical ideologists is the American Medical Association (AMA) and the separately organized American Medical Political Action Committee (AMPAC).

The persistent offensive against any forms of socialized medicine, focused particularly on the issue of medical care for the aged under social security, is phrased in terms of the classical ideology. "A tax-supported service must assume the duty of controlling the terms of the service."[31] But medicine, particularly, must be free of "federal controls"[32] since "medicine is a science which flourishes best in freedom."[33]

The statements of AMA leaders often portray the classical ideology in

[31] *AMA News* (August 19, 1963), 4.
[32] *AMA News* (January 6, 1964), 4.
[33] Statement by past AMA president George M. Fister, *Current Medical Digest,* 30 (September, 1963), 3.

broader terms than the specific medical issue. Upon his inauguration as the 117th president of AMA, Dr. Edward R. Annis stated:

> The great danger is that freedom can be nibbled away "because each decision turned over to the government is one less decision which may be made by the individual."
>
> . . . Physicians must have the courage and individuality "to fight for all our political, economic, and professional freedoms."
>
> . . . When our ancestors came to this nation "searching for freedom and opportunity," the pressures against the individual were generated mainly by kings and emperors, autocrats, and aristocrats. Today in America the threats are more subtle, more insidious. The pressures against freedom, the forces which would regulate us, tax us, coddle us, come largely from a hybrid breed of bureaucrats, some politicians, some economists, some sociologists, some educators.[34]

The AMA further displays its role in the classical creed by its affiliation. The AMA maintains membership in the Chamber of Commerce and sends "representatives to attend meetings of or to cooperate with the U.S. Junior Chamber of Commerce." The American Farm Bureau Federation is shown in Chapter 4 to be the agricultural representative of the classical creed. The AMA House of Delegates voted to commend the AFBF "for its vigorous leadership in opposing unwarranted government interference and regulation."[35] Although refraining from taking a position on the so-called "Liberty Amendment" to abolish the Federal income tax, the House of Delegates agreed that "it should be called to the attention of individual physician citizens."[36]

Traditionally, the doctor has not been an aggressive political force in the community. It is generally agreed that the strongest interest among doctors and medical students is the care and treatment of disease.[37] This occupational interest, it appears, is concentrated to a higher degree than in any other occupational group.[38] Since the field of medicine is a profession of high economic prestige and of high public trust, and one which can usually assure the doctor of a maximum amount of work,[39] the doctor's basic desire and interest seem well satisfied within the profession itself.[40]

Although the doctor spends long hours professionally engaged, he is

[34] *AMA News* (July 8, 1963), 2. See also *AMA News, Ibid.,* 7; *Human Events* (March, 1963), 49; *American Family Physician* (July, 1963), 230.

[35] *AMA News* (July 8, 1963), 8.

[36] *AMA News* (August 19, 1963), 20.

[37] William Glaser, "Doctors and Politics," *American Journal of Sociology,* 61 (November, 1960), 231.

[38] *Ibid.*

[39] The typical doctor handles 123 patient visits a week. This is actually limited only by the doctor's desire to work and the time he can put into his profession. "New Yardsticks for Your Practice," *Medical Economics* (December 16, 1963), 74.

[40] Glaser, 232.

also quite active in extraprofessional activities. In no way, however, do these activities reflect a natural affinity for politics. The typical doctor escapes occupational pressures by engaging in the community's relaxing pursuits made available through the facilities of the social, fraternal, and recreation clubs[41] rather than by undertaking the mental fatigue and stress of active politics.

The doctor's lack of natural enthusiasm for political activity could possibly be derived from the fact that the profession of medicine is guided by a set of humanitarian principles and values antithetical to those of the typical politician. As Robert M. Cunningham, Jr., editor of *Modern Hospital,* suggested: "Politics is a 'dirty hands' business and medicine has always been a 'clean hands' business; 'healing' and 'heeling' do not go together."[42] If the physician does actively participate in politics, he may run the risk of offending both patient and colleague within the profession who do not share his political views.

POLITICAL POLICIES OF ORGANIZED MEDICINE. The AMA—chief spokesman for organized medicine—has long recognized the precariousness of the doctors' political position and has traditionally limited its encouragement of their political participation to activities which raise the medical standards within the profession and to the regulation of these standards.[43] Yet, as government expanded its base of operation and invaded areas which organized medicine had previously controlled, organized medicine saw dangers in the possibility of economic revision and modification of the medical *status quo.* Thus the AMA opposed consistently every group plan and "voluntary medical plan" which was developed.[44] Immediately the AMA forgot the doctors' individual interests and began to urge them to participate actively in defeating these "changes" in order that their freedom might be protected. Emotion-filled phrases like: "You can't socialize the Black Bag," "Beware of the Welfare State," and the now famous phrase of Lenin's, "The Keystone to the Arch of Communism Is Socialized Medicine," all aided in encouraging political activity. One conservative physicians group—the Association of American Physicians and Surgeons—has taken

[41] Harry W. Martin, "Physician's Role Conflict in Community Participation" (unpublished Ph.D. dissertation, Department of Sociology and Anthropology, University of North Carolina, 1957), p. 64.

[42] Robert M. Cunningham, Jr., "Can Political Means Gain Professional Ends?" *Modern Hospital,* 77 (December, 1951), 52.

[43] Martin, p. 195.

[44] Hyde and Wolff explain that the only time the AMA has come out in support of a "voluntary health plan" has been when a governmental plan—a plan much more extreme—has gained popular support. David R. Hyde and Payson Wolff, "The AMA: Power, Purpose, and Politics in Organized Medicine," *The Yale Law Journal,* 62 (May, 1954), 976.

it upon itself to protect "all Americans" from any type of governmental intrusion, including socialization of farming, power, housing, and social security.[45]

A great many physicians have seriously heeded the warnings of organized medicine and, disregarding the traditional position of limited political participation, have allowed a "new philosophy" of politics to play a leading part in today's political milieu.

THE "NEW PHILOSOPHY" OF POLITICS. This new philosophy, based upon successful techniques utilized by labor, business,[46] and other politically active occupational groups, is best summed up in the words of Dr. Gunnar Gundersen, active leader of the American Medical Political Action Committee (AMPAC):

> All of us would prefer to practice medicine in an atmosphere free from politics . . . it has come as something of a shock to discover that politics has moved into the practice of medicine uninvited and with the intention of staying put. . . . *If we want to keep politics out of medicine, we must get into politics as citizens.*[47] [Italics added.]

Advocates of this philosophy have incorporated it into an active three-part political program which covers the following areas:[48] (1) *political activity,* which includes direct candidate support through the expenditure of time or money; (2) *political education,* which stresses the role played by the doctor as a citizen and emphasizes precinct activity; and (3) *legislative activity,* which is organized medicine's attempt to influence public opinion in support of or opposition to specific legislation.

ORGANS WHICH ACCOMPLISH PROGRAM GOALS. To accomplish the goals set forth by the program, permanent associations have been assigned specific areas in which to work. The AMA and its affiliated state and county medical societies, for example, actively lobby to influence public opinion concerning medical legislation. Subjects of interest to the AMA range from those of specific medical interest, such as "the distribution of drugs," to the more obscurely related ones, e.g., the endorsement of fallout shelter legislation.[49]

The AMA also influences the public through its ease of access to the means of mass communication. Through its many specialty journals, its two

[45] Harry E. Northam, "AAPS—Its Principles and Objectives" (Chicago: AAPS, n.d.).

[46] The Chamber of Commerce and organized labor have most particularly had great effect on this "new philosophy."

[47] *Political Stethoscope* (AMPAC's newsletter), 1 (October, 1962), 1.

[48] *Political Stethoscope,* 1 (June, 1962), 4.

[49] "Washington News," *JAMA,* 185 (July 27, 1963), 18.

nonscientific publications, and its widely acclaimed *Journal of the American Medical Association* (*JAMA*), as well as its various radio and TV programs, the AMA attempts to influence public opinion pointing out the benefits of the present system of medicine.[50]

"Political activity" for many years created problems for the incorporated medical societies since they were relatively limited in their political activity by the Federal Corrupt Practices Act and the Hatch Act. With the creation of AMPAC and its affiliate PAC units in 1961, organized medicine was legally able to participate actively in support of selected candidates. At present AMPAC operates separately from the AMA and carries on its own political programs on its own budget of corporate dollars and membership fees.

ASSESSMENT OF POLITICAL ACTION. The success of organized medicine's "new look" can best be judged through the accomplishments and failures of the 1960 and 1962 elections. Successful fund raising helped AMPAC to distribute $250,000 to various state organizations. The AMPAC planned to raise at least $750,000 for the 1964 campaign for use by needy state units.[51] The AMA, active as well in 1962, spent a total of $83,075.87 in an effort to influence legislation.[52] This did not come close to the unprecedented $163,000 spent in 1961 in the AMA's all-out effort to defeat the King-Anderson Bill.[53]

The money collected, of course, only hints of their success. Of the four Senate races which were AMPAC-sponsored in 1962, two candidates were successful—Wallace Bennett (R, Utah) and Peter Dominick (R, Colorado).[54] In congressional races, AMPAC entered 75 to 80 and won in better than 70 per cent of the cases.[55] In commenting on AMPAC successes, Republican leader William E. Miller, chairman of the Republican party, stated: "They (AMPAC) were one of the bright spots of the last campaign. Their potential for the future is enormous and both parties recognize it."[56]

[50] American Medical Association, "AMA Background Information," a report of basic facts (Chicago: AMA, n.d.), p. 4.

[51] "Doctors in Politics," *Wall Street Journal* (July 2, 1963). COPE, labor's political education committee, spent close to $700,000 and succeeded only 58.7 per cent of the time.

[52] "AMA Leads 1962 Health Lobbyists with Expenditures of $83,000," *Medical World News* (October 11, 1963), 8d.

[53] *Congressional Quarterly Almanac,* 87th Congress, vol. 18 (1962), 944–945.

[54] In both South Dakota and Connecticut, AMPAC candidates Joe Bottom (R, South Dakota) and Horace Seely Brown (R, Connecticut) lost to the opposition.

[55] "Does Politicking Pay Off?" *Medical Economics* (November 5, 1962), 269.

[56] "1963—Year of Preparation: 1964—The Year of Decision," a twenty-minute film scriptbook (Chicago: AMPAC, 1963).

Physicians are, on the whole, an extremely cohesive and influential group. Because of their desire for professional unity, and a lack of any formidable opposition, doctors form a political front impressive enough to make the opposition deviate from their political pathways. When in effect they unite their strength and energies with others within the healing arts, and with other occupational groups of similar "conservative" philosophies, they magnify their power and become a very active part of a large voting bloc which commands respect from every member of the opposition.

THE SMALL BUSINESS IDEOLOGY

The ideology of small business is essentially a minor variation of the classical ideology. It differs on only a few major points, such as the economic division of interest between big and small business, subversive elements in the country, and the generally higher emotional tone of the small business ideology.

Generally the classical business ideology incorporates most of the economic issues favored by small business. A major exception, of course, is that of interest in government aid to small business (defined by the Senate Small Business Committee as any firm with less than 250 employees, $500,000 in total assets, and $1,000,000 in business volume). The NAM leadership is made up of firms who, by this definition, are almost always big business men. Hence it is only reasonable to assume that the small business administration is of less concern to the NAM than to small business groups.

Apart from special economic advantage, the small business ideology seems to differ from the classical ideology more in its *tone* than in its content. On the issue of Communist subversion, particularly in schools, the small business men and certain other grass roots groups are much more incited than is the NAM and the classical ideology. Some analysts, such as Seymour Martin Lipset, have attributed this support, even of McCarthyism, to a traditional agrarian populist ideology that continues to flourish among nonindustrial segments of the country.

Also, the bigger business leaders in both the NAM and the CED value education more highly, it appears, than do the small business men who seem afraid of and even alienated by the "egghead," "dreamer," "social planner," and "intellectual" types who inhabit universities and whom they suspect of "un-American" thoughts and activities. John Bunzel points to this difference on educational ideology between big and small business as one of their main distinguishing features. Thus the small business man, even though he may send his children to college, wants to make certain that they are studying something "practical" and, above all, are not being tainted with any ideas of "socialism," which he frequently equates with big government, deficit financing, or Keynesian economics.

The small business man in America is generally given more attention as an ideal or as part of the American ideology than he is in actual public policy. For, while the virtues and values of the small business man are extolled more consistently and frequently than those of any other group, with the possible exception of the farmer, the small business men are not nearly so well organized or nearly so powerful on the national scene as their numbers might suggest. Small business men, however, frequently exercise considerable influence in state and local government and party organizations.

There have been many small business groups organized to promote the interest of American small business. Few of these organizations, however, have endured or developed into powerful organizations to lobby for and influence small business interests. Today, the National Federation of Independent Business, Inc. (NFIB) is perhaps the largest and most vocal of the pressure groups representing small business on the national scene.

This organization, which was founded and is still controlled by C. W. Harder, was begun in 1943 in California. Since then its membership has developed to around 100,000 members, at which point it appears to have stabilized. The federation employs 150 salesmen throughout the country to recruit and maintain memberships, and it hires a full-time lobbyist in Washington and a legislative researcher who prepares the organization's publication *The Mandate*. This is a tear-off, self-mailer ballot that is the cornerstone of the group's activities and a device for polling the members to learn their opinions on various domestic and international issues. The results of such polls are sent to congressmen and used by the association's lobbyist in attempting to influence legislation.

The major objective of the association's lobbyist has been to fight for consistent enforcement of the antitrust laws and oppose the expansion of big government and big unions. The Senate Small Business Committee, an agency whose main function is to make loans to small business, became a permanent committee in 1950, and the NFIB takes general credit for this development. It also claims to have been instrumental in aiding the passage of the Celler-O'Mahoney-Kefauver Act of 1949, an act which plugged up some loopholes in the antimerger laws of the Clayton Act. Furthermore, when general issues of union or government power come before Congress, the NFIB, needless to say, stands with those of the classical ideology such as the NAM and the United States Chamber of Commerce.

The persistence of the agrarian spirit is strongly enunciated in the statements of the small business man.

To the small businessman the best government is the one that has the least to do and say, reflecting again his attachment to the political and economic way of life that flourished before the rise of industry and the effects of urbanization. Apprehensive of the complexities of modern living, the small businessman is concerned with preserving what he feels are the true ideals and guarantees which the Constitution, drawn in pre-industrial setting, made the basis of our free-enterprise system.[57]

Spokesman groups, such as the Conference of American Small Business Organizations, founded in 1941 and active for a decade, warned continually that small business must fight for its life against "ever increasing competition conducted by government under the rules of socialism." The National Federation of Independent Business continues to express similar attitudes.

As with other holders of the classical ideology, the small business man decries the "assassination of Adam Smith" and stresses the virtues of individualism. Further, while both the NAM and the NFIB evidence strong dislike of large-scale organizations and the increasing concentration of political and economic power, the classical ideologists (i.e., NAM, United States Chamber of Commerce) define such evil as due to big government and big unions. The small business man, however, will include big business as well. The evils of the latter group are quite obviously and consistently overlooked by the NAM.

The small business ideology, while varying from the more commonly heard version of the classical ideology, is nonetheless basically a minor variation of it. Depending upon how fine a distinction one wishes to make between American business creeds, one could classify it either as a distinct and separate ideology or as merely the utilization of a well-known body of ideology by a small business group rather than by a big or bigger business group. Thus despite the difference in attitude toward business concentration, subversion, and emotional content of ideological statements on most major domestic economic issues, the small business ideology will essentially differ little from the classical ideology.

In terms of political power to influence national policy, the small business men appear to be disproportionately weaker, in comparison to the NAM and the CED, than their numbers in the population suggest. This discrepancy only points out the contention made in Chapter 1 of this book that the power of a group is not determined solely by numbers, for the small business man alone is seldom able to influence greatly or win battles involving the arbitrage of national power. In fact, Harmon Zeigler, in *The Politics of Small Business,* takes a position completely opposite to that of Bunzel. Zeigler argues that "there is no small business interest."[58] In his analysis of the NFIB, for instance, he feels that "the way the small business

[57] John H. Bunzel, "Ideology of Small Business," *Political Science Quarterly,* 70 1 (March 1955), 95–96.

[58] L. Harmon Zeigler, *The Politics of Small Business* (Washington, D.C.: Public Affairs Press, 1961), p. 66.

associations conceive of their clientele suggests they do not perceive of small business as a separate segment of the business population having unique interests and goals."[59]

This disagreement between such scholars as Bunzel and Zeigler on the actual role and power of small business points up how nebulous and ill-defined the role of the small business man as a power group is. Thus even an ideology, except along the broad general lines sketched above, is difficult to assume as a consensus of small business feeling. Owing to this very factor, the power of the small business man as a maker of public policy is fractured and necessarily limited.

THE MANAGERIAL IDEOLOGY

The managerial ideology is often thought of as a contemporary version of the classical business creed. It is modern inasmuch as it accepts Keynesian economic theory and attempts to work with the environment of expanded government to attain its ends. It represents professional management of big more than small or even middle-sized business: The Committee for Economic Development (CED), for example, is a group of 200 corporate executives and educators who work together to conduct research and formulate policy. The CED defines the purpose of such studies and policy guidelines as the making of recommendations which will contribute to "full employment at higher living standards and promote economic growth and stability and strengthen the concepts and institutions essential to progress in a free society." While many others also accept these basic positions, the CED is cited here because it is the most vocal group involved in disseminating this form of the business creed.[60]

As the managerial ideology maintains silence on many points, it is generally assumed that this silence indicates near agreement between its position and that of the classical business creed; there is, however, considerable difference between the two regarding what should be the proper function of government.

The managerialists accept a considerably greater role for government than do the traditionalists. As the editors of *Fortune* magazine express it, "It is now almost universally accepted that . . . in the event of a serious depression, government . . . undertakes very large counter-cyclical spending

[59] *Ibid.,* p. 24.

[60] The CED is financed by contributions of over 3,000 corporations which subscribe to the CED's philosophy and runs an annual budget of about $2 million for research, education, information, etc. The information division in 1961 alone reports distribution of 3,716,676 books and pamphlets. [Source: CED, *Report of Activities* (New York, 1961), p. 16.]

programs."[61] Even though Keynesian economics may be finding an increasing acceptance in the managerial credo, it should be pointed out that the CED does resist the encroachment of government into traditional areas of management decision making, i.e., wages, prices, production, etc.

Perhaps the general attitude and political position of the CED and of the managerial ideologists can best be summarized in the terms of *Business Week,* which pointed out as the Eisenhower administration came into office: "There is a marked similarity between the CED and the new administration that involves more than the names of men. Both are representatives of a particular type of forward-looking businessman, a sort of progressive conservative."[62] Even President Eisenhower himself, when president of Columbia University, had been a trustee of the CED, as had his Secretaries of the Treasury, Humphrey and Anderson, as well as others of his appointees, such as Marion D. Folsom, Walter Williams, Meyer Kestnbaum, and James D. Zellerbach. All had been chairmen of the CED at one time or another, and eventually found high appointments within the Eisenhower administration.[63]

It must be pointed out that, in contrast to the classical ideology, the managerialist ideology is far from a completely neat, perfect theoretical system. Essentially, the managerial ideology deemphasizes the traditional forces of supply and demand as determining prices in the competitive market and stresses more the composite group decision making of government, business, labor, and the public consumer. It argues that management is a trustee who serves the interest of all groups, taking account of more than just the concern of his own stockholders for profits.

Why does the managerial group hold this position regarding the expanded role of government when such views are anathema to businessmen of the classical orientation? In addition to difference in personality structure and liberality of educational background, the managerialists are more adjusted to and less alienated from modern government. The "why" behind this realism is difficult to determine precisely, but it may well be that managerialists are convinced of the necessity of the expanded role of government to prevent deep depressions and possible radicalism. By accepting such a position, one held by most United States economists as well, they are facing the problem of determining how government can be most effectively utilized in our mixed market economy.

Perhaps one main reason why they appear less alienated from the government is that they frequently play an important role in it—either officially or as unofficial advisers. Their opportunities to serve as government appointees are not only due to the fact that part of them, particularly members

[61] Schriftgiesser, p. 224.
[62] *Ibid.,* p. 162.
[63] *Ibid.,* p. 161.

of the CED, have led some of the most important and best-known corporations in the country, but also because the managerial ideology is sufficiently pragmatic and flexible to permit them to work with politicians who are noted for similar qualities. Too often the rather extreme position of the classical ideology forces its followers to estrange themselves from politicians and others who must walk a more middle-of-the-road position.

Thus, those holding the classical ideology have difficulty in working with either Republican or Democratic administrations, since to win votes the party must take a central position to woo the largest possible majority of voters, especially in the big industrialized states which carry such heavy weight in their bloc votes in the electoral college. The classical group, therefore, tends to form a hard core of believers at the right edge of both parties, who rarely participate in a national administration—even though individuals such as Senator Wallace Bennett, former president of the NAM, are sometimes elected to Congress from non-labor-dominated states. The managerialists, on the other hand, are closer to the political center and thus have greater facility in working with the other center groups who generally comprise the country's political majority.

The managerialists hold their ideology because they believe their view of the economy and society is more realistic as well as more pragmatic or flexible and less estranged from big government.

Competition and Bigness

While managerialists accept without question the Sherman Antitrust Act and the need to prevent monopolies from developing, nonetheless there is concern within the managerial ideology that big business is criticized and threatened by government, not because of violation of antitrust action but because of its very size. This position is understandable when one notes that the membership of the CED, for example, includes the heads of some of the largest corporations in this country. Particularly in such mediums as *Fortune* magazine one finds the expression that big business is necessary for research and technology in our present big economy.

LABOR.   The area wherein managerialists desire competition the least is in their relations with labor, which will be more fully discussed in Chapter 3. The managerial ideology contends that labor has too much influence and power over the basic decisions of management. Because of labor's voting strength, the managerial ideology generally contends that labor has been unduly able to influence legislation to the detriment of business. Thus the majority of those holding the managerial ideology would doubtlessly feel that labor currently has an unfair competitive advantage over business due to favorable government action generally taken under a Democratic administration. This view is shared, of course, by the classical creed. Managerialists, however, often expound it less vociferously.

Although often more subtle about their opposition to labor than are their brothers in the NAM, the CED members frequently regard the expansion of labor power as their greatest challenge for control, seeming at times to fear labor's power increases even more than government's. This may be understood by remembering that in recent decades labor has continually encroached upon management decision-making prerogatives, not only in the area of wages, but in all other areas of on-the-job labor involvement. As labor has been able to achieve this through the passage of certain legislation and through pressure brought to bear upon parties in office at various times as well as through collective bargaining, the managerialists feel that they in turn can only ward off labor's power challenge by the same tools of government. Thus government is less a threat to them than labor as long as it does not encroach upon their decision-making functions, for it is a double-edged sword which can be wielded to the advantage of whoever holds it.

GOVERNMENT. Somewhat contrary to the NAM's feeling that government is always in the hands of those who would cripple business, the managerial group itself has often been deeply involved in government administration in the postwar era. Government, then, is the only instrument by which the managerialists feel they can curb labor's power. This is not to say that both the NAM and the CED were not involved in the passage of the Taft-Hartley and the Landrum-Griffin acts. It does say that the classical business group regards the government apparatus as its most direct threat, while the managerialists tend to feel that they can and must work with government. While representing a threat to management if controlled by the wrong groups, government also represents an apparatus greatly influencing business success.

The classical ideology views government as continually at war against classical business interests, while in the collective mind of the managerial ideology, government is viewed not so much as a group but rather as a mechanism whose controller runs the economy. Thus, the CED fears labor as a competing power group, vying with it for control of the governmental processes. Of course, in practice, the NAM is an efficient and well-organized pressure and lobby group which understands well the practical way in which public policy is made. It might first appear that the classical ideology hampers its own efforts in the struggle for control of government mechanisms; however, the classical ideology's war against big government is usually fought against those promoting programs detrimental to its interests. Actually, this makes for a more powerful ideological tool through identifying opponents as favoring "more government" or "socialism," for "big government" creates a degree of apprehension in this country.

It may be that psychologically the classicist tends to have a more uncompromising personality and the managerialist tends to have a more adjustable personality. A study of the remarks made by business executives around the country at the time President Kennedy put pressure on United States Steel to revoke its price increase in April of 1962 might well give an indication of the basic psychological differences between the managerial and the classical views. Both groups generally condemned vigorously the President's action as an infringement upon management prerogatives and as an intrusion into the freedom of management's decision making in the traditional areas of wage and price controls. Nonetheless, a number of executives expressed the opinion in the *Wall Street Journal* that Roger Blough had been imprudent in his unawareness of the President's position and that Blough's actions were made publicly to appear as a direct challenge to the President of the United States. As such, this constituted gross mismanagement by the United States Steel Company. The managerialists generally tend to make themselves aware of such political problems and to be more conciliatory toward government, or at least to take what they consider to be a more pragmatic position.

AGRICULTURE.   Perhaps the area of agriculture is the most dramatic area of common agreement between the two business creeds. The CED and the NAM feel that there should be a return to the free market situation in which demand and supply, not the government, establish prices and the market; and most United States economists agree with them on this issue. When the CED published a statement to this effect before Congress while the Kennedy administration was working out its agricultural program along considerably different lines, certain farm areas in the Middle West protested this stand and argued in support of government subsidies to agriculture. When these farm protests were put at the door of Sears, Roebuck, whose chairman had been involved in developing the CED policy statement, Sears, Roebuck was forced to say that the views were not necessarily its own, but merely the personal views of the head of the company.

While some companies might feel such pressure from certain of the farm groups, the basic alignment between the business power bloc and the Farm Bureau, the largest of all farm groups, would not be hurt by this policy because the Farm Bureau is essentially in agreement. In a sense the reason the business group as a whole and the CED in particular argue for a market solution to the farm problem is that no other policy appears to have much chance of solving the farm glut without complete regimentation and government of agriculture. The cost and tax burden of a subsidized farm program was simply too irrational for the business group to tolerate any longer. (For further discussion of agricultural policies see Chapter 4.)

Government Spending

One of the areas of sharpest disagreement between the classical and managerial business creeds is the issue of government spending and deficits. The CED has published a number of quite sophisticated statements on national policy regarding fiscal and monetary policy for high employment as well as statements on inflation and various papers on agricultural policy, prices, output, distressed areas, and so forth. The distinctive general policy of the managerial creed is an acceptance of Keynesian cyclical spending by the government as contrasted to the classical creed. While not champions of Federal lending, subsidies, or grants-in-aid, managerialists nonetheless are not opposed to government lending and spending in many areas in which the classical creed would be.

DEFICITS AND THE BALANCED BUDGET.   At the core of the argument over government fiscal policy is the issue regarding government deficit spending. Fiscal policy would be unnecessary if the government were forced to balance its budget annually. Yet only by large expenditures which normally result in a deficit can fiscal policy attempt to reverse a strong economic downtrend. Therefore, if Keynesian economic policy is accepted (i.e., the use of countercyclical spending and deficits), then an annually balanced budget is not always possible. Because of this fact, the managerial creed proposes that the government's budget be balanced over the whole business cycle and not necessarily each year, while the classical creed, being opposed to the idea of government fiscal policy to begin with, naturally opposes any deficits.

The argument between the two business groups over this issue is both real and deep, even though on the surface the two ideologies sometimes appear to be only slightly at odds. The managerial ideology argues for a balanced budget over the cycle rather than the classicists' annually balanced budget. Thus the time period over which the budget is to be balanced makes all the difference regarding the role government will play in regulating the economy. At times this issue may on the surface seem almost trivial, but upon deeper examination, it is clearly a vital point of conflict. The issues involved here are merely part of the whole basic approach of business to its environment.

Taxation

In the area of taxation policies, the managerial creed argues as strongly as the classical creed that it is essential to have a revamping downward of corporate and private income tax rates. Arguments are generally expressed in terms of the depressive effect that the current rates have on economic growth and venture capital. Policy statements by the CED and articles in

Fortune magazine bear out this point. Business has been presented with a ready-made issue of some economic validity by the national desire for greater economic growth. The high rates of corporate and personal income taxes undoubtedly do lower the national rate of investment and hence affect the growth rate of the country. Since it is obviously to business's best interest to gain a decrease in the tax rate, it is not difficult to understand the position of the classical and managerial ideologies on this problem.

Price Stability

The managerial ideology contends that the most effective means to control inflation is through the use of restrictive credit and fiscal policies. The role of government in this case is not limited to noninterference, as would be recommended by the classical creed, but rather to involvement in monetary and fiscal measures that would, it is hoped, reduce inflationary pressures in the economy.

Why has the CED taken the position that inflation can and should be handled by government fiscal and monetary policies? This may be due directly to their commitment regarding Keynesian economics rather than to fear of any small annual price increase. Certainly businesses in most instances can pass on such price increases and can even frequently make money from their inventories in the process. However, rampant inflation would undoubtedly result in government wage and price controls (which the managerialists are opposed to as a definite encroachment of their own powers, as is labor).

Additionally, it has been suggested that inflation may provide the managerialists with some worry over foreign competition and the balance of payments. How important this suggestion may be is difficult to determine since inflation as an ideological problem for the CED developed before the more recent balance-of-payments problems.

It would seem that inflation has been a popular ideological problem that has necessitated a response from most groups. Further, monetary and fiscal policy should be able to handle inflationary pressures. To admit otherwise would be an admission by the managerial creed that its basic economic theory is in some way defective. While most managerialists might not actually be overly troubled by small inflationary pressures, the fact that inflation had become a general ideological problem (because of its ideological use by other groups) required that the CED make certain studies and policy statements on the issue, as discussed above.

Distributed Shares of the National Income

The managerial ideology presents no particularly distinctive approach toward the problem of income distribution. Rather its approach is eclectic; it accepts the classical argument that the market should be the main determinant of the relative shares received by each group in the economy. However, the managerial group would generally temper the market were its results to be overly harsh toward any one group.

The managerial and the classical ideologies frequently take a joint line of defense concerning business profits. The argument is repeatedly made that profits are earned just as truly as wages are earned. Profits are merely the price paid for the risk taken by the firm and the investment of capital. They are essential for the growth of the economy and for providing society with basic services. The very fact, however, that both business groups feel constrained to defend business profits is indicative of the antibusiness pressures exerted by such groups as labor and the intellectuals.

Unemployment

As mentioned above, the managerial group espouses a version of Keynesian economics; that is, government should manage its fiscal policies in order to prevent or at least cushion downturns in the business cycle which result in unemployment. The deficit financing which may well be incurred should be offset later by surpluses on the recovery side of the cycle—thus the budget would be balanced over the cycle even if not in particular years.

The managerialists' principal concern over unemployment is that it may presage a downturn in the whole economy. On the other hand, business could hardly be opposed to a slight cushion of unemployment to ease labor's pressures on it. Only at some critical level can business find itself seriously threatened by unemployment. This is evidenced by the observation that business has had relatively little to say about the unemployment of between 5 and 6 million workers, while at the same time labor has said a great deal. The fact that this was not viewed by business leaders as a serious number portending business downturn is likely the reason.

Other danger signs, however, such as some of the leading economic indicators turning downward, brought moves from the managerialists as well as other groups to urge the Kennedy administration in 1962 to take fiscal policy measures to reverse the situation. While unemployment represents a decrease in the purchasing power of consumers, it is viewed as a serious problem by business only when it reaches proportions portending business downturn.

Economic Growth

As concerns economic growth, the managerial ideology again represents a rather interesting hybrid, formed of the classical creed's attitude toward the use of the market mechanisms combined with a generally liberal attitude toward government's intervention in the economy. As noted in the CED's publication *Economic Growth in the United States,* the profit and loss system is the basic background for growth: "This universal drive to expansion in search of profit, animating each one of millions of economic teams, has undoubtedly been the great generating force for the cumulative economic growth that has taken place in the whole society."[64] Nonetheless, a managerial creed points out specifically that unrestrained *laissez faire* is foreign to their concept of the modern system of capitalism. In contrast to this, the classical ideology apparently prefers a return to a laissez-faire economy.

The managerial ideology goes much farther than the classical creed in its concession of the role of government for economic growth. "That is, the powers of government can contribute to economic growth in special ways, other than by good public investment."[65] This statement obviously departs a long way from the accepted ideals of the classical ideology. But contributions government can make toward the stimulating of economic growth by promoting flexibility and mobility in the economy, by avoiding excessive taxation and undue fluctuations in production and prices, and by promoting international trade will open the lid of a Pandora's box of government activity. Even these many activities do not include public investment. Thus, the managerial creed would apparently not oppose a wider scope of government activity to promote economic growth if such activity did not compete or interfere with its own decision-making prerogatives.

Why does the managerial ideology favor government action to stimulate economic growth? Beyond the obvious concern about United States economic competition with the Soviet Union, the answer may lie in the preoccupation with growth typical of most United States corporations. Expansion is one of the main yardsticks by which management can be judged. Further, the size of a corporation is in itself a status symbol among corporation executives, and generally, the larger the company, the larger the salaries for top executives. However, in a slowly growing economy, it is difficult for individual corporations to grow rapidly. Hence, the managerialists will accept government activity, within the bounds noted, to stimulate the economy toward a higher growth performance. As noted earlier, one of their primary recommendations is a general downward tax revision of personal and corporate taxes.

International Trade

In the realm of international trade, the managerial ideology goes considerably farther than does the classical creed in urging free trade or "freer" trade. At least, as recommended in one of the CED statements on national policy, *A New Trade Policy for the United States,*[66] its position is that the

[64] Committee for Economic Development, Research and Policy Committee, *Economic Growth in the United States* (New York, 1958), p. 20.

[65] *Ibid.,* p. 45.

[66] Committee for Economic Development, *A New Trade Policy for the United States* (New York, 1962).

United States should adopt the basic program proposed by President Kennedy in 1962, in which he recommended flexible arrangements for changing tariffs in order to bargain with the European Common Market and other industrialized nations and allow for a general reduction of international tariffs so that freer trade might be developed among all countries.

As noted earlier, the managerialists obviously feel that there is more to be gained than to be lost economically from freer trade. Thus, the companies they represent, usually some of the largest in the country, feel that they can be sufficiently competitive on an international scale to benefit from general tariff reductions. The United States has generally had relatively low tariffs compared to most other countries, and if such companies have not been injured up to now, they are not likely to be hurt by freer trade in the future.

The International CED

An interesting new development has occurred within the CED regarding international relationships with other independent business-oriented research groups. To quote a CED pamphlet: "Increasingly close relationships are being developed with independent non-political research organizations in other countries. These organizations are composed of businessmen and scholars, [who] have objectives similar to those of the CED, and [who] pursue them by similarly objective methods."[67] In several cases, agreements for reciprocal distribution of publications have developed out of this cooperation, and many of the publications of these international research organizations can now be obtained in the United States from the CED.

The following countries and organizations are listed as belonging to this international "fraternity": Political and Economic Planning in England, the SMS in Sweden, the Committee for Economic Development of Australia, the CEPES (European Committee for Economic and Social Progress) of West Germany, the CEPES of France, and the CEPES of Italy. There is also the Committee for Economic Development in Japan. The interesting common denominator among these groups in various countries appears to be a combination of businessmen and scholars. Furthermore the advancements made in economic theory, especially through the acceptance of Keynesian theory to handle business cycles and hence increase the role of government in economic affairs, have apparently been generally accepted within these various international free world groups.

At one time the classical ideology represented the only business group in America and was essentially the extension of a foreign ideology, since it has traditionally acted, in a sense, as merely one branch of an ideology hav-

[67] Committee for Economic Development, *International Library Order Form* (New York, n.d.), p. 1.

ing an international body of believers. Now it appears that the same thing is developing within the managerial ideology and that the CED is correspondingly developing reciprocal relations with similar groups in other countries around the world.

A CASE STUDY OF BUSINESS IN POLITICS

Perhaps the easiest way to understand how business as a power group operates in the legislative market is to look at a particular case to see how such a group has performed and what its methods and performance have been. The case we shall consider here is the campaign spearheaded by the National Association of Manufacturers to pass the Taft-Hartley Act of 1947.[68]

While the NAM was organized in the 1890s basically to protect industry from foreign competition, nonetheless its major problem in recent decades has been that of attempting to stop the encroachments of labor's government on its own traditional domain of decision making. With the election of Franklin Delano Roosevelt in the early depression years and the wave of antibusiness feeling that swept much of the country in this period, the NAM felt itself strongly under attack; and it was. For with the passage of the Wagner Act (National Labor Relations Act of 1935) labor achieved its highest position in terms of legal rights in United States history. After the passage of the Wagner Act, the NAM launched a long, untiring campaign to replace the act by legislation it felt more conducive to its own tenets. Interrupted only by World War II, the campaign by the NAM continued until the passage of the Taft-Hartley Act in 1947. It continues today; for the NAM and the AFL-CIO regard each other, realistically, as basic antagonists who must be watched at all times to prevent one of them from gaining the upper hand.

In 1934 Senator Wagner attempted to establish a permanent agency to supervise labor relations. The purpose of this program was to protect unions against employer domination, coercion, discrimination, or interference of any kind. To this end, the National Labor Relations Board was established to hear complaints against employers and to decide whether an employer was guilty of such actions. If the employer was found guilty, he was to be ordered to cease discrimination or coercion and even to rehire his employees if the board felt that they had been wrongly fired. Further, the Board was to be able to order elections to be held in various companies to determine whether unions had a bona fide claim to represent the employees of a given plant. Needless to say, business felt this to be a direct

---

[68] This material is based upon an analysis by Robert E. Lane, James D. Barber, and Fred I. Greenstein, *An Introduction to Political Analysis,* 3d ed. (Englewood Cliffs, N.J.: Prentice-Hall, Inc., 1962), pp. 90–95.

threat to its prerogatives, to its power, and to the type of labor relations it had been accustomed to. Before the Senate Committee on Education and Labor, J. A. Emery, counsel for the NAM and a well-known lobbyist, testified that this measure was not only unconstitutional and immoral, but also a violation of states' rights and of "sound public policy." He was backed in this by representatives of thirty employer and business associations, twenty-seven businessmen, and twenty-one spokesmen for unions threatened by the measure. Backing up their Washington spokesman, the *Law Department Bulletin* of the NAM urged its readers, "You should make clear . . . to those charged with responsibility for the legislation your determined opposition to the enactment of this unjust and invalid legislation."

Despite these measures the National Labor Relations Act was passed with only ten dissenting votes in the Senate and without even a record vote in the House. The NAM realized that this was only the beginning of a struggle and that it had been defeated in the battle because of lack of organization and preparation. The first reaction of the NAM to the passage of the Wagner Act was immediately to challenge its legality in the courts. However, by 1936, the NAM realized that the Supreme Court recognized the constitutionality of the measure. Finding that attempts to repeal it were not likely, the NAM attempted to amend the act to cover unfair union practices. In 1936, the NAM settled down to begin a decade of attack against the Wagner Act and to attempt to present its view of labor relations not only to Congress but to the public in an effort to mold both public and legislative opinion for its amendment.

In this new publicity campaign, the NAM began by establishing an employer-employee service to provide assistance to firms wishing to publish a plant magazine, leaflets to be stuffed in the pay envelopes, posters, speech material, and films on private enterprise. Additionally, a regular news service, *The Six Star Service,* for weekly and other newspapers; a cartoon series, *Uncle Abner Says;* foreign language radio programs; a series of newspaper advertisements; an agricultural news service; a publication for foremen, *Industrial Facts;* and a shareholder letter were prepared by a greatly enlarged public relations staff. The direct attempt of these new publicity measures was to secure an amendment to the Wagner Act and to show abuses of union power to the public, Congress, and the news services through cartoons, radio programs, and other periodicals. This campaign met with success finally with the passage of the Taft-Hartley Act a decade later in 1947.

By 1939, some results of NAM pressure were paying off, and ten bills amending the Wagner Act and one repeal measure were presented to Congress. For a time the NAM focused its attention on what was called the Berg Bill, which was to include unfair labor practices under the law. The

NAM Law Digest said, "We urge you to study this matter . . . communicate your views to your Senators and Representatives in Congress." Attention shifted somewhat among the various bills and finally came to focus on three resolutions requesting an investigation of the NLRB; by gathering support for these measures, the NAM was able to get one of them through both houses of Congress. The NAM, realizing the difficulty of its fight and how unprepared it had been in the past to wage this type of campaign, particularly with the administration favorable to labor, announced in 1939 that it had considerably increased the number of members of its staff and had increased the number of formal and informal conferences between the NAM officers and members of legislative and executive branches of the government. It should be pointed out that in conjunction with the efforts of the NAM, the Chamber of Commerce in 1939 was also very active and is reputed to have held 27 simultaneous steak dinners at which 300 congressmen were entertained by delegates of the Chamber from the congressmen's home states.

At the same time that activities were increasing in Washington, similar activities on a lesser scale were evident in the state capitals around the country. The state manufacturers associations and local chambers of commerce were attempting to impress state legislatures with the merits of their cause, attempting to show that legislation had swung too far in overrepresenting labor. In an effort to develop individual state legislation favorable to it, the NAM in its *Law Digest* said, "Beginning in 1939 the second trend developed toward the regulation of labor union activities and affairs centering around restrictions on the closed shop, ending in boycotts, the petitions on the right to picket and the right to strike." Eight years before sufficient business pressure had accumulated in Congress to pass the Taft-Hartley Act, state legislatures were already beginning to move in the same direction.

In 1940 the most nearly successful prewar attack on the Wagner Act occurred. Congress, still reflecting its off-year nonpresidential election of 1938, and hence being more conservative than in 1937 or 1941, seemed generally receptive to business pressure, particularly since the fruits of the Smith Committee investigation on the power and activities of labor had been gathered in this year. The NAM attempted to give wide publicity to the information developed out of the Smith investigation and to see that both Congress and the public were fully informed. It is reported that during the first few months of the work of the committee, over 1,000 editorials commending its work and attacking the NLRB were published in magazines and newspapers in the country. Out of the Smith Committee investigations came the Smith Bill, embodying recommendations for limiting labor's power. The NAM attempted to support this bill with all its strength. It continued to tell businessmen that they were not making their position sufficiently clear to Congress on these issues. With a full-scale drive the

NAM was able to see the Smith Bill pass the House, despite the opposition of the House Labor Committee. It appeared for a while that the bill might threaten a major part of the Wagner Act; nonetheless, the opposition was able to see that it was pigeonholed in the Senate Committee on Education and Labor, and the NAM was frustrated in its attempts to bring the bill to the floor of the Senate. Of small consolation, however, was the fact that the House Committee on Appropriations managed to strip the NLRB of its economic investigation unit, and the investigation of the Smith Committee was able to force the removal and resignation of many of the Board's technical assistants on various charges of ideological defection or political practices. For example, its director, David Sambros, was a former socialist.

With World War II there was a temporary truce, relatively at least, between management and labor. Undercover conflict came out in the administrative branch rather than in Congress and in general publicity. It was not until 1945 that the NAM had again mobilized its Washington staff to continue its campaign against the Wagner Act and to attempt to amend it. Nine bills were introduced in Congress in 1945 to this end. Still, nothing came of them and the demands of the NAM went unheard until the following year. In 1946 labor very directly aided the efforts of the NAM by striking for higher wages on a scale never before seen in this country. More man-days were lost in that year than ever before or since in the history of the United States, and many of these lost days were in industries whose temporary shutdown produced what was close to a national paralysis. Considerable public sentiment was aroused against labor. Also, it should be pointed out that labor had gained increasing strength and power during the war years with a favorable administration in office and with the NAM in a state of relative truce toward labor. Labor entered the post-World War II world in a position of great power.

Just as public sentiment had swung against business in the 1930s, so then did public sentiment become critical of labor in the post-World War II era, at least to the point that the NAM was able to take advantage of the changing public sentiment and urge even more strongly the repeal or amendment of the Wagner Act. While in 1946 the Senate did pass a bill, even though amended, somewhat along the lines the NAM wished, nonetheless President Truman vetoed it. At that point Congress was unable to marshall a two-thirds majority to override the veto. Commenting on this veto, the *NAM News* ran a story under the headline "Case Bill Veto Assures Nation Periodic Paralysis as Truman Aligns Himself Irrevocably with CIO."

The 1946 elections changed the political situation and put President Truman in a position where he was unable to stifle opposition to the Wagner Act. A Republican Congress, the first in fourteen years, was elected and immediately went to work on the labor policy problem in fulfillment of many years of campaign promises. All congressmen were given a leather-bound copy of a booklet entitled *Now Let's Build America,* which contained the legislative recommendations of the fifty-first annual Congress of American Industry. This group, of course, was aligned with the NAM. Also, the Committee for Constitutional Government gave 100 copies of John Scoville's *Labor Monopolies* to each congressman. These were only a few of many such actions by the business groups. With the 1946 elections, business was finally able to get what it considered to be a sympathetic House Labor Committee. The labor opposition contended that the House labor bill was not written with the help of the Democratic members but was actually written by lawyers from the NAM. This produced a heated discussion between Democrats and Republicans, with an allegation that Democrats had been using CIO lawyers to draft their measures for many years.

In the meantime, the NAM was going to the country with an amount of publicity and pressure never before equaled in the organization. Radio broadcasts, special publications for particular groups, such as teachers and clergymen, program notes for women's clubs, and paid advertisements in the newspapers were used. The *NAM News* was estimated to reach 40 million readers; and in addition, the NAM issued special pamphlets for school use and supplied material to 7,500 weekly newspapers alone. The intensive campaign aimed not only at the public and congressmen, but also at the various committees of Congress, enabled the NAM and Chamber of Commerce finally to pass the Taft-Hartley Act, which in many respects was similar to the proposals embodied in the pamphlet *Now Let's Build America.* Because of the Republican Congress and the public reaction against labor in this period, President Truman's veto was successfully overridden and the National Labor Relations Act of 1935 was superseded by the Labor-Management Relations Act of 1947, which labor immediately swore to repeal or amend.

CONCLUDING SUMMARY

Traditionally, business has dominated government policy from the Civil War to the New Deal. The emergence of competing power groups in this century, particularly labor, continues to face businessmen with a new situation and a critical problem. They find themselves at times, as during the New Deal, often the underdogs in the fight to affect government legislation and regulation. The major change of the 1930s in business's power position in the economy began to awaken many businessmen to the need to mobilize to fight for public policy in harmony with their general ideologies. After more than a decade of defensive action, business was able to win two victories against labor in the Taft-Hartley and the Landrum-Griffin acts. Nonetheless, business still found there was no chance of returning to conditions of an earlier and "happier" era in which it had faced little successful competition in the political arena.

Business and its archrival, labor, struggle to influence both the presidency, where labor often has greater access, and the Congress, where business can often more easily win its way. In this struggle, what are the strengths and weaknesses of businessmen and their allies among professional people who join them in such groups as the Chamber of Commerce?

Businessmen's principal assets are:

1. The skills with which to plan legislative campaigns, which stem from businessmen's relatively high educational level, their wide experience in planning commercial strategy, and their manipulative skills as managers
2. The access to public officials (who often share the same background), which stems from businessmen's status as social and community leaders
3. Wealth, which not only finances trips to Washington, long-distance phone calls, and secretary-typed letters to influence public leaders, but also buys billboard space and prime-time television commercials during election campaigns
4. Well-organized Washington lobbies

On the other hand, modern business still suffers the following weaknesses:

1. Failing often to recognize that the best way to ensure that a congressman will vote for your interests is to aid his election—for many companies, such as Standard Oil of California, have tended to eschew participation in local election campaigns and concentrate on influencing whichever candidates are elected[69]
2. Failing in their national business organizations to match labor's unity of national political planning for assistance to important local political campaigns
3. Failing to match labor's numerical strength, although businessmen partially compensate for numbers by a high rate of voting
4. Failing to achieve the ideological unity among business groups (i.e., the classical and managerial business ideologies which split businessmen) that American labor has generally achieved

These strengths and weaknesses of business as a political power group indicate that while seriously challenged by competing groups, it may still possess the greatest influence over legislation of any *single* power group. With the rise of more groups with influence, national policy is inevitably

[69] Keith Melville, "The Techniques of Standard Oil of California in Influencing Public Policy," *Ninth Annual University Faculty Seminar, 1959* (San Francisco: Standard Oil Company of California, 1959), pp. 27–31.

determined by those groups with political skills who can create alliances necessary to obtain the legislative goals they desire.

Historically, the fundamental ideological division among businessmen regarding government's proper role and functions grew out of a critical intellectual development of the Great Depression of the 1930s. This development originated in Lord Keynes's *The General Theory of Employment, Interest and Money,* published in 1936. Keynes essentially argued that government was the only institution capable of preventing depressions in modern industrialized societies. The implication of greater power for government has resulted in a direct loss of power over many areas of decision making previously enjoyed by business. The pre-Keynesian business philosophy, called here the classical business ideology, is held essentially by such business groups as the NAM and the Chamber of Commerce, while a variation of it is maintained by small business men and the National Federation of Independent Business. The small business man exerts little power in the making of public policy. The post-Keynesian business philosophy, called here the managerial business ideology, is essentially embodied in the CED. This group is made up basically of professional managers of the nation's largest corporations. The managerialists pragmatically accept the newer and enlarged role of government and, under President Eisenhower, played an important role in government administration. Both business groups tend to favor the Republican party. However, the classical business group generally tends to favor right-wing Republican leaders, such as Barry Goldwater, and Southern Democrats, such as Harry Byrd. The managerialists, however, feel stronger attachment to more "progressive conservatives," such as Eisenhower, and such liberal Republican figures as George Romney, William Scranton, and Nelson Rockefeller. A divergence between the two groups, wider than generally realized, was displayed in 1964 by the open support of Lyndon Johnson over Barry Goldwater and his classical creed by Henry Ford and a bevy of Republican business leaders of the managerial ideology.

As one study found, political agitation on public policy (such as writing to Congress) proved to be a function of self-interest and ideology. When self-interest was reinforced by ideological considerations, then these businessmen were most active politically. Generally, too, it was found that the men from large companies and those with better educations were most active in pressing for their views on public policy.[70] The victory in mobilizing to defeat labor on the Taft-Hartley and the Landrum-Griffin acts was not a victory of business alone, but was accomplished with the aid of other major power groups and tactical errors on the part of labor itself.

[70] Raymond A. Bauer, I. de Sola Pool, and L. A. Dexter, *American Business and Public Policy: The Politics of Foreign Trade* (New York: Atherton Press, 1963), p. 220.

A large number of businesses have not yet recognized that their future public environment as determined by government may make the difference between their success and failure. The major business organizations, such as the NAM and the CED, do play the dominant role in presenting the general policy of businessmen in the political arena. As yet, however, not even all the largest corporations maintain Washington representatives or are effective in taking account of and influencing government regulation and legislation directly involving them. This reluctance to face a new era in which the government is a key factor in profits makes even the major business groups less powerful on the macro level of general public policy. But businessmen have little choice today—either they develop greater political sophistication and influence over public policy or they will find their decision-making powers on both private and public levels decreasing.

This chapter has outlined the main divisions of the business ideology and has attempted to point out what the specific goals and philosophies of these groups are on major issues. The contrasts and similarities among the ideologies of the basic business groups and the following major power groups should illuminate the essential issues of our public policy as held by those who make it.

3
labor

INTRODUCTION

Few power groups in America are as controversial as labor. To antagonists, labor is all too powerful; to supporters, labor has all too little power. The pitting of labor and business on opposite sides of most issues in our society focuses attention on the striking differences in their ideologies. These ideological differences are less extreme, however, than the gulf which separates European labor and business. There is often a pragmatic approach to problems common to both American business and labor groups which differs from the more doctrinaire and class-oriented approach frequently found in Europe. What American labor's ideology is and why it is held, and hence some of the differences that set it apart from the labor movement in other countries, will be considered shortly. First, certain facts about labor and its power should be pointed out.

Occupations establish interests that have political consequences. As America became increasingly industrialized and unionized, a new distribution of power developed. No longer is power divided primarily between business and agriculture. Labor as a group has been increasing in power for the past century.

The increase in labor's power in America was greatly accelerated with the passage of the National Labor Relations Act of 1935, commonly known as the Wagner Act. This law gave labor the right to bargain collectively without interference from employers. This was interpreted so overwhelmingly in favor of labor that it prohibited management from even expressing its views on labor questions to employees until 1941 when the Supreme Court rescued the right of free expression of management.[1]

The pendulum which had swung so far in favor of labor produced a reaction and began to swing backward as early as 1939. This culminated in the passage of the Labor-Management Relations Act of 1947, commonly known as the Taft-Hartley Act, and the Labor-Management Reporting and Disclosure Act of 1959, known as the Landrum-Griffin Act.

Today in America a more even distribution of power has been reached between business and labor. This does not mean that a standoff between policies favored by the two has been achieved. On the contrary, the gradual flow of social welfare measures, for which labor fights, seems likely to continue. However, the conservative groups in the society, such as the classical business group, will make themselves felt by forcing measures less liberal than labor and others may wish.

History appears to favor many of labor's desires. This is so, not because the membership of unions continues to grow, but because in a democracy there is a continuous trend toward developing programs which will attract the votes of the majority of citizens. In this sense, despite the curtailing of some of labor's power in the past decade or so, the liberal coalition, which normally controls the Presidency of the United States, is likely to win further welfare measures over the opposition of the conservative coalition, which often controls Congress. Labor, therefore, will benefit from acquisitive mass psychology even if the strength of unions as a single power bloc should decrease.

One reservation to this analysis lies in the changing class structure. The fact that there are now more stockholders than union members points to a fast-growing middle class which may become less welfare-oriented. For example, Richard Nixon evidently hoped that if he won the Presidency he could create a new Republican majority by appealing to the rising middle class.

Another reservation which should be kept in mind is that the number of voters is not the only factor in political success. Other factors such as wealth and strategic position can outweigh numbers if properly utilized. An example of this has been the success of medical groups who, though small in numbers, managed to defeat President Kennedy's Medicare program as well as previous medical programs supported by organized labor. General apathy is often so prevalent that a minority which becomes militantly aroused can greatly multiply the power which would be suggested by its numbers. Thus, in 1962 doctors utilized their strategic position aris-

[1] *National Labor Relations Board v. Virginia Electric and Power Company*, 314 U.S. 469 (1941).

ing from the personal confidence and friendship of their patients to urge them to write an astonishing total number of letters in opposition to Medicare to their Washington legislators. The unions and their allies failed to use the advantage of numerical superiority and thereby narrowly lost the Medicare vote in the Senate at that time by 52 to 48, even though the Democrats controlled the Senate by nearly two to one.[2]

Finally, one cannot be sure whether the relatively small but vocal conservative movement of recent years might grow significantly in size. For this to occur would probably require one of the following conditions: (1) a marked increase in "taxpayers' revolts" against the fact that approximately one-third of our national income is now taxed and spent by some level of government; (2) serious international setbacks which might strengthen the hand of those calling for a more militant anti-Communist foreign policy; (3) a renaissance of the classical "individualism" and "self-reliance" types of ideologies in protest against the "softness" of modern American life; (4) the development of a more widespread white backlash to Negro demands than has yet materialized. Although conservatism has developed muscle in the last quarter century, it is still a minority ideology.

Today the 17 million union members in America are only one-fourth of the approximately 70-million-member labor force. Union members are attached to approximately 189 national or international unions. "Unionism is strongest in manufacturing, construction, transportation, and mining. It is weakest in the service trades, agriculture, and white-collar work generally."[3]

Union membership has been falling recently, a fact which is naturally of great concern to union leaders.

The AFL-CIO has lost more members than it will admit. New Labor Department figures show the federation lost 256,000 U.S. members between 1960 and 1962. . . . Counting unfederated unions, total union membership in the U.S. was 16.6 million in 1962—30% of the non-farm labor force. That's 463,000 less than in 1960, when unions represented 31.4% of workers. And the total is down 906,000 from the 1956 peak of 33.4%.[4]

It is interesting to note that between 1953 and 1963 membership in the United Mine Workers declined by 100,000.[5] Also of significance is a report by the Center for the Study of Democratic Institutions. The study of 131 national unions shows that 49 suffered a net reduction in membership. Sixteen had cuts of 10,000 or more members. The most serious cutbacks occurred among the textile unions, with losses of 164,770 by the

---

[2] *Congressional Record,* 87th Congress, 2d Session (July 17, 1962), 12923.

[3] George H. Hildebrand, "Economics by Negotiation," *American Economic Review,* 49, 2 (May, 1959), 399.

[4] *Newsweek* (December 16, 1963), 63.

[5] *U.S. News & World Report* (April 29, 1963), 69.

Textile Workers Union of America and 44,000 by the United Textile Workers. The Amalgamated Association of Street, Electric Railway, and Motor Coach Employees of America reports a decline of 75,363.[6]

An official of the UAW recently expressed his concern over this decline in the labor movement:

The changing attitude of workers toward the trade union movement is really one of our major problems. All of us were shocked by the results of the union shop elections at North American Aviation, at Ryan, at Convair. Two unions were involved: the Machinists' Union and our union, the UAW. Lou Harris did some studies for us. . . . He found that the whole question of voluntarism is important in the workers' relationship with the union and their jobs. Another thing that came out very strongly was corruption in the trade union movement. . . . He found the attitude that unions were too strong and were not really democratic. He got the idea that workers were alienated not only from the corporation but also from the union.[7]

This statement shows some of the reasons why the labor movement is losing its impetus. As union leaders seek ways to halt this decline and increase the union movement, these points act as obstacles. Other problems facing labor leaders include the effects of legislation less favorable to labor than previous legislation, these being chiefly the Taft-Hartley Act and the Landrum-Griffin Act; the tactics of employers against unions; state right-to-work laws; the sullied image of unions; and union apathy and structural difficulties.

Of special concern to labor leaders is the fact that because of improved social conditions resulting from the many programs undertaken by the government, fewer and fewer people regard the laborer as an underdog. Many people who once favored a strong labor movement now feel such a movement is less needed because unions have achieved their greatest demands.

Union leaders also face automation, one of the chief factors behind the decline in the labor movement. As automation releases more workers from unskilled and semiskilled work—35,000 each week—[8] union membership falls both absolutely (in total numbers) and relatively (in relation to the total labor force). This results in a decline in blue-collar workers— the traditional base of union membership—and an increase in the number of white-collar workers, who have traditionally opposed joining unions. Between 1956 and 1962 there was a drop of 1 million blue-collar workers.

[6] Center for the Study of Democratic Institutions, *The Decline of the Labor Movement* (Santa Barbara, Calif., 1961), p. 11.

[7] Center for the Study of Democratic Institutions, *Labor Looks at Labor* (Santa Barbara, Calif., 1963), pp. 5–6.

[8] Harold H. Martin, "Big Labor's Big Worry," *The Saturday Evening Post* (December 15, 1962), 66.

During the same period, the number of white-collar workers increased 3 million.[9]

Union leaders are currently attempting to overcome the labor movement decline by drawing members from the ranks of the white-collar workers. Although about 2,500,000 out of the approximately 13,600,000 white-collar workers belong to unions, the majority of them have shown little desire toward union membership.[10] The labor leaders are, however, encouraged by the recent upsurge in organization among public school teachers. As shall be shown in Chapter 6, labor leaders are making a considerable effort to advance this movement.

While labor's power position is faced with problems in the future, it will likely benefit from the ability of representatives of the working class to create majority alliances with other power groups for "bread-and-butter" measures.

The creation of the AFL-CIO federation in 1955 brought charges from certain business groups that labor was creating a monopoly. In effect, while a new era of labor unity may have been achieved, it should be noted that the AFL-CIO is still a federation and that member national unions are still entitled to have their autonomy, integrity, and jurisdiction protected and preserved. These member unions have the right of secession. Nevertheless, sufficient unity and power exists in the AFL-CIO for it to carry out one of its principal functions—the formulation and advancement of the political objectives of labor in elections, in Congress, and within the governmental administrative agencies. The AFL-CIO is, therefore, the principal power group representing the interests of labor in America. By this very position it is one of the basic powers determining economic and social policy.[11]

Both on the level of the national unions and in the federation of the AFL-CIO, things are, in the words of V. O. Key, "smoothly managed by the controlling oligarchy of leaders."[12] "Union hierarchies represent the union member in negotiations with employers but, in turn, union hierarchies also govern the union members—within the range of union powers and subject to varying degrees of 'popular' control by the member."[13] The self-sustaining power of most union hierarchies is seen if an examination of

---

[9] "The Greatest Unresolved Problem," *Fortune*, 65 (February 26, 1962), 199.

[10] Sumner H. Slichter, "The Power Holders in the American Economy," *The Saturday Evening Post* (December 13, 1958).

[11] Political power and bargaining power of unions are somewhat different. The AFL-CIO is largely a political power, whereas bargaining power rests with the individual locals and international unions.

[12] V. O. Key, Jr., *Politics, Parties, and Pressure Groups*, 4th ed. (New York: Thomas Y. Crowell Company, 1958), p. 63.

[13] *Ibid.*, p. 64.

their elections is made. In most cases the "organization slate" of the national union officers runs without opposition. For example, Philip Taft reports that "between 1910 and 1944 no candidate in the International Association of Bridge, Structural and Ornamental Iron Workers contested the presidency."[14] In the case of the International Union of Brewery, Flour, Cereal and Soft Drink Workers of America, "in the five conventions held between 1936 and 1948, no opponent challenged the head of the union."[15]

Internal hierarchies control both the AFL-CIO and the affiliate national unions. On rare occasions, however, when a policy formulated by the AFL-CIO or a national union runs strongly counter to the economic interests of a local union, the local may actually refuse to accept the official line and announce its own policy on this particular issue. This would in some ways be similar to a local firm or trade association departing from the policy advocated by an aggregate group such as the NAM, where such policy runs counter to local interests. However, it is much more likely for a national union to differ with the AFL-CIO than for a local to disagree with its own national union. Thus the analogy of a trade association differing with the NAM is really more akin to the relations between a national union and the AFL-CIO.

Rebellion in unionism is more important with the national unions, which actually may be expelled from the AFL-CIO for corruption (e.g., the Teamsters) or Communist affiliation. Expulsion never seemed particularly to hurt the expelled union leadership of the Teamsters—James Hoffa and others.[16] They have managed to control their national unions so tightly that even the leadership of the AFL-CIO cannot shake their control over national union organization.

Traditionally, the political role of labor in America has been simply to reward its friends and punish its enemies through the ballot box. However, despite the injunction of Samuel Gompers that labor should not become a tail to any political party, organized labor leaders in recent decades have made their nonpartisan policy into one of being nonpartisan Democrats.

The application of labor's traditional nonpartisan policy was considerably strained by its endorsement of Adlai Stevenson for the Presidency in 1952—the first time that an official AFL endorsement for the Presidency had been given. After the 1960 presidential campaign, Nixon's forces claimed that labor was one of the three reasons for the Kennedy victory.

---

[14] Philip Taft, *The Structure and Government of Labor Unions* (Cambridge, Mass.: Harvard University Press, 1954), p. 42.

[15] *Ibid.*, p. 41.

[16] The Teamsters, despite expulsion from the AFL-CIO, still generally go along with it on national policies. Expulsion could perhaps be called more of an internal organization issue than conflict over national political issues.

President Kennedy himself said he could not have won without strong union support.[17]

A study made in 1956 of UAW members showed the information on party preference given in Table 1.[18]

TABLE 1. **Party Preference**

Democrat or strong Democrat	53%	
Not very strong Democrat	14	
		67%
Republican or strong Republican	3	
Not very strong Republican	4	
		7
Independent:		
Democrat leaning	13	
Republican leaning	4	
Neither Democrat nor Republican	9	
		26
Democrats plus Democrat leaning	80%	
Republicans plus Republican leaning	11	
Independents with no leaning	9	
	100%	100%

The same study showed that in the 1952 presidential election 73 per cent of the UAW workers interviewed voted for Stevenson, 24 per cent for Eisenhower, and 3 per cent refused to say.[19]

Occasionally, rivalry between unions will be a contributing factor if one of them supports Republican candidates. This appears to have been the case in Hawaii's first election after becoming a state. The Longshoremen's Union, independent of the AFL-CIO, supported the victorious drive of the Republican candidate for the Senate, Hiram L. Fong, a multimillionaire Harvard law graduate, who was the son of an indentured Chinese sugar laborer.[20] The rivalry between the AFL-CIO and the longshoremen, combined with such factors as Fong's "labor" origin and the fact that he was not ideologically anathema to labor, contributed to this novel endorsement.

The industrial unions of the CIO have traditionally been more aligned with the New Deal, while the AFL craft unions have been more nonpartisan. These differences still emerge upon occasion. In the 1962 Senate race in California, much of the CIO organization was working for Richard Richards, a liberal Democrat, while simultaneously many of the AFL craft

---

[17] *The New York Times* (December 9, 1961).

[18] Arthur Kornhauser, Harold L. Sheppard, and Albert J. Mayer, *When Labor Votes: A Study of Auto Workers* (New York: University Books, 1956), p. 38.

[19] *Ibid.*, p. 32.

[20] *The New York Times* (July 30, 1959).

unions, such as the building trade groups, were working for the reelection of Senator Tom Kuchel, a moderately liberal Republican.

The passage of the Taft-Hartley Act and the Landrum-Griffin Act, both of which labor leaders considered highly antilabor, aided in the consolidation of the AFL and the CIO, beginning with their federation in 1955. The Republican–Southern Democratic sponsorship of both bills has intensified labor leaders' view of the Republican party as the representative of opposing interest groups, especially business. While in the post-World War II era labor has lost these two important legislative battles, its power is still considerable. Yet the influence of labor organization should not be dismissed as of no import because labor-endorsed candidates do not invariably win. Organization doubtless reinforces the loyalties of the hard core of labor votes. At times labor leaders manage to get to the polls a larger vote than would be cast without their efforts. And on occasion their exertions may account for victory.[21]

E. E. Schattschneider has assessed the power of the AFL-CIO in presidential elections in the manner shown in Table 2.[22]

TABLE 2. **Organized Labor and Presidential Elections**

Total membership of AFL-CIO	16,000,000
Since only about half of the membership votes in presidential elections, subtract votes actually cast by AFL-CIO members	−8,000,000
	8,000,000
Democratic share of the labor vote (70% of 8,000,000)	5,600,000
Republican share of the labor vote Subtract Republican share of the labor vote from the Democratic share to get	−2,400,000
Net Democratic gain	3,200,000

Schattschneider notes that the 3.2 million, not including wives, are important; yet it would be only a fifth of the potential total vote of the AFL-CIO if leaders could mobilize and control it. He argues that even this figure overstates AFL-CIO power because it is doubtful that even half of the union members vote.[23] Furthermore, "organization" increases the Dem-

---

[21] Key, p. 78.

[22] E. E. Schattschneider, *The Semisovereign People: A Realist's View of Democracy in America* (New York: Holt, Rinehart and Winston, 1960), p. 50.

[23] Charles Lipsen, the sophisticated Retail Clerks International lobbyist in Washington, D.C., showed labor's awareness of this "low-vote" problem to one of the authors with the following figures drawn from a Lou Harris poll. Wage earners, representing 37 per cent of potential voters, produced only 26 per cent of the actual votes in the 1960 election. On the other hand, people in professional and executive positions also cast 26 per cent of the votes in 1960, although they comprised only 18 per cent of the voting-age population. See *AFL-CIO News* (May 5, 1962).

ocratic bias of workers by only about 10 per cent over unorganized workers. Polls suggest that endorsement of a candidate by organized labor (and similarly with other pressure groups) may have a "reverse effect," repelling more voters than it attracts.

The political activity of the AFL-CIO is centered in two departments: the Committee on Political Education (COPE), which is largely involved with supporting the election of friends of labor, and the lobbying section, which is known as the Legislative Department.

The AFL-CIO lobbying system is best characterized as a committee system. The AFL-CIO Executive Council, consisting of twenty-seven vice-presidents, governs the organization and sets the broad legislative policy that is to be pursued by the lower echelons. Directly under this group is the Legislative Committee of the Executive Council, which consists of four members of the Executive Council. It is in this group that policy regarding congressional programs is specifically argued out and formulated.

The direct burden of actual lobbying belongs to the 100 professional labor lobbyists who live in the Washington area. This group, known as the National Legislative Council, attempts to achieve cooperation among the lobbyists of diverse unions in connection with legislation dealing with labor relations and other issues of interest to the AFL-CIO. It is provided with an Administrative Committee which meets weekly and makes reports regarding tactical planning and current information to the Legislative Council. Below this are nine operating subcommittees of the National Legislative Council composed of lobbyists from unions most concerned with the particular areas of legislation. These subcommittees deal with aviation, civil rights, depressed areas, education, minimum wages, health, housing, labor relations, and social security. The subcommittees are the bases of labor's legislative lobbying system.

Among labor lobbyists there are three clearly distinguishable functional types. They are the testifier-expert, the contact man, and the campaign organizer.

The testifier-expert is the lobbyist who testifies for labor before congressional committees as an expert witness on particular subject matter, such as social security, labor relations, etc. He is usually either an economist or a lawyer who supplies Congress with data presented from the labor point of view. Testimony plays an important part in labor lobbying because of the committee system used in Congress. During the Eighty-sixth Congress, for instance, it is estimated that labor spokesmen testified on nearly a hundred separate occasions. The preparation of testimony consumes great time and effort and requires a large staff. The testifier-expert is frequently only a part-time lobbyist, and in such cases is hired only on a consulting basis.

The contact man plays the classic role of the lobbyist. He spends his time making contacts with the members of Congress and their staffs. On the basis of established personal relationships, he attempts to place before individual congressmen labor's argument on basic issues. The contact man believes that the legislative goals of his organization can best be achieved through influence gained and exercised by personal contact with congressmen. He may urge a given kind of action by the congressmen, such as requesting voting commitments. If a legislator will not make a commitment, the contact man may ask him to request hearings on a bill or let the bill out of committee. In opposing some issue, he will urge that certain action be taken to kill or table a bill. He may urge certain legislators to accept committee assignments or chairmanships, and then request the congressional leaders to consider his selections.

An important adjunct to the work of the contact man is his expense account, without which he could not properly wine and dine his legislative contacts. His personal acquaintance with legislators makes it possible for him to provide information not only about their public activities and their commitments but also about their private attitudes and foibles.

The campaign organizer has a different concept and role as a labor lobbyist. He considers his job to be basically one of organizing grass roots support for labor's programs.

The contact man and the campaign organizer both perform tasks necessary for attaining labor legislation. These two separate roles are generally considered to be more developed in the labor federation than among other power groups who may simply hire a Washington business representative without having any type of permanent campaign organizer at home. In this sense, while labor's lobbying program may be often insufficiently coordinated, it is generally more organizationally adapted to the basic functions of achieving legislative victory.[24]

A factor in the labor movement which must be considered, at least briefly, is the conflict and divisions which periodically arise among the unions themselves. Competition among products may in some cases lead to conflicts among unions. For example, at the present time the railroad brotherhoods are supporting—while the Teamsters are opposing—proposals to give railroads more freedom in ratemaking. An increase in freedom of ratemaking would increase the ability of the railroads to compete with trucks. The United Mineworkers are supporting—while the railroad brotherhoods are opposing—proposals for coal slurry pipelines from mines in West Virginia to Eastern markets.

[24] The above material regarding the organization and types of labor lobbyists is based upon Samuel C. Patterson's paper, "The Role of the Labor Lobbyist," given at the annual meeting of the American Political Science Association in Washington, D.C., September 5–8, 1962.

The hottest internal dispute in labor presently is between the building trades unions who are proselytizing industrial employers for greater contracting out of construction and maintenance. Industrial unions such as the Steelworkers and Auto Workers oppose contracting out, hoping to save these jobs for their internal plant maintenance forces. The Operating Engineers find themselves in a particularly interesting position. The parent union is involved in the attempts of the General Presidents' Committee on Contract Maintenance and the Construction Industry Joint Conference to promote contracting out of turn-around maintenance in oil refineries. However, the Petroleum and Allied Products Division of the Union, which is a relatively small group employed in oil refineries, opposes contracting out of such work.[25]

These conflicts cause labor leaders constant concern and impede the operations of unions to a considerable extent. Labor, for all its problems and divisions, is a highly potent power group. J. Mack Swigert, an authority on labor law, has listed the following factors as being basic to labor's power: public sympathy for unions, labor's political strength, favorable laws, favorable treatment from the press, the right to strike and boycott, the unions' picket system, the tradition of threats and violence, loyalty of members, compulsory membership, and unlimited size of unions.[26]

The familiarity of many of labor's ideological positions in the next section may startle the reader who has not been aware that such positions and arguments over current economic and political issues were those of the labor group. Since ideology is one of the most important tools used by groups to influence both their own group and public opinion, it is useful to look next at what might be considered the official ideology and overt goals of American labor as promulgated by the AFL-CIO.

THE IDEOLOGY OF LABOR

The Role of Government

The role of government in the American labor ideology, in many ways, is not too dissimilar from its position in the managerial business ideology. American labor argues for a governmental role which extends over monetary and fiscal policy, but which is sharply limited in regard to such areas as economic planning and wage and price controls. Labor favors essentially a large and even increasing role of government through government expenditures. As will be shown, labor has had little fear of deficit spending and of an increasing function of government in the affairs of the country through its spending processes.

[25] Letter from Garth L. Mangum, research director, Subcommittee on Employment and Manpower, U.S. Senate, September 5, 1963.

[26] J. Mack Swigert, "Where Labor Unions Get Their Power," *U.S. News & World Report* (January 21, 1963), 96–99.

Essentially, labor is not afraid of "big government" as long as government does not interfere with the prerogatives of labor in collective bargaining, in wage setting, and in its general relationship with business. The labor ideology does stress, however, that it is government's responsibility to solve basic economic problems such as unemployment, unfair distribution of income, and various welfare needs.

Unlike the classical ideology of business, labor does not advocate that government should take a laissez-faire position. Nonetheless, labor is very much opposed to having any of its prerogatives diminished, and it may be aligned with business itself in protesting the expansion of government wage and price setting.

The reason why labor holds this ideological position regarding the role of government is partially explained above. Additionally, it should be pointed out that labor regards government as essentially manageable through the political process. Labor, in recent years, has made increasing attempts to influence Congress and the various administrative agencies through its lobbying organization. The tide of social forces or social philosophy in the country, labor feels, is in its favor and will eventually sweep aside opposition to those issues it favors. Therefore, labor feels much less fear of the democratic process in regard to government and its political control than perhaps does business. Labor's rise to power has been directly aided, and it may have been made possible, by government legislation.

Despite recent political setbacks, labor still feels that the role of government should be a large and increasing one without restricting labor's own position. Labor has a different psychology regarding its relationship with government from that of the classical group of businessmen, who appear deeply and emotionally disturbed over the increasing governmental control in modern society. Undoubtedly, as long as labor feels that it has the opportunity of getting what it wants and being able to influence and manipulate government toward its ends, it will continue to favor most extensions of government that do not challenge its own decision making.

Government Spending

Labor's ideology regarding government spending and the balanced budget is far removed from that of the classical business group. Labor shows little fear, ideologically, that deficit spending will create any particular problem for the economy. Rather, the emphasis is on the positive aspects of monetary and fiscal control necessary to prevent unemployment. Labor essentially attacks the issue of the balanced budget with its own approach to the problem of unemployment (e.g., that it is the responsibility of government to create full employment through spending programs). It is understandable why labor takes this position, for if it were to argue for a balanced budget, as the classical business ideology does, then labor would be forced to throw out fiscal policy as a means for controlling the business cycle and preventing unemployment. Of necessity, therefore, labor must at times attempt to skirt the rather powerful moral appeal of the balanced budget.

The reason for not mentioning deficit spending as an issue in many of the ideological statements regarding the problem of full employment is also understandable. It is much simpler to urge that it is government's responsibility to see that unemployment is eliminated than to be forced into debating deficit spending. The tactic of the labor ideology regarding government spending is essentially a defensive one. It is designed to sidestep the balanced budget controversy and attack the basic issue on the stronger emotional grounds of unemployment and the necessity for various government services. The implication of this reasoning is simply that labor has little to fear regarding government spending. Labor consistently urges further government spending for welfare measures as well as to promote lower rates of unemployment.

The labor ideology argues that ours is an "unbalanced economy" because it is operating with considerable unemployment and idle machines. Also, there are too few customers to buy the rising volumes of goods and services that can be produced. Therefore, labor is not concerned about a balanced budget, but rather about fighting for a "balanced economy." Its solution to this problem is simply that government spending is necessary to increase levels of consumption, thereby raising demand and increasing jobs. "We cannot afford to regard every expenditure of the federal government as a 'mask for big government.' "[27] Labor argues that we already have a big government, that we have a big nation, and that the issue of big government is false and deceptive.

In summary, labor avoids direct discussion of deficit spending or an unbalanced budget, which would be ideologically weak. It stresses the imbalance in our economy because of its lack of utilization of manpower and plant capacity, claiming that here is the need for greater government spending.

A Planned Economy

As has been mentioned above, the labor ideology opposes the idea of government planning in those areas where it would result in a planned or centrally controlled economy, which would infringe upon labor's own decision-making powers in regard to collective bargaining (i.e., wages, benefits, and working conditions).

In one area of planning, however, the AFL-CIO definitely urges

[27] AFL-CIO, *Economic Programs and Policies for the 60's* (Washington, D.C., n.d.), p. 4.

greater expansion. This is in regard to the Council of Economic Advisers. Labor argues that the Council has not been fulfilling its basic function.[28] That is, it should be making and publishing overall economic projections for the economy. The essential idea is that by making long-range projections regarding plant and equipment expenditures, inventory spending, levels of public and private construction, spending, etc., the overall levels of capital investment in the gross national product could be estimated on a year-by-year basis. Government should stabilize the business cycle by adjusting consumption and investment through its own timely spending increases and tax reductions in the lower income brackets.

Labor accuses the Council of Economic Advisers of timidity, charging that they avoid forecasting government expenditures lest they be labeled as planners. Labor contends that the issue of centralized planning is not involved here at all, rather it is simply good economic sense to make forecasts. The word "planning" is generally omitted from the argument. George Meany and other officials of the AFL-CIO have stated that labor would join with business in fighting a planned economy. However, within a free enterprise framework labor wants the Federal government to coordinate and use the resources at its disposal for maintaining maximum employment, production, and purchasing power. It sees the Council of Economic Advisers as one method for accomplishing this. It accuses the Council of self-congratulation when more self-criticism is needed.

The reason for such a position on labor's part is not hard to find. Labor fully realizes that while it would be curtailed in its rights if a fully planned economy were developed, nevertheless, unless government attempts to develop fiscal and monetary policy more fully by doing some forecasting or "planning," then it may be impossible to reduce unemployment levels or to reduce the fluctuations of the business cycle in the economy. Therefore labor, in this instance, treads a rather narrow ideological path.

Inflation and Price Stability

By and large, labor never meets head-on the issue of inflation and rising prices. The labor ideology, as expressed by the AFL-CIO publications, stresses that wages and salaries must be increased as living costs rise, or else the buying power of wages is decreased. The argument maintains that rising wages are essential for a growing economy, and that sales, to increase in the economy and to provide full employment, must be backed by consumer demand, which in turn depends upon family income. Since the overwhelming majority of Americans work for wages and salaries, labor income is the main source of consumer income. Inflation is not particularly viewed as a problem or an evil as long as wages and salaries are corre-

[28] *Ibid.*, p. 11.

spondingly increased. In fact, the labor ideology stresses that all must benefit in the growing prosperity and that wage and salary earners are entitled to share in the fruits of rising productivity, which result in greater profits for industry.

It can be seen from this approach that the problem of inflation or price stability is an issue on which labor is basically defensive. This is understandable because much, though not all, of the inflation experience in the early postwar period was of a wage-push type. Prices have been frequently pushed up to new levels by the initiation of the unions in collective bargaining for higher wages and salaries.

Labor, therefore, is in no position to argue against inflation or to argue for price stability. To do so in either case would often undermine their arguments for higher wages. It is the fear of the anti-inflation ideology and the issue of price stability which makes labor leaders worry most about the imposition of governmental controls over wages and prices, since labor's freedom in collective bargaining with business could thereby be curtailed. On this issue, business and labor take a corresponding position. It is understandable why the labor ideology holds this particular position.

Wage policy should not only enable wages to increase with rising prices—to maintain buying power and living conditions. It must also permit wage and salary earners to share adequately in the gains of the national economy's rising productivity through increased buying power and improved living standards.[29]

Inflation, as an issue for the labor ideology in America, is one that essentially has to be sidestepped and fought with other ideological tools. In the words of George Meany:

Progress, in fact, was decried as a mask for inflation. Despite a lack of excessive demand pressures, despite the fact that overall demand fell so far behind possible supply that the economy turned downward twice, the threat of inflation was raised over and over again to warn a nation against the things it needed most: The [Eisenhower] Administration preached restriction in buying power lest inflation take its toll. . . . The [Eisenhower] Administration preached restriction in wage increases, despite the fact that real buying power had never kept up with the production potential. The message was so effective, business so convinced that wage increases were harmful, that real wages lost even the impetus that they had already gained by 1956. Since then, despite collective bargaining efforts and progress, real earnings have been rising at a slower rate than before.[30]

In this quotation Mr. Meany states the essential dilemma that labor faces should it oppose the issue of inflation. Another of labor's arguments against accusations that inflation is caused by higher wages is as follows: Wages are not the source of inflation, for productivity increases more than

[29] *Ibid.*, p. 35.   [30] *Ibid.*, p. 3.

offset the wage demands of labor. Therefore, what inflation there has been has resulted not from labor, but from administered prices of big business.

Labor's wage demands are hereby pictured as attempts to keep up with the general increase in prices which has been caused by business. This type of ideological argument is, of course, essential for labor's position. The basic tenet of "more" in American unionism would be handicapped if labor admitted that its efforts had resulted in inflation for the economy at large.

Welfare Measures

The labor ideology, while stressing the need for full employment, better working conditions, and higher wages, also takes up a number of so-called welfare issues. A few of the measures which can be considered part of this welfare cluster and which appear in labor's ideology as necessary legislation are the eradication of slums; the rehabilitation of rural areas; the removal of poverty; increased appropriations for education; health insurance; minimum wage laws; increased aid to the aged, the unemployed, broken families, the injured, and the sick; as well as the raising of incomes in the lower fifth of the income scale. In arguing for these various measures, labor asserts that its opponents use the mask of fear of big government to avoid the passage of needed welfare measures. Labor also attacks those who argue against deficit spending or increased government spending as weakening America by emphasizing the need for a curb on spending.

Few of those who fight appropriations for decent schools and decent housing or legislation for decent minimum wage laws will say that they want a poor America which lacks the educational standards needed in a technical society, or an ill-housed, ill-fed population, or a group of potential consumers who cannot even begin to afford to buy the products.[31]

The ideological opposition to most of these issues is seen stemming directly from business, and as such the labor ideology reiterates the view that ours is an unbalanced economy rather than simply one with an unbalanced budget. Labor argues that there is a definite return on "public investments." "The return, it is true, cannot be entirely measured in dollars, since many public requirements will not show immediate dollar returns."[32]

If labor is to maintain the support of its members and is to promote passage of welfare legislation, it is necessary to challenge the opposing ideologies which stress the need for a federally balanced budget, price stability, and fear of the increasing role of government. The need for welfare legislation is, therefore, always put in heavily loaded emotional terms when discussed in the labor ideology. For it is obvious that the use of

[31] *Ibid.*, pp. 3–4.   [32] *Ibid.*, p. 5.

emotionally loaded words can vastly strengthen the persuasiveness or effectiveness of labor's arguments for such measures.

This technique is part of labor's ideological attack against those who would oppose welfare measures. Otherwise stated, in order to extend minimum wage laws, to increase benefits to the unemployed, or to provide for a Medicare program, labor has to paint an effective picture of the misery, poverty, degradation, and grievances which certain members of society endure. The more effective this painting, the greater the support and sympathy aroused for labor to pass its welfare measures.

Ideologies inevitably rely on emotional arguments and upon the use of emotional or emotion-tinged symbols and words. In the case of welfare legislation there is little doubt that an effective labor ideology must make use of these tools. They have an effect particularly because of the greatly increased national concern for the underprivileged which grew out of the traumatic Great Depression of the 1930s, though employment and opportunity for self-improvement exist in much greater abundance today. President Johnson's "War against Poverty" philosophy can be traced to the New Deal era.

Working Conditions

Working conditions are part and parcel of the basic labor ideology. With the emphasis of the American labor movement on business unionism and the pragmatic demands of its workers to obtain more, in both wages and working conditions, such emphasis is only to be expected. Union leaders in America must agitate continually for, and obtain on occasion, an improvement in working conditions and benefits if they are to maintain their active positions in the union hierarchy. This is particularly true of local union officials and less so among the officials on national-international levels and leaders of the AFL-CIO.

Wages

The basic ideological argument put forth by labor for an expanding wage policy has been essentially outlined. However, it may be well to summarize it here. The labor panacea for an expanding economy and for the ending of recessions is an increase in the buying power of consumers through higher wages and salaries. Only by increasing real wages is it possible, according to this argument, for consumer markets to grow, for business to expand, and for employment to increase.

According to this ideology, rising sales are essential in an economy with increasing productive efficiency and with an increasing number in the labor force. Thus, only by increasing wages is it possible to increase consumer demands sufficiently to stimulate the economy so that an increasing number of jobs will be made available. While labor generally accepts Keynesian economics, certainly in regard to monetary and fiscal policies, this particular argument—that the simple cure for recessions is to increase wages—is not fully consistent with Keynesian economic reasoning. The labor solution to such problems is, to many economists, a considerable oversimplification.

Nonetheless, the labor ideology has many arrows in its quiver. Another argument relating to the need to increase wages is simply that with rising productivity there is a tendency for wage costs per unit of production to decline, resulting in increased profits. Labor obviously claims it is entitled to a share in such profits.

> When rising productivity reduces production costs per unit—by increasing the output produced in one hour—business can share such benefits with other groups in the economy. If business holds most of these benefits for itself, the lion's share will go only to business in the form of booming profits, as in the 1920's. Failure by business to share the fruits of industrial progress with other groups creates economic distortions—excessively high profits and insufficient buying power—that are followed by production cutbacks and unemployment, as in the depression of the 1930's. In the long run, such economic policies have a bad effect on business, as well as on workers.[33]

It can be seen that the labor ideology asserts that unless business shares its profits from increased productivity, in the long run a lack of purchasing power develops, and ultimately this results in depression or recession. This reasoning appears to ignore the fact that profits, as a share of national income, have been declining in recent years.

Another argument used by labor in favor of increasing wages is that they are essentially necessary for a fully employed, growing economy. Growth is attributed to increasing sales based on increasing real income. Only in this fashion can economic growth and socially desirable conditions be created. "A dynamic wage policy is essential for the continued growth of a dynamic American economy. The forward advance of the economy requires rising real wages and salaries.[34]

Labor firmly states: "The A.F.L.-C.I.O. and its affiliated unions are dedicated to gaining continuing improvements in wages, fringe benefits, and living conditions. Through wage policies and legislative programs, trade unions attempt to establish the foundation for an expanding and prosperous, full-employment economy."[35]

This statement strongly indicates that the labor ideology is dedicated to the basic idea of increasing wages and benefits to its members. It notes that legislative programs are to be utilized by the unions to establish the basis for this program.

[33] AFL-CIO, p. 33.
[34] *Ibid.*, p. 35.
[35] *Ibid.*

Why does a nation which proclaims that all men are created equal tolerate an economic double standard that sets wage-earners apart, expecting them to live and eat and raise families year by year on an income that may fail them hour by hour, when almost everybody else in our economy receives steady income whether production is high or low?[36]

The above quotation illustrates another long-run goal of labor, namely, to obtain a guaranteed annual wage—or eventually to make wage earners into salaried workers.

The above statements provide an indication of the basic philosophy of American labor toward increasing workers' benefits. No labor group can hope to be successful in this country or to keep its membership cohesive without being able to promise, and to some extent deliver, actual economic benefits. The program of American labor is the tangible one of promising and delivering material benefits to its membership. The ideology is to relate these demands to a theory of prosperity and economic growth based upon high mass purchasing power. The pull of more theoretical ideologies or utopian visions has little impact upon the average American worker.

The Workweek

Traditionally we have always taken part of the fruits of advancing technology in the form of improvements in our material standard of living and part in the form of increasing leisure. This process will continue both through legislation and through the flexible mechanisms of collective bargaining which permit adjustment of the length of the workweek to the facts of each situation.[37]

Labor is ideologically committed to a current reduction of the standard 40-hour workweek without loss of pay. For example, during the almost 3½ months of the New York City newspaper strike which terminated in April, 1963, the longest-lingering issue was the demand of the photoengravers to cut their workweek from 36¼ to 35 hours. Even more remarkable, in the previous year the New York construction electrical workers postponed only under heavy pressure a decision to strike to cut their workweek to 20 hours without cutting wages.[38]

Labor's position on workweek reduction is somewhat vulnerable to attack on the grounds that a reduction would decrease the nation's economic growth. Governor Nelson Rockefeller has suggested that we have

[36] United Automobile Workers of America, "Workers' Problems Are Democracy's Problems," UAW Special Collective Bargaining Convention, April 27–29, 1961, p. 23.

[37] *Ibid.*, p. 78.

[38] *Wall Street Journal* (January 2, 1962).

been cutting the workweek by 3½ hours each decade and that if we forgo further cuts in favor of increased output, this would put a 5 per cent growth rate well within our reach.[39] This presents a paradox for the labor ideology since economic growth is heavily stressed in other sections of its creed.

Labor maintains that "more jobs can be created by agreement on a shorter workweek or a shorter workday with no loss in pay."[40] This would aid in reducing the number of unemployed in the economy, since additional workers would have to be hired to keep up the same levels of production. George Kirstein argues that "for each hour that the workweek is reduced 300,000 workers will be added to the payrolls across the nation. A standard 35-hour week would thus absorb approximately 1,500,000 additional workers, or one-third of the present unemployment."[41]

This presents an approach for collective bargaining sessions by which labor can ask for both increased wages per hour and decreased working hours. Such demands on a per hour basis would result either way in augmenting hourly wages. It appears that these demands could not currently be obtained in their entirety, since opposition to a 35-hour week is still great on many fronts. However, the rallying cry of increased leisure time to many well-paid workers is certainly one which has many supporters. A recent Gallup poll showed that 42 per cent of laborers favored a reduced workweek.[42]

It is also significant to note that although President Kennedy and Secretary of Labor Willard Wirtz opposed a reduction in the workweek as a solution to the problems caused by automation, on September 28, 1963, Kennedy said that the United States is a changing country and that "we had a 58-hour week, a 48-hour week, a 40-hour week. As machines take more and more of the jobs of men we are going to find the work week reduced."[43]

Such statements give considerable weight to labor's demands for a reduction in the workweek. This is an issue which will become more and more significant as automation increases.

Unemployment

The ideological issue of full employment has been covered under several of the above headings. It is evident that labor's greatest fears are of high unemployment levels. Certainly unemployment is the rallying cry by which

[39] *Business Week* (November 14, 1959), 33.

[40] United Automobile Workers of America, p. 27.

[41] George Kirstein, "Labor's Ebbing Strength," *The Nation,* 195 (September 1, 1962), 88.

[42] Dan Wakefield, "Labor Shudders at Leisure," *The Nation,* 196 (April 20, 1963), 326.

[43] *Salt Lake Tribune* (September 29, 1963).

labor attempts to gain support from its members and with which it demands various programs from both government and business. The unions' fear of widespread unemployment is, of course, understandable. High levels of unemployment not only result in misery for some workers' families, but also weaken labor's bargaining power. Furthermore, the leadership positions of the elite become vulnerable from growing discontent in their ranks as increasing unemployment develops. Unemployment as an ideological issue strikes at the heart of the "more" philosophy of American labor.

Labor is placing increasing emphasis upon the role of government to solve the problem of unemployment. While in past times more emphasis might have been placed upon business as the job creator, today labor's economists view government as the basic means of lowering unemployment levels through fiscal and monetary policies.

Labor generally advocates four basic policies by which unemployment should be curbed:

1. Labor suggests government buying and spending, not only for defense, but for schools, medical care, housing, urban redevelopment, mass transportation, aid to economically distressed communities, and many other types of programs. The idea is, of course, to put more money into the economy to raise the basic demand level.
2. Labor advocates that consumer buying power should be increased through continued improvement in wages, salaries, and fringe benefits. Particular emphasis is placed upon raising the income and buying power of low-income families, even though they may not belong to unions. This is to be done by increasing the coverage of the Fair Labor Standards Act to many unprotected workers, raising the legal minimum wage as well as improving standards and benefits of unemployment insurance.
3. Labor continues to favor easy money and low interest rates which essentially act to stimulate and encourage the economy.
4. Labor believes the tax structure should be completely revised to eliminate the advantages for the wealthy and to ease the tax burden on low-income families. Most of the above policies, of course, merely fall into categories of monetary and fiscal policy, which labor strongly advocates should be used by government.

Labor expresses few fears about the increased role of government or problems of deficit government spending. Further, it argues that the Council of Economic Advisers should increase its role to include forecasts regarding necessary levels of consumption and investment required to maintain increased employment. If such forecasting were done, labor argues, much more careful and skillful planning of government spending could be achieved, which could result in smoothing out the business and employment cycles.

All in all, most of the policies of labor hinge upon an increased role of government in solving the basic problems of unemployment and in creating an environment in which labor can bargain and negotiate successfully.

Taxation and Redistribution of Income

The labor ideology has long agreed with business that a major tax reform has been necessary, but at this point the similarity between the two groups ends. Labor argues that the objective of tax reform is to increase tax revenue by eliminating loopholes and to decrease tax rates on lower-income groups. If this could be done, the growth and stability of the economy would be increased. This aim reveals the basic social use of taxation as promulgated in the labor ideology. Labor argues that the personal income tax "is riddled with special privileges which are corroding its basically fair characteristics. The special treatment for capital gains, the special tax credit for dividend income, the continuing existence of tax-exempt interest are but a few examples."[44]

Labor ideology strongly argues against excessive depletion allowances for minerals and against continuing to allow income to be taxed differently according to its source: income from wages one tax, income and dividends another, and income from oil wells still another.

While agreeing with business on the desirability of a tax cut, labor argues that a cut should occur whenever unemployment exceeds 7 per cent of the work force, that tax reductions should not exceed $100 per year per tax return, and the tax cuts should benefit those in the lower income brackets.[45]

In other areas of taxation, however, labor strongly urges that the various loopholes mentioned above be eliminated from both individual and corporate income taxes and that the estate and gift taxes be made a more effective source of revenue by developing a single coordinated system for the two tax programs. In this regard, labor states:

> The present estate and gift taxes have hardly tapped the potential revenue involved in the transfer of funds by gift and inheritance. Nor have these taxes acted to reduce inequalities or to deter significantly the buildup of family fortunes. At present these taxes provide relatively liberal exemptions and deductions.[46]

The labor ideology regards tax reforms as a device to enforce greater equality. In its view of taxation and the redistribution of income American labor is perhaps at its most "socialistic." Whether this reflects socialistic or only American popularistic ideology is difficult to tell, for the results are essentially the same in this instance.

[44] AFL-CIO, p. 50.
[45] *Ibid.*, p. 46.
[46] *Ibid.*, p. 50.

Few issues that the labor ideology raises are apt to arouse as much consternation among business and other groups as labor's attack on capital gains taxes, dividends, certain areas of corporate income taxes, and estate and gift taxes. The idea of inherited wealth strikes at the heart of labor's egalitarian ideology. Furthermore, some labor leaders may have ideological carry-overs from socialist backgrounds. To an extent, such a carry-over from socialism undoubtedly does influence and affect a certain segment of labor leadership and results in programs aimed at redistributing wealth along more egalitarian lines.

Economic Growth

On the issue of economic growth, the labor ideology argues first that economic growth is necessary and essential for the economy. Second, it argues that the way to obtain economic growth in this country is through the stimulus of more customers. This is to be achieved by government spending and tax cuts for lower-income-bracket consumers. Labor disagrees with the emphasis on increasing business profits and investment for economic growth. Rather, it argues that there have been high levels of investment in this country, particularly through the retained earnings of the corporations. Labor refers to this as "costless capital." Such investment, labor claims, has not necessarily provided steady economic growth over the whole business cycle. Instead, it has only aided in promoting wide cyclical variation. The labor ideology, therefore, attacks the notion that tax cuts for corporations and the wealthy are necessary to initiate and sustain upward growth of investment.

Agriculture

The labor ideology has little to say about agriculture. Since unions generally represent urban groups, they are forced to be concerned with higher food and tax subsidies that result from the agriculture control programs. Nonetheless, the labor position is generally one of support of the subsidy program.

On one issue, however, labor does have considerable concern about agriculture, and most of its pronouncements regarding agriculture are usually related to this area. This is the issue of migrant farm workers. Labor is hostile to the current Bracero program which permits Mexicans to cross into the United States during certain seasons to aid in agricultural production. Furthermore, labor is very insistent about obtaining a minimum wage for agriculture and covering migratory farm laborers with social security.

Labor considers agricultural workers as a potential source for recruitment. It has had relatively little success in this program, and such an atomistic group will continue to be difficult to organize.

The unions have been aligned politically with the Farmers Union. However, considering the diminishing political power of farmers and the fact that agricultural stabilization programs are costly to union families, there is no guarantee that this informal AFL-CIO alliance with the Farmers Union will be permanent. (For further discussion of the Farmers Union see Chapter 4.)

Trade

The issue of freer international trade within the AFL-CIO has at many labor conventions been a hot political issue. Many individual unions which fear the competition of foreign firms with low wage levels, such as the garment and textile workers, are opposed to freer trade and the lowering of tariff barriers. Nonetheless, the basic policy taken by the AFL-CIO is favorable to the idea of increasing international trade and lowering tariffs.

At the opening of a trade conference held in late 1962, A. J. Hayes, president of the International Association of Machinists, reaffirmed their position that "withdrawal from world trade and isolationism from world problems is no longer possible." At the same meeting, AFL-CIO president George Meany outlined to the delegates a foreign trade program that included provision for Federal assistance to workers, communities, and industries hurt by foreign competition in an expanded reciprocal trade law.

Labor policy has become favorable toward lowering tariffs. The basic reason for this apparently rests on economic grounds. Labor generally appears to feel that in the long run it is self-defeating for a union or any business to shelter itself with high tariffs which permit inefficiency and perhaps the losing of customers and hence jobs. In this case it would appear that labor is following general economic reasoning, despite the resistance of particular union groups.

A CASE OF UNION LOBBYING

Unions are generally considered to have one of the most effective lobbying systems in America, especially when fighting for "bread-and-butter" programs which have broader appeal than for union members alone. Nonetheless, the passage of the Taft-Hartley Act in 1947 and of the Landrum-Griffin Act of 1959 represent two of the worst defeats that have occurred for organized labor in more than a quarter of a century, and the first since the high point of labor power under the New Deal. The case that will be considered here is the passage of the Landrum-Griffin Act. It is of considerable interest, because despite the highly organized union pressure and lobbying system, it shows how lack of political insight and inept pressure tactics can help defeat a major group.

Employer groups sensed that with the dramatic exposés of labor racketeering by Senator McClellan's committee in the late 1950s a favorable climate had developed for legislation to restrict many union practices. The goal was not only to pass legislation to rid labor of racketeers but, as could be expected in such a power struggle in our legislative arena, to achieve some dislodging of unions from their positions of power. To achieve this end, the supporters of labor reform legislation, largely business and certain agricultural groups, organized a coordinated and sustained grass roots campaign to convince legislators of the deep public desire for labor reform laws.

Under these circumstances, labor chose to be obdurate—a rather unfortunate tactic. For, by and large, the public and most legislators believed that some type of legislation was needed to protect labor from itself—certainly from the gangster elements that had received considerable publicity. Labor, however, at first refused to compromise on any type of government regulation of itself and thereby lost what might have been considerable middle-of-the-road support. Much of this began with the McClellan Committee hearings and their disclosure that certain unions had considerable criminal elements in them. The Dave Beck case and the actions of Jimmy Hoffa aided the antilabor groups in pressing for legislation. Further, Senators Ives and Douglas, during investigations between 1935 and 1955, found considerable misuse of union pension and administrative funds in a number of unions.

In the face of all these public disclosures, it is somewhat puzzling that labor refused to be more amenable to legislation enacted to prevent such actions in the future. Rather, George Meany, head of the AFL-CIO, appeared as a somewhat unfriendly witness before the Senate Subcommittee on Labor. He argued that labor had adopted self-regulating codes of ethics and that it would clean its own house in its own way. Thus labor lost the support of many of its friends in intellectual and academic circles who had become convinced that since, in many cases, government sanctioned compulsory union membership, it also had the obligation to guarantee and protect the rights of these workers.

In the spring of 1958 Mr. Meany appeared before Senator Kennedy's Labor Subcommittee and agreed to certain legislation which would entail publication of detailed financial reports by the unions and regulation of union trusteeships. However, the price for such agreement was that certain long-sought amendments to the Taft-Hartley Act be passed as well. At first it appeared that labor's demands would be met and that Congress would accept the price for the passing of certain necessary labor reform measures. Momentum, however, was developing among employer groups for stronger legislation.

Outright and clandestine opposition on the part of some labor spokesmen to the whole idea of any kind of labor regulation was sufficient to bottle up the Kennedy-Ives Bill—the original bill that labor agreed to accept, for a price—in the House Education and Labor Committee.

When it became apparent that the House Education and Labor Committee was not going to act on the bill, Speaker Sam Rayburn called up the Kennedy-Ives Bill for House consideration under suspension of rules. This procedure required a two-thirds affirmative vote to approve the bill, with debate limited to only forty minutes and no amendments permitted. The conservatives felt the bill was too weak, so it failed to get the necessary two-thirds majority. This, as it later turned out, was the last opportunity for labor to secure a reform bill which at least officially was to its liking. While the Senate Labor Committee, which was composed of a majority of members generally friendly toward labor, approved a bill in 1959 very similar to the one that had been rejected by the House during the previous year, considerable opposition to "soft" labor legislation was growing.

Despite the fact that the election of November, 1958, had changed the composition of the Senate in labor's favor, there was a general feeling, even among labor's friends in Congress, that it was necessary to restrict abuses of union power. The Kennedy-sponsored bill had much tougher going in Congress during the next session; for fifty-two amendments were introduced. Out of this number, many stronger legislative proposals were introduced into the bill, both with reference to internal union affairs and with provisions dealing with questionable union tactics in collective bargaining.

The most dramatic moment of the struggle occurred when Senator McClellan presented an amendment with a "bill of rights" for union members. This included such features as: (1) the guarantee of equal voting rights and equal protection of union rules to all members; (2) the requirement that dues could be raised only through a vote of the union member; (3) authorization of union members to sue union leaders who deprived them of rights; and (4) freedom of speech and assembly guaranteed to union members.[47]

The vote on this amendment put many Democratic senators, who regularly publicized their affection for the workingmen, in an awkward position of appearing to vote against rights of the members because the union leaders were so adamant against this amendment, which, they argued, would permit harassment and chaos. Senator Hubert Humphrey, who would have voted against the amendment, was away campaigning for the Presidency. This left an even split (45–45) in the vote. Vice President Nixon broke the tie, however, in favor of the "bill of rights."[48]

At this point the AFL-CIO expressed categoric opposition to the

---

[47] *Congressional Record*, 86th Congress, 1st Session (April 22, 1959), 6475–6476.

[48] *Ibid.*, 6492–6493.

Kennedy reform legislation as it emerged from the Senate. It denounced the bill as unacceptable, insisted that it would only agree to the original bill which had been approved by the Senate Labor Committee earlier, and declared that labor would not accept any amendments to it.

Labor hoped to recoup its losses with the Senate-approved bill when it appeared in the House before the Committee on Education and Labor, which contained several former labor organizers and was composed of a majority generally very favorable to labor's cause. Nonetheless, the mounting pressure for labor reform legislation was such that the committee would not adopt, in total, the original bill favored by labor. Since the AFL-CIO's rigid position against any other bill left no room for compromise, those members of the committee favorable to labor were left with little they could do but formulate measures that would inevitably be opposed by labor. The combined pressure, both pro and con, upon the House committeee became so intense that it appeared it would be unable to report out any bill. However, pressures on the House for reform legislation became dominant, and after five weeks the House finally reported out the Elliott Bill, which was more favorable to labor than had been the Senate bill. Nonetheless, the AFL-CIO spokesmen still refused to have anything to do with this bill because it was not along the lines of their original statements. As it turned out later, this was a serious mistake.

The House Democratic leadership put its full support behind the moderate Elliott Bill, but the AFL-CIO continued to object to it. This situation resulted in a division of the prolabor forces within the House. At first, supporters of the labor position had no particular bill which they favored. Finally, Congressman John Shelley of California introduced the labor-favored bill. He asserted that he knew the labor problem firsthand because he had been "beaten by 17 thugs," had his teeth "knocked out of my mouth by brass knuckles," and had "had a plaster cast over his whole torso for 14 weeks."[49] This revelation of his experience with labor goons had the unintended effect of horrifying some moderate congressmen and moving them to favor a stronger measure than the Shelley Bill, which was accused of having "foam rubber teeth."

At the other extreme a coalition of Southern Democrats and Republicans united behind the Landrum-Griffin Bill, which had won President Eisenhower's acclaim and had been carefully designed not to go "too far," so it was able to win a majority.

Thus, essentially three bills were vying for passage. The AFL-CIO continued to press for the Shelley Bill, even though it was generally conceded that the bill did not have the slightest chance of passage, and it was actually defeated by a 2 to 1 vote. With the prolabor forces divided between

---

[49] *Congressional Record,* 86th Congress, 1st Session (August 11, 1959), 15528.

the AFL-CIO-sponsored Shelley Bill and the Elliott Bill, which was somewhat more middle of the road, labor was unable to find enough votes to pass either bill. On the other hand, Republicans succeeded in closing their ranks (with only a few exceptions) for a bill favored by the administration and, with a number of powerful Southern Democrats, were able to pass the Landrum-Griffin Bill by a majority of 28 votes.

The Landrum-Griffin Bill was passed partly because of the tactics of the AFL-CIO itself. If the AFL-CIO had been able to recognize that politically the Elliott Bill was their best hope and had actively pushed for it, they would have had a better chance of receiving legislation more in line with what they wanted.

During the whole affair the AFL-CIO's lobbyists on Capital Hill continued to attack the Elliott Bill, and by so doing pushed certain Democrats and Republicans, even liberal ones, closer together to vote for the Landrum-Griffin Bill. Obviously, labor miscalculated its own strength. The vote on the reform issue makes it evident that labor does not have enough power to carry Congress on an issue which is at odds with the moderate elements in Congress and on which labor stands largely alone against the majority of the other power groups.

After the House approved the Landrum-Griffin Bill, representatives of the Senate and House had to meet together to iron out differences between the Senate-approved bill and the House-approved bill. It was up to Senator Kennedy and his Democratic colleagues, Senators McNamara, Morse, and Randolph, to pull labor's chestnuts out of the fire. This turned out to be a very difficult task. The majority of House conferees, led by Congressman Bardon of North Carolina, favored the strongest measures they could secure.

The task of the Senate Democrats was made more difficult by another blunder committed by James Carey, president of the International Electric Workers and a vice-president of AFL-CIO. Just as the conferees were about to start their work, Carey wrote a crude and tactless letter threatening the 229 congressmen who had voted for the Landrum-Griffin Bill with reprisals in the 1960 election.

A deadlock by the conferees could have resulted in the adoption of the Landrum-Griffin Bill without modification because there was little chance that Congress would have adjourned without passing a labor bill. The consensus of Capitol Hill was that the smart congressman had to vote for labor legislation in 1959. Most of the power blocs in the country favored some type of legislation. Senator Kennedy was, therefore, in a very disadvantageous bargaining position. Nonetheless, he was able to succeed in obtaining a number of important concessions in the original bill.

The bill, as finally passed, included the previously mentioned "bill of rights" and other key features essentially as follows:

Requirements were established for detailed public financial reporting by unions

Former felons and Communists were barred from holding a union office for five years after conviction or leaving the party

Employers were required to report spending to influence workers

A secret ballot was necessary to elect union officers at maximum intervals of five years for international officers and three years for local officers

State courts could take over smaller cases declined by the National Labor Relations Board

So-called "blackmail" picketing was banned for twelve months after employees had rejected a union in an NLRB election or where the employer lawfully recognized another union

Secondary boycotts were curbed both by prohibiting employees of one firm from inducing employees of a second firm to strike against the other firm and by banning employees' coercion of their employer not to do business with another firm

"Hot cargo" agreements, wherein an employer agreed with his employees not to do business with another company, were banned.[50]

The last three of these provisions were among those most hotly contested. The *New York Times* concluded that "the economic power of legitimate unions" was cut by these provisions.[51] Another disinterested observer, Roscoe Pound, former dean of the Harvard Law School, argued that the effort "to adjust the situations in labor today to rational principles" is not an effort to destroy them but to end their treatment as "peculiar favorites of government at the expense of the general public interest."[52]

Overall then, labor's actions were such that by a number of unwise moves they minimized their actual support in Congress. They wound up with a labor reform bill that was in many ways the worst bill—from their own point of view—that could have been passed in the face of their tremendous power.

Labor leaders made three critical mistakes. First, they took a completely adamant stand against any compromise, meaning they were heedless of the political realities that govern legislation. Second, labor did very little to attempt to stem the tide of adverse public opinion. Public opinion was fanned and utilized to demand the passage of strong reform measures. At the last minute, labor's contact men saw the need for grass roots support. Over 2 million leaflets, "Get Crooks, not Labor" were distributed. It was, however, too late to turn public opinion, and the labor lobbyists reported that there was virtually no prolabor group on the Hill. Labor brought in

[50] See *United States Statutes at Large*, 86th Congress, 1st Session, 73 (1959), 519–546, and *The New York Times* (September 3, 1959).

[51] *The New York Times* (September 14, 1959).

[52] *Congressional Record*, 86th Congress, 1st Session (August 11, 1959), 15560–15561.

ninety field people to aid in its contact operation, but by then it was too late to be effective.[53]

Labor's third mistake was its attempt to threaten congressmen that they would be defeated unless they acted for labor's bill. This rather blatant approach to lobbying is considered not only in poor taste but very bad psychology. To begin with, any politician is aware of the strength of labor and of the chances that without labor's support he may be defeated. To call this to his attention and to the attention of the public, in an attempt to force him into acting publicly as a puppet for labor, may be enough to turn other groups in his district against him and thus cause his defeat in another way. Furthermore, this approach touched upon a very delicate subject, the ego of the politician. The fact that most politicians are not independent, but are representatives of certain power groups, is one that few politicians ever wish to admit, even to themselves.

As this case so well illustrates, for any one power group in the country, even labor, to pass an important piece of legislation, compromise and conciliation are required among the other power groups in the economy and their representatives in Congress. Further, America today is very much a plural society. Power groups do not operate individually to secure legislation without the support of at least a minimum of other groups.

The results of this case are likely to force labor to develop policy and political strategy to match its highly developed political organization and consequently to become more adept at legislative compromise. It would appear that in the future all the basic economic power groups—business, labor, agriculture—are going to become, out of necessity, increasingly active politically, while at the same time growing in political sophistication.

CONCLUDING SUMMARY

Labor unions as a power group face these problems:

1. Less than half of the union members generally vote. A large minority of those who do vote respond to cross pressures such as family tradition, religion, television appeals, a candidate's personality, and comments of friends in lodges and clubs. Many labor votes are cast contrary to the desires of union leaders.
2. The numerical position of unions in the population is declining as automation helps speed the increase of professional and white-collar jobs at the expense of unskilled jobs.
3. The public image of labor's political power induces a substantial political reaction.

[53] The information in this case is drawn from Samuel C. Patterson, "The Role of the Labor Lobbyist," given at the annual meeting of the American Political Science Association in Washington, D.C., September 5–8, 1962.

4. The Taft-Hartley Act of 1947 and the Landrum-Griffin Act of 1959 have curbed some of the instruments of power, such as the closed shop, which unions enjoyed from 1935 to 1947, and which assisted them in their rapid growth.
5. Unionism as a cause no longer induces the same militance, loyalty, and zeal that it did during the Great Depression.

In order to overcome these difficulties, unions are attempting the following devices:

1. Intensively organized "get-out-the-vote" campaigns in working-class areas
2. More effective political education of workers on union interest and ideologies
3. Winning the election of a Congress and President sufficiently prolabor to repeal antagonistic labor legislation such as the Taft-Hartley provision which permits states to enact right-to-work laws
4. Selling their position to the public not only during election campaigns but to a degree through regular sponsorship, for example, of prolabor news commentators
5. Recruiting new union members particularly in such low-union sectors as the white-collar workers and farm workers
6. Developing alliances with unorganized workers, the Farmers Union, and other power groups sympathetic with the liberal ideology

Most Americans view themselves as members of the middle class; class consciousness and class warfare have not been prevalent. American unions, consequently, differ from European labor unions in this aspect of their ideology. European unions have for the most part adopted the socialist ideology of class conflict with the goal of working-class domination of a government which owns, or at a minimum controls, the instruments of economic production and distribution.

American unions are less interested in overturning the social, economic, and political system. At times, as during Nikita Khrushchev's visit to the United States in 1959, union leaders are even more vociferously anti-Communist than many business leaders.

Thus, labor ideology in the United States is not doctrinaire but is preponderantly pragmatic. In its simplest form it boils down to the demand for higher wages, better working conditions, and fringe benefits obtained through collective bargaining, government-guaranteed full employment, and increased government welfare programs within the broad framework of a mixed economy.

The labor ideology justifies these demands with an equalitarian concept of justice. The ideology ties the demands of the welfare of the nation to a theory of economic development based upon the stimulus of mass purchasing power. Government, in the labor ideology, is to play a dynamic economic role designed to stimulate employment through liberal fiscal policies, as well as to provide security to workers through increasingly generous welfare programs. Redistribution of wealth from the rich to the poor is also to be accomplished by these welfare programs. They are to be financed heavily by progressive income taxes, by increased estate and gift taxes, and by closing tax loopholes used by wealthy people.

The case study on the victory of the Landrum-Griffin Bill illustrated that labor is much stronger when joined in an alliance to achieve social legislation for a broader group than its own membership. When it is fighting strictly over the rights of unions, especially in the face of hostile public opinion, its forces must be very skillfully mobilized if it is to avoid defeat.

4

agriculture

INTRODUCTION

In the history of the United States, few domestic policies have been more thoroughly criticized for prodigious waste in human, natural, and capital resources than has our farm policy. Alexander Hamilton failed as a prophet when he wrote in the seventeenth *Federalist* paper that it was "improbable that there should exist a disposition in the federal councils to usurp the powers" to supervise and control agriculture "because the attempt to exercise those powers would be as troublesome as they are nugatory." He was "quite right, however, in foreseeing the consequences" of such action. Barry Goldwater expressed the views of many liberals as well as conservatives when he noted that "Federal intervention into agriculture has . . . proved troublesome."[1]

The effort by the government—costing more than $20 billion—to guarantee high prices without adequate production controls has been declared a failure on all sides.[2] Farm income has not been stabilized, and agricultural surpluses seemingly mount year by year beyond all imagined storage facilities of an earlier era. While some government agencies pay

[1] Barry Goldwater, *The Conscience of a Conservative* (New York: Hillman Books, 1960), p. 39.

[2] Official Department of Agriculture statistics listed the cumulative cost as $15,009,100,000 as far back as the end of fiscal 1957. U.S. Department of Agriculture, *Realized Cost of Programs Primarily for Stabilization of Farm Prices and Income, Distributed by Fiscal Years and by Commodities, Where Possible*, Appendix, 7.

farmers not to grow certain crops and impose acreage and marketing controls, still others teach them techniques to expand their production; and in many instances even pay them to do so.

Evidence of the advancing technology and resulting increase in production is clearly shown by the fact that "farm output in 1960 was 50 per cent higher than in 1940, an increase of almost 2 per cent per year . . . even though acreage planted declined slightly and the farm population fell by almost one third."[3] Scholars commonly observe, "Clearly something has gone wrong with our farm policy,"[4] and it is generally acknowledged that the "policy has gone wrong primarily because organized farm groups, the policy-making processes in Congress, and executive leadership have all failed to achieve agreement on the character of our basic agricultural problems and on the direction of remedial instead of a palliative action."[5]

Economists generally favor government intervention in many aspects of the economy, particularly through anticyclical fiscal policies. Yet a survey of elementary economics texts reveals that an overwhelming majority of economists favor a partial withdrawal of the government rather than increased government intervention in the agricultural area. "It is hard to find well reasoned defenses of American agricultural policy," notes one economist, "because economists are almost always on the other side."[6] In a typical statement, one economist said, "Pricing of farm products should be returned as rapidly as possible to the free market, keeping only the safeguards against depression."[7] Another echoed, "Free markets should be restored in agriculture by the gradual elimination of price and income supports."[8] John Kenneth Galbraith, a prominent liberal, noted this unanimity among economists and commented:

> In sharp contrast with the growing popularity of farm policy has been the position of the economists who have spoken on this subject. . . . What is remarkable is the unanimity with which this policy has been condemned by the professional students. . . . There have been almost literally no expressed partisans of the fixed guarantees. In the current climate of professional attitudes, approval of the present farm policy, one senses, would be not alone exceptional but eccentric.[9]

[3] Lloyd G. Reynolds, *Economics: A General Introduction* (Homewood, Ill.: Richard D. Irwin, Inc., 1963), p. 267.

[4] Merle Fainsod, Lincoln Gordon, and J. C. Palamountain, *Government and the American Economy*, 3d ed. (New York: W. W. Norton & Company, 1959), p. 156.

[5] *Ibid.*, p. 156.

[6] Rendigs Fels, *Challenge to the American Economy: An Introduction to Economics* (Boston: Allyn and Bacon, Inc., 1961), p. 106.

[7] Reynolds, p. 275.

[8] Campbell R. McConnell, *Elementary Economics: Principles, Problems and Policies* (New York: McGraw-Hill Book Company, 1960), p. 622.

[9] John Kenneth Galbraith, "Economic Preconception and the Farm Policy," *American Economic Review*, 44 (March, 1954), 41.

Yet, after analyzing the position of "the professional students" referred to above and expressing his concern over the possibility of economic preconception, Galbraith himself admits that "the policy seems . . . to have serious faults."[10]

Economists are also in agreement that "the only ultimate solution" to the farm problem of overproduction "is to reduce our surplus of farmers."[11] "Knowledgeable people on both sides recognize that price supports are no solution for hundreds of thousands of very poor farmers, whose only possible salvation lies in changing occupations."[12] In effect, these economists are saying that the trend of the last century must continue, for in 1960 only about 8 per cent of the United States population worked on farms compared to 27 per cent in 1920 and 53 per cent in 1870.[13] Yet this solution strikes at the very heart of what is perhaps the most cherished symbol among farmers and farm groups—the preservation of the American farm family.

To most Americans, the family farm is the lingering symbol of the American heritage. Somehow the rugged pioneer and the family farmer seem to live on coeternally in the hearts of men, women, and children everywhere. It is this sentimentalism which makes the family farm an appealing ideological symbol to both organized farm groups and aspiring politicians. For example, in his 1956 presidential campaign, Adlai Stevenson made the following statement.

. . . there is another thing that our people need to be told about farming, perhaps the most important thing of all. . . . They don't realize that farming is the way many Americans live, and that the family farm is the backbone of American agriculture, as it once was the backbone of American Society.

They don't realize that on a family farm the most precious thing that's raised is not corn or cattle, but children—children who go to rural schools and rural churches and who inherit the earth they live on and work on. People don't realize that when the family farm is in trouble, more, much more than dollars and cents is involved. What is involved is the whole fabric of American rural life. . . .

The real tragedy . . . is the human tragedy of young people forced off the farm, cherished belongings put up for sale, of human heartbreak, of the end of a family's chosen way of life.[14]

It is probably more to this symbolism than to any other that the advocates of high price supports appeal. The entire ideology of the National Farmers Union, as will be shown later, is expressed in terms of the

[10] *Ibid.,* 52.

[11] Paul A. Samuelson, *Economics: An Introductory Analysis* (New York: Mc-Graw-Hill Book Company, 1958), p. 419.

[12] Fels, p. 106.

[13] Daniel Hamberg, *Principles of a Growing Economy* (New York: W. W. Norton & Company, Inc., 1961), p. 28.

[14] *The New York Times* (September 23, 1956), 66, quoted by Fels, pp. 99, 100.

"farm family" and the "family farm," and the NFU is by far the strongest advocate of high price supports of the major farm organizations.

The success of this appeal can be illustrated no better than in the portion of the United States budget spent on agriculture. "In its fiscal year 1963, the federal government spend almost $6 billion on agriculture. This was seven percent of the total federal expenditures, and 20% of the federal expenditures excluding national security."[15] Yet, in 1963, only 4 million of the 56 million United States families were farm families. Even recognizing that not all of the agricultural budget goes to farmers, certainly no other occupational group in America has been supported so liberally by government.

Yet in spite of heavy government subsidies, inefficiency in farming continues, and government policy only seems to add to the problems. For one thing ". . . the prime beneficiaries of the price-support program are the farmers who produce the most—the large commercial farmers. The farmers who have little or no marketable surplus are almost totally excluded from the benefits of price supports."[16] For example, "One of the world's largest farmers collected $1.2 million in benefits in four years, and in addition received $14 million a year for storing . . . surplus wheat and other grains."[17]

In a lucid presentation of the farm picture, the CED has pointed out that if a total production of as little as $2,500 worth of farm products each year were to be used as a standard for determining farm efficiency, the 44 per cent of the farms which would qualify as efficient would produce 90.8 per cent of all marketed products, while the remaining 9.2 per cent of the products would be produced by the 56 per cent of the farms which produce less than that standard.[18] It seems, therefore, quite obvious why economists, looking beyond the symbolism and emotional issues of preserving the traditional family farm, are in agreement that what is best for the marginal farmer may not be the marginal farm, even if it is a "family farm."

Thus, economists generally agree that if the government stopped intervening in the market while adopting a phase-out program, the law of supply and demand would bring about an adjustment. Agricultural surpluses could ultimately be eradicated, per capita farm income would be higher, farm poverty would disappear at least in part as marginal farmers shifted to other areas and occupations, and the government would cease to waste billions of dollars annually subsidizing farm products which cannot be consumed. On the other hand, the difficulties of supporting a policy of a

---

[15] George Leland Bach, *Economics: An Introduction to Analysis and Policy* (Englewood Cliffs, N.J.: Prentice-Hall, Inc., 1963), p. 398.

[16] Hamberg, p. 30.

[17] Bach, p. 400.

[18] *Toward a Realistic Farm Program* (New York: Committee for Economic Development, December, 1957), pp. 12, 13, quoted by McConnell, p. 604.

tightly controlled agricultural production system are that the prices of farm products to consumers are higher, the advantages of a free market economy are lost, and economic regimentation could possibly lead to political control. Yet a few economists do support this solution, as will be shown later.

While an economic solution appears simple, the political answers are not. When the Committee for Economic Development recommended solutions along free market lines, Sears, Roebuck and other companies whose management suggested such measures as members of the CED were forced by the reaction of farm groups and by farmers' protests to claim that company officers backing such programs were speaking only for themselves and not for the companies concerned. This reaction is mild, nonetheless, compared to what some rural politicians would be likely to face were they to support such an "easy" solution.

Certain of the farm organizations strongly favor increased government control of agricultural markets, and since opposition from such groups could well mean defeat for particular congressmen, it would be an unusual politician who would not in such circumstances represent the basic power groups of his constituency. In fact, congressmen frequently have long membership in these groups. Further, since a return to a free market in agriculture would result in a number of small farmers being forced to leave the farms, certain rural congressmen might find their own congressional districts abolished by the next census count. Thus the political problems are difficult and involved, even if an economic remedy is relatively simple in this case.

The question may be asked: "If farm families scarcely represent 8 per cent of the population, how is it that they exercise such dominance in legislative policy on agriculture?" The answer lies partly in the fact that farmers have traditionally been overrepresented in state legislatures which draw congressional district lines and are slow to give the growing metropolitan areas their proper congressional apportionment. Many rural congressional districts have less than 250,000 residents, whereas urban districts often have in excess of 600,000 residents. Another factor is that although farmers are a minority, they are a big enough group in many districts to swing elections from one candidate to another. Finally, farm districts dominate the House and Senate agriculture committees which can bottle up legislation not to the farmers' liking.

Farmers, nevertheless, are decreasing in political power. The reapportionment of congressional seats following each decennial census reduces the percentage of farm-oriented congressmen, and this process will be accelerated as a result of the intervention of the Supreme Court into the redistricting controversy of underrepresented Tennessee citizens in *Baker v. Carr* in 1962. Furthermore, farmers and farm workers comprise the only major occupational group which is rapidly diminishing in number. The

Labor Department projections estimate that between 1960 and 1975 the number of farmers and farm workers will drop 28 per cent.[19]

If, as the above quotations argue, our farm policy has gone wrong because of failure to achieve agreement on a consistent policy among the farm groups, and consequently in Congress, an understanding of the identity and goals of the basic farm groups is the key to understanding present farm policy. Familiarity with the areas of agreement and disagreement and the causes of deadlock will aid in understanding what one may realistically expect for American farm policy.

THE POWER GROUPS OF AGRICULTURE AND THEIR IDEOLOGIES

Although there is an array of associations among farmers fully as complicated as that among either unions or businesses, three major power groups dominate the agricultural bloc and, on the macro level, represent the major positions of American agriculture. These three national organizations are the Farmers Educational and Cooperative Union, the National Grange— Order of the Patrons of Husbandry, and the American Farm Bureau Federation. Besides these three general associations, numerous specialized farm organizations proliferate. These specialized groups are based on the common economic needs of farmers engaged in similar specialties, such as the cattlemen, the sheepmen, the poultry producers, and the citrus growers. Each particular group has its own "trade association" similar to those of the business community. As in business, general agricultural lobbying (outside of special group interests) is conducted for the most part by the major power groups—the Farmers Union, the Grange, and the Farm Bureau. These three associations correspond in many ways to the roles played by the NAM and Chamber of Commerce for business and the AFL-CIO for labor.

Further, all three groups focus their attention upon changes in government policy as a primary means of gaining the desired degree of stability consistent with their ideology and programs. Determining the stand of each of these groups on basic issues is not always easy. Because of the profusion of statements and standards often taken on an issue, it is sometimes difficult to pin down the precise position that a group is taking. This difficulty is further accentuated because the position of the leadership of a group will not necessarily always represent the majority opinion of its membership. Thus, the position and goals of a group on some issues may be deliberately stated in somewhat obscure language.

By and large, however, there are three basic ideological positions taken

[19] "Unemployment—The No. 1 Worry," *Business Week* (January 25, 1964), 84.

by these groups. If the ideology of each is kept clearly in mind, its basic position on major issues is much easier to follow and to understand. Let us look, then, at these three organizations.

The Farmers Union (The Farmers Educational and Cooperative Union)

The Farmers Union, which is the second oldest and the third largest of the farm groups,[20] was founded in 1902 among low-income farmers in Texas. The Union was organized following the collapse of the Populist movement —a rural protest movement which had remonstrated against deflation by supporting greenbacks and free silver, called for greater democracy including the direct election of senators, and demanded political reform through the establishment of a universal civil service.[21]

From the organization's constitution, we learn that its purposes are "to discourage the credit mortgage system, to eliminate gambling in farm products, to secure and maintain profitable and uniform prices for cotton, grain, livestock, and other products of the farm."[22] As might be expected, the Farmers Union gained its primary strength among farmers in areas hazardous to farming, particularly in the Great Plains area from the Dakotas south, where the insufficiency of rainfall makes farming insecure. The economic insecurity of its members accounts for the Union's more or less consistently radical or liberal position on most economic issues. Its ideology is the farthest left, or the most liberal, of the three major farm groups.

In efforts to further the economic security of its members, the Farmers Union early emphasized cooperative buying and selling. Many of the cooperatives that it originally organized, such as the Farmers Union Grain Terminal Association, have been extremely successful, and today they are valuable aids to the internal cohesion of its membership. However, by the 1920s the Farmers Union found that cooperatives alone were insufficient as a means of achieving economic stability for its members. Concentration then turned toward promoting Federal legislation that would guarantee farmers the cost of production and thereby decrease agricultural instability and economic insecurity.

As might be expected from the background of its members, the Farmers Union has been concerned, as well, with the problems of subsistence

[20] Their president listed NFU as representing over 250,000 farm families. *Statement of James G. Patton, President, National Farmers Union,* before the Senate Foreign Relations Committee, June 27, 1963, p. 1.

[21] Fred A. Shannon, *American Farmers' Movements* (Princeton, N.J.: D. Van Nostrand Company, Inc., 1957), pp. 70–74.

[22] Orville Merton Kile, *The Farm Bureau Movement* (New York: The Macmillan Company, 1921), p. 31.

farming and tenancy and has at times attempted to use strikes to prevent milk and other products from reaching the market in hopes of increasing market prices on those products.

The Farmers Union has expanded into approximately twenty-two states, with its membership concentration stretching throughout the Middle West and Northwest, particularly in wheat-growing areas. As would naturally follow from its ideology, the Farmers Union is more closely allied with the AFL-CIO on most issues than are any of the other farm groups.

FARM POLICY. The ideology and goals of the Farmers Union, as revealed in its policy statements, give additional insight into its orientation toward public policy. In its general agricultural policy, the Union argues for a National Agricultural Act, paralleling the Employment Act of 1946, which would provide for the Department of Agriculture to determine annually a specific national production goal for all major commodities. Further, price levels for these commodities would be assured through an income-parity type of index. Thus it asserts the necessity of having an agricultural plan with governmental controls on both production and prices— or at least subsidization of prices through a parity program in which the government would assure farmers of price levels sufficient for an income on a parity within a given year. In the words of the Farmers Union:

> This agricultural policy is necessary in order that farmers not be subject to an "auction-hammer" type free market which would be forced on them in the absence of farm programs because of the basic weakness of their economic organization. Other segments of the national economic structure are not subject to this type of a market and could not survive under it.[23]

The philosophy of this statement is simply that a free market should not be permitted to function in agriculture because of the inherent weakness "of the farm position." In other words, this means that because of the highly competitive nature of farming and because of the hazards of weather, etc., farmers should be given additional income and production assurances. The Farmers Union argument is that agriculture, being the most competitive industry in the nation, faces competition which makes it extremely difficult for farmers to protect themselves against abnormal price fluctuations. It points out that in most industries, such as automobiles and steel, only a few large companies compete for the market, and price competition is neither as intense nor as dangerous to them as it is in agriculture.

As pointed out earlier, the Farmers Union expresses its ideology in terms of preservation of the family farm, and as such, it opposes large-scale operations. For example, the Farmers Union argues that the

[23] *Policy Statements of the National Farmers Union,* adopted by the delegates to the annual convention, New York, March 20, 1963, p. 7.

. . . concentration of farmland ownership and of farm operation into larger than family units should be discouraged. The conditions that cause sub-standard family farming should be eliminated as far as possible. The bargaining power of family farms in commodity and credit markets must be balanced with the rest of the economy through programs and policies of the federal Government which provide the means for producer management of supply and include strengthening farmer-owned cooperatives. The central issue is whether we will be able to maintain our family farm pattern in agriculture or go down the road to factory-in-the-field agriculture.[24]

As this statement brings out, the Farmers Union directly challenges the idea of agriculture moving to larger productive units where greater efficiency and lower costs can be achieved, and it is opposed to a "factory-in-the-field agriculture."

The desire of the Farmers Union to safeguard its membership is understandable; but from an economic point of view, it appears irrational to attempt by force to perpetuate smaller units of farming than might be the most economically efficient. Furthermore, the increased size and efficiency of farms has not necessarily shifted them from family to corporate ownership. Family-owned farms continue to dominate farm ownership by accounting for more than 90 per cent of all farms.

As is to be expected, then, the basic program of the Farmers Union appears to be oriented toward maintaining the income of the "family farm." To this end, the Farmers Union recommends a farm commodity program, amounting to a system of international and Federal supply-stabilization and income-improvement plans, which would rely on marketing quotas, or acreage allotments, based upon the past crop history of a farm. Taking this stand, however, the Union stresses the necessity of "protection to be afforded individual farm units from encroachment by large factory-in-the-field operations."[25]

The government, according to the Farmers Union, should make available special credit facilities for farm ownership loans to farm families in order to end tenant farming and to further the ideal of "farming as owner-operators of fully adequate family farms."[26] To accomplish this it advocates a program of low-cost loan funds and emergency credit, to be administered by the Farmers Home Administration, and it believes this action is needed immediately "to fully supplement credit made available on conventional terms through . . . other sources."[27]

The NFU further advocates that the government should continue to improve and expand its Federal crop insurance program "until it is available to family farmers in every county in the United States for all crops," providing greater protection against the risks of weather and other such

[24] *Ibid.*
[25] *Ibid.*, p. 10.
[26] *Ibid.*, p. 11.
[27] *Ibid.*

farm hazards. Again underscoring its emphasis on family farms, NFU says, "Production greater than the family farm maximum on any unit should not be eligible for Federal crop insurance."[28]

In the area of agricultural conservation and land use, the NFU maintains that "technical assistance in soil and water conservation should continue to be extended through local soil conservation districts, governed by democratically elected committees." Under this program "each family farmer and rancher should have conveniently available to him competent federally financed technical assistance and . . . programs . . . to develop and put into operation his own . . . conservation program." Once again NFU declares that "larger than family farm units should not receive cost-sharing payments on that part in excess of a family unit, and should be required to pay full cost for technical assistance . . . for such excess."[29]

The NFU calls for the establishment of effective farmer committees to administer Federal farm programs, with these committees more responsive to the needs of family farmers.[30] It also supports increased appropriations to expand agricultural research and increase protective and marketing services.[31] Likewise, aid in the form of vocational training, credit, and other services should be "utilized to the fullest extent to assist families with low income to establish themselves . . . so that the causes of poverty will be wiped out."[32]

COOPERATIVES. In regard to cooperatives, the Farmers Union has a separate section in its policy statements devoted to expanding and strengthening patron enterprises. Rural telephone and electrification cooperatives are given special emphasis, and the government is urged to continue the existing low interest rates of 2 per cent and the long-term amortization loans to such groups. In addition, it urges that taxation of cooperatives be kept at the present "favorable position."[33]

FISCAL AND MONETARY POLICIES. Contending that the recent average rate of national growth (3.5 per cent of gross national product) is too low to bring about full employment, the NFU urges that the gross national product be increased by at least 5 per cent annually. It argues that the proper governmental use of monetary policies, especially the lowering of interest rates, is the best insurance of this increased economic growth.

Concerning taxation, the union supports "the principle of the graduated net income tax," and calls for tax legislation to "close income tax loopholes and assure that the system accurately reflects the ability to pay."[34]

28 *Ibid.*
29 *Ibid.*, pp. 12, 13.
30 *Ibid.*, pp. 11, 12.
31 *Ibid.*, p. 12.
32 *Ibid.*
33 *Ibid.*, p. 14.
34 *Ibid.*, p. 19.

In a *Statement of the National Farmers Union* delivered to the House Committee on Ways and Means on March 12, 1963,[35] the NFU took the position that "the underlying cause of the dilemma in which we find ourselves in this so-called affluent society is actually underconsumption, not overproduction." To increase consumption, the Union argued for a personal income tax reduction along the lines proposed by the President in his message to Congress, but strongly opposed a tax cut for corporations, saying that it could see "no valid reason for reducing corporate taxes."

In addition to supporting a reduction in personal income taxes to allow more consumer spending, the NFU also called for increased government expenditures and stated that "the problem of the public debt is grossly exaggerated." It continued, "If the federal government had not assisted state and local governments, the federal cash budget would show a surplus."

BUSINESS. The Farmers Union takes an extremely harsh view of the business community, and it advocates programs of governmental price and policy determination affecting corporate business activity that are certain to make the NAM and other such groups shudder with horror.

For example, NFU maintains that business

. . . corporations in key basic industries, such as steel and chemicals, should be required to submit their plans and justifications for price increases to an appropriate Federal agency for review, public hearing, analysis and publication of the implications to the entire national economy before they may be put into effect.[36]

In his speech to the Joint Economic Committee of Congress on February 14, 1963, James G. Patton, president of the Farmers Union, took a vigorous swing at corporations and big business.[37] "The contention that lack of capital expansion is caused by the profit squeeze, that profits are too low, and that capital investment will not increase until industry is given tax relief is completely fallacious." He blamed the "prices of steel and other durable goods" as the cause of declining consumer demand in the 1950s, and added that "despite tax incentives, including the one in 1962, industry has not invested adequate funds in capital expansion. We, therefore, are opposed to any more tax inducements to large corporations."

Patton also argued that there is no need for expansion as long as industry continues to operate at less than full capacity. "It would seem

[35] *Statement of the National Farmers Union in Regard to Proposals by the President for Tax Reduction and Reform,* presented by Angus McDonald to the House Committee on Ways and Means, March 12, 1963, pp. 1, 2.

[36] *Policy Statements,* p. 17.

[37] *Statement of James G. Patton, President, National Farmers Union, on the Economic Report of the President,* presented to the Joint Economic Committee of the Congress of the United States, February 14, 1963, pp. 5, 6.

logical," he continued, "to stimulate demand before attempting to pour more billions of tax exemptions into industry" to encourage expansion "when a portion of the plant is already standing idle." He concluded that if there were no idle capacity in industry, "there would be no federal deficit and there would be no unemployment in this country except possibly a small amount usually referred to as technological and seasonal." He then urged a vast program of public works "of no less than $50 billion for the next three years" to solve the problems of idle plants and unemployment.

Thus, while the NFU can hardly expect to gain support among business groups for its position, it is quite possible that if its proposals clearly did not impinge on labor's own decision-making powers, support for such programs might be forthcoming from the AFL-CIO.

LABOR. The Farmers Union backs legislation which would protect the rights of all employees to organize, bargain collectively, and protect their organization. Minimum wage legislation should be expanded to cover all employees and should be fortified by such Federal protection for employers as may be needed to enable them to pay just wages.[38] The Farmers Union's position on labor legislation and taxation is very similar to that of the AFL-CIO. In fact, the ideology of the Farmers Union, as outlined above, stresses many liberal programs also favored by labor.

SOCIAL LEGISLATION. The Farmers Union believes that:

All phases of the National Social Security program and Old Age, Disability and Survivors Insurance should be expanded and improved. Special emphasis should be placed on providing adequate medical care for the aged within the Social Security program.[39]

The Farmers Union favors a vast public works program to relieve unemployment. This program would be administered by a national commission on unemployment and planning which would be directly responsible to the President. The NFU feels that special emphasis should be likewise given to the growing problem of youthful unemployment. "Legislation should authorize training programs and . . . a youth conservation corps."[40]

INTERNATIONAL TRADE. The foreign trade policy of the NFU is especially interesting. It recommends that:

Programs and policies affecting agricultural imports and exports should be designed to provide full parity returns to the domestic producers in ways that will be as consistent as possible with the objectives of the Reciprocal Trade

[38] *Policy Statements*, p. 19.   [40] *Ibid.*, p. 16.
[39] *Ibid.*, p. 22.

Agreement Act and the needs for furthering trade and economic cooperation with other countries of the free world, including Pacific and South American countries, the European Common Market and developing nations. When any program of trade expansion threatens, however, to weaken or destroy the opportunity for any group of consumers or primary producers to earn a livelihood based on United States living standards, the cost should be shared by all the citizens of the United States in accordance with ability to pay.[41]

The Farmers Union urges renewal of the Reciprocal Trade Agreement Act, but with "sufficient safeguards to fulfill these objectives." Thus, it argues that farmers should not be required to face competition from imports whose price would be less than full parity.

The NFU states that "safeguards should be maintained to prevent the destruction or weakening of commodity bargaining power programs by imports of competing farm commodities or products or substitutes therefore."[42] From this statement it appears that the Farmers Union has considerable reservations about freer trade of a nature which might weaken the bargaining position of agriculture in relation to competing products and imports.

INTERNATIONAL AFFAIRS. The NFU believes that the United States should attempt to preserve and strengthen the United Nations. The International Court of Justice should also be supported in order that International disputes may be settled, aggression prevented, and aggressors brought to trial.[43] The NFU also advocates a system of world law with intensified activity by the United States arms control and disarmament agency. It likewise favors long-term legislation for economic aid to the underdeveloped countries of the world.

Thus the Farmers Union adheres generally to liberal programs on almost all national and international issues.

The National Grange (The National Grange—Order of the Patrons of Husbandry)

Founded in 1867, the Grange, as it is commonly called, is the oldest and today the second largest of the three major farm groups. As with the other groups, the size and strength of the Grange has varied, depending upon the economic crises facing its member farmers. Modeled on a type of Masonic order for farmers, the Grange approached 900,000 members at the peak of its strength in 1875, owing in part to the panic of 1873 and the critical conditions of farmers during that period. Since then, the number

[41] *Ibid.*, p. 29.   [43] *Ibid.*, p. 26.
[42] *Ibid.*, p. 11.

of Grange members has fluctuated, but it has maintained its relative position between the larger Farm Bureau and the smaller Farmers Union. Although the Grange is national in scope, its principal strength is found in New England, New York, New Jersey, Pennsylvania, and Ohio. According to David B. Truman, this geographic concentration "may help to explain the fact that the organization at present assumes a policy position far different from that of its radical youth."[44]

The Grange's original constitution had formally eschewed "political activities," but it soon shifted to satisfy the demands of farmers to do something about "the infernal monopolies."[45]

The Grange Blue Book of today points to its role in working for farmer-oriented legislation.

The focal point of National Grange activities is Washington, where policy established by democratic Grange processes throughout the Nation is vigorously administered by the national officers. In the course of a year, Grange leaders make scores of appearances before Congressional committees and hold numerous conferences with leading officials of government and business.[46]

Political activity, however, does not detract from the social function of the Grange. It is organized on a social basis, providing membership for men, women, and children through 4,500 subordinate Grange-owned halls in various communities throughout the country. Further, the Grange provides fire insurance, automobile, casualty, windstorm, and in some states even hail insurance to Grange members. In their own words, "While it is difficult to put a dollar and cent sign on money the Grange either saves, or in effect, makes for Patrons in a year's time, it is clearly apparent that Grange benefits far exceed the small membership dues."[47]

The Grange cautions its members not to feel that their position in the economy is secure or safe. "These savings cannot be taken for granted, for the legislative experience of the Grange shows that there must be an ever-increasing effort to protect and expand the opportunities of rural families."[48] Thus, the Grange openly declares not only that the focal point of its activities is in Washington, but also that those activities are directed toward affecting legislation favorable to the agricultural interests of its members.

Besides being in between the other two farm groups in size, the Grange

[44] David B. Truman, *The Governmental Process* (New York: Alfred A. Knopf, Inc., 1955), p. 88.

[45] L. Harmon Zeigler, *Interest Groups in American Society* (Englewood Cliffs, N.J.: Prentice-Hall, Inc., 1964), p. 168, citing DeWitt C. Wing, "Trends in National Farm Organizations," in *Farmers in a Changing World*, 1940 Yearbook of Agriculture (Washington, D.C., 1940), p. 946.

[46] *The Grange Blue Book* (Washington, D.C., n.d.), p. 1.

[47] *Ibid.*, p. 17.   [48] *Ibid.*, p. 17.

is in between them ideologically as well, being essentially a middle-of-the-road group. In fact, its *Summary of Legislative Policies and Programs, 1963,* appears somewhat equivocal on most major issues.

FARM POLICY.   While the Grange feels that "action necessary to cure social and economic ills of agriculture is a primary responsibility of those engaged in agricultural pursuits," it nevertheless takes the position that the "magnitude and complexity of action necessary" to remove such ills is often such that "it can only be undertaken with the help of the Federal Government."[49]

One such problem is overproduction. "Farmers," declares the Grange in its guidelines for public action, "must have the help of Government in solving the continued problem of overproduction." Producers, of course, must face their responsibilities too. They cannot, for example, "expect taxpayers to support prices of commodities already in excess supply" if the producers themselves refuse to accept responsibility for effective supply, control, or management.[50] The Grange takes the position that while effective action does not call for government control, "it is the responsibility of Government to provide programs through which producers can effectively control, regulate, or manage their own commodities."[51] This assistance should be tailored to meet the needs of individual commodities, however, and should be financed by consumers rather than the taxpayers.

The Grange also feels that farm programs should be designed to preserve and strengthen family-type farms as a basic pattern for American agriculture.[52] This statement draws on the same ideological symbol as do the Farmers Union programs. The Grange continues, however, by suggesting that vocational training, rural development, and other programs be expanded to increase off-the-farm opportunities for families whose farms are inadequate. The impossibility of small family farmers doing well through farming alone is recognized by the Grange, a position which differs from the Farmers Union's stand on family farms.

The Grange also advocates the vigilant safeguarding of the profit motive and the free enterprise system. Here the Grange is seen attempting to carry water on both shoulders—walking the middle of the road between programs favoring the return to a free market and those calling for the maintenance of farm income through government intervention. The following quotation exemplifies this quite well:

The Grange supports policies which tend to stabilize the economy against violent business cycle fluctuations. It believes in the profit motive and the free

[49] *Summary of Legislative Policies and Programs, 1963* (Washington, D.C.: The National Grange, 1963), p. 5.

[50] *Ibid.*

[51] *Ibid.*

[52] *Ibid.*, p. 7.

enterprise system, being forever vigilant to safeguard the country against those forces that would destroy that system.[53]

The Grange views itself as ideologically unaligned with either the supporters of a free market or the advocates of government controls; hence, it may side temporarily with either the liberal or conservative camp, depending on the issue. This flexible ideology, needless to say, does not prevent the Grange from uniting with the other farm associations in support of any particularly advantageous programs for rural groups, such as rural free delivery; production, utilization, and marketing research; Federal crop insurance, and other such programs.

The Grange has long been a strong advocate of better credit facilities for rural people. It supported legislation resulting in the creation of the Farm Credit Administration, and it has worked closely with both Congress and the Farm Credit Administration in obtaining better credit for farmers. It nevertheless opposes excessive paternalism or governmental control of credit agencies, agreeing with the Farm Bureau that the farmer, not the government, should control these agencies. It likewise continues to support a program of cooperative farm credit as opposed to governmental lending.[54]

COOPERATIVES. As do the other farm groups, the National Grange traditionally supports farmer cooperatives for marketing, purchasing, and services. It therefore "opposes any change in tax laws that would hinder or handicap farmer-owned cooperatives in the performance of their needed economic functions."[55] On rural electrification and rural telephones, the Grange, as other interest groups, merely supports its own constituents.

FISCAL AND MONETARY POLICY. The Grange is ideologically quite close to the Farm Bureau on fiscal policy. Like the Farm Bureau, the Grange opposes deficit spending and argues for a balanced budget "except during periods of extreme emergency." It further demands "a balanced budget as a prerequisite to a cut in Federal Taxes."[56]

The Grange is concerned with the increase of national, state, and local taxes. "The Grange believes that government can curtail expenditures through greater efficiency, economy in purchasing and the elimination of many non-essential services."[57] In opposition to the Farmers Union, the Grange argues that present tax policy has reached the point where it harms both individuals and businesses. However, even on such issues as this, the

[53] *Grange Blue Book*, p. 5.
[54] *Ibid.*, pp. 5–6.
[55] *Summary of Legislative Policies and Programs, 1963*, p. 10.
[56] *Ibid.*, p. 26.   [57] *Ibid.*

Grange is not nearly so ideologically committed in its public statements as is the Farm Bureau.

BUSINESS. In its declaration of purposes, the Grange states its attitude toward business.

For our business interests we desire to bring producers and consumers, farmers and manufacturers, into the most direct and friendly relations possible.

We wage no aggressive warfare against any other interest whatever. On the contrary, all our acts and all our efforts, so far as business is concerned, are not only for the benefit of the producer and consumer, but also for all other interests that tend to bring these two parties into speedy and economical contact.

We long to see the antagonism between capital and labor removed by common consent, and by an enlightened statesmanship worthy of the twentieth century.[58]

Concerning the issue of government participation in private enterprise, the Grange feels that the government should share the opportunity of power development with private enterprise. Cooperation should exist between these two in order "to make available ample supplies of power at the lowest possible cost."[59] However, the Grange qualifies this position with the statement that:

Government participation in commercial and financial enterprises in competition with private business should be strictly limited to enterprises which cannot be economically or efficiently performed by private business.[60]

The Grange includes the development of atomic energy sources among those in which government should participate. It supported legislation "authorizing construction of two demonstration atomic reactors in conjunction with municipal and rural electric cooperatives."[61]

Thus, on the issue of business, the Grange aligns itself with the Farm Bureau, although its position is somewhat less intense.

LABOR. On the issue of labor relations, the Grange fundamentally backs right-to-work laws; however, it is moderate in claiming that the right-to-work laws are the responsibility of the states and also by stating that inasmuch as unions have been oppressed on occasion, the right-to-work laws may not necessarily be in the best public interest in all cases. Public interest, the Grange believes, has priority over the demands of either union or business. It also believes that it is in the public interest to maintain stricter control over unions. The Grange is opposed to monopoly control—

[58] *Grange Blue Book*, p. 19.
[59] *Summary of Legislative Policies and Programs, 1963*, p. 19.
[60] *Ibid.*, p. 21.   [61] *Ibid.*, p. 19.

. . . whether exercised by an individual, a corporation, a labor union or any other organization. Thus provisions of laws to prevent monopolistic powers of corporations should apply to labor unions as well.[62]

On this issue, then, the Grange would side with the Farm Bureau, though not taking as extreme a stand or defending it as fervently.

SOCIAL LEGISLATION. While the Grange feels that much social legislation is needed, it is becoming increasingly alarmed at the gradual trend toward centralization of government authority and responsibility. The Grange is an advocate of community development programs planned and conducted "self-help" style. It emphasizes "self-help" as the solution to most social problems. The National Grange opposes Federal aid to education, though not so strongly as does the Farm Bureau.

INTERNATIONAL TRADE. The Grange is presently working diligently to promote freer trade "except where it is in the national interest to protect a domestic industry."[63] Much of the current trend toward the elimination of trade barriers in the interest of agriculture is the result of pioneering efforts by the Grange. Its stand, of course, corresponds closely to that of the Farm Bureau.

INTERNATIONAL AFFAIRS. The Grange has traditionally supported the United Nations as well as certain types of foreign aid through economic and military assistance.

Programs of foreign military and economic assistance should be directed toward economic progress consistent with political and economic objectives of the United States and the free world. Surplus food and fiber should replace dollar aid wherever possible. In accordance with their ability, other industrialized nations should play a larger role in military and economic programs for maintaining security for the free world.[64]

While the Grange will support economic and military foreign aid, it is nonetheless very cautious about doing so. It is undoubtedly far less generous in its approach to this problem than is the Farmers Union, at the same time being less conservative than the Farm Bureau.

In summary, the Grange is seen to side at various times with both liberal and conservative groups, yet it becomes apparent after carefully analyzing its programs that the Grange may be slightly to the right of center—at least on issues regarding United States domestic policy. Thus, domestically, it favors a balanced budget and opposes unrestricted use of fiscal policy; internationally, it favors freer trade while expressing some hesitancy about foreign aid.

[62] *Ibid.*, 1962, p. 16.
[63] *Grange Blue Book*, p. 9.
[64] *Summary of Legislative Policies and Programs, 1963*, p. 15.

The Farm Bureau (The American Farm Bureau Federation)

While the Farm Bureau is the newest of the formal major farm organizations (having been organized on a local basis in 1903, one year after the Farmers Union, and having become a national federation in 1919), it is the largest and most important farm group in existence.[65] Unlike the Grange and the Farmers Union, its organization did not arise out of agricultural crises. It spread in the areas of increasing mechanization and specialization in agriculture, particularly in the cotton South and the corn-hog Middle West.[66] Rather, the Farm Bureau developed to promote the control of plant diseases and to increase farm production. Understanding its origin helps to explain why the Farm Bureau has enjoyed such a close relationship with the Department of Agriculture throughout its history. It should be added that these ties have been both formal and informal, for in 1914 the Smith-Lever Act established a system of grants-in-aid to state colleges of agriculture to support programs on extension education for the improvement of farming techniques. With this encouragement, the county agent system spread rapidly throughout the country, taking with it the Farm Bureau as part and parcel.

Under this act, the states were required to match funds in order to gain the maximum Federal allowance. In determining conditions for extension work, most state legislatures required the establishment of an organized group of farmers as a cooperating body. In fact, some state legislatures specified that such groups be known as Farm Bureaus. By 1916, most of the local groups were known as county Farm Bureaus. Additional Federal funds have been added from time to time, continually strengthening the liaisons between Farm Bureaus and county agents. Today, the size and power of the Farm Bureau is in no small measure related to its history of association and cooperation with the Federal Government.

While the Farm Bureau has had its formal connections severed from governmental activities in certain areas, it has shifted its program toward the promotion of favorable legislation for its members. As David B. Truman has noted: "This shift was dramatically symbolized by the formation and operation of the first 'farm bloc' in the 67th Congress (1922), in which the Farm Bureau was a major factor."[67]

As has already been noted, the Farm Bureau is considered the most

---

[65] Accurate figures on the size of the major farm groups are difficult to determine precisely, since all groups do not measure by the same unit. That is, some base their total figures on member families, and some use simply members. The Farm Bureau, for instance, claims over 1½ million member families; the Farmers Union lists more than 250,000 families; whereas the Grange lists over 800,000 members. Since a number of Grange members may come from one family, it is therefore difficult to determine precisely its size in regard to the other groups.

[66] Zeigler, p. 174.   [67] Truman, p. 91.

conservative of the three farm groups. In this regard it is highly interesting that the one group which has been nurtured by the government would turn out to be ideologically the most hostile of all three farm groups to government intervention.

FARM POLICY. In the following statement, the Farm Bureau takes a rather unusual stand for a farm interest group, declaring that the availability of free competitive markets is essential to agriculture.

It is abundantly clear from years of experience that needed adjustments are made more readily and the economic well being of farmers is better served in those areas of agriculture which have not been subject to government control and price support programs. . . .

We vigorously oppose all attempts to depart from the market price system in areas of agriculture still operating under this system. In those areas of agriculture where farm programs have led to a departure from the price system, we urge a return to this system as rapidly as possible. . . .[68]

Ideologically, the Farm Bureau differs most widely from both the Farmers Union and the Grange in that it argues for effective and widespread competition as a means of promoting individual incentive and effective use of resources. "If farm people are to enjoy freedom, we must accept the discipline of competition. . . ."[69] To other farm interest groups, free competitive markets for their goods appear to be the last thing they desire.

The Farm Bureau also recommends a relatively stable general price level in order to avoid what it feels are the painful economic and social disruptions that inevitably result from inflation and depression. While stable prices are set forth as a basic objective of all three farm groups, the Farm Bureau seems to be the most vocal. Yet, in spite of its concern for general price stability, the Farm Bureau takes a strong stand against rigid price supports. "Experience has clearly shown that programs to fix prices and control production do not ensure satisfactory farm income." It once again calls for the return to the "market price system" as rapidly as possible in order to "more effectively serve the interests of farmers at a greatly reduced cost to the tax payers."[70] The Farm Bureau thus opposes price and production controls, urging that they be removed speedily, but with an orderly transition. The only price supports acceptable to the AFBF would be based upon market prices rather than artificially fixed or discretionary levels.

Of all the farm groups, then, the Farm Bureau is the strongest advocate of the free market. In fact, on page 6 of the *Farm Bureau Policies for 1963*, it argues that government programs should promote efficiency in

[68] *Farm Bureau Policies for 1963* (Atlanta, Ga., December 13, 1963), p. 6.
[69] *Ibid.*   [70] *Ibid.,* p. 7.

farming, adhere to the competitive principle, be consistent with the law of supply and demand, strengthen the free market, and stimulate market expansion; further, the government should not continue price fixing, freezing historical production patterns, stimulating excessive production, and usurping individual freedom by making farmers dependent upon government payments.

Nonetheless, the Farm Bureau does favor a voluntary land retirement program and those marketing and regulatory functions of the government where necessary on a local or regional basis—but not as production control measures. It feels that the important issue concerning Federal Marketing orders is that they should not be used as a device to control agricultural production or as a tool for the further intervention of the Federal government in the management of agriculture. It firmly opposes this "use of federal marketing orders on a nationwide basis."[71]

While it appears that on most issues the Farm Bureau ideology calls for the elimination of government intervention, it should be noted that on a number of specific commodities, e.g., tobacco, cotton, and rice, the continuation of the current program is recommended. Apparently to maintain unified organizational control of its membership, the Farm Bureau has felt the necessity of making specific exceptions to its overall philosophy. It insists that these specific commodity exceptions are not to be permanent, but only transitory—until the market can be stabilized to ensure all farmers adequate income, as well as government nonintervention. Needless to say, this is a large order.

The Farm Bureau contends that "farmers should be able to obtain credit necessary to their operations at lowest rates of interest consistent with the actual cost of money."[72] On this point, the Bureau states further:

We recognize the value of the enactment during recent years of a series of laws, beginning with the Farm Credit Act of 1953, which provides for an independent bipartisan Farm Credit Board, retirement of government capital, preservation of revolving funds, and decentralization of authority to increase farmer ownership and control of Farm Credit institutions. We support the continuation and development of these principles. We oppose efforts to establish federal budgetary control over Farm Credit institutions or the surpluses existing therein.[73]

Thus, while favoring low-interest credit, the Bureau prefers farmer rather than Federal control where possible. Bitter memories of farmers' being unable to pay high interest charges and having their mortgages foreclosed in past decades are a key ideological symbol in the universal demand of farm groups for low-interest credit.

As would be expected from an interest group, the Farm Bureau, de-

[71] *Ibid.*, p. 15.
[72] *Ibid.*, p. 53.
[73] *Ibid.*

spite its opposition to government aid to education and other areas of the economy, nonetheless approves of aid in certain areas of its own interest. "We recommend appropriation of federal, state, and local funds to support the Cooperative Agricultural Extension Service in keeping with the needs of our rapidly advancing agriculture."[74] Thus, as with any group, its ideology is not fully consistent, but is generally shaped by its own interests.

COOPERATIVES.   Along with the other farm groups, the Farm Bureau stoutly maintains that cooperation is necessary between the Federal government and cooperatives if they are to remain a vital part of the private competitive enterprise system. The Farm Bureau also advocates the continuation of support to rural electric and telephone cooperatives and the Farmers Home Administration which provides direct and insured loan programs for farm housing.

FISCAL AND MONETARY POLICIES.   Farmers resent the steady upward rise in the prices of the equipment and services they purchase, and the battle against inflation involves key ideological symbols. The Farm Bureau opposes deficit spending by the Federal government, arguing that the government must balance the budget and reduce the national debt if stable prices are to be achieved.

The Employment Act of 1946 should be amended to make it clear beyond any doubt that it is national policy to stabilize the purchasing power of the dollar as well as to maintain a high level of employment.[75]

We recognize the need for a substantial downward adjustment in federal taxes to create a better climate for economic growth; however, the current budget deficit and our mounting national debt make it mandatory that a cut in federal expenditures accompany any general reduction in taxes.[76]

Thus, the Farm Bureau is committed philosophically to tax policies that would balance the budget and aid in reducing the national debt and therefore act as counterinflationary measures. The Farm Bureau further believes that:

Tax programs should be designed to maintain our private competitive enterprise system and to bring about a fair and equitable distribution of the tax burden. . . . Extreme graduation in income tax rates tends to discourage the incentive to save and invest.[77]

BUSINESS.   The issue of public power is faced somewhat equivocally by the Farm Bureau. While, as noted above, its ideology on many issues

74 *Ibid.*, p. 52.
75 *Ibid.*, p. 22.
76 *Ibid.*
77 *Ibid.*

resembles closely that of the NAM, it previously has supported the Tennessee Valley Authority, which benefits directly a segment of its membership. As a matter of policy, however, the Bureau argues that the Federal government should enter the power business only when circumstances would not otherwise permit the adequate development of power.

It becomes obvious why the Farm Bureau is thought of as an agribusiness group, for its ideology currently shows considerably greater fear of government and union monopolies than of business monopolies. In this regard, therefore, it is one with the NAM and the CED and has much less in common ideologically with the Farmers Union. Where business monopoly is concerned, however, the Farm Bureau is against the so-called "fair trade" pricing practices, which it holds to be inconsistent with a competitive economic system.

LABOR.   The basic position of the Farm Bureau in regard to labor relations is best summed up in the following quotation: "Any program involving compulsory arbitration or recommendation for settlement by a public fact finding board will tend to destroy collective bargaining and create problems more serious than it may solve."[78] The Farm Bureau not only supports the Taft-Hartley and Landrum-Griffin acts, but would also apparently favor restricting labor's power further in collective bargaining and arbitration. "The concentration of economic power in labor unions permits a resort to measures which, if used by any other economic group, would result in drastic anti-trust action."[79] Thus, the Farm Bureau argues that "unions, like other groups, should be subject to anti-trust laws."[80]

The Farm Bureau further argues in favor of a national right-to-work law as contrasted with the Grange position favoring state determination of the issue. As would be expected, therefore, the Farm Bureau is highly opposed to any efforts to unionize farmers and to bargain for farm prices through union methods. Obviously, the enrollment of farmers into unions would represent a direct attack on the membership and power of the Farm Bureau as well as on its basic ideology.

SOCIAL LEGISLATION.   In the whole of the United States it would be difficult to find two organizations more opposed to each other on social legislation than the Farm Bureau and the Farmers Union. The Farm Bureau, for instance, argues that in order to avoid further tax increases, social security programs should not be increased and extended; and, what is more, that present social security legislation should be modified. Under the present law, social security would have to be drastically reduced if taxes are not to increase. The Farm Bureau is opposed to Federal sub-

78 *Ibid.*, p. 41.
79 *Ibid.*, p. 40.
80 *Ibid.*, p. 41.

sidies for medical care or to a social security program which would include medicine.

In regard to unemployment, the Farm Bureau recommends "appropriate action to eliminate current abuses of the unemployment insurance program." It also opposes "extension of coverage under this program."[81] The Farmers Union, of course, takes an opposite position on all these issues.

Like the Grange, the Farm Bureau opposes Federal aid to education and the use of Federal grant funds for the construction of buildings and major facilities at land-grant colleges, state universities, and other institutions of higher learning. Although the Farm Bureau admits that additional aid must be given to education, it argues that it must come from local and state sources. Property taxes, however, should not provide the means for increasing school support.

The Farm Bureau aligns itself with the advocates of states' rights, placing itself behind the Southern and less frequently the Middle Western complaints against the increasing power of the Federal government and the judiciary.

INTERNATIONAL TRADE. On this issue, the Farm Bureau follows the traditional position of farmers who felt that protective tariffs merely raised the prices of the machinery and consumer goods they purchased. The Bureau advocates the expansion of freer international trade on the basis of mutual advantage. The Farm Bureau supports the Trade Expansion Act of 1962 which "authorizes the President to negotiate substantial reductions of trade restrictions, tariffs, and other barriers which are imposed against U.S. exports," and it calls for the vigorous administration of this act with "full utilization of the authority granted by Congress."[82]

Although generally favorable to freer trade, the Farm Bureau argues that the European Common Market is a threat to this development and that the United States must negotiate censuring trade restrictions with the Common Market. The nations of Western Europe and the European Common Market are urged to abandon those "policies which discriminate unjustly against other nations of the free world." For example, "Japan's inability to earn foreign exchange through trade with Western European countries could impede the opportunity" for expansion of United States agricultural exports to that important industrial nation as well as "create pressures in this country against imports from Japan."[83]

INTERNATIONAL AFFAIRS. Because a number of new countries have recently been admitted into the United Nations, making it difficult for

---

[81] *Ibid.,* p. 26.
[82] *Ibid.*
[83] *Ibid.,* p. 28.

policies favored by the United States always to be adopted, the Farm Bureau states:

> We are opposed to proposals to establish new agencies within the United Nations through which large sums of U.S. money will be channeled for economic development programs. We are also opposed to programs which would channel a major portion of U.S. surplus agricultural commodities through such agencies.[84]

In a potentially isolationist view, the Farm Bureau openly states its doubts about the usefulness of the United Nations for United States policy and is adamant against allowing that body to dictate policy to the United States.

Consistent with its attitude toward other international organizations, the Farm Bureau maintains reservations in regard to the World Court. It contends that there is no clear distinction between domestic and international matters and therefore the United States should not delegate to the International Court of Justice the power to determine whether it has jurisdiction over disputes involving the United States. Consistent with this general attitude, it urges the United States to maintain its sovereignty in all matters of international jurisdiction.

The Farm Bureau favors effective international disarmament; yet "the United States must not reduce its military capability without complete assurance that the entire soviet bloc is fulfilling its commitments under such an agreement."[85]

Even though the Farm Bureau is organized nationally, much of its membership is concentrated in the corn belt, and the organization tends to reflect this fact—particularly in that this area has always been noted for its isolationist tendencies. Thus, the generally conservative nature of its international program is understandable. Despite the reflection of Middle Western and Southern conservatism, however, the Farm Bureau, in advocating the relaxation and removal of government price controls and the establishment of free competitive markets, represents a divided membership.

In studying the local newspapers in many areas of the country where the Farm Bureau is dominant, one finds considerable reaction against the Farm Bureau's national policies of ultimately removing artificial price supports and production controls. While farmers are generally opposed to government controls, they are nonetheless considerably worried about facing a fully competitive market.

Thus, as has been stated earlier, organizational leadership sometimes dominates the policy-making process—even though democratic proceedings are used. This is not to argue that the Farm Bureau does not represent

---

[84] *Ibid.*, p. 34.   [85] *Ibid.*

a majority of its membership on this issue (there being no adequate way to determine what the majority opinion is without voting), but there does appear to be some opposition to the general Farm Bureau line among part of its members. This lack of unanimity is evidenced by the mention made earlier of the specific commodity exceptions (cotton, rice, and tobacco) to the policy of returning to a free and competitive market.

FUTURE FARM POLICY

In examining the ideology of the major farm groups, it has become apparent that recourse to the institutions of government is a natural outgrowth of the policy of having to provide for the economic interests of groups representing dispersed membership—regardless of what the general ideology may be. The overrepresentation of rural areas in both state and national legislatures has historically given additional power and impetus to the farm groups in gaining special-interest favors. In addition, sympathy-waking ideological symbols, such as the family farm as the basis of a healthy society, the fears of farm bankruptcies, and the fact of depressingly low average farm incomes, have aided farm groups. Thus, farmers have perhaps been the most successful of all economic segments in obtaining special legislation for their interests. Certainly this is so if one considers the relative size of the various interest groups in the country.

Yet, in spite of its favored position, American agriculture has never been able to obtain a program to satisfy all its own interests, and agricultural power is dwindling. The Farmers Union and the Farm Bureau were perhaps farther apart in 1963 than at any time in their history, and the future looks even less promising. It may be, however, that some of the startling events of 1963 will provide a clue to what may be expected in the future.

As each new administration has come to power, it has promised a solution to the farm dilemma. The Kennedy administration was no different. Under the direction of Willard W. Cochrane, director of agricultural economics in the Department of Agriculture, a new farm philosophy, called "supply management" or "supply adjustment," was developed.

"Dr. Cochrane's thesis," says Hans Landsberg,[86] "is that the farmer above all lacks the 'market power' that is standard practice in industry." In industry, he points out, "It is considered a mark of prudent management to prepare market calculations that indicate what output the market can absorb at the price the producer knows he must get." Farming, however, lacking this mechanism, proceeds by trial and error. " 'It is time,'

[86] Hans Landsberg, "A New Approach to the Farm Problem," *The Reporter* (April 12, 1962), 34–37.

says Cochrane, 'for a change. . . . Farming must move into the twentieth century in the marketplace—as it has already done in technology—and be furnished an arsenal of economic weapons similar to those long possessed by industry.' "

First, Cochrane proposed that government economists estimate the quantity of farm products that could be sold at alternative prices. "A fair price would then be set, and the demand at this price calculated." Adjustments would be made for foreign trade and other government programs, and the resulting production goal would then be "allocated among the producers in proportion to their share in growing the crop in past years." If the estimates and calculations were accurate, no unwanted surplus would result.

One of the big problems with agricultural programs designed to control or freeze the existing production patterns is that they tend to perpetuate the inefficient farmer. Under Cochrane's plan, this problem would be solved by issuing a "marketing certificate" to each farmer permitting him "to sell a given share of the national quota for his crop." This has been called farm licensing. Each farmer could then either use his certificate or sell it. Thus a market would be created in which the more efficient producers "would bid eagerly for these negotiable certificates," while less profitable producers would find it to their advantage to sell their certificates rather than produce. This, he believes, would lead to the concentration of these certificates in the hands of the more efficient producers, thus combining "administrative convenience, a handy control measure, and a shot of competition" all into "one neat package."

In 1961, the Kennedy administration presented a farm proposal to Congress with much of Cochrane's program included in it, plus a request for additional powers to be granted to the Secretary of Agriculture and farm commodity groups in determining farm policy. Not only was Congress disturbed by what seemed to be an attack on its rights to set policy, but the proposal was widely attacked by agricultural interests from the farmer to the processor. American Farm Bureau President Charles Shuman termed the bill "a bid to concentrate unprecedented power in the hands of the Secretary of Agriculture and Executive branch of the government."[87] When Congress finished, little was left of the original proposal.

Supply adjustment legislation was again presented to Congress in 1962, but in a much more limited form. Once again the critics, who refer to the program as "agricultural birth-control," attacked the proposal. Finally, it was decided to call for a national referendum in which farmers themselves would have an opportunity to express their feelings. This effort culminated in the National Wheat Referendum of May 21, 1963, and provided a

[87] *Ibid.*

classic example of the differing ideologies and roles of the farm groups and the bitter struggle which they wage against each other.

The administration, backed fully by the Farmers Union, and supported by the National Grange, went all out to obtain the two-thirds majority necessary to put the proposed program of supply management into operation.

President Kennedy threw his full support behind the proposal by personally campaigning for it. He boldly declared that if the certificate program were defeated, farmers could expect no new wheat legislation for there would be none forthcoming. Secretary of Agriculture Orville Freeman and others traveled throughout the country urging a "yes" vote. By far the most active farm group in this campaign was the Farmers Union. Tons of literature were distributed, not only urging a "yes" vote, but also predicting the most severe and catastrophic consequences if the program were defeated.

On the other side of the issue stood the American Farm Bureau, supported by former Agriculture Secretary Ezra Taft Benson and other prominent Republicans. The Farm Bureau published, among numerous other things, a pamphlet entitled *Questions and Answers on the 1963 Wheat Referendum,* in which it attempted to present its side of the issue involved. Keeping firm in its position of favoring a free market system, it dramatized the dangers of complete government control by asking, "Who will manage our farms—farmers or the federal government?" It then analyzed point by point the proposed plan and concluded that to vote "no" would be to vote for freedom while to vote "yes" would be to submit to the merciless hand of government planners and thus become only a slave to the will of the Federal government.

By the time the shouting was over, each side had so bitterly attacked the other that the passage of time and greatly changed circumstances would be necessary for any reconciliation ever to be achieved. Never before had so many persons become so involved, and never had such an intense campaign been waged among farmers. Because not only the farmers themselves were able to vote, but also their wives, children, and even hired servants who shared directly in the income of the farm, much of the attack was carried to their level. Particularly important were the small growers who plant less than 15 acres of wheat and who for the first time were permitted to vote in a national referendum.

When the farmers finally went to the polls on May 21, they overwhelmingly rejected the supply management program in a record vote. Only 47.8 per cent[88] of the 1.2 million votes cast supported the wheat certificate program—far less than the two-thirds majority required. The

[88] *U.S. News & World Report* (June 3, 1963), 40.

vote thus dealt a heavy blow to the Kennedy administration and represented a bitter defeat for the National Farmers Union, the National Grange, and others who had supported it. To the American Farm Bureau, however, the vote came as a sweet victory in its struggle to see agriculture returned to the free market system, and immediately the Farm Bureau appeared in Congress to introduce an alternative farm bill.

Many congressmen, particularly Democrats, issued statements suggesting they would not back new wheat legislation. President Kennedy, at his May 22 press conference, issued a statement "accepting" the "judgment" of the wheat farmers and said he hoped "that this will prove to be a wise choice for wheat farmers and the country." He promised to look at any bill aimed at reducing surpluses and maintaining farm income and which did not cost too much, but added, "I think it would be difficult to get a bill by the Congress."[89]

As the heat of the campaign died down, however, congressmen were back at work again trying to solve the mystery of agriculture. Clearly the wheat farmer had spoken his mind. For the first time, the American farmer had voted not to accept price supports with government controls, but rather to face an uncertain future with the knowledge that he was free to manage his own farm, succeeding or failing by his own decision. If nothing else, it was a courageous stand.

Without controls, it was predicted that wheat production would soar to record heights, resulting in greatly reduced sales prices. Additional surpluses would flood the market, and old surpluses would not be moved unless new markets were found. The fact that this did not take place for the 1963 and 1964 crops mitigated what otherwise might have become an explosive new farm issue.

In the fall of 1963 a new issue arose which could temporarily solve part of the problem of a new market, but which could erupt into another violent clash between farm and nonfarm groups. It involved the sale of wheat to Russia and other Communist satellite countries.

With the announcement that Canada had agreed to sell 500 million tons of wheat to Russia, American farm groups saw an opportunity to relieve the surplus problems in the United States by likewise opening trade with the Communist nations. President Kennedy agreed to permit negotiations, and a team of experts arrived from Russia and other European Communist nations to begin discussions. Again, some groups opposed the sale on the basis of not wanting to feed an enemy, especially through subsidized sales on our credit, but these critics were in the minority. Even with the sale of wheat to Russia, American farmers still have a long way to go before the problems of agriculture will be solved.

[89] "Wheat Farmers Reject Kennedy Control Plan," *Congressional Quarterly Weekly Report,* 21 (May 24, 1963), 795–796.

The answer will not come in one easy lesson, nor can one expect the future to bring its own solution. The struggle between farm interest groups is likely to continue, but with the overall power of agriculture decreasing, arguments over economic ideology will continue to be mixed with arguments over morality as illustrated by one of many such statements by former Secretary of Agriculture Ezra Taft Benson: "The supreme test of any government policy, agricultural or other, should be, 'How will it affect the character, morale, and well-being of our people?' We need—the world needs—a strong America in the critical years ahead."[90]

THE CASE OF A LOOPHOLE

The Packers and Stockyards Act Amendment of 1958 is an interesting case showing how the major farm groups may take diverse positions on an issue and how many different trade associations become involved and aligned with one group or another in the process. The case sounds rather prosaic if judged only by the title; nonetheless, it is a fascinating example of legislation in action on a highly sophisticated level.

The case began when the Federal Trade Commission (FTC), whose responsibility it is to enforce certain antitrust laws, attempted to prosecute a large supermarket chain called the Food Fair for unfair trade practices. The FTC soon found to its surprise, however, that it had no authority in the case; the reason being that the Packers and Stockyards Act of 1921 had transferred from the FTC to the Department of Agriculture the enforcement of unfair trade practices for all packers and stockyards. This particularly surprised the FTC because the definition of packer under this act was any firm owning 20 per cent or more of a packinghouse—regardless of all their other business and economic activities. It turned out, therefore, that Food Fair, while by most calculations a supermarket chain, was a packer under the terms of the 1921 act because it owned at least 20 per cent of a small packinghouse. Food Fair was therefore legally a packer and could be prosecuted only by the Department of Agriculture.

The Department of Agriculture had traditionally done little, however, to enforce fair trade practices within its jurisdiction. Thus, it became evident that all any company needed to do was to buy into a packinghouse in order to avoid prosecution for unfair trade practices.

All this brought to light the fact that from 1950 to 1957 the FTC had referred twenty-nine complaints to the Department of Agriculture, all of which were against such so-called packers, but no significant action had been taken in any of the cases. Since the Department of Agriculture had

[90] Ezra Taft Benson, *Cross Fire: The Eight Years with Eisenhower* (Garden City, N.Y.: Doubleday & Company, Inc., 1962), p. 603.

essentially no staff for investigating and enforcing fair trade practices, no action could be expected against those firms falling within its jurisdiction. Thus, companies like Armour and Wilson, which had many other large businesses in other industries, were not touched by existing law enforcement.

At about the same time all this came to light, the dairy groups were attempting to get a cease and desist order against Armour and Company for implying that their margarine was butter by advertising it as "freshly churned." The dairy industry became alerted to this problem by the fact that no results were forthcoming in their action. Since Armour and Company was very much a packer, it could only be prosecuted by the Department of Agriculture, which was to say that no action would apparently be taken against it.

A number of trade groups began to get involved at this point also. The retail stores became interested because the packers could practice price discrimination against various stores with no fear of prosecution. Non-vertically integrated and small businesses were hostile to the packers because they gave price advantages to chain competitors; so the small businesses became interested in affecting legislative changes.

The major farm groups were split on the issue. The Farm Bureau, because of close association with agri-business groups, sided with the packers (on the national level at least), urging that antitrust power over the packers be left with the Department of Agriculture. The Farmers Union, as might be expected, opposed the Farm Bureau's stand and argued that the small stockman needed to be protected by changing the law. The Grange also reacted typically, standing somewhere in the middle between the positions of the Farm Bureau and the Farmers Union. The Grange's middle-of-the-road position had little effect on either side of the issue.

Of necessity, the arguments used by those on both sides took the tone of "what is the best solution?" In this case it was impossible to come out and say that anyone was not in favor of enforcing the antitrust laws. Rather, as noted above, the semantics of the whole dispute veiled the real problem. The chairman of the House Agricultural Committee, Harold Cooley (D, North Carolina), argued that things should be left as they were and that the Department of Agriculture only needed more money for enforcement. Cooley and the Farm Bureau, therefore, were on the same side. It was unusual, however, for Cooley to be defending the Department of Agriculture under a Republican administration. It happened in this case because he wished to keep as much power as possible in the Agriculture Department since he was chairman of the House Agricultural Committee.

Cooley and many of the members on the House committee seem to have been influenced by Aled Davies, representing the major meat-packers' lobby. He was successful in aligning most of them with the policy of the packers and the Farm Bureau. Realistically, the Farm Bureau is the most important farm group in the home states of these congressmen. Its position was not, therefore, to be taken lightly. Also, the packers are frequently generous contributors in election years—a fact of some importance. At this point, therefore, it appeared that no bills regarding this issue would come out of the Agricultural Committee, and the case might have died except for the following developments.

Congressman H. A. Dixon and Senator A. V. Watkins, Republicans of Utah, had been pushing the issue, partly on the initiative of a shared staff member, Dr. Reed Frischnecht. Feeling that an amendment of the 1921 act was needed and was of basic interest to the major groups they represented, they pursued a new tactic. After it became evident that the House Agricultural Committee would not initiate any legislation, Dixon introduced a new bill to amend the Fair Trade Act, at the bottom of which there was a section also amending the Packers and Stockyards Act. This rephrasing of the bill helped get it assigned to the House Judiciary and Commerce committees. Both committees became interested because of their involvement with antitrust matters.

The key point in lobbying developed next as the lobbyist for the Western States Meat Packers Association, Blaine Liljenquist, who had long pushed for action against the packers and had been partly instrumental in getting Dixon and Watkins involved, attempted to rally support. Liljenquist's association represented small and independent Western meat-packers who felt they were being driven out of business by the big packers who could dump products in their areas to force down prices and put them out of business. No prosecution had been brought effectively against the large packers, because of the act of 1921 and the lack of enforcement by the USDA. In this issue Liljenquist became the key organizer of a coalition of interests. Some of the twenty-seven groups he helped rally against the large packers were dairy groups, retail trade associations, small business associations, the Farmers Union, consumer groups, National Wool Growers' Association, Utah Cattlemen's Association, and the Utah State Farm Bureau (even though the Farm Bureau on the national level took an opposing stand). In addition, a few other groups were essentially neutralized. Thus the lines were drawn.

While Dixon and Watkins of Utah normally supported Secretary of Agriculture Benson (also from Utah), this issue was unusual in that while they took an opposing stand to his, they generally praised him in the hearings. Politically, of course, Dixon and Watkins had more to gain than to lose by their position on this issue—as is evidenced from the fact that the Utah Farm Bureau opposed its national organization on the matter and that the Utah Cattlemen and Wool Growers, among other Utah groups, were in favor of stricter enforcement of trade practice laws.

Dixon and Watkins were able to gain additional support with Congressman Celler (D, New York), chairman of the House Judiciary Committee, introducing a consumer-oriented bill against the packers, and Senator O'Mahoney (D, Wyoming) joining Watkins against the packers. Celler and O'Mahoney both found such action attractive, as Celler represented a consumer-oriented constituency and O'Mahoney knew that most cattlemen in Wyoming traditionally felt oppressed by the large packers.

By this time, sufficient publicity had been developed to force the Agricultural Committee to push through a minimal bill of its own to forestall action by the other committees. The final bill was a compromise transferring all nonmeat activities (e.g., margarine, sporting goods, and chain stores) of the packers to the FTC, but leaving all meat activities with the USDA for enforcement of fair trade practices.

All the groups whom Liljenquist of the Western Packers had brought together were now satisfied—except his own! For it was the meat activities of the big packers that Liljenquist was really after. However, the legislative process did not end quite then. As experienced lobbyists maintain, nothing in the legislative process ever ends, it merely goes on from one round to another, and often shifts between the legislative and executive branches. Under these circumstances, Liljenquist transferred the focus of his actions to the Department of Agriculture. The issue had created enough publicity so that the Department took an interest in attempting to enforce the law. Such matters take time, however. It took two years to bring about passage of the amendment in 1958, and it was not until June, 1960, that Congressman Dixon was able to write to his constituents that the Department of Agriculture had established a Packers and Stockyards Division and had commenced enforcement activities. Even within the Department of Agriculture the politics were not open and shut, for the meat-packers were strong allies of Secretary Benson and his farm program, and he was not eager to antagonize them. Benson realized, however, that the law must be administered, even after a hiatus of several decades; and thus the USDA, under fire from various pressure groups and feeling itself exposed to the national publicity generated over the issue, moved to upgrade its enforcement activities.

CONCLUDING SUMMARY

The major ideological differences among the three peak agricultural organizations are seen in the following summary.

The Farmers Union is the smallest and second oldest of the three farm groups. It is adamantly opposed to leaving farmers at the mercy of the free market with its many uncertainties. It has been the most ardent advocate of high price supports and it continues to demand a government-guaranteed supply management program, wherein supply and prices will be so planned as to assure adequate income for farmers. The group supports protection against competing imports, low-interest government credit, more protective crop insurance, and favorable tax policies on cooperatives. This increased economic assistance and protection by government is demanded through the ideological emphasis on the symbol of the family farm which must be protected against all enemies including "encroachments by large factory-in-the-field operations."

The Farmers Union also wants low interest rates assured by government as a means of stimulating faster economic growth. The members favor corporations in key industries submitting proposed price increases to a public agency for review and analysis before they are put into effect. The Farmers Union supports extension of the minimum wage to cover all workers and favors legal protection of unions as part of its ideology of government aid to the needy. It wants a vast expansion of public power developments. It supports international cooperation and aid programs.

The Farm Bureau, the newest and largest of the three organizations, takes a strikingly different ideological position from the liberal Farmers Union. The Farm Bureau deprecates supply management by government as necessarily depriving farmers of their freedom to farm. It favors essentially a free competitive market for agriculture as well as for business and labor. It opposes budget deficits and favors debt retirement. It supports the Full Employment Act and wants stable prices included in legislation. It favors freer international trade, legislation to restrict the powers of the Supreme Court, and more states' rights. In welfare legislation the Farm Bureau expresses the classical ideology in favoring limited government. The Farm Bureau's position would require cutting back present social security programs and would tighten up administration of unemployment compensation. In line with both its market economy and individual freedom ideology, the Farm Bureau favors a national right-to-work law terminating compulsory union membership as well as subjecting unions to the antitrust laws. It also attacks fair trade pricing by business as eliminating price competition. Consistent with its ideology against big government, it opposes Federal aid to education, even for construction at land-grant colleges. The Farm Bureau accepts the development of major new public power projects only where the development cannot be satisfactorily accomplished privately.

The Farm Bureau ideology against big government restricts its requests for Federal aid to agriculture. Nevertheless its ideological emphasis on a "rapidly advancing agriculture" permits it to favor healthy financial support from all levels of government for the Agricultural Extension Service, its traditional ally, as well as cooperation between the Federal government and cooperatives, and Federal credit to farmers at lowest interest consistent with the government's cost of borrowing.

The Farm Bureau favors freer trade but is more nationalistic than the Farmers Union regarding world affairs. The Farm Bureau particularly wishes to assure that the United Nations shall not take over the United States' prerogatives or sovereignty.

The Grange, the oldest and second largest of the farm organizations, in general takes a middle-ground legislative position. It supports the general position that the government should assist in developing "producer-bargaining and supply-management programs" tailored to the needs of individual commodities, and financed by consumers rather than taxpayers. Any program should require approval of producers in a referendum. The Grange recognizes, however, that there is no panacea in agriculture. Consequently it calls for programs to increase off-the-farm opportunities for families whose farms are inadequate. The Grange also calls for the vigilant safeguarding of the profit motive and the free enterprise system. It views itself as being unaligned with advocates of either free market agriculture or government-controlled agriculture. This leaves the Grange flexible. Along with the other farm groups, it supports the traditional programs benefiting agriculture, such as agricultural research. The Grange favors freer trade, except where it is in the national interest to protect a domestic industry. The Grange is conservative in fiscal policy, favoring a balanced budget and tax structure conducive to investment. The Grange favors right-to-work laws but feels they are a state rather than a national responsibility. It supports existing tax structures for cooperatives. Like the Farm Bureau, the Grange favors local rather than Federal aid to education. It supports the United Nations and cautiously supports foreign aid. In other words, consonant with the Grange ideology of moderation in both domestic and international policy, the Grange is less liberal than the Farmers Union and less conservative than the Farm Bureau.

The sometimes acrimonious ideological differences among the agricultural groups help to prevent agriculture as a whole from realizing its potential power. Even though farmers now represent less than one-tenth of the work force, their potential power is considerably greater than this because of their relatively greater access to both the Senate and the House through rural overrepresentation in each. In addition there is the possibility of an alliance with important agri-business segments. Should such unity and alliance be achieved, the limited available wealth of farmers, due to the fact that income is relatively low and assets are largely fixed and not easily convertible to political use, would be more than compensated by other power factors.

However, the ideological split in agriculture, combined with numerous varying and often conflicting interests among commodities and regions, makes such unity impossible in the foreseeable future. Meanwhile a further decrease in the number of farmers with the shift of more congressional districts and states from a dominantly rural to a dominantly urban constituency, together with further court-enforced reapportionments, will cause agriculture to lose much of its historic strategic advantage of overrepresentation in Congress and will minimize the significance of what overrepresentation remains.

The amazing result of these divisions has been that while almost no one is willing to defend existing agricultural policies, still it is almost impossible to organize an effective majority to change the *status quo* in any given direction. On the surface it would appear that, if both the classical and managerial segments of business strongly favor returning to a freer market with price support programs, with the support of the Farm Bureau, the largest farm organization, they should surely be able to defeat the Farmers Union, which has only the somewhat lukewarm support of the labor unions for its programs.

The fact is that by and large the groups favoring a freer agriculture are generally able to defeat the Farmers Union–sponsored programs, but the Farmers Union is also able to veto a return to a freer market.

Thus, in 1954, President Eisenhower vetoed a congressional enactment to extend high, rigid price supports in agriculture. This returned the "basic" commodities to an earlier law with flexible supports with a minimum of 70 per cent. The agricultural committees of the House and the Senate, however, are dominated by the basic commodity interests. Therefore they presented several costly subsidy measures to the Congress, none of which were enacted because the Benson-Eisenhower team opposed them. Interestingly enough, most of these programs were defeated right on the House floor, to the embarrassment of Chairman Harold Cooley of the House Agricultural Committee.

If there was a majority against more costly farm programs in the House, particularly, why could not this same majority return agriculture to a freer market? The answer to this gives some insight into the congressional process with its dependence upon standing committees. Major legislation is almost never done on the floor. It must come out of the appropriate standing committee, after which it is debated, frequently modified, and either approved or rejected on the floor. Since agriculture committees are dominated by the basic commodity interests, they cannot be expected to draw up and to recommend to the Congress legislation to curb subsidies. Yet such legislation would probably be too intricate to be expected to succeed if it were simply presented on the floor as an amendment with limited debate time. So, for an extended period, the advocates of both a freer trade and a more controlled agriculture can veto each other's plans but cannot succeed in enacting their own.

One event could work toward breaking this stalemate. On May 21, 1963, wheat farmers "revolted" against a tightly controlled production plan, even though they had been warned by President Kennedy that to do so would mean a cut in their net income. The referendum on the new plan required approval of two-thirds of the wheat growers. Yet only 47.8 per cent approved. This surprise victory among farmers themselves for the Farm Bureau ideology of freedom to farm may strengthen the forces in the legislative process favoring programs for a freer agriculture. On the other hand, there is still a possibility that experience with low wheat prices might make more farmers penitently resign themselves to tight government controls in exchange for guaranteed high prices.

In conclusion, the profound divisions within agriculture have prevented it from realizing its power and have resulted in a politics of deadlock, making it almost impossible to change an irrational and costly farm policy. Even if the aftermath of the wheat growers' rebellion against controls facilitates the development of a more coherent policy, the divisions within agriculture are likely to continue. With the trend toward fewer farmers and political reapportionments, the overall power position of agriculture will decline further. With such a change in agriculture's power position, the fate of agriculture may be decided increasingly by the other power groups.

5

negroes

INTRODUCTION

The previous chapters in this book have dealt with occupational groups and the extent of their influence and persuasion upon the national government. In this chapter we turn to Negroes—an ethnic group. Dissatisfaction with widespread low occupational status is part, but certainly not all, of the binding force that has recently made the Negroes a dynamic and effective power group.

The history of the Negro influence on American policy extends back to revolutionary times, although the Negroes themselves did not play an important role in achieving whatever place in society was granted them. Their presence caused the three-fifths compromise concerning the counting of slaves in the Southern states to be written into the Constitution, and emotions about Negro slavery were among the dominating passions that divided North and South during the Civil War. The Negroes did not display their contemporary potency until the 1950s when Congress passed its first civil rights legislation of the century in 1957. Negroes themselves date their effective influence on national policy as beginning with the Supreme Court decision in 1954 in *Brown v. the Board of Education,* which nullified the doctrine of "separate but equal." This was the first major triumph of an organized Negro body.

To understand the power the American Negro exerts on our political system, we should consider that Negroes are no longer a provincial group without electoral representation. A shift of 50 per cent of the national Negroes to the urban North has been a dramatic influence in the past sixty years. They are now a major pressure group influencing urban elections in the North and West Coast areas. Twenty million Negroes make up 12 per cent of the population of the United States and are represented in their political goals by several major organizations. Most of these share the same broad ideological goals; however, there are significant differences among them, and the ideology of one major organizational group takes issue with the dominant Negro ideology.

The Negroes are one of the most volatile of the power groups, and their beliefs and desires are having an impact on the American political system. Their rapid growth in power and recent "inventiveness" in finding methods to accomplish their purposes display that the Negro power group is not static and that new methods of exerting influence may continue to make it the most dramatic of all groups.

Whether or not the American Negro influence will continue to grow at the rate it has grown in the past decade, or whether as it accomplishes its goals it will lose its militancy and therefore its dramatic appeal, will be determined in large part by the several organizations which are reviewed in this portion of the book. We can briefly identify the major organizations and their leaders as follows:

The National Association for the Advancement of Colored People (NAACP) is the largest and oldest (400,000 members, founded 1909) of the organizations. It is directed by Roy Wilkins, the executive secretary. It has traditionally used the American courts and legislatures in its approach to solving Negro problems, but has recently followed other groups into more militant action.[1]

Another Negro aggregation, the Southern Christian Leadership Conference (SCLC), is a loose confederation of religious groups supporting "nonviolent" action. Its leader, Dr. Martin Luther King, Jr., has been recognized as the most "popular" spokesman for the Negro cause.[2]

The Congress of Racial Equality (CORE) and the Student Non-Violent Coordinating Committee are examples of groups that have risen to prominence as innovators of types of action that have won Negro battles. Their methodology marks their only ideological differences with the NAACP and the SCLC. James Forman and John Lewis direct the Student Non-Violent Coordinating Committee (SNCC—pronounced SNICK), and James Farmer leads CORE.

The National Urban League, directed by Whitney Young, operates

[1] Louis Lomax, *The Negro Revolt* (New York: Harper & Row, Publishers, Incorporated, 1962), pp. 101–120.

[2] *Newsweek* (July 29, 1963), 31.

within the Negro community to create "first-class" citizens ready to enjoy the victories won by its sister groups.[3]

All the above groups share a basic ideological commitment to the policy of Negro equality as citizens of the United States, and therefore they demand the same opportunities of citizenship that whites have. One major group, religious in nature, the Black Muslims, is ideologically opposed to the integration of the Negro into the existing stream of American life. Elijah Muhammad teaches his Nation of Islam, or Black Muslims, a doctrine of black supremacy and separatism.[4]

IDEOLOGY

These people are citizens of the United States, not merely citizens of the states wherein they reside. As such, they are entitled to the protection of the Congress of the United States against the infringement of their rights under color of any local or state law or custom.[5]

This statement, coupled with the statement below, summarizes the Negro doctrine of militancy.

The Negro American has been waiting upon voluntary action since 1876. He has found what other Americans have discovered: voluntary action has to be sparked by something stronger than prayers, patience and lamentations. If the thirteen colonies had waited for voluntary action by England, this land today would be a part of the British Commonwealth.[6]

The Negro ideology depends on many key symbols: citizens, rights, equality, action, custom. Negroes as *citizens* demand the *equality* conferred by that citizenship, by *action* they want the rights that *custom* or laws often deny them. Both concepts are a part of the ideology: the concept of equality and the concept of action to achieve that equality.

Equality is probably best defined, according to the Negro concept, as having the same rights, privileges, rank, etc., as other men; it would be extended to convey the thought that opportunity must be evenly proportioned and balanced and must have a uniform effect on whatever is being done. In his book *Nobody Knows My Name,* James Baldwin attempts to sum up the Negro ideology in seven words: "Negroes want to be treated like men."[7]

[3] Lomax, pp. 209–220.

[4] *Ibid.,* pp. 164–177.

[5] From the text of the testimony given by Roy Wilkins before the Senate Commerce Committee, July 22, 1963 (New York: National Association for the Advancement of Colored People, 1963), p. 3.

[6] *Ibid.,* p. 6.

[7] James Baldwin, *Nobody Knows My Name* (New York: The Dial Press, Inc., 1961), p. 67.

This concept repudiates the notion of inherent inequality, but recognizes perhaps an environmental handicap—the environment that the Negroes want changed. Few opposing this ideology disagree openly with the denial of inherent inequality, but both Negroes and whites have expressed opposition to that part of the ideology that deals with the kind of change in the environment, the rate of change, and the method used to achieve that change. Most of these critics would be classified among those favoring gradual evolution. They have a "don't rock the boat" attitude. Some offer no opposition to the equality concept but strenuously object to its Federal enforcement, contending that Federal intervention encroaches on constitutional rights.

S. B. Fuller, a Negro entrepreneur and millionaire, favors the gradual evolution with an economic approach. In answer to the question, "In general what do you think is the answer to the race problem in this country?" he replied:

Well, the problem is one the Negro has to work out for himself. Negroes are not discriminated against because of the color of their skin. They are discriminated against because they do not have anything to offer that people want to buy.

The minute that they can develop themselves so they excel in whatever they do—then they are going to find that they don't have any real problems.

An example is baseball. There was discrimination in the big leagues. But when the owners of the big leagues found out that the Negro could play just as well as whites, discrimination in the big leagues ended as far as Negro players are considered.[8]

John C. Satterfield, past president of the American Bar Association, speaking out against the civil rights legislation proposed in 1963, summarized the counterideology of the white South:

Never in the history of nations governed by elected officials has the head of any State demanded naked untrammeled power such as is embodied in this Act, except when such State was on the verge of becoming a dictatorship. If it is enacted the checks and balances set up by the Constitution of the United States will be destroyed. The States will be little more than local governmental agencies, existing as appendages of the central government and largely subject to its control.[9]

The Negro demands for equality are sometimes stated generally, but have very specific ramifications. Any examination of the Negro ideology must consider what these specifics are and how they are being achieved.

[8] *U.S. News & World Report* (August 19, 1963), 58.

[9] John C. Satterfield, *Unlimited Federal Control of Individuals, Businesses and the States* (Washington, D.C.: Co-ordinating Committee for Fundamental American Freedoms, 1963), p. 1.

Employment

Whereas non-Negroes are often concerned with improving their working conditions and wage scales in specific jobs, Negroes are concerned with enlarging the total number of jobs available to their race. Aware that unemployment is a national problem, Negroes fight for fair job distribution —fair employment—where job shortages exist. The unemployment rate for Negroes is twice that of the rest of the population.

Negro demands for more and better employment have taken many forms—pressure for high informal quotas of government jobs, pressure from the government to increase Negro hiring by private industry, legislative programs, and economic sanctions on uncooperative employers.

The biggest increase in the number of jobs available has come from within the government, where Negro employment comprised 17 per cent of the hirings during fiscal 1962. Negroes, with 12 per cent of the total population, counted 12.9 per cent of the government working force at the end of 1961, with the figures increasing. There were 293,353 Negroes on the Federal government payroll in June, 1962. In order to get such a count, departmental supervisors had to take a "head count," as government records no longer indicate race.[10]

As the government, under executive pressure, increases its labor force among the Negroes, it is also putting pressure on private industry doing business with the government to hire more Negroes—and apparently with success. President Lyndon B. Johnson, when he was Vice President, headed the executive committee which insisted on government contractors employing Negroes where qualified without discrimination.

Negroes themselves have been employing economic force to achieve their goals. In some large urban areas, such as Philadelphia, when a company is accused of not employing a representative working force, the Negro community may boycott the firm's products until its demands are met. The Negroes have been making specific and detailed rather than vague and general demands, and reports indicate a high degree of compliance.[11]

A chief stumbling block in the road to increased job opportunity is the increasing need for skilled workers. The Negro population has a substantially lower rate of trained workers. Automation has done away with the jobs of many unskilled workers and created a demand for workers in jobs that Negroes are not trained to fill. Business and government are actively recruiting Negroes from colleges and training schools, and they report generally lower scores on examinations taken by Negroes than by whites. Trade union discrimination has been a particularly sore spot to

10 *U.S. News & World Report* (July 22, 1963), 41.
11 *U.S. News & World Report* (August 12, 1963), 30–32.

the Negroes because of the declarations of sympathy and unity of purpose that have come to the Negroes from labor leaders. Often the reasons for nonequality are local in nature, ranging from strong competition to strong racial feelings. Legislation has been introduced in Congress to set up a commission which would investigate and adjudicate claims of racial bias in hiring of workers.

Housing

In Negro "intellectual" literature—the vast majority of which centers on the lack of equality—the word "ghetto" often appears. A ghetto is defined as that section of a city where minority groups are forced to live because of social, legal, or economic pressures. Negroes resent not only the quality of their housing, but also the attempts of white men to move them into better yet still segregated housing. Ghettoes are not inherently slum dwellings, according to Negro ideology. Ghettoes are simply locations where Negroes are forced to live because they are Negroes.[12]

On November 20, 1962, President John F. Kennedy issued an Executive Order prohibiting discrimination in all Federally assisted housing. This order had long been a goal of the NAACP, whose efforts to achieve the goal of equal opportunity in housing have been primarily directed at new projects constructed partly with Federal funds. The right to deny the sale of your house to a man because of race is a right that the Negro groups are attempting to do away with. Despite Negro efforts, most white neighborhoods usually resist the sale of a home to a Negro, and if the resistance fails there is a flurry of home sales in the area, causing prices to drop and bitterness to ensue.

Education

Best known of the specific points of the doctrine of equality as espoused by the American Negroes is the concept of segregation versus integration in the nation's schools. The Federal court order prohibiting school segregation in public schools was a dramatic legal turning point for the Negroes. However, for Negroes and whites, the order to integrate the public schools did not end the argument. It merely rekindled it, and the decade following the decision has been marked by consistent legal actions demanding the integration of specific schools, districts, and universities.

It was a school crisis that first called out the Federal troops in Little Rock, Arkansas, and again at Oxford, Mississippi, attracting world attention to American racial problems. There are those who feel that if Negro

[12] Baldwin, p. 65.

power groups stayed out of the school issue, "things would work themselves out." Roy Wilkins does not agree.

A great many southerners want nothing more than that the Negro's destiny shall be left to their decision. This is their historic position. This is their cry today in the school desegregation issue. Nothing in the history of the past five years suggests even faintly that if the NAACP were to bow out, the school desegregation would have a better chance of success. No so-called moderate group has ever intimated it would get on with desegregation if the NAACP were not in the picture.[13]

Most Negroes have objected not only to segregation "by law," but also to segregation "in fact," and have demanded that their children be transported out of their normal school area and sent to a school in a predominantly white area, thus integrating that school. Pressure to end *de facto* segregation has been exerted in the large cities, particularly Chicago in late 1963 and New York City in early 1964. Emotions become heightened when children of white parents are scheduled to be taken by bus out of a white school to a Negro one. School boycotts in New York and a school superintendent's resignation and rehiring in Chicago resulted in stalemates with only partial accomplishment of Negro aims. The issue has not been settled nationally by litigation. In California in June, 1962, the State Board of Education issued a policy statement agreeing with the Negro position that segregation by law or in fact denies an equal opportunity for education.

Despite Negro protests that they will not be satisfied with "tokenism," there is really no substantial school integration in the South. Washington, D.C., is an exception, where the public schools were integrated shortly after the Supreme Court decision—which encouraged many white families to join the flight to the suburbs. Only 10 per cent of the schools have been integrated in the South—and the NAACP has been gradually shifting its area of greatest concentration to the Northern urban areas which house as many Negroes as the South.

Voting Rights

We are sending our diplomats abroad, writing notes to other nations and issuing white papers demanding free elections in Asia, Africa, Germany and the satellite countries, but we don't have free elections in our own country—in Alabama, Mississippi and elsewhere.[14]

The above remark of Roy Wilkins made to the Capital Press Club in 1959 describes a situation which is peculiar when contrasted with that

[13] *Roy Wilkins Speaks Out* (New York: National Association for the Advancement of Colored People, 1962).
[14] *Ibid.*

before the turn of the century. Strange as it seems now, in 1896 Negroes made up a majority of those registered in twenty-six parishes in the Deep South state of Louisiana. Six years later they did not comprise a majority in any parish. Stated numerically, Negro registration plummeted from 130,334 to 1,342 during this brief period. The Louisiana move to white political supremacy characterizes what took place in the rest of the South because of Negro economic dependence on the whites and judicial and legislative decisions weakening the intent of the Fourteenth Amendment.[15]

Devices used to keep Negroes from voting included long residence requirements in the particular voting district, permitting only those whose grandfathers qualified as voters to vote, literacy tests, poll taxes, and white primaries.

Both Negro and white leaders have preached the doctrine that the Negroes can never fully achieve their aims until they are fairly represented by a ballot box. The slogan of the 1962 convention of the NAACP was the "Battle of the Ballots." Restoring the Negro voting rights has long been a goal of the various power groups, and to some extent they have been successful. Negro voters have registered in increasingly large numbers since the *Smith v. Allwright* decision in 1944 which outlawed the white primary. In 1963, about 28 per cent of the voting-age Negroes were registered voters.[16]

How to increase the total number of registered voters among Negroes is a major problem facing the leadership. Registration drives are not usually publicized by Negro groups because they fear that possible failure to arouse Negroes out of apathy will be made more conspicuous. Legal measures making registration easier have been proposed. These would strike down prohibitive literacy tests, and they were part of the civil rights legislation fought out in the 1964 congressional session.

All major groups within the Negro community, excepting the Muslims, have supported movements fostering increased Negro suffrage, sometimes cooperating one with another.

Opponents of the civil rights bill rarely discussed their opposition to Negro voting, but often defended the doctrine of states' rights. Southern attorneys contended that setting the requirements for voting is a state prerogative and that for the Federal government to interfere in such a matter would be unconstitutional. The bill provided for specific measures designed to help Federal officers protect the rights of Negroes to vote. It gave the officers the right to referee elections in areas where less than 15 per cent of the potential Negro voters were registered, established a sixth-grade edu-

[15] Gaylon L. Caldwell, *American Government Today* (New York: W. W. Norton & Company, 1963), pp. 306–312.

[16] Donald R. Matthews and James W. Protho, "Social and Economic Factors and Negro Voting Registration in the South," *American Political Science Review*, 57 (March, 1963), 27.

cation as presumption of literacy, and in other ways increased control over national suffrage.[17]

Another point on which the Negroes have been very militant is the demand for access to public facilities, including transportation, eating places, theaters, hotels and motels, and public parks and playgrounds. Negroes have demanded equal rights to use all such facilities and have used legislative, judicial, economic, and mass demonstration methods to emphasize their demands. The commerce clause of the United States Constitution has been used to prohibit discrimination in some areas and has been proposed for expansion into other areas.

These are some of the specifics that are included in the Negro ideology. Previously mentioned in brief were some of the organizations in existence to make this ideology a reality. An examination of these groups, their backgrounds, leaders, and ideological differences in terms of the causes they are generally associated with and methods they use is now in order.

DISTINCTIVE CHARACTERISTICS OF NEGRO GROUPS

National Association for the Advancement of Colored People

Meeting on Abraham Lincoln's birthday, February 12, in 1909, a group of fifty-three white and Negro leaders issued the first policy statement of the National Association for the Advancement of Colored People. The statement came in the form of a call upon "all believers in democracy to join in a national conference for the discussion of present evils, the voicing of protests, and the renewal of the struggle for civil and political liberty."[18]

On the early rolls of the organization were the names of hundreds of prominent educators and social workers. Representing the Negroes was Dr. W. E. B. DuBois, leader of the so-called "talented tenth" of the race and professor of economics at Atlanta University.

In a pamphlet published in its fiftieth year the NAACP reviewed its accomplishments, shedding light not only on the organization but also on the changes in the Negro movement since 1959. In 1909 the feeling of Negroes was illustrated by the following:

> We are 46 years from the Emancipation and yet today is this race oppression so wide-spread that a gathering of this kind is imperative. At the same rate of retrogression, in 46 more years, the then 20,000,000 colored people will be veritable serfs.[19]

[17] *The President's Civil Rights Program* (New York: National Association for the Advancement of Colored People, 1963).

[18] *Then and Now* (New York: National Association for the Advancement of Colored People, 1963), p. 3.

[19] *Ibid.*, p. 7.

It is the contention of the NAACP that through their efforts the status of the North American Negro has improved significantly. The "impressive advances" listed by Mr. Wilkins in 1959 would not be so termed today. The major contributions of the NAACP have come through American courts and legislatures. Their basically nonmilitant position was justified by the statement "Basic inequalities remain, but unlike 1909, they are diminishing, not increasing."

Abolition of lynching, revival of Negro voting in the South, enactment of fair employment practices acts in fifteen states and twenty-six cities, passage of the Civil Rights Act of 1957, and the legal ban on segregation in public elementary and secondary schools are listed as accomplished goals by the NAACP.

In order to win acceptance, each Negro group must prove itself to American society as a whole, but in addition, each must compete for recognition in the Negro ranks. Long a part of the liberal movement in the civil rights area, the NAACP has been left appearing quite conservative compared with its more militant "sister" groups.

The Southern Christian Leadership Conference

The closest thing in the Negro power structure to a one-man organization is the Southern Christian Leadership Conference. It had its beginnings in Montgomery, Alabama, where on December 1, 1955, a Negro seamstress in a department store, Mrs. Rosa Parks, refused to relinquish her seat in a bus to a white man. Her arrest prompted the calling of a protest meeting, in which a boycott of the buses was arranged. As a part of the bus boycott, a young minister named Martin Luther King, Jr., formed the Montgomery Improvement Association to implement the Negro demands that the bus company seat passengers on a first-come, first-served basis and hire Negro drivers. These events led ultimately to the formation of the SCLC.

Sixty-five groups in Southern cities, under the direction of ministers, form the loosely confederated SCLC. It has its headquarters in Atlanta, where Dr. King is now a pastor in a Baptist church, but he does not maintain an office in the headquarters of the SCLC. Administration is headed by Rev. Wyatt Walker. Gandhian nonviolent militancy has been the hallmark of the SCLC. Rev. Mr. Walker listed the active areas of his group's influence in 1960 and 1961 as being voter registration in Alabama, Mississippi, and Georgia, acting as Southern coordinating center for freedom riders, engaging in citizenship training, and aiding the Student Non-Violent Coordinating Committee with its sit-in programs.[20]

The personal popularity of Dr. King has been measured by pollsters and has been found to be the highest of all the Negro leaders. Lomax

[20] Lomax, pp. 81–100.

attributes King's popularity to his ability to communicate with the people on a highly emotional basis.[21]

What is Dr. King's philosophy of action in achieving the goals of the Negro?

The purpose of our action program is to create a situation so crisis packed that it will inevitably open the door to negotiation.

In no sense do I advocate evading or defying the law as a rabid segregationist would do. This would lead to anarchy. One who breaks an unjust law must do so openly, lovingly . . . and with a willingness to accept the penalty. I submit that an individual who breaks a law that conscience tells him is unjust, and willingly accepts the penalty by staying in jail to arouse the conscience of the community . . . is in reality expressing the highest respect for law.[22]

Opposition even to the type of civil disobedience proposed by Dr. King is typified by New York City Judge William Ringel.

You cannot decide what laws to obey and what laws to disobey. You cannot demonstrate in a way in which people can be injured.

If you don't like the law, the remedy is to go to the legislature, to the trade unions, to the city fathers—not to take the law in your own hands. This will result in anarchy.

The National Urban League

Founded two years after the NAACP, the National Urban League was traditionally the group that helped Negroes adjust to the complexities of their rapidly urbanized lives, while the NAACP fought to improve conditions. As Negro groups became more militant, the National Urban League became less effective and its prestige dropped. Only in recent years has its prestige risen again. A large part of the new success of the Urban League is due to Whitney Young. In 1961 Mr. Young outlined his group's objectives:

We will do an action research job—the sort of job that not merely identifies the extent of poor housing, employment and general social disorganization; but a research which concerns itself with community attitudes towards these social ills. Yesterday these attitudes generated resignation and despair. Today they are more likely to be expressed in resentment and hostility.[23]

Mr. Young feels that if Negro groups openly discuss Negro problems and place their opinion of the cause of the problems on the record, the problems will be eliminated faster.

21 *Ibid.,* p. 86.
22 *U.S. News & World Report* (August 12, 1963), 6.
23 Lomax, p. 211.

He is especially concerned about breakdowns in the Negro family relationship. He thinks that these problems can be overcome through closer cooperation between Negroes and social welfare agencies and the continuing League fight for more jobs for Negroes. He has brought college presidents and corporation employment executives together to discuss methods of increasing Negro employment. He has been so successful that he has found more good jobs than there are Negroes trained to fill them.

The League expects its action research program to explain the causes of Negroes being in prisons and to aid in bringing down the Negro crime rate.

In order to bring the Negro environment up to where the League thinks it ought to be, Mr. Young proposes that the Negro masses be certified as an underdeveloped people, and that they be given special, accelerated training and treatment in order for them to assume full responsibilities in American society.

A few years of "deliberate inclusion and special programming" are needed to help the Negro catch up, he feels.[24]

CORE and SNCC

The Congress of Racial Equality was formed by a group of Negroes and whites in 1942 because they felt that "legalism" was not sufficient to win the battle against segregation. James Farmer, its first national chairman, is now its national director.[25]

Since its organization CORE has achieved a number of quiet, though very real, gains, but has not been thought of as among the top Negro leadership organizations. The group's membership in 1962 was 40,000, and it has been growing, mainly because of the notoriety of its particular method of fighting the ideological battle.

James Farmer first took a "freedom ride" in 1947 under the sponsorship of the Fellowship of Reconciliation. The objective of this ride was to test discrimination on trains engaged in interstate travel.

At the beginning of 1961, James Farmer resigned as program director of the NAACP to become national director of CORE. He assumed the new position on February 1, and on March 13 announced that CORE would conduct freedom rides to test discrimination in interstate travel terminals. Freedom rides, the method that was to make CORE famous, began on May 4. A biracial group left Washington, D.C., for New Orleans. There were thirteen participants, six whites and seven Negroes, on that first ride. On May 17, other Negro groups joined the ride, but the credit remained with CORE.

[24] *Ibid.*, p. 213.   [25] *Ibid.*, p. 133.

It was another device, the sit-in, that caused the creation of the student Non-Violent Coordinating Committee. The sit-ins, which ultimately led to the organization of SNCC, began in Greensboro, North Carolina, under CORE sponsorship. Dr. Martin Luther King, Jr., came to offer advice. The NAACP sent its youth secretary, Herbert Wright, to aid the students in their sit-in plans. The sit-in movement spread all over the South, and the participating students were organized as SNCC. Although the group got its start with sit-ins, it has expanded to boycotts, freedom rides, and voter registration. Northern college students and the Southern Christian Leadership Conference are the principal financial backers of the group. James Forman, a former Chicago school teacher, is its executive director. Although it has a humble background, Louis Lomax feels that it could become "*the* organization to be reckoned with in the Deep South."[26]

The Black Muslims

The Christian religion has failed. Your leaders of that religion have failed. Now the government of America has failed you. You have no justice coming from no one. It is written that you are like sheep among wolves . . . every wolf taking a bite at you. You want justice, you want freedom; you want equality . . . but get none. . . . The only thing for you to do is to separate from the white man and have some land of your own.[27]

This is the essence of the philosophy of the Nation of Islam, a group of more than 100,000 Negroes, and is, of course, in direct contradiction to the generally accepted ideology of the American Negro community. The Black Muslims, as they are called, are the largest and most dynamic Negro group opposing the general consensus.

Mr. Farrad Muhammad founded the movement in Detroit, where he sold African silks. He preached to his buyers the glories of the Koran and the evils of the white man. One of his followers, a former Baptist minister named Elijah Poole, became the new Muhammad and is called Elijah Muhammad. Most militant of the Muslim leadership is minister Malcolm X, a former convict whose inflammatory statements in 1963 resulted in Elijah Muhammad curtailing his national activities. This resulted in his breaking with Elijah Muhammad and forming a separate splinter group.

The militance of the Muslims is directed toward extreme black nationalism, and the religion's teachings emphasize the evil nature of the white man, the supreme position of the black man, and withdrawal from outside society.

The importance of the Muslims could be magnified if the groups seeking equality through integration fail and Negroes turn to the opposite position. A concerted Negro effort at complete withdrawal from all American

[26] *Ibid.,* pp. 127–129.   [27] *Ibid.,* pp. 169.

society would appear to create more difficulties in America than the drive toward integration.

THE WHITE REACTION

Although it is difficult for Negroes to measure the tangible results of their protest, some legal and specific effects of the "revolution" may be calibrated. A definite goal of the Negro ideology is to convince whites to treat Negroes "like men" or in effect, to change an attitude. Journalist Stewart Alsop and public opinion analyst Oliver Quayle made a study of the success or lack of success in this effort. Their conclusion: "The white North is no more ready to accept genuine integration and racial equality than the deep South." This was based on a statistically typical sampling which showed that as the word "equality" comes in for heavy use in Negro terminology, the word "but" comes in to equally heavy use in reaction to that ideology.

Typical of the comments reported were "They have been held down too long, but they are pushing too hard." "The colored got rights, just like us whites, but I don't see why we got to mingle together." "They are human beings just like the rest of us, but I wouldn't want one living next door."

Of those interviewed, 16 per cent reported that they felt innately superior to the Negro, another 27 per cent said they thought Negroes were inferior, but traced the inferiority to education and environment. "All out" integrationists formed only 23 per cent of those queried. One-third of those asked replied that they felt that the race question was the most important facing the country today; 63 per cent indicated approval of President Kennedy's civil rights program. Concerning schools, 75 per cent approved of the Supreme Court order ending legal segregation in public schools; 17 per cent preferred to have their children attend an integrated school; 42 per cent preferred to have their children in an all-white school, and 41 per cent did not care.

As to the question of a Negro's right to buy a home in an all-white neighborhood, only 23 per cent felt that the Negro had a right to do so, and 77 per cent felt that the homeowner had a right to refuse to sell to the Negro.

Over half—51 per cent of the persons polled—felt that Negroes were treated "about right" in the United States today, and 38 per cent felt they were not treated well enough.[28]

The above statistics seem to indicate that as long as the questions of Negro ideology are kept in general terms, the majority of whites approve,

[28] Stewart Alsop and Oliver Quayle, "What Northerners Really Think of Negroes," *The Saturday Evening Post* (September 7, 1963), 17–21.

ut that Negroes have not yet succeeded in changing the attitudes of most Northern whites on specific demands of their ideology. As Negroes emphasize cultural characteristics similar to those of white Americans and as Negroes increase their economic status, much as the Japanese have done, their social status should go up and their ideological demands will be more easily met.

THE CASE OF THE MARCH ON WASHINGTON

Acting on the belief that "legislation is enacted under pressure. You can't move senators and congressmen just because a measure is right," some 200,000 people marched on Washington, D.C., on August 28, 1963.[29]

It was the largest march on the nation's capital ever held and was the climax, both emotionally and in amount of participation, to the Negroes' most militant year. Of the 200,000 people, about 10 per cent were white. Negroes and whites had streamed into Washington from all parts of the country for that one brief day. The idea was initiated by A. Phillip Randolph, president of the Brotherhood of Sleeping Car Porters, and was carried out in detail by representatives of all the leadership groups. Actual planning of the March took place in New York City during most of the summer of 1963, under the direction of a former secretary to Martin Luther King, Jr., Bayard Rustin.[30]

Undertaking the March was a calculated risk. The Negroes faced the problem of violence on the part of the participants, which would have been an unseemly climax to a nonviolent campaign. Mr. Randolph announced that he could not promise that there would be no violence. Another risk, poor turnout, would have severely injured the Negro cause.

The Negro leaders hoped, by means of the March, to demonstrate to congressmen that the pending civil rights action was supported by a sufficiently large number of Negroes to be politically important. In the manual published to help guide the marchers, the specific goals of the action were listed. Among them were, first, a comprehensive and effective civil rights legislation from the sitting Congress to guarantee all Americans access to public accommodations, decent housing, adequate and integrated education, and the right to vote.

Other demands were for the withholding of Federal funds from all programs in which discriminations existed, total school desegregation in 1963,

---

[29] *The National Observer* (September 2, 1963), 1, quoting A. Phillip Randolph.
[30] Harvey Swados, "Revolution on the March," *The Nation* (September 7, 1963), 104.

a massive Federal program to train and place all unemployed workers, Negro and white, on meaningful and dignified jobs at decent wages.[31]

In a speech at the National Press Club on August 26, Mr. Randolph explained the purpose of the March:

Now is the opportunity to advance the frontiers of freedom, the frontier of human dignity, equality and social justice. This is the reason for the March-on-Washington movement and all of the demonstrations throughout the nation in whatever form they take. This is the reason for the Civil Rights Revolution—a full dress revolution.[32]

Most dramatic speech of the afternoon of the March came from Dr King. In part he said:

So we have come here today to dramatize the shameful condition. In a sense we have come to our nation's capital to cash a check. When the architect of our republic wrote the magnificent words of the Constitution and the Declaration of Independence they were signing a promissory note to which every American was to fall heir. The note was a promise that all men—yes, black men as well as white men—would be guaranteed the inalienable rights of life liberty and the pursuit of happiness.[33]

The reaction to the March is also a part of history. Many of the demands made were not acted upon; the civil rights bill was not passed in 1963, and resentment against Negro militancy increased. Negro leaders, however, viewed the March as a limited success. It displayed a large number of Negroes demonstrating without violence before the government and the nation, and represented a type of massive insistence that the nation give in to the demand for equality.

CONCLUDING SUMMARY

In summary, we may view the Negro revolt as a series of activities on the part of several groups to overcome racial prejudice in a number of specific areas. These areas—education, housing, voting rights, the right to all public accommodations, and fair employment—are all part of a central ideology of equality.

The groups have all been born of the necessities of the times. The National Association for the Advancement of Colored People was founded at a time when legal action alone on the part of a few was necessary because of the attitude of servitude on the part of most Negroes. The National Urban League was organized to provide assistance to the influx of Negroes moving

[31] *U.S. News & World Report* (September 9, 1963), 34.
[32] *U.S. News & World Report* (September 9, 1963), 82.
[33] *The National Observer* (September 2, 1963), 9.

o the cities. The more militant groups were organized during and following World War II, when Negroes began to fight for democracy at home as well as freedom abroad. The most recent militant groups, CORE and SNCC, are outgrowths of the surge of hope generated by the Supreme Court desegregation decision of 1954. Negro action since that time has seemed to indicate a feeling that "if it is possible for us to achieve equality, it should be possible now."

The gradual evolution that has drawn Negroes closer to the whites in standard of living and education has quickened in recent years, and the Negroes are pushing to accelerate it further.

Success of the revolution depends on unity within the Negro ranks, difficult to achieve because of the differences of opinion on how the revolution ought to be run, and on white reaction to increased Negro militance. As the militance increases, the resistance may be expected to increase also. Negro progress in the North has taken place in a vacuum of opposition. If serious opposition develops, the pace of the revolution's success will be slowed. An increase in programs designed to end segregation by custom rather than by law may be expected, and an increase in economic pressure for change may also be expected.

Negro rights will remain a political issue, and the Negro stands to gain because of his increased political importance. If the revolution were to be substantially set back, then an increase in black nationalism, typified by the Black Muslims, might be expected to increase quickly in political importance. The passage of the civil rights bill in 1964 was a major gain for the Negro cause. Its implementation and interpretation in the courts will have a major effect in aiding the Negro to achieve his ideological goal of "equality." The passage of the bill is ample proof of the power of the Negro as a major power group in America today.

6
public school teachers

INTRODUCTION

The public school teachers, in the last decade, have emerged as one of the nation's major organized power groups—particularly at the state and local levels. In the future it is probable that they will become increasingly powerful at the national level as well. Currently, however, most of their efforts are being concentrated on the local and state levels in order not only to increase their income and status, but to improve school facilities and to participate with boards of education in the control of educational policy. Thus, their power struggle becomes involved on three levels: (1) with state and national government for economic gains, (2) with the general public for due recognition of their services, and (3) with the school boards for control of educational policy and decision making.

Because it is primarily on the local level that policies are made which affect not only teachers' salaries but also their working conditions, released-time benefits, teaching requirements, and other matters which directly concern them, the power struggle with the school boards has become, and will continue to be, very prominent. Because of historic local control of education in the United States, it is from the local level that examples are most appropriately drawn in discussing the teachers as a power group influencing the making of public policy.

Notwithstanding, teachers have exercised their influence at higher levels through their lobbying activities in the national Congress and state legislatures, particularly for "Federal" and more "state" aid to education. The teachers have been temporarily thwarted in their national drives for Federal assistance for the nation's primary and secondary schools, principally because of controversies over racial integration and aid to parochial schools. Yet educators are optimistic because of congressional enactment of the Higher Education Facilities Act (December, 1963). This bill provided $1.2 billion in construction funds for the nation's colleges and, aside from the land-grant college program, set up the first Federal aid program to help in their expansion. All of the nation's 2,100 colleges, public and private alike, are eligible for grants under this program.

Teachers, with a strong conviction that the Federal government should share with the states and local communities a greater responsibility for the support of public education, expended considerable effort in aiding the passage of the Higher Education Facilities Act and supporting the "Federal aid to education" bill. Nevertheless, the financing of public education continues to be determined largely at state and local levels, and consequently, teachers national associations are directly aiding their state and local affiliates in their struggles with school boards and state legislatures.

The rise of the teachers as a power in the making of public school policy has occurred mostly since 1950. Prior to that time the expression of their wishes seemed not to come from a concert, but rather from a discordant rehearsal. Teachers have now become more articulate in their petitions, their associations or unions have become more solidified, and their power has been increasingly felt each year.

Several reactions are involved in the transformation of the public school teachers into a dynamic, aggressive, and sometimes militant power group. In addition to reactions against low salaries and uncooperative school boards, one of the most important has been their reaction to public criticism and abuse. The revolution in education, which has been going on (sometimes quietly, sometimes violently) during the last thirty years, has helped to make them a center point for criticism. Their position has been further questioned since the sudden advent of Sputnik I and the ensuing avalanche of probes into American education attempting to ascertain the basic causes of our failure to surpass the Russians in space.

Many teachers have deeply resented the following public image of them and their professional preparation:

The teachers' colleges, stuffed with dull and repetitive courses in "method" grind out the annual crop of neophyte instructors who have only a halting command of the subject matter they are supposed to impart to their future students. Presumably an intelligent neophyte could go on to get up his chosen specialty for himself. But brainy lads and lasses are repelled by the teachers' college curricula in the first place, and the few lively individuals who put up with their "miseducation" just to get coveted jobs soon discover that they are expected to take more dreary courses in nothingness just to qualify for salary increases.[1]

Certainly this type of criticism may be severe and exaggerated. The point is that whether true or not, it triggers a reaction of resentment and of retaliation among public school teachers. The thrust of this reaction is centripetal—a force which binds the teachers together in defense of their ideology. As to the reaction of retaliation, it is significant to note that the largest national teachers organization in the United States, the National Education Association, publicly states that it welcomes all objective criticism of education. However, its legal organ, the NEA Defense Commission, is quietly building a file on the more outstanding critics of education. The file will contain appropriate dossiers which could be used by the association for discrediting such critics.[2] The commission, in the 1960–1961 *NEA Handbook,* states:

A major step forward during the 1959–60 period was the initiation of a four-year project in which the commission's extensive files on the critics of education will be reorganized and reclassified. An additional staff member has been secured to prepare fact sheets on all the major critics of education.

For more than a decade, teachers have been increasingly venting their feelings that local school boards have not concerned themselves sufficiently with educational problems and that they have been too paternalistic and dictatorial toward the teachers. Teachers feel the boards have oftentimes overruled teachers' educationally sound judgments. The point in question concerns the school boards (generally composed of laymen and considered at times by the teachers to be uninformed) desiring only "economy" and "fundamentals." Furthermore, teachers feel that the public has not accorded them due deference and status. They want to cut this Gordian knot, and they are willing to play aggressive politics to achieve that end. On the local level, money may in some instances be incidental to the power struggle. As

---

[1] John Chamberlain, review of *The Miseducation of American Teachers,* by James D. Koerner, *The Freeman* (Foundation for Economic Education, Inc.) (September, 1963). Biting criticism is also made concerning some dissertations for the Ph.D. or Ed.D degree.

It is notorious that the Ph.D. or the Ed.D. has actually been awarded to people for grinding out wordage on such topics as "A Performance Analysis of the Propulsive Force of the Flutter Kick," or "The High School Students' Perception of Most-liked and Least-liked Television Figures."

Ibid.

[2] "Big Brother Is Watching You," *Council for Basic Education Bulletin* (October, 1962), 4, cited by John M. Ashbrook, *Congressional Record,* 88th Congress, 1st Session (June 25, 1963), 10884. See also *NEA Handbook,* (Washington: National Education Association of the United States, 1960–1961).

Raymond Moley stated: "It is a matter of management and control of the public schools."[3]

Foreseeing the possibility of organized teachers obtaining control of the schools, Sterling McMurrin, former U.S. Commissioner of Education, made a surprising statement:

> But while we guard against "federal" control, we should not lose sight of the possibility of "national" control—control of education by the bureaucracies of large and powerful educational organizations.
>
> These bureaucracies are just as real, and exhibit all the vices of a Government bureaucracy. Their control of the schools is not beyond possibility unless their leaders are genuinely responsible to their constituents, and there is no reason for believing that such control would be any more desirable than federal control.[4]

The teachers have generally solidified their positions, and have given much more power to their national organizations in an attempt to find a solution to their problems. The trend has now developed to a point where a more precise articulation of purpose is carried to the public. The influence is felt from local school boards to Congress, and the spectacular growth and power accretion of some local teachers unions or organizations have had a tendency to inspire, as if by charismatic influence, an individual dedication to this power growth. Through the use of sanctions or strikes, these organizations have made their influence felt in such states as Connecticut, Minnesota, Rhode Island, New York, Illinois, and Utah.[5] So important have these techniques become that several states, since 1955, including Alaska, Florida, Illinois, Massachusetts, Minnesota, New Hampshire, Rhode Island, and Wisconsin have enacted laws authorizing the state or its political subdivisions to deal with teachers organizations (sometimes compelling them to do so) in a "collective bargaining" atmosphere.[6]

As a result of the teachers' power position, some of them will no longer abide by the rulings of a seemingly "dictatorial" local board of education. An interesting instance occurred in New York City where the teachers of a school placed a large advertisement in a widely circulated newspaper, calling public attention to their disagreement with the board of education and to the conditions in their school which they felt were "intolerable." The advertisement attracted sufficient attention to trigger a visit from Mayor Wagner. The need for the repairs of their "rat-infested" school were adequately demonstrated when a rat did run across the gymnasium floor in

---

[3] Raymond Moley, *New York Herald Tribune* (June 22, 1963).

[4] *American School Board Journal,* 147 (December, 1963), 31.

[5] Sterling D. Spero, "The New York Teachers' Strike," *Good Government,* National Civil Service League Official Bulletin (September, 1962), 39.

[6] Howard L. Cherry, "Negotiations between Boards and Teacher Organizations," *American School Board Journal,* 147, 3 (March, 1963), 7.

front of the Wagner inspection team.[7] Significantly, the National Education Association, which was not involved in the New York City incident, has adopted a policy which permits its affiliates to seek similar recourse in cases where its teachers feel they are under duress.[8] This case was demonstrated in Utah where the Utah Education Association threatened to instruct its teachers to withhold their services from the schools unless certain conditions were met by the state legislature.[9] Although the National Education Association did not adopt a Utah resolution at its 1963 Detroit convention, which would have imposed nationwide sanctions against Utah schools, it did support the Utah group in its usage of NEA-adopted policy within the state.

There are two major national teachers organizations which have come to represent the consensus of a vast number of the teachers in the United States: the American Federation of Teachers (AFT), with a membership of 81,798 teachers, and the National Education Association of the United States (NEA), with a membership of 859,505, approximately 95 per cent of whom are teachers and the balance principals and other administrators (the AFT does not include administrators in its organization). There were 1,511,251 teachers in public school rooms in October, 1962, according to the U.S. Office of Education statistics. Therefore less than half, approximately 43 per cent (655,000), of the nation's teachers do not belong to either of the above organizations. (Figures for the individual organizations are as of May, 1963.) In the treatment of the teachers and their ideology, however, it is appropriate to refer to these national organizations, for they literally have come to be the "voice" of the majority of teachers in the United States.

CHARACTERISTICS OF THE NATIONAL TEACHERS ORGANIZATIONS

American Federation of Teachers

The AFT is almost entirely oriented to the traditional approaches of organized labor. It is an affiliate of the AFL-CIO, and its own locals openly employ the personnel, organizing techniques, procedures, and some of the finances of that massive labor combine in order to achieve their goals.[10] The real support for the teacher-labor movement is coming from Walter Reuther and his Industrial Union Department (AFL-CIO). Reuther's dream is the

---

[7] *Newsweek* (September 16, 1963).

[8] National Education Association of the United States, *Guidelines for Professional Sanctions* (Washington, D.C.: NEA, November, 1963).

[9] *Ibid.,* p. 14, *n.* 19.

[10] *American Teacher Magazine,* American Federation of Teachers (April, 1962), 19.

unionization of millions of white-collar workers, including public school teachers. Capitalizing on the organizing drive among the school teachers, Reuther reveals that two part-time organizers from the Industrial Union Department of the AFL-CIO have been assigned to the American Federation of Teachers. In addition, three full-time American Federation of Teachers organizers are subsidized by the IUD drive, and financial support is being furnished to the AFT for twenty-three part-time organizers.[11]

Reuther's Industrial Union Department was instrumental in the AFT's 1961 New York City victory in which one of its locals, the United Federation of Teachers, won initial concessions from the New York City Board of Education, later developing into collective bargaining rights. This was the first major teacher organization victory in the United States over the traditional policy-making prerogatives of a school board. The union was so successful in its New York City drive and its bargaining with the New York City Board of Education that similar organizing and bargaining efforts have been extended to other major cities in the United States. Carl Megel, president of the American Federation of Teachers, has reported to Walter Reuther that:

> As a result of IUD support, teacher organizers are now at work in Boston, Philadelphia, Newark, Cleveland, Chicago, Detroit, Dearborn, Milwaukee, and elsewhere. In Milwaukee, the AFT defeated the local National Education Association affiliate by a substantial majority in a collective bargaining election. In Gary [Indiana], union teachers conducted a successful one-day strike to achieve recognition as majority representatives of the school system's teachers. . . . The importance of a growing, active teachers' union to all of U.S. labor cannot be too greatly stressed.[12]

The extent to which Walter Reuther intends to push his organizing efforts is exemplified in the $3,000,000 he has set aside for union organizing purposes.[13]

The American Federation of Teachers outlook on education, until the middle of 1963, was almost entirely limited to the improvement of the teachers' welfare through the attainment of higher salaries, time releases, sabbaticals, and other money considerations, and to the acquisition of a degree of governing control over the public schools.[14]

[11] Walter Reuther, "Reports to the Industrial Union Department of the AFL-CIO," Fifth Constitutional Convention, Washington, D.C., November 7–8, 1963.

[12] *Ibid.*, p. 22. The election referred to by Mr. Reuther was held among teachers in the vocational high school in Milwaukee. Subsequently, a system-wide election was held among all the teachers in Milwaukee, and AFT lost this election by a narrow margin. This later election did not negate the election at the vocational high school. Here the AFT is still the collective bargaining agent for that group of teachers.

See also Victor Riesel, "Labor's Vast White Collar Drive: Teachers Serve as Base," *Deseret News* (April 23, 1962).

[13] Victor Riesel, "New Unionization Program Shoots for Million in Schools and Colleges," *Deseret News* (November 18, 1963).

[14] Riesel, "Labor's Vast White Collar Drive."

Sterling Spero, a professor of political science at New York University and an advocate of teachers' bargaining rights, feels that there is a faction in the AFT which seems to think "that 'militancy' and intransigence is a sign of trade union virility, that teachers must demonstrate that they are an honest-to-goodness part of the labor movement like the coal miners of 1936."[15] Though this group of which Spero speaks is a minority and does not permeate the entire federation, its influence is strongly felt, for it seems to be the organization's consensus that it is a "craft" rather than a "professional" organization. This, in fact, singles out one of the main self-viewed differences between the AFT and the NEA. The NEA, though flirting at times with a semblance of labor union techniques,[16] maintains that it is a "professional" organization composed of professional teachers and administrators.

The AFT is not so concerned with "professionalism," and openly uses the mechanisms of mandated collective bargaining, strikes, and picketing to further its aims. It has shown on occasion that it will engage in these activities even in open defiance of the law.[17] Although its methods are held in disdain by some observers, the techniques have proved effective in furthering the organization's expressed goals—improvement of teacher welfare and participation with school boards in the control of the public schools. Although its methods are contrary to the traditional American system of public school government, the AFT feels that this is the only way its members will receive remuneration and status commensurate with the value of their services. Walter Reuther stated in his report to the fifth constitutional convention of the AFL-CIO, held in 1963:

This year, the United Federation of Teachers, New York affiliate of the American Federation of Teachers, won significant new gains through collective bargaining. Included . . . were provisions that will raise the professional status and confidence of teachers and will benefit the children and community. Collective bargaining has proved through performance to be the most effective answer for the educational dilemma and the plight of the nation's teachers.[18]

The AFT, though small in total numbers, is strong in the heavily populated urban centers, such as New York City and Chicago. Its power in

[15] Spero, p. 38.

[16] As in Utah, where it threatened to withhold teachers' services from the public schools unless certain demands were met.

[17] Spero.

[18] Reuther, p. 21.

The control of the local schools has traditionally been invested in local lay people, elected or appointed to boards of education, which generally have not shared their policy-making power with teachers organizations. However, centralization of educational control has been done in Hawaii, and is permitted by the constitution of Alaska (though in practice the control is still local in Alaska). Teachers organizations prefer to deal with a central body, as they feel that their lot will be more favorable there than with local school boards.

these urban areas oftentimes is much greater than that of the NEA. Through the help of organized industrial labor, it has made gigantic strides in the 1960s in organizing and marshaling the nation's urban teachers to a point of militant action. Because of its aggressiveness, the relatively small size of the AFT belies its actual influence on the American educational scene.

The National Education Association

Since the NEA is composed of administrators as well as teachers, its policy has been moderated as it applies to power politics. Administrators are in a "middle-of-the-road" situation, for, in order to be effective, they not only must maintain a degree of rapport with classroom teachers, but also must demonstrate allegiance to their employers—the boards of education. As these administrators have interacted with the teachers, they have tended to temper the latter's sometimes militant views. This was demonstrated during the NEA 1963 Detroit convention when the question of imposing nation-wide sanctions against Utah in support of the Utah Educational Association, an affiliate of the NEA, was debated.

The Utah legislature had raised its public education budget by 14.5 per cent, which fell considerably short of the 31 per cent jump which local education groups insisted was necessary. The NEA Delegate Assembly supported the recommendation of the NEA Executive Committee, which had recommended that the Utah resolution *not* be adopted; however, the resolution had *previously* been adopted by the NEA's Department of Classroom Teachers (DCT), *which includes about 95 per cent of NEA membership.*[19]

Nevertheless, the spectacular early successes of Local No. 2 of the American Federation of Teachers in New York City, and similar teacher union successes elsewhere, have challenged and stimulated the National Education Association to devise new methods to compete effectively with the American Federation of Teachers. Some observers feel that the NEA is entering the throes of a desperate struggle, one in which it will attempt to keep its ranks somewhat professional as it competes with the successes of labor's American Federation of Teachers. Raymond Moley suggests that: "One reason for the energetic actions of the NEA is its fear that unless it gets deeply into collective bargaining and coercive action, its membership will drift into the AFL-CIO American Federation of Teachers."[20] This may be an extreme view; but significant is the fact that during the 1963 Detroit convention the NEA adopted policies and finalized guidelines for collective pressure applications which it hopes will permit its members to

[19] See, for example, *The New York Times* (July 2, 3, 4, 6, and 7, 1963).

[20] Moley.

See also Elaine Exton, "NSBA at the Crossroads," *American School Board Journal,* 147 (December, 1963), 33.

retain the cloak of professionalism and yet not be outflanked by teacher labor unions.[21]

As was stated by T. M. Stinnett, NEA's assistant executive secretary for professional development and welfare:

The inroads of labor legislation already in four states which, in effect, place teachers and school boards within the confines of labor techniques, in matters having to do with salaries and other welfare considerations, presumably against their will, simply force the teaching profession to seek professional approaches through law. The obvious interest to extend this labor legislation to other states, *leaves no choice except to get there first with the most and best procedures, or find that it is too late.*[22] [Italics supplied.]

John Scanlon, in the *Saturday Review,* concludes that the power struggle between the NEA and the AFT will continue and that it will be waged with greatest intensity in the large urbanized centers.[23]

The NEA and its affiliates have consequently developed a special kind of "unionism." To counter the position of the AFT and its collective bargaining privileges, the NEA has developed the concept of "professional negotiations." Also, to offset the attractiveness to teachers of labor's strike mechanism, the NEA has developed a policy of "professional sanctions."

In its "professional negotiations," the National Education Association espouses Exton's doctrine of the "consensus."

That consensus is an essential element in professional negotiation was made plain by Allen M. West, NEA's special assistant for Urban Affairs, who in his remarks at NEA's Detroit convention, stressed the importance of "establishing acceptance of the philosophy that the goal of negotiation is the reaching of a consensus—not merely the making of a decision."

The goal of "reaching a consensus" is also featured in the current NEA Resolution on Professional Negotiation which says in part: "The National Education Association insists on the right of professional associations, through democratically selected representatives using professional channels, to participate with boards of education in the determination of policies of common concern, including salary and other conditions of professional service. . . . The seeking of consensus and mutual agreements on a professional basis should preclude the arbitrary exercise of unilateral authority by boards of education and the use of the strike by teachers."[24]

This is different more in terminology than practice from the American Federation of Teachers concept—and practice—of collective bargaining with bilateral decision making. Both professional negotiations and collective bargaining have essentially the same basic aim—written agreements between

[21] See NEA, *Guidelines for Professional Negotiations,* and *Guidelines for Professional Sanctions* (Washington, D.C.: NEA, November, 1963).

[22] Cited by John M. Ashbrook, *Congressional Record,* 88th Congress, 1st Session (June 25, 1963), 10884.

[23] John Scanlon, "Strikes, Sanctions and the Schools," *The Saturday Review* (October 19, 1963), 51.

[24] Exton.

teacher organizations and school boards on matters of mutual concern, including participation by teachers in the determination of school policy. School boards flatly remonstrate this collective pressure technique of the teachers, and they resolved in their 1963 Denver convention that

School boards, subject to the requirements of applicable law, shall refrain from compromise agreements based on negotiation or collective bargaining, and shall not resort to mediation or arbitration, nor yield to threats of reprisals on all matters affecting local public schools, including the welfare of all personnel. They shall also resist by all lawful means the enactment of laws which would compel them to surrender any part of their responsibility.[25]

By divorcing itself from labor, the NEA would probably (1) remain outside the jurisdiction of existing labor laws which it fears it would be subjected to if it advocated the concept of collective bargaining as such, and (2) retain within its ranks education supervisors and administrators who it fears would be excluded under an industrial-labor-type arrangement of collective bargaining.[26]

The NEA believes that, as a means for preventing unethical or arbitrary policies or practices that have a deleterious effect on the welfare of the schools, "professional sanctions" should be invoked.[27] The "professional sanction" offers a diversity of application to accommodate the degree of gravity of almost any situation (including internal policing of its own

[25] National School Boards Association, *School Boards in a Changing Society* [Proceedings of the 1963 convention of the Association at Denver, Colo., April 27–30] (Evanston, Ill.: The Association, 1963), p. 329.

[26] See *Guidelines for Professional Negotiations, passim.* An expression of the reasons for keeping the negotiation machinery out of the labor pattern is also found in the 1962–1963 *NEA Handbook*, p. 64.

[27] Sanctions, within the context of this statement, are defined as a means to prevent the violation of a right or responsibility. A community should support its schools; school boards should discharge their functions with integrity and impartiality; administrators should use the procedures essential for the democratic administration of good schools; teachers should make every effort to provide the best possible learning experiences for students. Against those who fail to act by such standards, organizations of the education profession may impose sanctions.

As used by a professional education organization, sanctions mean censure, suspension or expulsion of a member, severance of a relationship with an affiliated association or other agency; imposing of a deterrent against a board of education or other agency controlling the welfare of the school; bringing into play forces that will enable the community to help the board or agency to realize its responsibility; or the application of one or more steps in the withholding of services. Sanctions are used only to improve educational opportunities through the elimination of conditions detrimental to effective education. The most severe types of sanctions should be invoked only as a last resort where conditions are such that it is impossible for educators to give effective professional service.

NEA, *Guidelines for Professional Sanctions,* p. 9.

ranks). However, in ultimate form, when applied to political subdivisions, it differs very little from AFT's concept of the strike. In a "strike," the teachers simply quit work; in "professional sanctions," they collectively refrain from signing contracts and do not resume work at the opening of schools in the fall. As John Scanlon has stated: "When teachers vote to withhold their contracts and urge other teachers not to man their positions, the result is the same as when teachers vote to strike and throw up a picket line to keep other teachers out of the classroom."[28] "No contract—no work."

Although obligatory mediation is not an official policy of the NEA, an example of the extent to which some wish to go is found in the wording of a resolution submitted by the resolutions committee of the NEA's Department of Classroom Teachers, which suggested that final authority for the resolution of differences should be vested in an appropriate educational or professional state agency.[29]

School boards generally are suspicious of the doctrine of the "consensus" and are particularly concerned about the possibility of obligatory mediation of conflicts. They view in "consensus" a diminution of their statutory authority and in mandated mediation an illegal delegation of power which they feel the law forbids. They state that "the authority of the board of education is established by law and this authority may not be delegated to others. Strikes, sanctions, boycotts, mandated arbitration or mediation are improper procedures to be used by public school employees who are dissatisfied with their conditions of employment."[30] Teachers contest the ethics and the legality of such assumptions, thus placing the educational function in an unsolved conflict—teachers on the one hand and the school boards on the other.

Ideologies of the AFT and the NEA Compared and Contrasted

As we have seen, public school teachers are willing to declare open hostilities with school boards and pressure the public in an effort to achieve

[28] Scanlon, 51.

[29] The concluding paragraph of the resolution urges:

Teachers in states not now recognizing or accepting such policies (mandated bargaining in mediation), through their local and state associations, to press for legislation to legalize such procedures *and to vest final authority for the resolution of differences in an appropriate education or professional state agency.*

The italicized portion following the word "procedures" was disputed by Robert Klemmer of the Montgomery County chapter of the Pennsylvania State Education Association and after discussion was voted down by the Department of Classroom Teachers delegate body, which adopted the rest of the resolution. Elaine Exton, "Teachers' Groups Challenge Lay School Board Control," *American School Board Journal,* 147 (August, 1963), 29.

[30] NSBA, p. 329.

their concept of the all-American system of education. The general teacher ideology and justification for all these actions is to promote the growth of all peoples, in an optimum atmosphere, in the areas of "intellectual qualities, civic competence, international understanding, moral and spiritual values, cultural and aesthetic appreciation, vocational and economic capability, conservation of human and natural resources, and constructive use of leisure time."[31] The teachers are able to rationalize group action and promote inner cohesion by clearly espousing their ideology—shared by all Americans—that the goals of American education should be to promote the opportunity for every individual to develop his full potential for responsible and useful citizenship, for the "ultimate strength of the nation lies in the social responsibility, economic competence, and moral strength of the individual American."[32] That they sincerely believe in these goals makes their ideology all the more potent. For certainly the school boards (their chief opponents) desire these same aims. The difference, of course, is that in specific goals the teachers differ from boards of education frequently on how these ideals should be realized.

Besides this general type of ideological agreement, the two national organizations have developed a number of areas of specific agreement.

1. Both groups espouse the desirability and necessity of a strong power position.
2. Both groups express distrust of the motives, efficacy, and aims of local school boards.
3. Both groups believe in a *right and a necessity* to participate in bilateral decision-making authority with the school boards.
4. Both believe that the public does not accord them due deference or status, or reward them adequately for their services.
5. Both share a distrust in the application of teacher-competency evaluation and merit-pay standards.

These issues will be taken up in turn.

A STRONG POWER POSITION. Both the NEA and AFT have come to feel that to satisfy their membership they must attempt to realize their aims and goals more rapidly. They both lobby extensively in local and national levels of politics, and both groups are vigorously soliciting new members to increase their power positions. Fred M. Hechinger has stated: "Whether the future will favor the UFT [New York City Local No. 2 of AFT] or the NEA, it is clear that both organizations will put greater pressure on the unorganized teacher to stop going it alone."[33] There is little doubt that teachers are increasingly aware of their power growth, whether it accrues from membership in a professional association or a labor union.

[31] *NEA Handbook, 1962–1963,* p. 50.
[32] *Ibid.,* p. 66.
[33] Fred M. Hechinger, *The New York Times,* Western Edition (September 18, 1963).

The teachers feel that from a position of power the day of the school boards' "handing down commands" will be over. They want the boards to recognize that teachers are "human beings and that it [would be] profitable to channel their individual values, [management goals] through an orderly, organized system"[34]—in other words, the teachers organizations.

The public school teachers also believe that it is only from a position of power that they can command attention from the Federal government and influence it into improving the economic situation of its teacher employees. The NEA has notified the White House that unless there is some legislative action to remedy the deplorable economic situation of teachers employed by the government in its overseas schools for military dependents, "it would appear that the NEA would be called upon to impose sanctions."[35] Overseas teacher salaries averaged $4,720 in 1964 as compared with a national average of $5,963. The overseas teachers received a $100 increase in 1964, but a group of teachers in Ankara rejected this raise as an insult.

Some contend that the largest United States teachers group, the NEA, has moved into a pivotal power position in the areas of accreditation of teacher training colleges, certification of teachers, and the establishment of professional standards of teachers. As all three of these are somehow involved in the type of education a prospective teacher receives, the power over accreditation has a tendency to have *de facto* influence over who will be certified and the standards by which he must abide. The control comes through a voluntary organization, without legal status, known as the National Council for the Accreditation of Teacher Education (NCATE), which is largely influenced by the National Commission on Teacher Education and Professional Standards (TEPS). TEPS, on the national level, was established in 1946 as a commission of the NEA.[36]

NCATE is being criticized because of its attempts to bring national conformity to certain teacher preparation standards through holding out the threat of nonaccreditation of a teacher training college or university if certain requirements are not meet. Dr. Burton Brown, of the University of Wisconsin, has stated that the present trend of "unification via NCATE" is

Dangerous to our traditional democratic system of checks and balances, dangerous to the academic freedom of institutions that prepare teachers, and dangerous to the continued development of a sound program of accreditation in the field of teacher education.

Certain certification officers and proponents of rapid professionalization of

[34] Raymond W. Pasnick, "The Human Frontiers in Education," *American Teacher Magazine* (October, 1960), 7.

[35] *Salt Lake Tribune* (January 5, 1964).

[36] James Bryant Conant, *The Education of American Teachers* (New York: McGraw-Hill Book Company, 1963), p. 16.

teachers, working effectively through . . . TEPS are trying to make the education profession march boldly forward "in step to the same piece of beautiful music" and attempting to reduce greatly or eliminate altogether diversity, irregularity, and multiplicity of "weak and detrimental" certification requirements and professional standards standing in the way.[37]

This extension of bureaucratic empire building is a subtle but effective way of influencing public policy. The only problem here is that the teachers in the bureaucracy may have overextended themselves temporarily.

DISTRUST OF LOCAL SCHOOL BOARDS.   The public school teachers feel that school boards generally have been too paternalistic and dictatorial with them, and they are unhappy with this present arrangement which makes them "second-class" members of society. Inasmuch as boards of education have generally not shown a willingness to share their control of the schools, teachers interpret this as an indication of a distrust of them as professionals. They reciprocate the feeling of distrust toward the boards, and their assumption is that the boards do not make their decision in an atmosphere which sufficiently considers the teachers' viewpoint.

For three centuries, lay boards and voters (those who supply the money for the public schools and therefore feel it is their legitimate right to control them) have made the policies under which the schools have functioned, seeking advice, and accepting it when they felt it wise, from the professional teacher and administrator.[38] This historic concept is now under fire. Many teachers feel that school boards in general are incapable of rendering adequate decisions concerning education because they are composed of laymen, sometimes uninformed, who are either unwilling or unable to support the needs of education or make the effort necessary to improve the educational system. Teachers were extremely bitter during the 1963 "Federal aid to education" conflict in Congress, for example, because the school boards generally opposed this legislation. Significantly, the boards saw in the legislation a mechanism wherein the Federal government might begin to strip them of their local power over the schools, the very area of power which the teachers now decry as being too unilateral, and which should be shared, to some degree, by them.

The men and women who comprise the boards of education believe that local lay control is a vital factor in the quality of American education. They see themselves as a necessary safeguard for democracy in order to prevent public servants from becoming public rulers. School board members in general believe that their efforts in preserving a democratic institu-

[37] Bob Burton Brown, "Dangers in the Misuse of NCATE Accreditation," *Journal of Teacher Education*, 14, 3 (September, 1963), 326.

[38] Gordon McCloskey, "Who's Responsible for What?" *Phi Delta Kappan*, 44 (May, 1962), 369.

tion should not be interpreted by the teachers as a lack of confidence in them. They draw the analogy of the situation between the military Joint Chiefs of Staff and the President of the United States. The President, an elected official, through consultation with his staff advisers and within the scope of legislation, makes the policies under which the military functions. It is the Joint Chiefs of Staff who carry out the policies tendered by elected governmental officials. School board members hasten to point out that in almost every country where the military, or any other group without elective controls, has ascended to power, the democratic institutions have become shattered. They resist, therefore, the struggle of the teachers to an ascendancy of policy-making power.

Board members also point out that they too are extremely interested in educational progress and in achieving the type of education which will offer maximum opportunity for individual attainment of the highest goals. They point out that school boards *also* "work to maintain and improve the professional status of the teaching profession, and . . . encourage potential candidates for teaching who will exemplify the highest ideals." [39]

A SHARE IN DECISION-MAKING AUTHORITY. Nevertheless, the teachers feel that the boards are too cumbersome, too closely linked with the *status quo,* and too uninformed. Teachers want to accelerate the attainment of their goals, and they feel that by gaining a share in the school boards' decision-making power, they will more readily achieve their ambition. That the NEA and the AFT are actively seeking to gain participation in decision-making authority with boards of education, and thus break with tradition, is a fact of life school boards are going to have to accept.[40]

Whether this is necessarily good or bad for education cannot be treated here. The concept is an emotionally charged one in which varying opinions have been and will continue to be vigorously expressed. The AFT pioneered the idea of sharing in the decision-making authority with boards of education. The knowledge of this became widespread, specifically during their activities of 1960 and 1962 with the New York City Board of Education. Victor Riesel has indicated that the whole movement was brought about when labor leaders of the AFL-CIO began to believe that "union accomplishments in industry-management relations could carry over into educa-

[39] NSBA, p. 329.

[40] John Scanlon has stated:

Teachers are making it increasingly clear that they want a voice in school affairs and that they are willing to fight for their rights, if necessary.

This means that stubborn school boards will find it increasingly difficult to run the schools by unilateral action, and that ignoring the legitimate demands of teachers will increasingly involve some peril.

Scanlon, p. 52.

tion."[41] As has already been pointed out, the success of some of the AFT's demands in New York City was partly due to the organizing help and financial aid provided it by the AFL-CIO. Labor is proud of these gains into the traditionally sacred ground of the school boards. An article in *Newsweek,* scoring the plight of the nation's urban schools and minimizing the gains of labor in their latest negotiations with the New York City Board of Education, triggered a response from the president of the involved local of the AFT, which embodies the emphasis of this section.

> You refer to the "minuscule" salary increase for the current year obtained by the United Federation of Teachers. You failed to mention, however, the substantial increase in salary for the second year of our two-year contract period. You failed also to mention the numerous other benefits obtained by us, *with particular reference to the tremendous increase in the share of control in the administration of the school system.*
>
> The actual picture of gains is one of great magnitude and quite different from the picture that you have painted in your article.[42] [Italics supplied.]

The NEA has followed AFT's policy example in this area, despite its reluctance to be "nonprofessional." It realizes that it must meet the competition, particularly since the dramatic recent successes of AFT in its negotiations. A reporter at NEA's 1963 Detroit convention stated:

> Watching the fireworks touched off whenever the subject of "teacher sanctions" or "professional negotiations" came up for discussion at the business session of the National Education Association's Representative Assembly (of about 6,800 official delegates) held during the NEA's 1963 convention, June 30–July 5, in Detroit's Cobo Hall, it was apparent that many of its teacher-delegates are intent on seeking a stronger, if not a dominant, voice in the decision-making and operation of the public school policies and programs.
>
> Leadership for these efforts is being furnished by the top echelon of the NEA which will wage an extensive campaign in coming months to instruct its members in the ABC's of launching these potentially dangerous firecrackers at state and local levels.[43]

The NEA feels that the teaching profession must be responsible for identifying the knowledge necessary to teach and for the competence of those who do teach.[44] Therefore, the profession should share in the decision making of who can or cannot be employed by a local school district. The NEA also feels that it is necessary to develop the autonomy of the organized teaching profession in determining standards of professional competence and conduct, and the freedom, within broad public policy, to establish and carry out educational programs.[45] The character of educational programs

---

[41] Victor Riesel, "Labor's Vast White Collar Drive."
[42] Charles Cogen, "Letter to the Editor," *Newsweek* (September 30, 1963), 4.
[43] Exton, "Teachers Groups," 29.   [45] *Ibid.,* p. 55.
[44] *NEA Handbook, 1963–1964,* p. 52.

generally has been determined, after consultation with the professional staff, by boards of education. The "sharing" of decision-making authority, teachers feel, must also include additional policies of common concern including salary and other conditions for professional service.[46] This "would include negotiations regarding personnel policies, working conditions, fringe or non-wage benefits, salaries, employment standards, in-service education of personnel, class size, teacher turnover, communications within the school system, curriculum planning, and teaching methods."[47]

The school boards oppose this threat to their statutory authority and remind the teachers that "the authority of the board of education is established by law and this authority may not be delegated to others."[48] School boards fear that teachers, if allowed mandated collective participation with them in the determination of school policy, will use the threat of a strike or a severe "professional sanction" if the boards do not capitulate on almost every major issue. They feel that the continuity of public service, a basic requirement of the public good, must be a paramount consideration of all its citizens, including those employed by the public. The boards believe that employees should not use any power, either statutorily or by permission, to bring public service in any category, schools included, to a standstill. They point out President Hoover's statement, "If [public] servants are to strike, they are striking against the government, they are striking against the entire people, and there is no right or justification for that." [49] Boards also rely on the stature of the great advocate of the common man, Franklin Delano Roosevelt, who indicated that because of public employees' peculiar relationship to the source of money from which their check comes, that is, the taxpayer through the legislative process, they "should realize that the process of collective bargaining, as usually understood, cannot be transplanted into the public service."[50]

[46] Resolution of 1961 NEA Delegate Assembly.

[47] National Education Association, *Classroom Teachers Speak on Professional Negotiations* (report of the Classroom Teachers National Study Conference on Professional Negotiations, November 23–24, 1962), pp. 5–6. Also of interest is part of resolution No. 18 found in the *NEA Handbook, 1962–1963*, p. 64, which states:

> The National Education Association insists on the right of professional associations, through democratically selected representatives using professional channels, to participate with boards of education in the determination of policies of common concern, including salary and other conditions of professional service. . . . The seeking of consensus and mutual agreement on a professional basis should preclude the arbitrary exercise of unilateral authority by boards of education and the use of the strike by teachers.

[48] NSBA, p. 329.

[49] Felix A. Nigro, *Public Administration Readings and Documents* (New York: Holt, Rinehart and Winston, Inc., 1951), p. 300.

[50] *Ibid.*, p. 294.

INADEQUATE REWARD. That the teachers have resorted to a degree of militance in an attempt to increase their economic status is evidence of the intensity of their feelings on this issue. They point out that "the quality of education reflects the ideals, motives, preparation, and conduct of the members of the teaching profession"[51] and that one of the determining factors of the level at which these ideals, motives, and conduct operate is established by the value the public places on teachers' services. The teachers feel that they are not being remunerated according to their degree of preparation and professional status.

Compared with other professions requiring approximately a four-year college degree, teachers rank lowest in starting salaries. In 1962, salaries paid beginning engineers were $6,648, accountants, $5,856, salesmen, $5,616, and teachers $4,800.[52] The teachers' salaries, of course, are for nine months and are sometimes increased by summer employment. In comparing the average salary paid to teachers with the average wage paid to workers in jobs covered by employment security laws, teachers, in 1960–1961, were only 7 per cent above the covered worker average, and in 1961–1962 only 11.7 per cent.[53] The significance here is one of education, as the "average wage in covered employment" is the average total payment received by all persons employed by business and industry subject to unemployment compensation laws. Managerial as well as clerical, technical, and production employees are included as part of the overall average, and the bulk of these are not required to have any college education for their employment. Teachers point out, further, that their purchasing power in 1962 was only approximately 109 per cent of the 1935 average while per capita personal income purchasing power was up 158 per cent. Relatively speaking, they say, 1935 was more financially favorable to teachers than 1962.[54] And a study in 1964 by *School Management* pointed out that the average United States teacher purchasing power, due to inflation, was only $99 more then than it was in 1958, six years before.[55]

Both NEA and AFT point out that only if adequate salaries are available to attract and hold qualified people in the teaching profession will Americans ever be able to achieve an optimum educational system and realize the goals which the teachers have set. As a standard of measurement, both organizations have set a "professional" salary schedule toward which

[51] *NEA Handbook, 1962–1963,* p. 66.

[52] *NEA Research Bulletin,* 41, 2 (May, 1963), 48.

[53] *NEA Estimates of School Statistics, 1961–1962,* Research Report 1961–R22, December, 1961.

[54] Utah Education Association, "Economic Status of Utah Teachers 1962–1963," *NEA Research Bulletin* (December, 1962), 23. See also National Education Association, "Economic Status of Teachers in 1962–1963," *NEA Research Bulletin* (August, 1963).

[55] *School Management,* 8 (January, 1964), 106.

they are driving. The schedule has a $6,000 minimum beginning salary and continues through eight to ten annual increments of $1,000 each to a top of $14,000 a year, adding amounts up to $1,000 for advanced degrees.[56] These amounts are considerably more than those which teachers receive in most parts of the United States.

TEACHER EVALUATION. Many extraeducational organizations, such as the Chamber of Commerce of the United States, advocate some sort of differential stand with respect to the teachers' salary question,[57] in order that the exceptionally qualified may be appropriately rewarded. Many teachers admit that the idea is good in theory, but they have steadfastly resisted its suggested application in any of its multiple forms. Their universal reservation flows from a fear of subjective ratings. Although the National Education Association feels that it should support the development of methods to measure teacher competency "objectively," it does not believe that ratings should entail any subjective evaluation whatsoever.[58] Furthermore, the association "believes that use of subjective methods of evaluating professional performance for the purpose of setting salaries has a deleterious effect on the educational process. Plans which require such subjective judgments (commonly known as merit ratings) should be avoided. American education can be better served by continued progress in developing better means of objective evaluation."[59]

Teachers fear that such things as personality clashes with their superiors might militate against their advancement. They generally prefer one of a variety of "single-salary" schedules in which salary advancements are based on the number of years of experience and the quantity of educational preparation of the individual rather than primarily on ability or effectiveness. In a recent study, the NEA found that the reasons for giving up merit-pay systems in some school districts which had attempted to implement them into practice

. . . appeared to be that no satisfactory plan had been developed for selecting the superior teacher. The corollary, stated with equal frequency, was that the plans had created dissension. Words such as ill-will, misunderstanding, and suspicion, were used in reporting the negative reactions.[60]

---

[56] See, for example, *Deseret News* (August 19, 1963); Carl J. Megel, "Merit Rating Is Educationally Unsound," *American Teacher Magazine* (February, 1961), 20; and *NEA Handbook, 1962–1963,* p. 59.

[57] Chamber of Commerce of the United States of America, *Policy Declarations* (Washington: The Chamber of Commerce, 1963), p. 62.

[58] *NEA Handbook, 1962–1963,* p. 61.

[59] *Ibid.*

[60] National Education Association, "Why Have Merit Plans for Teacher Salaries Been Abandoned?" *NEA Research Bulletin* (May, 1961), 62.

Teachers fear that the ill will and dissension created by the instigation of merit-pay plans would thwart their progress toward the optimum goals which they seek in education. They feel that education can be better served by the elimination of factors which create ill will and dissension. It is significant to note that some teachers associations have requested their boards (and some boards have acceded) to withdraw their differential salary schedules which rewarded excellence, simply because the policies were such that the teachers feared their application would militate against a majority of them.[61]

The position of the AFT is most adequately presented by its president, Carl J. Megel, who indicates that the basing of teacher salaries on merit rating is educationally unsound, that it was administratively impossible thirty years ago, and that it would be even more impossible in our modern technological society. He fears that the rating of one teacher above another for the purposes of remuneration would be done by school boards only to make teaching rewards appear higher than they are. "We know that merit increases will be given to a relatively few teachers in order to blunt demands for across-the-board increases for all teachers."[62] Megel further states that "experience has shown that the only way to protect the superior teacher from unfair, inadequate, inept, or vindictive rating is by the use of an adequate single salary schedule based upon training and experience."[63]

Areas of Ideological Disagreement between the AFT and the NEA

Two main areas are involved here—the question of the participation of administrators in an organization ostensibly designed for teacher employees,

[61] *Ibid.*, 63.
[62] Megel, 20.
[63] *Ibid.*

Mr. Conant, past president of Harvard University, makes this observation:

The intent of teachers' groups and school boards has no doubt been to find ways of rewarding meritorious teachers with salary increments that go beyond those attached to mere seniority. Attempts to measure teacher merit, however, have not yet proved clearly valid, and teacher groups have violently resisted proposals to adopt a merit system. One suspects they would oppose any system that defined merit in such a way that particular teachers would almost certainly be denied access to the "meritorious" category. . . .

Despite their constant charge that the American Federation of Teachers has a "trade union" rather than a "professional" bias, the NEA affiliates have been as adamant as has the AFT in opposing any kind of salary schedule except one based on length of training and experience. . . . I must express my dissent from the position that the mere accumulation of further college credits provides evidence that a teacher deserves a raise in salary.

Conant, p. 188.

and the ethics of associating with industrial labor unions for a desired power position.

ADMINISTRATORS AND EMPLOYEES.   The AFT takes the position that all administrators must be excluded from their unions, for under any other pretext a union would end up being administrator-dominated, a "company union" by industrial labor relations' definition. The AFT fears that such an organization would fail to heed the voice of the teacher employee. It feels that "unrestricted administrator membership is wrong because it leads straight to a totalitarian form of government."[64] A belief in nonmembership for administrators is certainly not synonymous to a belief in noncooperation with them, its members say.

The NEA takes a radically different position. It believes that the *exclusion* of administrators is not appropriate for a professional organization. NEA members generally equate their professional status with that of doctors, lawyers, and dentists. They state that associations of these groups enroll all practitioners in a given area, hence, so should those of teachers. The NEA also contends that, since administrators and teachers must work together, they should be in the same organization. It feels that labor is one important element in society, but that there are other important ones also; that education should represent all of society, and not single out one portion with which to identify itself. It feels that alignment with labor means identification with labor and that this can result in a very exclusive situation, one which will not enhance the totality of education. For these and other reasons, the NEA maintains that an organization containing contributing influences from all facets of education will enhance the whole movement, avoid much friction between employee and administrator, and permit a greater interchange of ideas.

THE INVOLVEMENT OF LABOR.   Much has been implied already in this chapter concerning the gulf between the manifest views of the two organizations on this issue. The American Federation of Teachers is a labor union, views itself as such, and employs all the recognized techniques of labor to achieve its goals. Charles Cogen, president of Local No. 2 of the AFT, has said: "We utilize various pressure tactics [to achieve our goals] such as mass petitions, rallies, and whenever necessary, a strike. We consider ourselves a militant organization, one that is constantly on the alert when necessary."[65]

The paradox in the case of the NEA is that even though its members reject this type of procedure as being unprofessional, they nevertheless have

[64] Myron Lieberman, "The Battle for New York City Teachers," *Phi Delta Kappan,* 43 (October, 1961), 4.

[65] Letter from Charles Cogen to F. LaMond Tullis, September 30, 1963.

set up a policy structure in their own organization which permits them to employ similar, though more diplomatic, techniques. This fact was pointed out earlier in this chapter.

SOME OBSERVATIONS. Even though members of the AFT are deeply committed to their course of action, it is very probable that they have not entirely considered the price they may have to pay in the long run for their association with labor. There is no guarantee, for example, that they might not be called on to participate in "sympathy" strikes at some time in the future, or even be required to assist labor in battles with management which may be distasteful to the teachers. Once teachers become identified with, or convey the image of, labor unionism, they must be prepared to accept a complete reevaluation of their claim to professionalism. It will be difficult for the public to associate professionalism (as the term is generally understood in our society, notwithstanding some interpretational objections from labor) with "laborism," and still retain the traditional professional image of the teacher. "Certainly, the public and other professions will not be inclined to regard a teacher as a professional if he desires the peculiar advantages enjoyed by labor."[66] Finally, teachers might have difficulty in presenting objectively to their students a perspective on labor-management relations, once the teachers had chosen one side.

The implications for the NEA are also potent. If it becomes involved in an aggressive and sometimes militant power struggle, it also may have to reevaluate its claim to professionalism. The signs are ominous, for the NEA is in a power struggle with the AFT on the one hand and with the school boards and the public on the other, an involvement which may require a complete reevaluation of its image. Inasmuch as the NEA power struggle roots are well established, the projections are, then, that this organization will increasingly become more militant, and in the future may be expected to implement vigorous pressure techniques on school boards and the public.

THE CASE OF LABOR'S AMERICAN FEDERATION OF TEACHERS IN NEW YORK CITY[67]

This case takes up specific examples of the public school teachers as a power group and their influence on the formation of public policy. It is not intended to represent the activities of all teachers local organizations or, indeed, of a majority. The intent is simply to demonstrate the leverage,

[66] William W. Brickman, "Teachers' Organizations and Labor Unions," *School and Society* (March 11, 1961), 96.
[67] See *The New York Times*, 1959–1963.

power, and influence which one large teachers organization has been able to obtain through a dedicated and engineered use of techniques heretofore generally used only by industrial labor. Whether this situation will be repeated, or even become widespread, depends upon the new approaches of the educational power groups who are keeping the New York City example vividly in mind.

This case and the developments behind it began in New York City in January, 1959. At that time there was no one representative teachers group in the area. Rather, the public school teachers were members of some forty organizations, which, among them, represented the two national groups and a host of independent ones. Some of these were "parochialized" into such systems as evening high school teachers, day high school teachers, junior high school teachers, and elementary school teachers. They all had diverse claims to authority and jurisdiction; some condemning others for actions, then occasionally resorting to those same actions themselves.

Many factors were responsible for the teachers' dramatic turn to militancy. They were victims, and in a sense, they sometimes victimized. The urban school problems were legion, and their plight was compounded by the middle-class flight to the suburbs, leaving a vacuum for depressed, but opportunity-seeking, minority groups to enter.

The teachers' rapid rise to power, as a result of militancy and pressure, began with the Evening New York City School Teachers about January, 1959. These teachers had felt for some time that the board of education and Superintendent Theobald of the New York City School District had been forcing them to the wall. They had not received any pay increase for a number of years, and their teaching responsibilities were growing. On the other hand, the administration had its problems also, among them mounting financial difficulties. Whether the parties attempted in good faith to resolve their differences and find a common ground, short of militancy, can be answered both yes and no, depending on who answers the question. The following, however, points out the facts of the case as it unfolded.

On January 1, 1959, the association representing the evening high school teachers made a statement to President Silver of the New York City Board of Education and to New York City Mayor Wagner that 95 per cent of its members would resign *en masse* on February 2 unless salaries were raised. They were seeking a total of $18 per night. The board of education declared that there were no funds available for an increase at that time, but that teachers who did wish to work longer hours could receive more pay, for the board lacked teachers to staff all its evening stations anyway. This compromise suggestion was rejected by the association. Several meetings, which became emotionally charged at times, were held between association representatives and Superintendent Theobald. From one of these the superintendent stalked out, accusing the association of "sarcasm."

On February 2, the evening high schools were struck; only 52 out of 425 teachers reported for work; the board terminated from employment all the recalcitrants and attempted to recruit other teachers to replace them. (They were able to hire only 29 replacements.) The board then set up temporary central evening high schools in all boroughs and staffed them with the 100 teachers it was able to retain on the job; striking teachers picketed the high schools; the teaching staff dwindled at the central temporary schools to a point where the board found it necessary to close all evening schools; the superintendent said that the board could not better its pay offer, but that when the schools reopened, priority appointments would be given to teachers who had remained on the job. The teachers association then suggested to Mayor Wagner and Superintendent Theobald that the money New York City had saved in snow removal the previous winter be given to the board of education to be used for teachers' salaries; a compromise plan was worked out in which the teachers agreed to receive a slight pay increase and the board of education agreed to make no reprisals against striking teachers. On February 25, twenty-three days after the strike began, the teachers voted to return to work and the evening high schools were reopened.

The troubles for the board of education were not ended, however, for in March the day high school teachers, seeing what their evening colleagues had obtained through militancy, decided to test their strength. Mayor Wagner stated that the reason the day teachers had not received their anticipated salary increases was that the New York State cuts in requests for new tax levies had forced New York City to withhold part of the budget which had been set up to be allotted to the board of education, and therefore it was impossible to meet the pledged pay rise. The day high school teachers, represented by the Teachers Guild, took this as a "breach of contract" and voted to stop work. Superintendent Theobald warned the teachers that he would invoke the penalties of the state's extremely harsh antistrike Condon-Wadlin Act (for public employees) in the event of a work stoppage, and furthermore, he ordered all principals to list the names of absent teachers when the stoppage occurred, together with the reasons for their absence.

The teachers were aware that the Condon-Wadlin Act, if invoked, would not only deprive them of their jobs but also subject them to heavy fines and perhaps imprisonment. Notwithstanding, two other associations, the Teachers Association and the Teachers Union, voted to back the guild and honor its picket lines. At the eleventh hour the guild called off the strike, for the board had agreed to work out a salary schedule with them. The final compromise was a $300 across-the-board increase. This compromise, resulting from a militant threat to the education system, resulted in two advances for the Teachers Guild: (1) the guild was to be allowed to participate with the board in arriving at salary schedules, and (2) its member teachers received a pay rise. These concessions were significant, for they formed stepping-stones to greater concessions which would be received later.

During or shortly after this strike threat, the AFL-CIO sent organizing aid and money assistance to one of the affiliates of the American Federation of Teachers in New York City.[68] This, together with other factors, gave birth to a combine of organizations which came to be known as the United Federation of Teachers, AFL-CIO,[69] with a membership of 21,000, half the school teachers in New York City. Immediately following their organizing victory, the newly elected president, Charles Cogen, threatened the Board of Education with a strike if his teachers were not supplied with higher pay, collective bargaining rights, dues checkoff, and other benefits. President Silver of the board and Superintendent Theobald asked the board of estimate (New York City's budget-dispersing body) for a $15 million increase in the schools' budget in order that teachers' salaries could be increased. The board of estimate did not approve the total request; the UFT voted an indefinite work stoppage, and again, at the eleventh hour, the strike was avoided only when the board of education agreed to give the UFT collective bargaining rights, and permit a referendum in the near future to allow one organization to represent all the teachers in the New York City school district. The board granted sick pay for substitute teachers, a demand of the UFT, and also dues checkoff.

As the summer months of 1960 passed, the UFT began to feel that the board of education was not moving rapidly enough on the collective bargaining arrangements which had been agreed upon, and so they called a strike. There was bitter opposition to this strike, even from associations outside the UFT which had teachers in the New York City school district. The Teachers Union condemned the strike as being against accepted trade union policy and practice inasmuch as the strike threat was called when there was no general pay issue at hand. However, the UFT wanted more than a pay increase. It wanted a voice "as a union in school policy. [It wanted] to participate in the selection of textbooks, in their preparation, in their coverage. . . . [It wanted] to participate in the development of child guidance services, in the creation of community centers, improvements of the schools and [it wanted] the teachers to have a strong say in the setting up of curricula."[70] The strike was called for November 7, 1960; the schools were disrupted and the UFT demonstrated its growing militant power.

A volume could be written on the New York teachers' strike of No-

[68] Riesel, "Labor's Vast White Collar Drive."
[69] *The New York Times* (March 26, 1960).
[70] Riesel, "Labor's Vast White Collar Drive."

vember 7, the subsequent granting of all collective bargaining rights to the United Federation of Teachers, after a teacher referendum, and the myriad individual involvements of policy, tradition, and militant force for change. The UFT made good its threat to gain *policy decision-making authority* with the board of education in teacher recruitment, class size, curriculum, and improvement of certain schools, particularly those in slum areas, besides gaining numerous teacher welfare advances.

Final Considerations

Can the United Federation of Teachers measure up to its responsibility as a "joint power" in policy-making areas of the school system? Will the union be progressive in academic policy, research, and general improvement areas while being progressive in terms of salaries and working conditions? Traditionally, teachers, like many other professionals, prefer the *status quo* to change. Fred M. Hechinger, writing in the *New York Times,* puts it this way:

> Educators. . . tend to like things as they are. Both UFT and NEA have generally been leaning toward the status quo against new ideas, from television to teacher aids. It is often left to lay boards and to able superintendents to lead or push schools towards the future.[71]

The teachers, on the other hand, contend that *they* are the ones who are pushing for change and that they are having to drag the school boards and administrators along with them.

CONCLUDING SUMMARY

The public school teachers are seeking a stronger power position from which to impress the public with the importance of recognizing their needs. Teachers are finding that these power patterns can be achieved through strong associations or unions, and therefore, a tendency does now exist wherein the teachers are solidifying their strength in local, state, and national organizations.

There are two principal national teachers organizations: the National Education Association of the United States and the much smaller American Federation of Teachers. The main difference between the two is their attitude with respect to administrators and labor unions. The NEA shuns labor unions, as such, and permits administrators within its ranks. The AFT endorses labor unions, in fact is a labor union, and excludes administrators from its ranks.

[71] Fred M. Hechinger, editorial, *The New York Times* (September 18, 1963).

The AFT engages in militant activities with fervor reminiscent of that of labor unions in the 1930s in order to achieve its goals. The NEA is being challenged by the gains of labor in teacher welfare. Though ostensibly abhorring labor union tactics, it has found it necessary to construct a policy which permits it to engage in techniques which resemble those employed by the AFT and which are more militant than earlier NEA policies. The NEA has adopted the policy of the so-called "professional negotiation" and "professional sanction" which, it hopes, will prevent it from being outflanked by teacher labor unions.

In its "professional negotiations" the National Education Association espouses the doctrine of the "consensus," which is different more in terminology than practice from the American Federation of Teachers concept —and practice—of collective bargaining with bilateral decision making, as exemplified in the New York City school district. The NEA "professional sanction" offers a diversity of application to accommodate the degree of gravity of almost any situation (including internal policing of its own ranks). However, in ultimate form, when applied on political subdivisions, it differs very little from AFT's concept of the strike. In the "strike," the teachers simply quit work; in the "professional negotiation" they do not resume work at the opening of the schools in the fall.

Both the NEA and the AFT advocate sweeping school reforms, but in their aggressive or militant conflicts with school boards the questions of real importance to them have been those of salary, other money or time-release considerations, and a share in policy-making authority traditionally held exclusively by local boards of education. These organizations feel that they have had to resort to pressure tactics because the public has failed to recognize its own "miscarriage of justice" and has not adequately supported public education. The teachers' demands for improvement of their own position is blended with an idealistic desire to help the school children and improve America. Further illumination is provided about the idealism and the liberalism of teachers in the following chapter on the intellectuals.

The teachers' pressure applications have been both successful and unsuccessful as well as indeterminate. They have won considerable concessions for increased salaries, time releases, and participation in decision-making authority with boards of education in some parts of the country. They have failed to vigorously sponsor a progressive outlook in some facets of education in which the public may require further change. The indeterminate aspect of their new-found power position is the extent of the total effect on the image of the teacher and his ability to function in his culture as a "professional" while enjoying the peculiar power position of labor.

7

intellectuals

INTRODUCTION

Any attempt to assess the role and ideology of influential occupational groups must go beyond such formally organized ones as business, labor, and agriculture. Among the rising and powerful informal groups of major significance stand the intellectuals. The consensus and power of the intellectual community are little recognized, but without this recognition the policy-making process in modern America cannot be fully understood.

Membership in the intellectual community is heterogeneous, and definitions of intellectuals are varied. In one sense, an intellectual might be considered anyone who creates or purveys ideas, or anyone "who specializes in generalities,"[1] or one who represents "the life of the mind."[2] He might be thought of as one engaged in productive research and speculative thinking. Malcolm Cowley's characterization of an intellectual is pertinent to this study. He said an intellectual is one having an attitude "open to ideas" and one who believes "that society can be improved by finding the right ideas and putting them into practice."[3] Seymour Martin Lipset also suggests a broad definition including among intellectuals

[1] George Lichtheim, "The Role of the Intellectuals," *Commentary* (April, 1960), 295.

[2] Richard Hofstadter, *Anti-intellectualism in American Life* (New York: Alfred A. Knopf, Inc., 1963), p. 7.

[3] Malcolm Cowley, "Who Are the Intellectuals?" *The New Republic* (February 25, 1957), 14.

all those who create, distribute, and apply culture, that is, the symbolic world of man, including art, science, and religion. Within this group there are two main levels: the hard core or creators of culture—scholars, artists, philosophers, authors, some editors and some journalists; and the distributors—performers in the various arts, most teachers, and most reporters. A peripheral group is composed of those who apply culture as a part of their jobs—professionals such as physicians and lawyers.[4]

In the study of power groups in this book, physicians were considered separately from intellectuals and were identified in Chapter 2 as supporters of the classical ideology. Public school teachers were also presented separately, in Chapter 6, because of dramatic problems emerging from their recent militance and swift numerical growth. This chapter deals with other professional elements in the intellectual community, focusing upon those whose occupations involve them most directly in speaking and writing on public policy, i.e., social scientists and journalists.

A fundamental problem relating to intellectuals is whether it is legitimate to classify them as a group, albeit an informal one. The ideal of intellectual diversity is illustrated in William James's oft-quoted commencement address warning that Harvard should never "stamp a single fast and hard type of character upon her children."[5] Many intellectuals tend to guard jealously their self-image as individualistic and autonomous creators and critics. One scholar, commenting on the idea of this chapter, asserted that genuine intellectuals are a small group, who rarely acknowledge any single employer and "have no corporate sense and would die in the attempt to foist one on them."[6] Most of the people referred to as intellectuals by the definitions used in the present chapter are viewed by this critic as merely "brain workers" chained to tasks and ends set by others. At best such intelligentsia are "Machiavellis to princes of industry, finance or public affairs."[7]

A similar distinction between the creator and the expert is discussed by Hofstadter, who notes that when educated people "go into the service of government, business or the universities themselves, they do not suddenly become intellectuals."[8] Hofstadter distinguishes between intelligence as "manipulative, adjustive and practical" and intellect as "critical, creative,

[4] Seymour Martin Lipset, *Political Man: The Social Bases of Politics* (Garden City, N.Y.: Doubleday & Company, Inc., 1960), p. 310.

[5] Nathan M. Pusey, *The Age of the Scholar* (Cambridge, Mass.: Harvard University Press, 1963).

[6] Letter from Paul Tillett to Mark W. Cannon, September 23, 1963.

[7] *Ibid.*

[8] Hofstadter, p. 428. See also Henry A. Kissinger, *The Necessity for Choice: Prospects of American Foreign Policy* (New York: Harper & Row, Publishers, Incorporated, 1961), p. 352.

contemplative."[9] Yet Hofstadter does count a contingent of mental tech-nicians among the intellectuals and hopes that "the intellectual community will not become hopelessly polarized into two parts, one part of technicians concerned only with power and accepting the terms power puts to them, and the other of willfully alienated intellectuals more concerned with main-taining their own sense of purity than with making their ideas effective."[10] He says it will be tragic if hired intellectuals who serve power lose their con-nection with and responsibility to "the intellectual community."[11]

A related problem in the effort to classify intellectuals as a political power group is the implicit objection of some intellectuals that interest groups represent greed, whereas their own political values tend to approxi-mate the public interest. In fact, this altruistic posture is one of the ideologi-cal strengths of their liberal intellectual position, although it is at the same time an irritant to other groups. In reality, the ideology of virtually every power group attempts to identify its positions with the public interest. Those most hostile to the intellectuals, the classical ideologists, insist that they themselves are the greatest defenders of the public interest because, they assert, they are almost alone in helping to preserve individual freedom through their demand for a laissez-faire economy. Yet many intellectuals would contend that the "classical creed" would more appropriately be labeled "classical greed." The title of an article by Fred J. Cook, "The Corrupt Society: A Journalist's Guide to the Profit Ethic" suggests the attitude of many intellectuals toward the business community.[12] Classical ideologists, in return, are likely to assert that many self-righteous intellec-tuals want to assume the role of deity for society through their Olympian prescriptions.

The analysis of intellectuals in this book consequently views them broadly as including creators and critics as well as many of the advisers and mental technicians. It is obvious that the intellectuals do not comprise a cohesive formal organization which operates with the traditional methods of mobilizing money and votes and lobbying to obtain specific political outcomes. It must also be recognized that the positions taken by intellec-tuals range more widely than the requirements of their direct self-interest. Yet this analysis concludes (1) that there is an abundance of evidence demonstrating sufficient political consensus among intellectuals to enable us to classify them as a political community or group, (2) that they have sufficient influence in public policy to be important in the analysis of key

[9] See discussion in Richard Gillman, "The Intellect and Its Enemies," *The New Republic* (July 13, 1963), 19.

[10] Hofstadter, p. 429.

[11] *Ibid.*, p. 430.

[12] *The Nation* (June 1–8, 1963), 453–497.

power groups, and (3) that their ideology is not unrelated to the interests emerging from their position in American society.

CONSENSUS AMONG INTELLECTUALS

Included among intellectuals are thinkers of marked diversity, from Ayn Rand, Russell Kirk, and William F. Buckley on the right to Murray Kempton and Howard Fast on the left. Notwithstanding, intellectuals "develop group attitudes and group interests sufficiently strong to make large numbers of them behave in the way that is usually associated with the concept of social classes."[13]

In referring to the liberal consensus emerging from these shared values, Richard H. Rovere commented that "something like 70% of those whom Mr. Buckley and I could agree to call intellectual would acknowledge support of this common body of doctrine. The percentage might be higher, but 70% seems to me quite enough to make a consensus."[14] Mr. Rovere points out that there does appear to be a concurrence of opinion among intellectuals that permeates their writing, speech, and thought regarding most public questions. S. M. Lipset also recognized a "somewhat left of center" coalescence of much of American intellectual thought.[15] Hofstadter agrees that "if there is anything that could be called an intellectual establishment in America, this establishment has been, though not profoundly radical (which would be unbecoming in an establishment), on the left side of center."

This left-of-center position appears to differ from that of the nation as a whole. With the growth of conservatism since World War II, more Americans have come to adopt the label of "conservative" than that of "liberal." A poll by Lou Harris showed that 24 per cent of the voters classify themselves as liberal, 34 per cent conservative, and 42 per cent as middle of the road.[16]

The leftward proclivity of intellectuals stems from a traditional desire anciently expressed by Omar Khayyám to break "this sorry scheme of things entire . . . and then remold it nearer to the heart's desire." Since government is viewed as the fastest and most powerful instrument to alter contemporary society, intellectuals favor a strong positive role for government. With the desired extent and role of government being a primary measuring rod of their position in the political spectrum, the intellectuals' support for energetic government is a factor in placing them on the left.

[13] Joseph A. Schumpeter, *Capitalism, Socialism, and Democracy*, 3d ed. (New York: Harper & Row, Publishers, Incorporated, 1950), p. 146.

[14] Richard H. Rovere, "Shall We Let Buckley into the Establishment?" *Harper's Magazine*, 225 (September, 1962), 40.

[15] Lipset, p. 39.   [16] *Deseret News* (November 18, 1963).

The advent of the Great Depression of the 1930s shifted the concern of most intellectuals (particularly the economists, political scientists, and other social scientists—the most politically articulate of the intellectuals) toward the problem of full employment. This area of basic domestic concern has continued and widened to emphasize such problems as economic growth. The conservatives of the 1930s had no dramatic program to solve unemployment. Furthermore, the conservative position of isolationism coupled with the Republican protectionistic trade policies (e.g., economists sought unsuccessfully in the early 1930s to have Hoover veto the Smoot-Hawley Tariff, the highest tariff ever passed in the United States) alienated most intellectuals from the conservative and Republican positions.

Pro-New Deal sentiments in Chicago in 1937 were found among a remarkable 84 per cent of the social science professors and 65 per cent of natural science professors, compared to 54 per cent among manual workers, 17 per cent among lawyers and physicians, and 28 per cent among engineers.[17]

Two decades later a sampling of more than 2,400 social scientists revealed that nearly twice as many voted for Stevenson as for Eisenhower in 1952, a year when the great political appeal of Eisenhower drew almost half the manual workers and trade unions into casting Republican ballots.[18] Even more dramatic, this 1955 survey of social scientists teaching in colleges revealed that of the two-thirds who classified themselves with a major party, the division was three to one for the Democrats even though their parents, of high socioeconomic status, should have produced overwhelmingly Republican progeny.

As Clinton Rossiter commented, "Even a casual survey of departments of English, history, sociology, physics, or mathematics at almost any college in the country would reveal a similar pattern, and anti-Republican urge would be even stronger among painters, poets, dramatists, musicians, entertainers, and others engaged in esthetic or intellectual pursuits."[19]

Since political scientists would appear to have greater opportunities to communicate their political values in the classroom than have the members of any other single discipline, it is highly significant that a recent study of a sample of 213 political scientists identifies 73.7 per cent as Democratic compared with only 16.4 per cent Republican. (Others were 8 per cent Independent, 1.4 per cent Socialist, and 0.5 per cent Liberal.)[20] Regarding

[17] Arthur Kornhauser, "Attitudes of Economic Groups," *Public Opinion Quarterly,* 2 (April, 1938), 264.

[18] P. F. Lazarsfeld and Wagner Thielens, Jr., *The Academic Mind: Social Scientists in a Time of Crisis* (New York: The Free Press of Glencoe, 1958), p. 14.

[19] Clinton Rossiter, *Parties and Politics in America* (Ithaca, N.Y.: Cornell University Press, 1960), p. 103.

[20] Henry A. Turner, Charles G. McClintock, and Charles B. Spaulding, "The Political Party Affiliation of American Political Scientists," *Western Political Quarterly,* 16 (September, 1963), 652.

this preponderant orientation toward the Democratic party, the investi
gators concluded:

> Moreover, this alignment with that party cannot be attributed to the per
> sistence of family influence. Instead, it appears to represent largely consciou
> choices based on evaluations of the policies and leadership of the party and or
> information and attitudes gained in the political science profession.[21]

The evidence in individual universities generally substantiates thes
more collective studies. Alex Gottfried, in a study he made of facult
members of a large Western university, concluded that there was a hig
degree of identification of academic voters with the prototype of "egghead,"
with Stevenson having received a ratio of eight financial contributions from
faculty members for every one received by Eisenhower in 1956.[22] Gott
fried also found from the research that the largest group of faculty mem
bers identified themselves as Democrats, while the next highest group
called themselves Independents. The Republicans were last in both the
1956 and 1960 polls.[23]

Robert Yee in a survey of three colleges in Washington state dis
covered that two-thirds of the faculty members associated themselves with
one of the two major political parties, with Democratic party identifier
outnumbering Republican party identifiers by a ratio of two to one.[24]

Harvard professors were thought to have supported John F. Kennedy
over Richard M. Nixon in 1960 by as much as 75 per cent.[25] Yet the
reputed liberalism of the Harvard faculty has not been uniform. For
example, in 1952 a postcard poll of Harvard faculty members suggested
that Eisenhower was their favorite over Stevenson by a 379:298 ratio
This was not the case among social scientists. The business and medica
school faculties provided the main Eisenhower strength. The law schoo
faculty favored Stevenson at about a 2:1 rate.[26] By 1956 at Harvard there
had been a net shift in favor of Stevenson and some Eisenhower supporter
were insufficiently enthusiastic to respond. Thus a postcard faculty pol
showed Stevenson the favorite, 243:145.[27]

Journalists also, while maintaining a posture of independence, tend to
be liberal. As Rossiter concluded, "The journals of America may be owned
by Republicans, but they are largely written by Democrats."[28] This di-

[21] *Ibid.*, 665.
[22] Alex Gottfried, "Political Attitudes and Behavior of a University Faculty,"
Western Political Quarterly, 14 (September, 1961), 45.
[23] *Ibid.*
[24] Robert Yee, "Faculty Participation in the 1960 Presidential Election," *Western Political Quarterly*, 16 (March, 1963), 219.
[25] Letter from Joseph M. Russin, President, *Harvard Crimson*, to Mark W.
Cannon, August 15, 1963.
[26] *Ibid.*, referring to *Harvard Crimson* (November 3, 1952).
[27] *Ibid.*, referring to *Harvard Crimson* (November 3, 6, 1956).
[28] Rossiter, p. 103.

chotomy between the newspaper owners and the working press was suggested by comments of the press secretaries to the 1960 presidential candidates. Pierre Salinger asserted that only 16.4 per cent of the newspapers with only 15.8 per cent of the circulation gave editorial support to Kennedy. These figures were prepared by *Editor & Publisher,* which reported that 57.7 per cent of American dailies with 70.9 per cent of the circulation were editorially for Nixon.[29] Herbert Klein, the Nixon aide, however, contended that "most of the reporters who covered the presidential candidates appeared to favor Kennedy" and "most columnists supported Kennedy."[30] Klein questioned whether interpretive reporting had gone too far.

Even editorially the press supported the Democratic presidential campaign in 1964. A *New York Herald Tribune* survey, something more than a month before the general election, indicated that editorial endorsements had gone to Johnson over Goldwater in a ratio of 6 to 2.

Kruglac's analysis of foreign correspondents identifies them as favoring Stevenson over Eisenhower in a survey made in 1955 by 59 per cent to 36 per cent with 6 per cent undecided.[31] Because of the desire for a change, the foreign correspondents had favored Eisenhower in 1952 by 55.8 per cent to 41.7 per cent with 2.5 per cent undecided. Partly because of their conclusion that Eisenhower "could not control the Republican Party," these correspondents switched strongly to Stevenson as noted above.[32]

The Democratic proclivities of the intellectuals contrast markedly with Republican tendencies of other college-educated people—many of whom are in professional and managerial occupations and who tend to vote Republican. One of the most marked dichotomies among the college-educated was the 1948 presidential election. Only 8 per cent of the Truman voters were college-educated, whereas 43 per cent of the Dewey voters were college-educated. Yet by contrast the foreign correspondents favored Truman by 55.7 per cent to only 29.9 per cent for Dewey with 15 per cent undecided. Supporters of Progressive party candidate Henry Wallace amounted to only 1.3 per cent, suggesting that the leftward tendency rarely reaches radical proportions. Similarly, the social scientists who voted divided almost 66 per cent for Truman, less than 30 per cent for Dewey, less than 5 per cent for Wallace, and a mere 0.6 per cent for Dixiecrat candidate Strom Thurmond.

Thus, diversity among the intellectuals is acknowledged, and the need

29 Robert E. Blackmon, "Bias in the 1960 Presidential Election Campaign," *Nieman Reports* (October, 1961), 20, 22.

30 *The New York Times* (December 3, 1960).

31 Theodore Edward Kruglac, *The Foreign Correspondents* (Geneva: Librarie E. Droz, 1955), p. 88.

32 *Ibid.,* p. 89.

for more data is recognized. Yet, the mounting evidence of a left-of-center political consensus among a great majority of an opinion-forming elite group of artists, journalists, and academicians, especially social scientists, demands that intellectuals be analyzed among "the makers of public policy." The next question which must be considered is "How do intellectuals influence public policy?"

INFLUENCE OF INTELLECTUALS

The first key to understanding the influence of the intellectuals is recognition of their current rapid numerical growth. This is most dramatically demonstrated by the growth in academicians—currently the fastest growing of any of the groups considered in this book. College faculties may triple in size between 1940 at 146,900 and 1970, estimated at between 400,000[33] and 450,000.[34]

Although academicians are not a wealthy class, they have gained increasing power, as against boards of trustees, over the use of wealth through greater control over policies in the use of college facilities and policies over the hiring and promoting of personnel in the colleges. Other controls over wealth include assistance in management-channeled budgets of vast tax-exempt foundations, and partial control over the still relatively small, but growing, educational television systems. To give just a hint of the money being invested in higher education, estimates on the amount of money which must be spent for new buildings alone during the 1960s have varied from $16.3 billion to former President Kennedy's estimate of $22.9 billion.[35] An illustration of academic power over the use of these facilities was the Yale faculty's successful pressure against permitting segregationist Alabama Governor George C. Wallace to speak at Yale in one instance in 1963.

The significance of intellectuals in America is suggested by some comparisons. It is estimated "that during the past twenty years the United States has done something like 80 per cent of the science and scholarship of the entire Western world."[36] It is similarly estimated that "more than

---

[33] Homer D. Babbidge, "Staffing the Nation's Colleges and Universities: Some Perspectives," *AAUP Bulletin,* 47 (autumn, 1961), 212.

[34] Robert D. Calkins, "Government Support of Higher Education," in Dexter M. Keezer (ed.), *Financing Higher Education: 1960–70* (New York: McGraw-Hill Book Company, 1959), chart opposite p. 184.

[35] *Statement of Roger A. Freeman before Subcommittee on Education of the Committee on Labor and Public Welfare,* U.S. Senate, May 27, 1963, pp. 17–18.

[36] Sir Charles Snow, "On Magnanimity," *Harper's Magazine,* 225 (July, 1962), 40.

80% of the world's political scientists are in this country."[37] Put in another way, there are more than 2,000 colleges and universities in the United States[38] compared with about fifteen in Great Britain, one in Norway, and one in Sweden. The paradox is that only a successful and advanced capitalist nation can afford so many intellectuals—who in turn have an interest in "social unrest."[39] Thus capitalist civilization "creates, educates and subsidizes" a group which, according to Schumpeter, may dig capitalism's grave.[40]

The size of the growing academic community suggests a major source of the influence of the intellectuals—the communication of their values to the leading elements of the oncoming generation through lectures and books. Lazarsfeld and Thielens discovered that "in each age group, the proportion of Democratic voters is greater, the higher the professional eminence of the respondent."[41] The future college teachers are those most heavily exposed to liberal values.

Since the bulk of new Ph.D.s is produced by a score of eminent universities containing a high share of the most productive scholars, the oncoming generation of academicians is evidently taught by the most preponderantly Democratic group of scholars.

While the proportion of responsibility of the faculty cannot yet be precisely assigned, studies indicate that students tend to become liberalized while they are in college. Jacob, in one of the few studies which failed to show significant changes, still recognized that there are a few "potent" colleges for producing changes in values.[42] Other studies have been more dramatic. Newcomb, in a study of Bennington College, published in 1943, found significant change from conservatism to nonconservatism between freshman and senior years.[43] Sanford also concludes that "between the freshman and the senior year in college there is, in general, change in the direction of greater liberalism and sophistication in political, social, and religious outlook."[44]

Directly pertinent to the type of political liberalization is an increased

[37] Ralph J. Bunche, "Presidential Address," *American Political Science Review,* 48 (December, 1954), 962.

[38] Babbidge.

[39] Schumpeter.

[40] *Ibid.*

[41] Lazarsfeld and Thielens, p. 16.

[42] Walter T. Plant, *Personality Changes Associated with a College Education,* (Washington: U.S. Office of Education, 1962), p. 5, referring to P. E. Jacob, *Changing Values in College* (New York: Harper & Row, Publishers, Incorporated, 1957), p. 5. For a criticism, see David Riesman, "The 'Jacob Report,'" *American Sociological Review,* 23 (October, 1958), 732–738.

[43] Theodore M. Newcomb, *Personality and Social Change* (New York: The Dryden Press, Inc., 1943), pp. 171–174.

[44] Nevitt Sanford, *The American College* (New York: John Wiley & Sons, 1962), p. 806.

preference for the use of government to solve social problems. A study of National Merit Scholars showed liberalization during college. On the question "Should the government provide medical and dental care for citizens who cannot afford such services?" favorable responses increased from the end of the freshman year to the end of the junior year. For Merit Scholars in the humanities and mathematics the approval vote increased from approximately 54 to 69 per cent. By contrast, the approval vote among Merit Scholars in engineering dropped from 56 to 47 per cent. Partywise, the Merit Scholars divided at the beginning 30 per cent Republican, 17 per cent Democratic, and 50 per cent Independent. After two years the humanities majors reduced their Republican vote considerably. For men, the change was mostly to Democratic; for women, to Independent.[45] Many mathematics majors also shifted from Republican to Independent. The study also showed a substantial decline from about 89 to 60 per cent in the proportion who felt a need to believe in a religious faith,[46] which often correlates with political conservatism.

Polls of students at Harvard regularly display a net migration toward the Democratic party as they move from their freshman to their senior years. In 1952 Harvard College (the undergraduates) preferred Stevenson over Eisenhower 1,223 to 1,202, yet the freshman class strongly favored Eisenhower 335 to 209. (Business school students similarly favored Eisenhower 240 to 73.)[47] This was, incidentally, the first Democratic victory at Harvard College since Wilson won a minority plurality over Taft and Roosevelt in 1912. Similarly in 1956, upperclassmen gave Stevenson the nod by 75 votes, yet Republican strength in the freshman class was enough to turn the tide, putting Eisenhower ahead in the college 1,368 to 1,338.[48]

In 1960 the undergraduates at Harvard College gave an overwhelming victory for Kennedy over Nixon, 1,953 to 1,186.[49] Even the freshmen were Democrats, 482 to 310. Yet the liberalization pattern prevailed, with seniors giving Kennedy his strongest support.

There is no conclusive proof that Democratic professors are responsible for the liberalization of college students. In fact an interesting comparison by Walter T. Plant has been made between college-aspiring young people who did and who did not attend college. He found that both groups decreased in ethnocentrism, authoritarianism, and dogmatism, but in different amounts. He concluded, consequently, that the collegiate experience

---

[45] Harold Webster, Mervin Freedman, and Paul Heist, "Personality Changes in College Students," in Nevitt Sanford, *The American College* (New York: John Wiley & Sons, 1962), p. 827.

[46] *Ibid.*, p. 826.

[47] Russin, referring to *Harvard Crimson* (October 31, 1952).

[48] *Ibid.* (October 26, 1956).

[49] *Ibid.* (October 27, 1960).

facilitated changes already underway in college-aspiring youth.[50] It would be interesting to have a similar study comparing the changes in political ideology between college and non-college attenders. However, the evidence which is available that college students become more politically liberalized and that many of them attribute the change to their texts and professors (as is shown in the following surveys) enables us to conclude that the influencing of students' political values is one of the means by which intellectuals affect the policy-making process.

Samuel Lubell, in a 1960 survey of students on 33 campuses, concluded that the influence of the New Deal professors and the emotional magnetism for President Kennedy effectively resisted the so-called "conservative revival" among the college students. He found a net shift of students from the Republican to the Democratic party. Among students who changed parties from those of their parents, one out of six with Republican parents shifted to the Democrats, while one in ten students from Democratic homes changed to Republicanism.[51] Lubell reported that "nearly a third of the students shifting from Republican leanings gave as one reason for the change the fact that 'our professors are Democrats.' "[52]

A survey of twelve colleges conducted by Educational Reviewer, Inc., Russell Kirk, president, showed that nearly 70 per cent of the students interviewed reported significant changes in their political beliefs since entering college. In all but two of the twelve colleges considered, the change had been toward a liberalization of politics. "Lectures and/or assigned reading courses" were listed by two-fifths of the students as the primary agent for their change. "Personal contact with the faculty" was listed by 10 per cent as one of the major influences.[53]

The fact that there is not a more monumental political liberalization should be credited to the efforts of many academicians to eliminate or minimize the advocacy of personal values; the existence of a degree of conflict and cross currents rather than a united front, especially on details, and the heavy weight of such external pressures upon the students as family tradition and, to a degree, occupational expectation. The vast and growing college audience, a segment of which is affected by the professors, is conservatively estimated to reach 6,312,000 by 1970.[54]

Not only are values presented in the lectures, texts, and other books written by intellectuals, but the value judgments of journalists also sometimes became intermingled with the reporting of the facts. Nixon was not

---

[50] Plant, pp. 71, 74.

[51] Samuel Lubell, United Feature Syndicate, Inc., New York, June 17, 1962.

[52] *Ibid.*

[53] "A Survey of the Political and Religious Attitudes of American College Students," *National Review,* 15 (October 8, 1963), 281.

[54] Freeman, p. 15.

alone in attributing part of his loss of the Presidency in 1960 to the favorable treatment given Kennedy by the working press. The vinegary *New York Daily News* asserted that 75 per cent or more of the reporters assigned to cover Nixon's campaign were Democrats. The *News* added:

> They slanted their dispatches against the Republican candidate. They left out incidents and sidelights which might have been helpful to him. They frequently underreported the size and enthusiasm of the crowds that gathered to hear him speak.
>
> In campaign press conferences with Nixon himself, some of these crooked crusaders for Sen. John F. Kennedy insulted and badgered Nixon instead of asking him honest and pertinent questions.[55]

After losing the California governorship in 1962, Nixon cried in anguish that the reporters should have given his "opponent the same going over" that they gave him.[56] Recognizing that most candidates feel they have not received fair and adequate treatment by the press, Nixon still probably had some legitimacy to his assertions. The reporters who were against him may well have outweighed the less frequently read editorials in his favor. As Douglass Cater noted, "There are many moments in a reporter's work-day when he silently accepts the fact that the formulation of news is not exactly a scientific process foreign to the reporter's thoughts, feelings and ambitions."[57]

Journalists are also cited by congressmen, and their statements are placed in the *Congressional Record*. Suggestive of the proximity of views of Walter Lippmann, for example, to the Kennedy administration was the fact that partial data from 1961 indicate that Democrats inserted approximately 89 per cent of the Lippman columns which were placed in the *Congressional Record*.[58]

In addition to shaping public attitudes on governmental questions, intellectuals affect government even more directly in advisory capacities and through training those who obtain responsible positions in government. This process takes place in both administrations, but to a lesser degree in Republican than Democratic administrations. V. O. Key, in a presidential address to the American Political Science Association, argued that academicians seldom realize the impact they have on government. He pointed out that "many well settled governmental practices were but a few decades ago regarded as impractical schemes emanating from the ivory tower."[59]

---

[55] Blackmon, 20, citing *New York Daily News* editorial (November 14, 1960).

[56] *The New York Times* (November 8, 1962).

[57] Douglass Cater, *The Fourth Branch of Government* (Boston: Houghton Mifflin Company, 1959), p. 16.

[58] Eugene J. Webb, "To Tell a Columnist," *Columbia Journalism Review* (winter, 1963), 20.

[59] V. O. Key, Jr., "The State of the Discipline," *American Political Science Review*, 52 (December, 1958), 962.

It is noteworthy that almost half (17 of 35) of President Kennedy's top appointees had taught previously on a college level.[60] Kissinger noted that intellectuals with reputations are now called upon for help so frequently that they become as harassed as the policy makers and may lose their creativity and ability to supply perspective.[61]

The close association between influential civil servants and academicians is illustrated by an organization such as the American Society for Public Administration. The organization normally alternates its presidency between top government administrators and professors. Approximately two-thirds of the 6,326 members are practitioners, and one-third are academicians.[62] Many members fill both these roles in their lives. Some time ago, Pendleton Herring noted that nearly one-half of the American Political Science Association members were not employed by universities,[63] and subsequently V. O. Key indicated that possibly one-third of the Ph.D.s and more than one-half of the Master's degree holders go into government service.[64]

In the jubilee presidential address at the American Political Science Association, Ralph J. Bunche noted "the considerable and encouraging traffic between campus and bureaucracy."[65] He also commented:

No doubt our most distinguished past president, Woodrow Wilson, were he with us, would be highly gratified by the increasing extent to which members of the profession, particularly in the past two decades, have emerged from the academic realm to render invaluable assistance to governments—local, state, and national—and to international organizations and agencies.[66]

Economists are also playing a major role in government. Edwin E. Witte pointed out in a presidential address to the American Economic Association:

More economists today spend part of their active careers in government service than ever before. It is becoming commonplace that economists are in and out of government service several times during their lives and quite a number are working simultaneously for the government and in academic teaching or in research positions.

Thousands of economists are employed in government. A former president of the American Economic Association is a distinguished U.S. Senator. A few

---

[60] Joseph Kraft, "Kennedy and the Intellectuals," *Harper's Magazine* (November, 1963), 112–116.

[61] Henry A. Kissinger, "The Policymaker and the Intellectual," *The Reporter* (March 5, 1959), 33.

[62] The membership figure is current as of September 30, 1963. Letter from Mrs. Janice Bowen, Administrative Assistant, American Society for Public Administration, December 19, 1963.

[63] Pendleton Herring, "On the Study of Government" (Presidential Address), *American Political Science Review*, 47 (December, 1953), 971.

[64] Key.　　　　　　　　　　　　　　　　[66] *Ibid.*, 963.

[65] Bunche, 966.

other members of the Congress hold membership in the Association. The Council of Economic Advisers is constituted of economists. Other economists are bureau chiefs and a somewhat larger number have held such positions. Thousands of economists are civil service employees of the national, state and local governments.[67]

In spite of all this involvement in government, Witte feels the principal influence of economists in public policy is ultimately through their roles as scholarly writers and teachers. Witte recognized, as did Kissinger and others, that the intellectual advisers are primarily problem solvers rather than decision makers in government, yet this distinction should not obscure the fact that the interplay of ideas proffered by the advisers often does affect basic policy decisions.

While primary sources of the intellectuals' political influence have been noted in terms of their roles as teachers, writers, and advisers, the additional role of political campaigner should not be overlooked. A substantial share of political scientists have run for office, and the fact that Republicans are a small minority has not curbed their political activity. Those who had run for office comprised 28.5 per cent of the Republican political scientists and 14.6 per cent of the Democrats.[68] The fact that nearly twice as many Republicans as Democrats had run for office may result partly from the fact that the Republicans generally are older than the Democrats. Compared with other occupational groups, a high share of political scientists had participated actively in political campaigns, comprising 60.5 per cent of the Democrats and 51.5 per cent of the Republicans.[69]

The fact that Adlai Stevenson twice received the Democratic nomination for President, in 1952 and 1956, and was pushed so hard for the vice presidential nomination in 1964 was partly attributable to his strong support among the intellectuals.[70]

It could be argued that there is such a strong anti-intellectual current in America as to prevent intellectuals from exercising any real power. It is true that there is an anti-intellectual current, only mildly symbolized by a joke told by President Eisenhower, wherein he defined an intellectual as "a man who takes more words than are necessary to tell more than he knows."[71] Eisenhower's Secretary of Defense, Charles E. Wilson, described an egghead as "a man who doesn't understand everything he knows."[72]

One explanation of this anti-intellectualism was in terms of the gulf resulting from the intellectuals' inability to divest themselves of the Euro-

---

[67] Edwin E. Witte, "Economics and Public Policy," *American Economic Review,* 47 (March, 1957), 2–3.

[68] Turner et al., 659.   [71] Hofstadter, p. 10.

[69] *Ibid.*   [72] *Ibid.*

[70] Cowley, 15.

pean aura and the European's dislike for things American, e.g., super-markets, organizations, and public relations; along with their lack of self-criticism.[73]

Hofstadter presents a significant conclusion that contemporary resentment against the intellectual is a manifestation not of a decline in his position but of his increasing prominence.[74] The orbiting of the first Russian satellite "highlighted the difference between ignorance and knowledge" and made the stock of the intellectual soar.[75]

> Once the intellectual was not needed; now he is fiercely resented because he is needed too much. He has become all too practical, all too effective. He is the object of resentment because of an improvement, not a decline, in his fortunes. It is not his abstractness, futility, or helplessness that makes him prominent enough to inspire virulent attacks, but his achievements, his influence, his real comfort and imagined luxury, as well as the dependence of the community upon his skills. Intellect is resented as a form of power or privilege.[76]

Thus, anti-intellectualism in America today does not mean that intellectuals are weak. It means they are strong—and must be studied among power groups.

CAUSES OF INTELLECTUALS' LEFT-OF-CENTER IDEOLOGY

There are several traits that seem to be held in common by the majority of intellectuals in this country. Although the financial prospects of academicians are improving, those who have joined the intellectual professions, such as teaching, during the past quarter century have known they were much less likely to become wealthy than their contemporaries, in business particularly. In fact, the real purchasing power of the college teachers' take-home pay declined 5 per cent between 1940 and 1954.[77] (Academicians were virtually the only group to suffer such a decline.)

The educators' enthusiasm for American capitalism is not intensified by the fact that the average professor earns less than twice what the average worker earns in the United States, while Soviet professors' earnings are eight times as much as those of Soviet workers.[78]

[73] Michael Novak, "The Brain Curtain: Why America Distrusts Its Intellectuals," *The Nation* (December 10, 1960), 457.

[74] Hofstadter, p. 6.

[75] Helen C. White, "The Association in 1958," *AAUP Bulletin* (April 25, 1958), 394.

[76] Hofstadter, p. 34.

[77] Dexter M. Keezer (ed.), *Financing Higher Education, 1960–1970* (New York: McGraw-Hill Book Company, 1959), p. 10.

[78] *Ibid.*, p. 11.

During the period that faculty purchasing power declined 5 per cent, physicians' purchasing power increased 80 per cent (partly because prosperity enabled patients to pay their doctor bills). These contrasting economic shifts explain the jealousy which sometimes is exhibited by teachers toward doctors. The teachers believe their work with the human mind is no less, and probably more, worthy of reward than doctors' assistance to the human body. Supply and demand, however, has come to the rescue of the professors. Increased demand for their services, induced particularly by the arrival of the wave of war babies in the colleges, has moved salaries up at an accelerated pace. Yet a doubling of the average college teacher's salary between 1960 and 1970, which is not impossible, would still not quite give the academician the relative salary position he held in 1940.

The intellectual has had to be more idealistically inclined and less business-oriented to choose the profession he entered. In a society where income is used commonly as a yardstick of success, this disparity creates considerable strain on the individual who has renounced such an objective measure of his success. American society is a highly "success"-oriented culture, and this makes the problem all the more difficult for those in intellectual professions.

It appears that the majority of American intellectuals (as well as most members of our society generally, though on perhaps a lower level) espouse the ideal of equality. The very strength with which this egalitarian principle is held in our society may well cause some of the frustration that American intellectuals feel. For with a much milder class system than that found in Europe, intellectuals here cannot retreat either ideologically or socially to the protection of a European (say German) type of class structure which automatically declares that they are superior or successful. Interestingly enough, the classless-society ideology of communism does not necessarily eliminate the elitist concepts of the European intellectual, as is shown by a study of Polish college students.[79]

By espousing the creed of equality, intellectuals cut off another route to "success." At least, intellectuals in this country (according to Lipset) feel that they hold much less "status" than what surveys among other groups in the society actually attribute to the intellectuals. Thus intellectuals in America have had a strong feeling that they failed to receive adequate "recognition."[80] Regardless of the fact that studies among the rest of society seem to hold intellectual professions at generally very high levels of status, the view the intellectual holds of his social status appears to be considerably different.

While, as Lipset has noted,

[79] Stefan Nowak, "Egalitarian Attitudes of Warsaw Students," *American Sociological Review,* 25 (April, 1960), 219–231.
[80] Witte, 1.

. . . much of the self-deprecating image which the American intellectual projects to justify his feelings of alienation from his society turns out to be invalid, there have been strong anti-intellectual tendencies in this country; and these further account for the historic lack of a sizable group of politically conservative intellectuals.[81]

The current ultraconservative attacks against intellectuals by groups such as the John Birch Society, and, a decade earlier, by McCarthyism, point out a fundamental antagonism existing between the far right and the intellectuals. Even intellectual conservatives such as William Buckley have attacked Robert Welch, head of the John Birch Society. Whether these rightist movements are merely continuing ripples of a Populist wave of half a century ago or not, they help explain the absence of a large politically conservative intellectual group.

The preceding discussion may help to explain another characteristic of American intellectuals, which until recently has been bothersome to them— that is, their general feeling of alienation from contemporary society. Their role as critics developed a fear of lack of respect and success within the society. This was somewhat demonstrated by Lazarsfeld and Thielens's interpretation of the teachers' preference for the Democratic party as a sign of "occupational protest."[82] These investigators found that a higher share of Democratic professors felt dissatisfied with their professional "image" than did businessmen, congressmen, and university trustees. Democratic social scientists stated teachers have a higher occupational inferiority feeling than other groups and "are consistently more inclined to think that nobody loves the professor!"[83]

Interestingly enough, the most permissive professors were the most highly Democratic (91 per cent in 1952) and also they ranked highest in reading three liberal journals, *The Reporter, The New Republic,* and *The Nation,* and were most prone to join "controversial" political groups.[84]

Yet, as previously indicated, the intellectuals are now in a new era of widespread recognition of their importance. Even though this does continue to foster resentment, it may also reduce the intellectuals' sense of alienation. In fact, there is a real question as to how the intellectuals will change as a result of their new-founded success and recognition. Hofstadter says that the intellectuals' real fear is that they will become conformists since their tie with American society has become so close.[85]

The "rich and powerful" now make a place for the intellectual; the abstract painter today finds his paintings in demand. Beatniks on the university campus are also "in demand . . . where they are received as entertainers and

[81] Lipset, p. 336.

[82] Lazarsfeld and Thielens, p. 131.

[83] *Ibid.,* pp. 14–15.

[84] *Ibid.,* p. 132.

[85] Hofstadter, p. 393.

turned into esoteric comedians of the sophisticated."[86] Authors of social criticism like C. Wright Mills, Vance Packard, David Riesman, and William H. Whyte are now among the most widely read and popular writers in the field.

All told, then, the intellectual in a modern technical democratic and affluent society will undoubtedly continue to play an important role in forging public policy, a role that, it would appear, will continue to grow in importance.

From the discussion of the previous section, a majority consensus among the intellectuals does appear to exist which exerts considerable power upon the shaping of public policy even if only on an informal level. The following section considers some of the general contours of the intellectual consensus.

THE IDEOLOGY OF THE AMERICAN INTELLECTUALS

The authors agree with Richard Rovere: "A quick and by-and-large accurate way of stating it [an intellectual consensus] could be to say that the consensus was embodied in the declared aims of the Kennedy Administration."[87] Although President Kennedy achieved only partial legislative success before he became the victim of an assassin's bullet, a selection of his statements and policy positions continues to be highly interesting as a summary (though necessarily an imprecise one) of the intellectual consensus during the peak of their power.[88] Kennedy's representation of an intellectual consensus was comparable to the earlier expression of the writings and platforms of Adlai Stevenson.

Important Role for Intellectuals

One reason why a selection of the expressed aims of John F. Kennedy can depict the general contours of the intellectuals' ideology is that Kennedy's statements were to a great degree developed and written by the distinguished group of intellectuals who advised him. In fact, Kennedy's providing an important political role for these intellectuals was the first point of shared ideology.

During Kennedy's campaign for the Presidency in 1960, the *Wall Street Journal* noted in an article on "Kennedy's Brain-trust" that:

[86] *Ibid.,* p. 418.

[87] Rovere.

[88] Kennedy speeches which are not cited can be found by date in *The Speeches of Senator John F. Kennedy, Presidential Campaign of 1960* (Washington: Government Printing Office, 1961).

No politician in American history, not even Franklin D. Roosevelt, can match Senator Kennedy in the sheer size of his brain-trust. For campaign purposes, the professors will help prepare position papers on one hundred and twenty separate subjects. The number of professors involved in this question, directly or indirectly, could easily exceed one hundred. The universities represented range from Harvard to Rutgers to Michigan to California.[89]

Joseph Kraft suggests that Kennedy attempted to establish rapport with the "egghead reformers of the Democratic Party."[90] He suggests that the Kennedy administration "made of culture a form of patronage" in an attempt to woo the Democratic intellectuals away from the image of Adlai Stevenson—still their "principal hero."

President Kennedy's hiring of intellectuals was reinforced by his statements about their role. At an Amherst College convocation, he lauded the criticism of artists because "power corrupts and poetry cleans."[91] He declared that artists strengthened the nation by aiding self-comprehension.

Many intellectuals similarly believe that they are of crucial importance to progress since they comprise the "stratum which incorporates the main evolutionary tendency."[92] Social development will increasingly depend on "the capacity of the intellect to introduce order into the environment."[93] Gerald W. Johnson believed that the return of men with ideas to the national administration under Kennedy was so significant it would restore American prestige.[94] Arthur Schlesinger, Jr., showed the necessity in policy making of the intellectual ideology in a response to anti-intellectual moves in some Democratic areas. "A party which seeks to qualify itself for responsibility in an age of national and international crisis is not well advised to begin to do so by blowing out its own brains."[95]

Positive Role of Government

Social scientists, deeply aware of the growing complexity of society, are likely to point out at their conventions the increasing Federal role in the problem areas they are studying in this "age of the service state."[96] Spencer Parrott, for example, at an American Society for Public Administration convention, asserted that "the people who are doing the most for metropolitan

[89] *Wall Street Journal* (August 4, 1960).

[90] Kraft, 113.

[91] *Provo Herald* (October 27, 1963).

[92] Lichtheim, 304.

[93] *Ibid.*

[94] Gerald W. Johnson, "Return Flight," *The New Republic* (January 30, 1961), 10.

[95] Arthur M. Schlesinger, Jr., "Death Wish of the Democrats," *The New Republic* (September 15, 1958), 8.

[96] Witte, 7.

planning today are sitting in Washington." He also noted that the Federal government "may be in it a lot deeper before long."[97] Intellectuals generally supported the theme of a vigorous administration and Presidency, which ran as a persistent thread throughout all of John F. Kennedy's campaigning for the Presidency in 1960. Kennedy's acceptance and support of Richard Neustadt's thesis of the necessity for a strong President is well known, and Lyndon Johnson's personality made him even more capable of utilizing the techniques of strength than his predecessor. Neustadt believes that the office of the Presidency has great potential power that Eisenhower failed to utilize. He feels that the President must personally make decisions on the basis of alternatives presented to him, not merely acquiesce to compromises among his lieutenants. The President also must take the vigorous and dramatic steps necessary to see that his decisions are implemented. Neustadt served in advisory capacities to President Kennedy.

The posture of power and vigor presented by John F. Kennedy, undoubtedly influenced by the intellectuals themselves, was very appealing to a group intrinsically desiring to make changes and remold society—particularly in such areas as eliminating racial discrimination. At times intellectuals criticized him for considering the political elements of issues too strongly. Yet his posture in terms of action, as well as his public statements, often came close to the demands of his intellectual critics. Interestingly, Lyndon Johnson is generally viewed as a stronger President than his predecessor, yet intellectuals have been slow to elevate Johnson to hero stature because his personality background and former associations (e.g., oil interests, the South) make him less personally attractive than Harvard overseer John F. Kennedy.

In fact there was a resignation of such key intellectual advisers as Arthur Schlesinger, Jr., John Kenneth Galbraith, and Ted Sorenson after Lyndon Johnson became President. In a speech to the National Committee on Pockets of Poverty, Galbraith expressed doubt about the possibility of accomplishing significant changes by continued working in government.

To those who feel they can best serve by endowing the scene with their presence rather than pursuing their convictions, let me simply say that I agree it is a good life. But also a bit like being one of the warriors in the Washington parks. "The posture is heroic, the sword is being waved, but alas, movement is nil."[98]

It is perhaps illustrative of Johnson's style that he got along well with less idealistic intellectuals of the tough-minded variety such as McGeorge Bundy.

[97] *The New York Times* (March 26, 1958).
[98] *Time* (December 20, 1963).

Budget and Fiscal Policy

President Kennedy, in his first message to Congress on budget and fiscal policy (March 24, 1961), noted that the country could afford to do what must be done, publicly and privately, and further that the country had not approached the limits of its economic capacity. This line of reasoning is similar to John K. Galbraith's thesis in *The Affluent Society* that the country is privately rich but publicly poor. It should be noted that Galbraith, once his tutor at Harvard, was an important adviser to President Kennedy. Second, Kennedy mentioned a thesis which was almost identical with that proposed by the CED, that the budget be balanced over the business cycle. However, he did note the exception of national security needs. Third, Kennedy argued that it was the government's responsibility to aid and contribute to economic growth and maximum employment, thus outlining a policy not vigorously pursued by the Eisenhower administration. Fourth, while he noted that the economy should not spend money wastefully, nonetheless Kennedy emphasized that the government would not deny its people essential services or security. This was a somewhat different philosophy from that found in the Eisenhower administration and one more in keeping with the general intellectual consensus. Kennedy further warned and predicted that Federal nondefense expenditures can be expected to grow. The influence of Galbraith, Samuelson, and Harris, to name only a few academic economists advising Kennedy, can readily be seen in these statements.

While some intellectuals criticized President Kennedy for being less vigorous in subsequent actions than his policy pronouncements indicated, by 1963 Kennedy proposed a $98.8 billion budget for the fiscal year 1964, which topped even the highest wartime expenditure of $98.4 billion in fiscal 1945. The projected deficit of $11.9 billion at that point was estimated to be the second highest in peacetime. Kennedy's request for a tax cut, for example, elicited the signatures of 400 economists at 43 universities who "subscribed to the propositions of the President's tax program."[99] A subsequent survey of economists revealed that 84 per cent responded "yes" to the question "Do you favor a cut in federal taxes at the present time?"[100]

Kennedy's intentions received little criticism from the intellectuals, except for a minority on the right. The intellectuals felt increasingly hostile toward Congress for failure to pass Kennedy's legislation, or they criticized Kennedy for his inability to lead Congress. For example, at the national convention of the American Political Science Association in September, 1962, liberal Republican Senator Jacob Javits evoked enthusiasm by con-

[99] *Congressional Record*, 88th Congress, 1st Session (July 22, 1963), 12317.
[100] "Slow Growth Is No. 1 Problem," *Business Week* (December 7, 1963), 39.

demning President Kennedy, not for his programs, but for his inability to win their adoption.[101]

Monetary Policy

Traditionally, the Democratic party, and in recent years the intellectual group as well, has been opposed to the use of high interest rates as a means of controlling the business cycle. There was considerable criticism against the Eisenhower administration for using monetary policy—raising interest rates in order to repress inflationary pressures upon the economy. Critics of this method prefer fiscal policy, or compensatory spending by the government. They argue that high interest rates abnormally and disproportionately affect the small business man. The large corporations can divert profits into investment and thereby avoid the hardship of high interest rates on loans. J. K. Galbraith, for instance, wrote articles attacking the use of monetary policy on this very basis. During the 1960 presidential campaign, Kennedy made mention of the tendency of Republicans to adopt "dear" money policies. Kennedy, speaking before businessmen, urged the greater use of lower interest rates to stimulate the economy. The Federal Reserve, in his view, held onto high rates too long and helped bring on recessions.[102]

Monetary policy, therefore, under the Kennedy administration, was not an important device to affect the business cycle. The Kennedy administration basically avoided increasing the interest rate as a means of dampening the upward part of the business cycle. Its actions were simply to stave off any problems with the balance of payments, yet to maintain as low a general interest rate as possible. Monetary policy as a tool, which had been most actively used under the Eisenhower administration, was generally not considered to be a major tool within the kit box of President Kennedy's power —although the raising of the discount rate before the end of his administration showed some willingness to use monetary policy.

Price Stability and Inflation

On the issue of price stability instead of inflation, not even labor as a power group has directly challenged what appeared to be a major and generally accepted national ideology. Yet, the intellectuals appeared quite willing and ready to challenge the traditional ideology on inflation as evidenced in the proposals made to President Kennedy by his economic task force, headed by MIT's Paul Samuelson. The group noted that inflation or inflationary pressures might well develop in the economy. They formally warned that if prices and wages should rise before high employment was reached, then it

101 *The New York Times* (September 7, 1962).
102 Seymour Harris, *The Economics of the Political Parties* (New York: The Macmillan Company, 1962), p. 115.

vould be necessary to forge new types of tools to solve the problem in addi-
ion to the innovations of monetary policy in the 1920s and Keynesian fiscal
policy in the 1930s.

It might be noted that quietly and unofficially many intellectual advisers
.o Kennedy appeared to have a predilection toward wage and price controls
:o solve inflationary pressures, if necessary. Despite the general ideological
unpopularity of such measures, there is surprisingly little ideological bias in
intellectual writing against the utilization of wage and price controls as
planning techniques in general.

Kennedy argued, however, against using inflationary price increases as
a means to stimulate economic growth. Thus, he proposed an advisory
committee on labor-management policy in an effort to adopt sound wage
and price policies. Less than a year later, when Kennedy jumped on United
States Steel—in the person of Roger Blough—for raising prices against his
desired goal of price stability, the business community was highly upset.
Contrarily, however, the intellectual group appeared to endorse the President's actions in demanding and compelling Blough to retract his price
increase in steel.

Even more important to the President, however, was the use of fiscal
policy to reduce the rate of unemployment and promote greater economic
growth—goals that had greater priority in the President's mind than price
stability. Such goals appeared to be identical with the consensus of intellectual opinion in the country; in fact, judging from the economic advisers to
President Kennedy, these goals were undoubtedly proposed and initiated
by them.

Welfare Measures

A daring proposal in the field of human welfare, made by Carl J. Friedrich
in a presidential address to the American Political Science Association,
represented the general feelings of many intellectuals toward welfare.
Friedrich recommended that our modern social and economic rights be
incorporated into the Constitution of the United States.[103] He noted that
such rights as the right to education could thereby be made enforceable in
the courts. In proposing an expanded Bill of Rights, the eminent constitutional authority was referring to such rights as the rights to social security,
to work, to rest and leisure, to education, to an adequate standard of living,
and to participation in cultural life.

While not so fundamentally sweeping in his approach, John F. Kennedy, campaigning to win the Presidency, said on October 2, 1960: "I want
a $1.25 an hour minimum wage, medical care for the aged through social
security, Federal aid to help raise teacher's salaries, as well as schools, an
adequate program of . . . low rent housing, and a program of aid to areas

[103] *The New York Times* (September 6, 1963).

of chronic unemployment. . . ."[104] This brief statement sums up most of Kennedy's welfare aims for his congressional program—aims which had been shaped by the position papers of his intellectual advisers and which the bulk of the intellectuals in America had little trouble in accepting.

As will be seen in the following discussion of education, medical care, unemployment, liability insurance, housing, and depressed areas, welfare measures on a fairly broad front were advocated by Kennedy and supported by the majority of intellectuals in this country. The intellectuals' desire to shape the country into "the good society" makes such measures an essential ingredient for the molding of America into a more welfare-oriented state. Certainly, among groups in the economy which favor extended welfare, and against whom accusations of "welfare statism" can be made, the intellectuals and labor as groups stand out. Of course, individual sectors of the public and the economy benefit from particular welfare measures and thus produce certain sectional, regional, or specific interest groups whose pressure adds to any general leverage favoring such measures. The intellectuals have been particularly interested in civil rights for Negroes recently. They have often been called the "bleeding hearts" because of their concern and their espousal for welfare measures. In such areas as education, of course, intellectuals themselves have much to gain from the furthering of social legislation. Generally, however, the intellectuals' espousal of welfare legislation is basically idealistic. They would cheer the accomplishments wrought by a growth of Federal programs in health, education, and welfare and would generally not be averse to continuing increases in these expenditures which have been estimated, for example, to increase from $10.6 billion in 1956 to $61.2 billion in 1981.[105]

EDUCATION. The goal of a major educational improvement act, as Kennedy sometimes called it, had been a basic part of the Kennedy and intellectual ideology for some time. Before Kennedy was elected to office he campaigned on a program of extended benefits to education, and despite the continual rebuffs from Congress to many of his educational programs, Kennedy continued to press for broad educational aid. "Our twin goals must be," he stressed, "a new standard of excellent education and the availability of such excellence to all who are willing to pursue it."[106] Kennedy urged greater aid to education, but made clear that education must remain a matter of state and local control—a gallant attempt to placate those critics who condemn Federal aid to education as a means of Federal control of education.

[104] *The Speeches of John F. Kennedy, Presidential Campaign of 1960,* p. 1071.
[105] *U.S. News & World Report* (June 17, 1963), 49.
[106] John F. Kennedy, *To Turn the Tide,* W. Gardner (ed.) (New York: Harper & Row, Publishers, Incorporated, 1962), p. 129.

On another occasion[107] Kennedy urged that a strong educational system be developed. He proposed, first, that Federal aid to education for school construction and teachers' salaries be enacted; second, that aid to colleges and universities be extended to enable them to take care of the college population during the next ten years, which would require as many dormitories and classrooms as had been built in this country since 1775. On the issue of education, Kennedy and the intellectuals, by urging that Federal aid to education should be extended to teachers' salaries as well as construction, clashed with the dominant Republican position. Republicans argued against contributions for salaries on the basis that this would bring about Federal control. Few issues in the campaign of 1960 did more to alienate the intellectuals as a group from the Republican party than the latter's thoughts concerning education; certainly Kennedy did few things that won as implicit an acceptance by the majority of the intellectuals as his urging of greater aid to education. Subsequently in Congress, his education proposals became embroiled in a church-state controversy that prevented much effective legislation during his Presidency. This, however, did not turn the intellectuals from him or from the position that aid to education was needed. Henry I. Heald, president of the Ford Foundation, for example, felt that the needs of education were as great and vast as those of defense, social security, conservation, etc., and should be given the full weight of national support.[108]

MEDICAL CARE.   Few of the welfare measures proposed by Kennedy or the intellectuals themselves created as much organized resistance as Federal aid for better medical care for the aged. This program, opposed largely by the American Medical Association, the American Farm Bureau, and some of the more conservative business groups, such as the National Association of Manufacturers, was a very controversial issue in 1962. Although the President himself addressed a large rally at Madison Square Garden in New York and although there was considerable public approval of the program, it was rejected by Congress.

In short, this health insurance program under the social security system would be available to all those sixty-five years old or older. It would cover areas of hospital costs, nursing-home benefits, clinical diagnosis, and community visiting nurse service.

The President contended that "this program is not a program of socialized medicine, it is a program of pre-payment of health costs with absolute freedom of choice guaranteed. Every person will choose his own doctor and hospital."[109] The President also recommended Federal scholarships for

[107] September 7, 1960.

[108] *Higher Education and National Affairs* (American Council on Education, August 8, 1963), 5.

[109] Kennedy in Gardner, p. 139.

medical and dental students, construction aid for medical and dental schools, and funds for construction of nursing homes. There had been a long history of protest against the lack in the United States, compared to most European countries, of a health insurance program. Kennedy, in his statements, was attempting to offset the countering ideologies of the classical business group, and in particular the AMA, by asserting that this type of program coming under social security would not be a form of socialized medicine. Nonetheless, Kennedy never saw such legislation enacted. The typical trend of welfare legislation is that unless there is strong resistance the benefits and inclusions become, with time, broader and more generous. Whether or not the classical business group and the AMA can stay the tide indefinitely on Medicare remains to be seen.

The intellectuals' main service toward the passage of such legislation is through the molding of public opinion by means of communication, wherein they have considerable effect, and through the continuing advice and pressure brought upon the President.

HOUSING AND COMMUNITY DEVELOPMENT. Typical of the broad front of welfare legislation proposed to the Congress in the early days of Kennedy's administration was that involving housing and community development. The President outlined a policy to accomplish what he considered three basic national goals. "First, to renew our cities and assure sound growth of our rapidly expanding metropolitan areas. Second, to provide decent housing for all of our people. Third, to encourage a prosperous and efficient construction industry as an essential component of general economic prosperity and growth."[110] The President also recommended that the Department of Housing and Urban Affairs be created with Cabinet rank. This particular issue might have had greater success if the President had not virtually guaranteed that the position as head of this new Cabinet post be given to a Negro. This activated Southern opposition. In addition, the President argued for greater aid to the FHA-insured no-down-payment mortgage homes. The expansion of government aid to mortgage financing and housing received considerable support from the construction and building industry. Nonetheless, little of this program as originally proposed was finally enacted. The Kennedy administration, however, proposed much of the outline of the "brave new world" that the intellectuals as a group were demanding and recommending.

CIVIL RIGHTS. Few issues raise as deep an emotional cleavage within this country as the issue of civil rights. The intellectuals, by and large, are the most animate major group encouraging the use of government to achieve the extension of civil rights to Negroes. The emotional support for Negro rights is so strong that other rights may be sacrificed in the process. Prince-

[110] *Ibid.,* p. 91.

:on and Yale, while supporting the idea that citizens should listen to all opposing and hostile political ideas, at one time barred Alabama's Governor George Wallace and Mississippi's Governor Ross Barnett from their campuses. Even among the intellectuals it would appear that emotions sometimes outweigh support for the free marketplace of ideas.

Civil rights legislation is not limited to the Democratic party; in fact, it can only be passed by a bipartisan coalition. Strong support for civil rights legislation is inherent to the intellectual position. The concern of the intellectual for civil rights is heightened because of the interest of many Jewish intellectuals. Certainly the sting of anti-Semitic persecution in Europe under the Nazis, and periodically under the Communists, has focused their concern upon this problem, perhaps beyond that of other major groups in the country. Therefore, in the case of civil rights, as also in the case of education, the Jewish intellectual is deeply and emotionally involved and committed.

The civil rights movement is supported not only by the ideological symbols of justice and equal opportunity, but also by the commonly esteemed value of efficiency. In a presidential address to the American Economic Association, Theodore W. Schultz indicated that racial and religious discrimination still provide "hindrances to the free choice of professions."[111] A survey of university economists showed that 67 per cent said "yes" to the question "Does discrimination against minorities constitute a serious obstacle to economic efficiency?"[112]

UNEMPLOYMENT. One of the areas where economists, particularly, feel strongest is the need to use government to minimize unemployment. Arthur F. Burns, in a presidential address to the American Economic Association, said that "one of the triumphs of this generation is the progress that our nation has made in reducing economic instability."[113]

Leon Keyserling, also a former chairman of the Council of Economic Advisers, asserted that "the right to work . . . is a fundamental human right."[114] In a presidential address to the AEA, Edward S. Mason lamented that the ideologies of various interest groups blunt the use of fiscal and wage-price policy tools with which the government could attain stability and growth.[115]

111 Theodore W. Schultz, "Investment in Human Capital," *American Economic Review,* 51 (March, 1961), 13–14.

112 "Slow Growth Is No. 1 Problem," 39.

113 Arthur F. Burns, "Progress towards Economic Stability," *American Economic Review,* 50 (March, 1960), 19.

114 Leon Keyserling, "Eggheads and Politics," *The New Republic* (October 27, 1958), 17.

115 Edward S. Mason, "Interests, Ideologies, Stability and Growth," *American Economic Review,* 53 (March, 1963), 1–17.

Kennedy faced the trying problem of unemployment during his administration, and few Presidents have made as many verbal commitments toward eliminating it or easing it as he did. Within the contemporary American economy and under present economic circumstances, the problem is not an easy one to solve. This Kennedy realized, and in the message given to Congress on February 2, 1961,[116] he said that since the labor force is rising 1.5 per cent per year and productivity is also increasing, an expansion of 3.5 per cent of jobs annually must be provided just to prevent unemployment from growing larger. The continuing fact of 4 or 5 million or more unemployed remains untouched, and in fact, there were still 5.5 per cent unemployed toward the end of the Kennedy administration (seasonally adjusted).[117] The necessity for an active Federal fiscal policy to aid in grappling with the unemployment problem was realized by the Kennedy administration.

No President, whether Democratic or Republican, can easily face a high rate of unemployment. Certainly they all campaign on programs for greater economic growth and greater employment. Two basic approaches to the solving of the problem of unemployment were suggested and attempted by the Kennedy administration. One was a specific attack on the problem largely in the nature of on-the-job training, vocational education, trying to increase worker mobility, and providing area redevelopment programs. Both President Kennedy and the intellectuals, as well as many union groups, pushed for these programs, but in the summer of 1963 the conservative coalition narrowly defeated new financing for the area redevelopment program, arguing that its results had been inflated and were skimpy in relation to the cost.

The other approach attempted was the Keynesian or general approach. It is simply the policy of increasing fiscal spending and/or of lowering taxes to ensure high levels of spending and effective demand in order to increase the number of jobs and decrease the number of unemployed. While Kennedy gave considerable lip service to the use of such a general policy in his campaign for the Presidency, he invoked some intellectual criticism during his administration for not pursuing his proposed programs more ardently. In the latter half of his term in office, however, with the level of unemployment still high, Kennedy increasingly followed the advice of his economists, who urged and argued for tax cuts along with high levels of Federal spending and a larger deficit in the Federal budget along Keynesian lines to eliminate the problem of unemployment. In this sense it can be seen that Kennedy followed in the direction of his economic advisers in the attempted solution of the problem of unemployment and thus more in the direction of consensus with general intellectual support. Keynesian economics are, for the most part, accepted by the majority of intellectuals

[116] *Ibid.*, 82.
[117] *Wall Street Journal* (November 1, 1963).

n this country and might be considered to be the bases of their economic
deas and ideology.

Growth and Taxation

In his campaign for office in 1960, Kennedy concentrated strongly on
attacking the lack of growth in the economy and on demanding a high rate
of economic performance and accelerated growth. On at least twenty occasions in his campaign speeches, Kennedy discussed the issue of economic
growth. In a talk he gave on September 5, 1960, he stressed three facts
which he said were indisputable. They were:

Fact #1: Between 1947 and 1953, under the administration of Harry
Truman, our average annual rate of growth was 4½ per cent. Between 1953 and
1959, under a Republican administration, the rate was only 2¼ per cent—less
than half as much. And today our key industries such as auto and steel are
operating at much less than full capacity.

Fact #2: While our economy is crawling forward at an average rate of
only 2¼ per cent, the Russian gross national product is annually increasing at
7 per cent—three times as fast.

Fact #3: Our rate of growth was surpassed by almost every major industrial nation during the past years of drift and indecision—including Germany,
France, the Netherlands, Italy, and Japan. These are the facts which we must
face.[118]

The means by which Kennedy proposed to remedy the problem of
low economic growth rates in the United States were basically related to
monetary and fiscal policy, using expenditures for various welfare measures
which would act as a stimulant for growth in the economy. In particular
he suggested low rates of interest, coordinated monetary and fiscal policies,
and increased spending for education, housing, and social welfare. His
argument was that in time this would actually save both the government
and the economy money because, with a high rate of economic growth,
the taxes received by the government would be greater and thus his increased welfare policies could be afforded. In fact, at times, Kennedy
intimated that unless the country grew at a more rapid economic rate, it
could not afford the welfare measures that he was proposing. In a sense,
this was an ideological attack against the balanced-budget ideology that
the Republicans were using in opposition to him—an ideology which some
intellectuals suspected Kennedy shared to a greater extent than they might
wish.

The economic growth issue was one which economists had for some
time been discussing and one which Kennedy had adopted under the urging of his various intellectual advisers, Paul Samuelson being perhaps the
major economic adviser in his pre-election campaign. (Samuelson, Gal-

[118] *The Speeches of John F. Kennedy, Presidential Campaign of 1960,* p. 987.

braith, Rostow, and Harris, to name only a few, were some of the prominent economists who were privately and publicly advising Kennedy during
his campaign and after his election.) The issue of economic growth, calling for vigorous action to utilize unemployed resources of the economy,
had great appeal to the intellectuals. For example, a survey of economists
revealed that 65 per cent were not "satisfied with the U.S. economic growth
ratio."[119]

As noted above, however, Kennedy argued that the acceleration of
economic growth in the country was essential if welfare measures were to
be increased. Such statements gave great support to the intellectual group
who desired both welfare programs and faster economic growth. Thus,
government aid to education, health, and other welfare issues became
interwoven with the problem of economic growth itself.

Such a course had great appeal to a group which is interested in re-
molding the world nearer to its ideals of justice and equity. Further,
Kennedy found the issue to be one very much to his liking in terms of
political appeal and one well suited for a political campaign based upon
a posture of vigor. Nixon only gradually faced the need for greater economic growth. He stressed private incentives and tax reform to develop
greater growth from the economy. While urging tax cuts, Kennedy, nevertheless, focused his attention on those monetary and fiscal policies which
might be pursued to give increased aid to education, science, and natural
resources, as well as to solve the unemployment problem and to spur
economic growth.

Taxation was one of the major issues which Kennedy proposed to
revamp the American economy and to obtain greater economic growth. In
a message to Congress,[120] Kennedy urged that a tax system be developed
to provide for a more efficient and conducive method to promote economic
growth. While his proposals were made early in his term of office, Congress, nevertheless, was slow to act upon them.

Trade and Aid

Foreign aid has been a basic ideological issue of the intellectual position,
and it was elaborated by Kennedy on numerous occasions.[121] During his
first year in office, in a special message presented to Congress on foreign
aid, Kennedy began by enumerating three facts:

1. Existing foreign aid programs and concepts are largely unsatisfactory and
   unsuited for our needs and for the needs of an underdeveloped world as it
   enters the 60's.
2. The economic collapse of those free, but less-developed, nations which now

[119] "Slow Growth Is No. 1 Problem," 39.   [121] See, for example, Schultz, 15.
[120] April 20, 1961.

stand poised between growth and economic sustained chaos would be disastrous to our national security, harmful to our comparative prosperity and
offensive to our conscience.

3. There exists in the 1960s an historic opportunity for major economic assistance, effort by the free industrialized nations to move more than half of the
people of the less developed nations into self-sustained economic growth,
while the rest move substantially closer to the day when they, too, will no
longer have to depend on outside assistance.[122]

Intellectuals are internationally oriented and have long urged a greater
and more vigorous foreign aid policy. Kennedy expressed these demands
several times, both during his campaign and afterward, to Congress. Perhaps
his most dramatic successes were the establishment of the Peace Corps and
obtaining of permission from Congress to permit trading or bargaining with
the European Common Market in order to develop basic tariff relationships. The President was committed to a low-tariff policy that would
encourage trade with the underdeveloped countries, as well as with the
more developed European nations. Even before Kennedy had campaigned
for the Presidency, he had introduced in Congress bills proposing large
amounts of foreign aid to countries such as India. In the case of India,
in particular, he had proposed a bill which would commit the United States
to underwrite India's development program. Thus, it was not unexpected
that Kennedy would attempt to push a program for larger and more effective foreign aid. This, of course, was not only on the advice of economists,
such as W. W. Rostow and John K. Galbraith. It was also the more or less
sustained opinion of the intellectuals that one of the major means of com-
bating communism was to have a more aggressive and successful foreign
aid and trade program, particularly with the underdeveloped countries.
The argument upon which the intellectuals relied was simple but unproved.
The hypothesis was that as the underdeveloped countries developed economically, there would be less opportunity for the Communists to exploit
frustration and chaos and bring the emerging nations into their orbit.

Kennedy recognized the strains on the United States foreign aid policy
resulting from the pressure of rather delicate balance-of-payments problems concerning the outflow of gold from the United States. Therefore,
other countries that the United States had supported and aided, particularly in Europe and Asia immediately after World War II, were urged
to cooperate with the United States in providing economic aid for the
underdeveloped areas.

Certainly the intellectuals were concerned with the standard of living
in underdeveloped countries, and the desire among intellectuals to aid these
areas was undoubtedly significant. Nonetheless, a far stronger issue for the

[122] Kennedy in Gardner, p. 143.

general public was the desire to prevent underdeveloped countries from falling into the hands of Communists, and even this was insufficient to prevent major cuts in the foreign aid appropriations for fiscal 1964. Those in Congress, for instance, who oppose such foreign aid regard the problem of international communism as not particularly solvable simply by greater aid from the United States. They argue that countries such as Czechoslovakia can be absorbed into the Communist group even though they have very high standards of living. Nonetheless, the issues of international aid and trade are issues that the intellectuals consider an important part of their ideology. These, together with the diligent seeking of international cooperation and peace in other ways, represent the cornerstone of their foreign policy.

In fact the desires of such varied intellectuals as Erich Fromm, Fred Warner Neal, and D. F. Flemming for a rapprochement with Communist nations have produced an attack by such conservative columnists as Holmes Alexander and William F. Buckley for presumably inspiring a "no win" policy against Russia. Buckley asserted that "the people are less easy to frighten out of their wits than are the intelligentsia, who by all odds are the most easily frightened people in the world."[123]

THE CASE OF THE REPUBLICANS COURTING THE INTELLECTUALS

Introduction

American party politics are sometimes viewed as following a sun-moon pattern, with a dominant and a minority national party during extended periods. For example, there have been only three major reversals in United States history in which a dominant party was replaced by a new one. The first was the switch from the Federalists to the Jeffersonians in 1800 over the issue of popular sovereignty. The second was the switch from the Democrats to the emergent Republican party in 1860 over the issue of slavery. Third, following seventy-two years of Republican domination (with only two Democratic presidents), there was a switchback to the Democratic party on the issue of government intervention in the economy to try to cope with the Great Depression. The major issue in each case helped in the organization of a new sustained majority coalition.

Since 1932 the Republicans have controlled Congress only twice, 1947–1948 and 1953–1954, and have elected only one President, warhero Gen. Dwight D. Eisenhower. An understanding of the parties' ideological appeals, as they affect interest groups, helps to explain why the

[123] *Salt Lake Tribune* (September 9, 1963).

Republican party continues to be the minority party. The Republican emphasis on a balanced budget and on cutting Federal spending corresponds to its representation of taxpayer interests. The Democratic espousal of government-provided welfare and economic security financed by progressive taxes corresponds to its representation of the lower socioeconomic classes. Beardsley Ruml dealt the Republican party a serious blow by his pay-as-you-go income tax withholding system. This made taxpaying much less conspicuous and painful than when checks had to be written out and mailed to the Internal Revenue Service personally by all income tax payers, as many businessmen still have to do. The relative lessening of tax consciousness reduced the public heat under the Republican issue of thrift in government. Add to this the fact that Democratic programs benefit more people than they hurt since they involve some redistribution of wealth from the few rich to the many poor and the Republican dilemma is clear.

After the resounding Republican victory of 1952, some Republican analysts anticipated that a new turn in history had been marked. They believed that the liberalism of the Democrats had reflected the needs of the Depression and that a moderate Republican party in the Eisenhower image could retain the conservatives and win the middle-of-the-roaders and thus reflect a new majority coalition responsive to popular demands in a society with growing suburban, middle-class orientation during normal economic times. They hoped, in other words, that the Republicans had replaced the Democrats as the "sun" party on the issue of moderate versus liberal government. If this had not taken place, it was at least hoped that America had reached a new political style in which traditional voting patterns were less meaningful and that the parties could compete somewhat more equally than in the previous two decades to utilize issues and to create coalitions bringing victory. More flexible voting behavior was developing, but the hope of making the Republican party into the new majority party was dashed upon the rocks. Despite President Eisenhower's immense personal popularity, his lack of inclination to think in terms of the realities of coalition building and to organize the intensive program and drive necessary to accomplish this was not helpful. This contrasted with the skillful political leadership displayed by Franklin D. Roosevelt, who enticed such traditionally Republican groups as the Negroes into the Democratic party and joined together such diverse groups as the immigrant-dominated urban masses, protesting farmers, the traditionally Democratic South, and an intellectual elite. Roosevelt also effectively portrayed the Republican party as the party of the "economic royalists" and invited everyone else (which means virtually everyone) to join him in the party of the "people," the Democrats.

Democratic intellectual Arthur Schlesinger, Jr., subsequently presented his own view of how the Republicans could create a majority. Prior to the presidential nominations of 1960, he wrote a paper which was circulated to key Democrats and liberals. He contended that American politics followed a cyclical pattern with liberal spurts followed by conservative, or moderate, stabilizing periods. Thus he noted that the liberal enactments under President Theodore Roosevelt were followed by the conservative stabilizing period under President William Howard Taft. Then the innovations of Woodrow Wilson were followed by the "normalcy" of Presidents, such as Warren G. Harding and Calvin Coolidge. Finally, the crackling of new ideas and experiments of the New Deal era were followed by the moderation of President Eisenhower. Schlesinger contended that the nation was ready for a new liberal wave, but that the Democrats could not assume that they would automatically be the beneficiaries of the wave. Should the Republicans nominate Nelson Rockefeller, while the Democrats failed to mobilize their most effective liberal leadership, the Republican campaign might coincide with and take advantage of the new liberal wave that Schlesinger believed was in the making, as an earlier Republican, Theodore Roosevelt, had done.

The coalition which did elect Eisenhower and a GOP Congress in 1952 failed to be mobilized in the subsequent congressional elections. Thus even though "Ike" was reelected partly on the basis of his personality in 1956, he served all but the first two years of his eight years in office with a Democratically controlled House and Senate.

The disappointment of Republican leaders was particularly poignant after the election of 1958. There is a normal off-year trend which favors the President's opponents when he does not run. For example, during the past century there was only one instance in which the President's party improved its proportion in the House of Representatives during the off-year election. This exception occurred in 1934 during President Franklin D. Roosevelt's first term. The average number of seats lost has been thirty-six in off-year elections for the party controlling the Presidency.

But political parties do not automatically bow to such historic trends. It was hoped that the fact that the Democrats already had a substantial majority might enable the Republicans to reverse the trend and to nibble away at the Democratic majority. The recession atmosphere accentuated the normal trend, however, and in 1958 the Democrats achieved the largest off-year gain since 1946. The Republican percentage of the vote in the House of Representatives' races had dropped from 49.8 in 1952 to 43.7 in 1958. Put another way, the Republican House candidates polled approximately the same number of votes in 1958 as in 1950, 20 million. But with a growing electorate, the Democrats increased their votes from 20 million in 1950 to 25.7 million in 1958. The result was considerable soul searching by Republican party leaders. Meade Alcorn called a National Committee meeting at Des Moines, Iowa on January 22, 1959. In his opening comments, Chairman Alcorn emphasized the need to change the image of the Republican party and to broaden its base of support. He declared:

It's time we snatched off the "big business" false-face that the Democrats placed on us years ago.

It's time we erased the dollar signs they painted on our vest.[124]

Dr. Claude Robinson, president of Opinion Research Corporation of Princeton, New Jersey, made a presentation on "What Ails the G.O.P.?" He showed a series of charts on Republican voting strength which displayed discouraging losses of support over the last four congressional elections among farmers, white-collar workers, and union members. Even business and professional people were far from solidified.

Out of these meetings came renewed determination to improve the ingredients of successful campaigning—more attractive candidates, superior organization, and more appealing programs which would bring larger group segments into the GOP. In order to assist in building the image of a revitalized party which would meet the issues with attractive programs, President Eisenhower agreed to the appointment of a forty-member Republican Committee on Program and Progress. The committee was headed by Charles Percy, who had become president of Bell and Howell at the age of twenty-nine.

In naming the committee, the GOP leadership wished to avoid the apparent mistake of Chairman Paul Butler of the Democratic party when he appointed a Democratic Advisory Council of virtually all liberals, such as Eleanor Roosevelt and Adlai Stevenson. These people represented the "presidential" Democratic party, as did Butler, and received little serious attention by the two Texans, Sam Rayburn and Lyndon Johnson, who ran the House and the Senate, and their colleagues who were more conservative than the advisory group.

Thus House Minority Leader Charles Halleck and Senate Minority Leader Everett Dirkson were named to the committee in the hope of obtaining unity between the more conservative congressional leadership and the moderate presidential wing of the GOP which was represented by such people as Percy. The appointees gave representation to most of the basic power groups, including labor unions, as well, of course, as business and agriculture. Some of the others had rarely had much contact with labor leaders, and they found the comments of John Stender, vice-president of the International Brotherhood of Boilermakers, Iron Shipbuilders, Blacksmiths, Forgers, and Helpers, refreshing in bringing high-flown discussions down to earth.

[124] Meade Alcorn, "A Road to Victory: An Address by the Republican National Chairman" (Republican National Committee, 1959).

The Efforts to Woo the Intellectuals

It was particularly hoped that the committee could appeal to the intellectuals. It was anomalous to many Republican leaders that virtually all studies showed that college-educated people voted Republican in substantially higher percentages than did grade school– or even high school–educated people. Yet this correlation seemed to be reversed at the Ph.D. level, at least in the social sciences, and among the intellectual opinion leaders in general. This was dismaying to the GOP leaders because of the recognizable growth in power among the intellectuals through their influence upon other groups and their shaping of the views and ideology of the oncoming generations.

Meade Alcorn, an urbane Connecticut lawyer, felt a degree of kinship with the intellectuals and was particularly interested in winning their support. An expression of this interest was the fact that eight members of the Committee on Program and Progress carried the titles of Dr. or Professor. These included people such as Gabriel Hauge, Eisenhower's economic adviser, Lev Dobriansky, chairman, National Captive Nations Committee and professor of economics at Georgetown University, and Malcolm Moos, Eisenhower's speech writer and political science professor at Johns Hopkins University.

The committee did produce a well-thought-through "progressive" program which emerged from its task forces on national security and peace, human rights and needs, the impact of science and technology, and economic opportunity and progress. Chuck Percy was named to head the 1960 GOP Platform Committee a few months later. It is noteworthy that the platform adopted ideas from the committee report and was also "progressive."

In summary then Chairman Alcorn hoped the Committee on Program and Progress would formulate programs which through a long-range problem-solving approach would win over larger segments of various groups. He especially hoped that by using intellectuals on the committee, by the widespread communication between the committee and opinion leaders, and by the attractiveness to intellectuals of the idea of the committee's developing a long-range responsible program for the party, more of them would be attracted to support the Republican party. Fifty thousand copies of the "Percy report" were distributed, and the activities of the committee undoubtedly had some effect in the desired direction.[125] It was not more significant partly because sophisticated observers such as the intellectuals recognize that America does not have a responsible party system where the results of such an official party organization have any

[125] Representative Fred Schwengel, "Why Scholars in Politics," *Congressional Record,* 86th Congress, 2d Session, August 25, 1960.

binding relationship upon the legislators who may be influenced by a coalition of interests quite different from and more conservative than those represented at the committee sessions. Even the delegates to the Republican National Convention are a good deal more conservative than the presidential standard-bearer and platforms that emerge from the conventions. This was illustrated in 1961 when President Ernest L. Wilkinson of Brigham Young University polled the delegates to the previous GOP National Convention and announced that 81 per cent of the nearly two-thirds who responded opposed Federal aid for school construction.[126] Yet the platform clearly called for "Federal aid for school construction—pacing it to the real needs of individual school districts,"[127] and Richard Nixon supported such a program.

The Committee on Program and Progress was not the only device used by the Republicans to court the intellectuals. There had been concern for some time about the preponderance of intellectual support for the Democrats. Some of the principal reasons for this alignment appeared to have been the following:

1. Franklin D. Roosevelt had given the intellectuals a place of honor and power during the New Deal, e.g., the brain trust.
2. Many of the intellectuals associated with the Democratic administrations of the 30s and 40s had returned to teaching positions at the key universities where their values influenced a large segment of the oncoming crop of Ph.D.s who began teaching across the land.
3. The reluctance of Republicans to adopt policies favoring substantial intervention in the economy to try to ameliorate the traumatic Great Depression alienated many intellectuals who felt that, with up to 12 million able-bodied men walking the streets unable to find employment, any device which might aid the situation had to be attempted—in fact the Great Depression encouraged many social scientists to believe the Federal government was the primary motive power of the economy and society.
4. The traditional support of Republicans for high tariffs had alienated many free trade–oriented intellectuals, particularly economists.
5. The isolationism of the majority of key Republicans prior to World War II was repugnant to the internationalist ideology of the intellectuals.
6. The substantial influence which businessmen supporting the classical ideology enjoyed in the Republican party made intellectuals ideologically uncomfortable, as well as feeling that the GOP emphasized "property rights at the expense of human rights," did not want the services of the intellectuals, and was even anti-intellectual to a degree.

The feeling of the intellectuals that the Republicans did not care for them was valid for a segment of the GOP. Many Republicans had de-

---

[126] Ernest L. Wilkinson, *Federal Aid to Education* (Provo, Utah: Brigham Young University, 1961), p. 51.

[127] *Building a Better America: Republican Platform 1960*, p. 19.

veloped during the 1930s, particularly, and had retained a stereotype image of intellectuals as unrealistic visionaries, unappreciative of American traditions, and as alarmingly leftist in their ideology.

For years at least a narrow link had existed between the Republican National Committee and the political scientists through Dr. Floyd Mc Caffree. Furthermore, the Citizenship Clearing House (now the National Center for Education in Politics) operated a program wherein each year a political scientist affiliated with each party was hired to work for the national party chairman for a year. The cost was divided between the Citizenship Clearing House and the party.

Following the defeat of 1958, Alcorn took definite steps to ascertain methods of improving the relationship between the GOP and the social scientists, particularly the political scientists since they, more than any other single group, passed on political values and concepts to the oncoming generation.

On January 14, 1959, he convened a political science advisory committee, consisting of twenty-one political scientists, at the National Committee offices, telling them in his opening remarks: "The inadequate liaison between our party and the political science profession has disturbed me for many years."[128, 129]

The committee finally estimated that the political science profession divided about 75 per cent pro-Democrats to 25 per cent pro-Republicans and that it was not "fashionable" within the profession to admit publicly to being a Republican. One even suggested that to some intellectuals the idea of a Republican intellectual was "almost like a dog writing a poem."[130]

One of the most eye-opening series of comments centered on the feeling among political scientists that the Republican party was indifferent to them. Several instances were cited from various areas of the country where Republicans had failed to accept invitations to send representatives to both local and national academic meetings, whereas Democrats were represented by prominent people.

On the question of what political scientists could do for the Republican party, numerous ideas were set forth which are interesting in elucidating the means by which intellectuals can exercise power. They could ghost-write speeches and articles for Republicans, supply GOP solons with helpful articles to insert in the *Congressional Record,* encourage more Republicans to apply for the congressional internship program operated

[128] "Proceedings of Political Science Advisory Group Meeting" (Republican National Committee, January 14, 1959).

[129] One of the authors, Mark W. Cannon, observed most of the meetings referred to in this case. He has also referred to the available written materials about the various meetings.

[130] "Proceedings of Political Science Advisory Group Meeting."

by the American Political Science Association (APSA) to equalize the
party distribution among the participants, supply ideas to Republicans
holding top offices in the Eisenhower administration by the establishment
of an executive internship program, "translate" professional articles and
summarize the results of behavioral studies for *Straight from the Shoulder*
or other GOP publications, help define the party's philosophy, prepare a
campaign manual, advise on the use of specific issues, write letters to the
editor in favor of specific Republican positions, and help local candidates
with their campaigns.

The remainder of the meeting was devoted to a discussion of what the
Republican party could do to improve relations with the political science
profession. Ideas included the following: Use political scientists in administrative positions in government; invite political scientists to join with
professionals in small Republican work groups; hold an "open house" at
the national APSA convention; have Nixon and Eisenhower's key aides
set up a meeting at the White House; bring more intellectuals into prestigious party positions, as economics professor John Kenneth Galbraith
had been made chairman of the Democratic Advisory Council; convince
intellectuals the GOP sincerely wants their views and not merely "a front
for the party"[131]; distribute properly expurgated minutes of the Republican
National Committee meetings and various studies of the very able GOP
research staff to political scientists through the name plates of the APSA;
establish regular liaison between the National Committee and the APSA;
establish a permanent organization for Republican-oriented intellectuals,
such as had been temporarily supplied by the Committee on Arts and
Sciences for Eisenhower, which would go after all opinion formers, including teachers, editors, and ministers; have Nixon invite political scientists to consult with him on issues; and indicate the need for political
scientists to help Republicans in order to fulfill the objective of a recent
APSA publication on the desirability of having a responsible two-party
system.

Senator Thruston Morton of Kentucky replaced Meade Alcorn as
national chairman. Morton had the breadth of a former Assistant Secretary
of State, and he desired to continue Alcorn's efforts to woo the intellectuals.
A subsequent committee drew up specific recommendations for Chairman
Morton. Morton was urged to join the APSA, as Meade Alcorn had done.
The committee offered to draft a brochure on the value of "Operation
Social Scientists" to be mailed to Republican state officers and county
chairmen and officeholders across the country. This would give some cases
where social scientists had been helpful to the GOP, such as Professor
Paul Bagwell's political scientist speech-writing team when he ran for
governor of Michigan, Representative Fred Schwengel's use of a research

[131] *Ibid.*

team of faculty members and students at the University of Iowa, the use o political scientists for such projects as reapportionment by Republicans ir California, and Representative Henry Aldous Dixon's bringing a wide sector of the educational community in Utah into his following, which provided an unusual illustration of what could be accomplished when the educational community was brought into the Republican coalition.

Scarcely two weeks before the general election of 1954, Dougla Stringfellow, a widely acclaimed paraplegic war-hero Congressman from Utah, confessed, after he had been exposed, that his tales of war heroism such as having captured German atomic physicist Otto Hahn, were a hoax Among Stringfellow's many awards he had been chosen one of the te: outstanding young men of the nation by the National Junior Chamber c Commerce—the same year Billie Sol Estes was chosen to share this honor The Utah Republican party was struck by catastrophe, but it reacted with finesse and literally drafted the only man who had the personal popularit, to have any chance of winning, Dr. Henry Aldous Dixon, president o Utah State Agricultural College (now Utah State University).[132] Dixor defeated a former Congressman, Walter Granger, almost without a cam paign. He immediately began to draw upon the academic community to help him. This is illustrated by the fact that after he resigned after six year as a Congressman, the people in academic life who had worked on hi congressional staff numbered four political science professors—one c whom, Laurence J. Burton, became a Congressman himself in 1963 though he was hardly identified as a Republican before Dixon recruite him to Washington, D.C. A philosophy professor and a dean of wome were also among Dixon's former aides. The broad coalition that Dixor formed enabled him to win in 1956 by 61 per cent, tying the record fo any previous Republican candidate in Utah for the United States House, a well as to survive the Democratic wave of 1958.

The social scientists' committee offered not only to elucidate suc cases but to help brief Republican field representatives so they could bette persuade local GOP officers to pay more attention to intellectuals.

Other recommendations included a vast expansion in the list which ha then been gathered of 250 social scientists and opinion leaders who wer favorable to the GOP with mailings of materials which would help encour age their Republicanism; making directories of these sympathetic socia scientists, with indications of the work they would be willing to do, avai able to state and county party officials; Chairman Morton should give :

---

[132] Dr. Dixon has told the authors that what finally convinced him to accept th draft was the implied threat of then-Governor J. Bracken Lee that if Dr. Dixon turne down the state and the Republican party in such a time of terrible need, he woul undoubtedly find it difficult to defend his budget requests for the college before th coming legislature.

new address on "why social scientists should be Republicans" and mail it
to the full membership (6,000) of the APSA; Morton should personally
encourage articulate Republican intellectuals, e.g., "Kistiakowsky, Flemming, Derthick, Milton Eisenhower, Killian and John Hannah,"[133] to
address more conventions; hold a GOP reception during the APSA convention, and urge GOP congressional staff members to arrange more university speeches for their bosses.

Out of these exploratory meetings, several achievements came to be
realized. A permanent Arts and Sciences Division was organized. The
political science interns who followed Neil Cotter—Arthur Peterson, director of the Institute of Practical Politics at Ohio Wesleyan University and
chairman of the Ohio Civil Rights Commission, Earl Nehring of the University of Kansas, Robert J. Huckshorn of the University of Idaho, and
John Kessel of the University of Washington—all developed the arts and
sciences program.

A directory of 12,500 pro-Republican professors had been built by
1963, 4,000 of whom had "expressed a willingness to participate in some
political activity."[134] Dr. Huckshorn expressed the hope of doubling the
size of the roster. Similar state arts and sciences divisions were organized
in California, Oregon, Washington, Illinois, Indiana, West Virginia, Mary-
land, Colorado, and Utah. In Texas, GOP academicians formed an organization not formally affiliated with the state committee. Other states
such as New York, Pennsylvania, and Michigan were also working toward
the organization of arts and sciences divisions. Ohio led the way with
2,400 names. The directories were made available to local candidates and
party officials.

Better liaison was also developed with the APSA. Republican re-
ceptions were held at the national conventions. Top Republicans also
addressed the conventions, including Thruston Morton; his successor,
Chairman William E. Miller (who called for a breaking down of the
"Chinese wall"[135] between the Republican party and the academic community); and Senator Jacob Javits. In fact, after a panel at the 1962
convention in which Arthur Peterson participated, a comment was made
in the halls in jest that since the APSA was trying to be bipartisan, it was
an advantage to be a Republican in the profession because, being fewer
in number, they were designated more frequently for panel participation.

The Republican report was published and circulated together with

[133] Memorandum to Chairman Thruston B. Morton from Republican Political
Scientists, with recommendations on "Operation Social Scientists," June 1, 1959.

[134] Robert Huckshorn, "G.O.P. Pushes Drive to Win Support of Nation's Professors," reprinted from Newhouse Newspapers' Advance News Service, March 22,
1963.

[135] *Republican Report,* November, 1961.

other materials to the Republican academicians with items likely to suit their interest, e.g., civil rights, allegations that the Kennedy administration was attempting to erode the civil service merit system through expanded political clearance of Federal employees, and the state of other fights in which the GOP appeared to be on the side of the angels.[136]

The nomination of Barry Goldwater as the Republican Presidential candidate in 1964, however, lost to the Republican party much intellectual support which they had been laboriously establishing. Thus despite the explorations by the Republicans after 1958 defeats to gain greater support from the intellectual group, the *views* and *image* of the Republican candidate (particularly the Presidential nominee) are critical for galvanizing support. It appears that the major factor that attracts academicians and other similar opinion leaders is the nomination of candidates that they can identify with and who will respect them as well. Too often both the Republican candidate and the intellectuals as a group are suspicious of each other. Under these circumstances organizational efforts have only limited effect. President Kennedy is perhaps the prime illustration of how a candidate can achieve dominant support from the intellectual group. Kennedy's support, however, was based on both a liberal program and appeal as a writer and intellectual himself—not to mention organized efforts to make use of and keep the support of the intellectual opinion-forming community. Arthur Schlesinger, Jr., as a personal aid to President Kennedy, was largely in charge of this program. In this regard, President Kennedy was uniquely successful.

CONCLUDING SUMMARY

The intellectuals, one of the smaller of major power groups in numbers, rank next to business and labor because of the great influence they have on both political elites and followers through advisory positions and through other means of communicating stimulating ideas and analyses. The wealth of the intellectuals as a group is not great. Yet their influence upon the use of wealth has become significant through increasing control over the policies and communication systems of American universities, which represent billions of dollars worth of investment. Furthermore the giant tax-exempt foundations, worth approximately $15 billion, are of increasing consequence in the shaping of American ideologies, due to their ability to designate certain types of programs and investigations to receive financial assistance. These foundations often choose liberal intellectuals to manage their programs. Illustrative of this was the selection of Robert

[136] *Republican Report*, April, 1963.

Hutchins, president of the University of Chicago, to head the Fund for the Republic, an offshoot of the Ford Foundation.

Thus the power of the intellectuals lies not in their numbers, organization, or wealth, but in their strategic position, which enables them to influence people who do control the other tools of power. The intellectuals actually influence each of the major power groups. For example, the division in business between the classical and managerial ideologies is partly promoted by the intellectuals in the following manner. The breadth of understanding and penetration of thinking required to make decisions in modern industry has induced many companies to encourage their executives to obtain a liberal education. After World War II, Bell Telephone established a pioneering program of sending potential top executives to the University of Pennsylvania to study the classics, etc. The aim was to broaden their backgrounds by obtaining a liberal education—hence to liberate their thinking from the limitations of direct experience by exposing them to, and making them familiar with, a vast and varied spectrum of human experience and ideas. It was hoped that people who had received rather narrow training as accountants or engineers, for example, would broaden their scope and their skill at analyzing people and ideas by studying history, literature, and the social sciences.

The intent behind the Bell experiment has become common. In various ways many large corporations, such as General Electric, encourage liberal education for their budding executives, and increasing numbers such as Dr. Frank Stanton, president of CBS, have doctoral degrees. One of the most striking ways that liberal arts education is encouraged is through the contemporary emphasis of business and law schools on a liberal education as necessary background for entry. Many of the better graduate business schools take very few applicants who receive their undergraduate degrees in business. They are interested in recruiting promising young people with liberal educations from the social and natural sciences. Both the Ford and Carnegie foundations studies of business schools emphasized the need to make business school educations considerably broader and more liberal, and these studies are having an impact.

The effect of this movement has been to expose an increasing proportion of business executives to the values and ideologies of the intellectuals. The result is that many of these executives are less hostile to government intervention and social programs than were their predecessors. In other words, this movement contributes to the growth of the moderate managerial (CED) ideology among businessmen.

Labor is influenced by the intellectuals by the unions' hiring of professional economists and by joining forces politically with intellectuals in the Democratic party. Also a few of the people in the labor movement, such as Walter Reuther, might be classified as intellectuals.

Farmers are influenced by intellectuals through increasing necessity of obtaining college educations to compete in agriculture. The fact that colleges require courses in the social sciences and humanities exposes the budding agriculturists to the liberal ideologies of intellectual professors.

The professionalization process in the bureaucracy subjects it to the influence of the intellectuals as is taking place in business. For example, the rapid growth of the city-manager system has transferred effective power in many municipalities from local poorly educated commissioners to high-salaried managers, usually with Master's degrees and sometimes with doctorates. These men usually blend with their own predispositions the emphasis on urban planning taking precedence over property rights, for example, of their educational mentors. Similarly, the increasing emphasis on graduate degrees by the Federal civil service strengthens the link between the bureaucracy and the intellectuals. The enactment of the Civil Service Training Act prior to the decade of the 1960s enabled executive agencies to send up to 1 per cent of their employees away to universities on full salary with tuition paid to study subjects relevant to their work. Many of the people so chosen attend graduate work in public administration where they are exposed to the values of the social scientists. It is interesting to note that long before the Civil Service Training Act, both the Foreign Service and the Defense Department were sending personnel to universities. Many of these did graduate work in the social sciences, particularly international relations at Ivy League schools. The latest in the development of stronger links between the academic community and the bureaucracy deals with the congressional bureaucracy. In 1963 the Ford Foundation financed a program operated by the American Political Science Association to give scholarships as high as $14,000 plus tuition to congressional staff members for postgraduate study at prominent universities.

The fact, incidentally, that the officers who teach the social sciences to the cadets at the military academies frequently received their Ph.D.s from Harvard, Columbia, Princeton, and the University of California builds a bridge between the values of the intellectuals and the emerging military elites. While teaching at the academies has differences, such as a substantially greater emphasis on nationalism, this bridge appears to be one factor preventing the United States military from being as far removed from the ideologies of other important groups as has been the case in many countries.

This analysis of the influence of the intellectuals on other groups does not imply that intellectuals present only one side in their lectures and writings. Various sides of controversial questions are frequently discussed. However, depending upon the personalities involved, their personal values are presented and do influence listeners and readers to one degree or another. The facility for critical evaluation which is developed by students helps prevent them from blind absorption of the dominant values and ideologies expressed by the intellectuals.

There is a marketplace for ideas among the intellectuals. However, the marketplace is dominated, in terms of political and economic ideology, largely by the positions presented in this chapter.

In summary, the dominant intellectual ideology would include the following: (1) an emphasis on an energetic leader as President with the use of government as a primary instrument for creating the good society; (2) further shifts from private to public spending as necessary to satisfy "public" needs such as Medicare under social security, aid to depressed areas, more low-rent housing through slum clearance, and vast grants of Federal aid to education for instructional salaries as well as new buildings; (3) a willingness to use flexible fiscal policy to attempt to accelerate economic growth and reduce unemployment; (4) dramatic and forceful civil rights programs; and (5) internationalism, including support for the United Nations, international trade, arms control, and aid to underdeveloped countries. In spite of varying degrees of objectivity in varying areas of analysis, the majority of intellectuals can become righteously indignant over some of these issues, most particularly hostility to ultra-right-wing groups such as the John Birch Society, and support for expenditures for education, civil rights, and international programs. It is this quality of emotional involvement that helps make the majority position of the intellectuals an ideology rather than simply a consensus.

8

the civil bureaucracy

INTRODUCTION

Few aspects of national life in America are outside the interests or regulation of the Federal government. The nearly 2½ million civilian employees of the Federal government create a bureaucracy so vast that almost no one can comprehend its full ramifications. The American government is the largest and most complex business in this country as well as in the free world. For when state and local governments are included, almost one out of every six workers in the United States is employed by government. Further, taxes take almost a third of national income, and the government annually spends nearly $100 billion. Thus, in terms of its scope and function, the fact that it is the largest employer and the biggest spender in our economy gives the government, and therefore the bureaucrats who run it, tremendous power.

We might begin this discussion of the civil bureaucracy by asking first just why it has come into being and what are the causes of its growth. The decisive reason for the advance of bureaucracies is undoubtedly their purely technical advantage over any other form of organization. Max Weber stated that the "fully developed bureaucratic mechanism compares with other organizations exactly as does the machine with the nonmechanical modes of production."[1] In situations where only small institutions exist,

[1] Max Weber, "Technical Advantages of Bureaucratic Organization," in H. H. Gerth and C. Wright Mills (eds.), *From Max Weber: Essays in Sociology* (Fair Lawn, N.J.: Oxford University Press, 1946), p. 214.

222

where life is simple, and where interpersonal relationships are direct, one would not find an institutional situation which could be called bureaucratic.[2]

Even seventy-five or a hundred years ago, Ministers of the Crown and the more conscientious Members of Parliament could master the trifles from which policy is fashioned. . . . Sir James Graham could be personally aware of everything that happened at the Admiralty, and Palmerston was practically a one man Foreign Office, conducting the important correspondence of his Department in his own hand, and sometimes pursuing a policy all his own. Even in more recent times, Lord Salisbury, who never trusted his officials, could disregard them with more or less impunity.[3]

Prior to the beginning of the twentieth century, the civil bureaucracy of even the largest and most powerful nations of the world could be considered chiefly as a tool to be employed strictly to execute the policy established by the lawmakers. Lord Welby undoubtedly was thinking in such terms when he stated that the chief function of any civil servant was to do what he was told.[4]

World War I, the Depression of the 1930s, World War II, the Korean conflict, the challenge of communism, and the great urban surge have caused the functions of the Federal government to expand to a level undreamed of at the turn of the century.

In this study the term "civil bureaucracy" will refer to the Federal government employees who fill the ranks of the many Federal agencies, except for the military groups which will be considered separately. These employees are the technicians who make possible an operation of a scale which is based upon the coordination of many specialized functions.

The growth in numbers alone has given the civil bureaucracy an increasingly powerful position in the American governmental process. However, a greater part of the bureaucracy's power has resulted from the technical nature of the functions the government is concerned with and the growing recognition by the bureaucracy of its position in American society in general. Harold J. Laski has observed the growing power of the bureaucracy in these terms:

It has followed quite logically from the growth of governmental functions that the civil service should have accreted to itself continuously greater power in the state. The fact that the highest officials are permanent; the knowledge they inevitably acquire from daily familiarity with their problems; the necessary

---

[2] Marshall E. Dimock, "Bureaucracy Self-examined," *Public Administration Review,* 4, 3 (summer, 1944), 198.

[3] J. Donald Kingsley, "The Execution of Policy," in Robert K. Merton, Ailsa P. Gray, Barbara Hockey, and Hanan S. Selvin (eds.), *Reader in Bureaucracy* (New York: The Free Press of Glencoe, 1952), p. 216.

[4] *Ibid.,* pp. 216–217.

dependence upon them of any minister for the material which gives flesh and blood to his half-formulated principles; his inescapable reliance upon them for the measurement of ideal against fact—all this means their attainment of a position of authority different from that which any previous age has known.[5]

Any decrease in the powerful role being played by the agencies of government seems most unlikely inasmuch as the current trends point toward a continued increase in the size and functions of government. The executive director of the National Civil Service League has asserted that the future of the bureaucracy in the United States will be tremendously influenced by the worldwide challenge of communism and the great urban surge. Because of this situation he says that "strength in this modern day requires strength in government. In spite of the delusions under which some people labor, government is big, complicated, and necessary."[6] With reference to the challenge of communism, former Secretary of Defense Neil McElroy has said:

Our civilization is locked in a vast contest of ideologies, in which the very survival of human freedom is at stake. In this struggle there has fallen upon us the enforced, uninvited but obligated leadership of the free world. If we are to meet this obligation, it is essential that we build our strength in every part of our society. And I think it is clear that at the core of this society is our government. To be capable of world leadership we must have a strong and able government.[7]

The role of world leadership not only means an expanded role for government in terms of being able to check any outright aggression of a Communist power, but also places on the United States the responsibility of presenting to all the world an example of a system providing great economic and social opportunities—a system which is being observed very closely during the worldwide revolution of rising expectations.

Since the Depression of the 1930s, public opinion no longer tolerates prolonged economic depressions. The government is considered in a position to take remedial action. This general change in the attitudes of the public toward the job of government is one of the basic factors in consideration of the ideology of the bureaucracy. In 1956 former President Eisenhower said:

Experience . . . over many years has gradually led the American people to broaden their concept of government. Today we believe as strongly in economic progress through free and competitive enterprise as our fathers did, and we resent as they did any unnecessary intrusion of government into private affairs.

[5] Harold J. Laski, *Democracy in Action* (Chapel Hill, N.C.: The University of North Carolina Press, 1935), p. 100.

[6] James R. Watson, "The Public Service of Tomorrow," *Good Government,* 80, 3 (March, 1963), 9.

[7] *Ibid.*

But we have also come to believe that progress need not proceed as irregularly as in the past, and that the Federal Government has the capacity to moderate economic fluctuations without becoming a dominant factor in our economy.[8]

Along with a change in attitude toward the government's role has come an increasing realization of the nation's dependence on the bureaucracy for its welfare and security. Indeed, without the contributions of the experts within the agencies of government, our political system could not handle the increasingly complex demands being placed before it. The President and members of Congress cannot fully control how policy is executed, as they could in times past. Now they even find themselves looking to the bureaucracy for assistance in the creation of policy, thus permitting the civil servants to act as policy initiators as well as policy executors. As Wallace Sayre observed:

> The higher executives and professionals of the federal service stand, with the President and the Congress, at the center of the nation's policy process. Much of the process of decision-making is in their hands. The assemblage of information, the discovery of alternatives, the analytical appraisal of these choices, the synthesis of risks and opportunities into innovative yet realistic recommendations, the process of bargaining and accommodations which transforms proposals into accepted policies, the execution of resulting plans and programs—in each of these stages effective participation by the higher executives and professions is indispensable to the President and the Congress, being essential to the creation and execution of viable public policies.[9]

All the participants in the public policy-making process have come to depend upon the agencies of government in one way or another. The complexity of America's way of life, the mechanism through which the wishes of the public become law, and the desire of the branches of government and of power groups to influence rule-making and policy-making processes all combine to place the bureaucracy in a position which is quite different from anything anticipated by the drafters of the Constitution.

In order to understand the manner in which the bureaucracy acts as a power group, it is necessary to view it as being composed of many agencies, each acting as a power group in its own sphere of operation toward the procurement of its own objectives. Yet, inasmuch as each agency is striving toward an expansion of its own functions and jurisdiction, the bureaucracy can be observed in a general sense as encouraging the acceptance of a progressive role for government.

[8] *Economic Report of the President,* Transmitted to the Congress January 24, 1956 (1956), p. 10, quoted in Marver H. Bernstein, *The Job of the Federal Executive* (Washington, D.C.: The Brookings Institution, 1958), p. 205.

[9] Wallace S. Sayre, "The Public Service," in President's Commission on National Goals, *Goals for Americans* (Englewood Cliffs, N.J.: Prentice-Hall, Inc., 1960), pp. 292–293.

The following outline of some of the departments and agencies will indicate the extent to which some of the Federal government organizations have grown in size. Since nine-tenths of all Federal government employees fill positions outside Washington, D.C., these agencies are able to spread their influence broadly with a minimum amount of effort. It also makes possible the development of stronger legislative ties between the bureaucracy and individual congressmen. The further implications of this geographical distribution of employees will be treated in more detail in the following section. The size of the bureaucracy is delineated by the following employment figures for January, 1964.[10]

I. Departments:
  A. Defense: weapons evaluation, coordination of procurement, research and development, munitions, manpower, and military assistance (1,043,361)
  B. Post Office (595,571—20 per cent of Federal civilian employees)
  C. Agriculture: marketing, commodity control, research, Forest Service, and soil conservation (98,412)
  D. Treasury: internal revenue, customs, custody of funds, currency, debt, finance, narcotics control, Secret Service, and Coast Guard (84,779)
  E. Health, Education, and Welfare: social insurance, child welfare, food and drugs, health, education, and vocational rehabilitation (82,040)
  F. Interior: territories, Indian affairs, water and power resources, fish and wildlife, national parks, public lands, oil and mineral resources (61,963)
  G. State: foreign affairs and policy, cultural exchange, technical and economic aid (total employees, 42,357)
  H. Justice: Attorney General, FBI, immigration, Federal prisons, civil rights, and antitrust (31,682)
  I. Commerce: census, statistical services, maritime, public roads, promotion of trade, national production, Weather Bureau, and patents and standards (30,707)
  J. Labor (9,269)
II. Independent Agencies:
Fifty independent agencies had a total Federal government employment of 2,496,105.

These organizations are engaged in spending billions of dollars annually for projects which affect every segment of the American public. Large amounts of money stimulate the use of power and politics. The political and economic processes of the United States cannot be separated. Public policies cannot be devised which affect economics without affecting politics also. Inasmuch as the agencies are the spenders of this money, they become involved in power politics.

The role played today by the administrative agencies in the govern-

---

[10] U.S. Senate Committee on Government Operations, "Organization of Federal Executive Departments and Agencies," chart accompanying Committee Report no. 24 (1964).

mental process has some similarities to the functioning of the large formal power groups. *The bureaucracies not only help execute the law, they also strive to apply effective pressure at the critical points in the political process, placing them among the power groups which help forge public policy.* J. Leiper Freeman has elaborated on this political role of bureaucracies as follows:

> Since a public bureaucracy is concerned with special and limited aspects of public policy, to a degree it resembles the ordinary private pressure group. It is a congregating place for individuals concerned with the same subjects. . . . In this representative process perhaps the bureaucracy's most important function is to promote the idea that its special area of concern is important—be it education, air power, or mental health. The bureaucracy also promotes special solutions to policy problems in its area. Finally it promotes objectives which are of particular interest to its members *as bureaucrats*.[11]

The Federal agencies occupy what might well be considered the most advantageous spot in the policy-making process. Indeed, it is their strategic position which is most essential to their power role. The administrative agencies enjoy a day-to-day liaison with congressmen, the committees of Congress, and high officials of the executive branch. They can frequently rely upon the support of clientele groups, which themselves are often counted among the most effective power groups. Much of the power of some agencies comes from the support of its employees, who in some cases are organized and act as power groups themselves.

The pressure activities of the agencies comprising the bureaucracy are directed generally toward expanding policy-making and rule-making powers and specifically toward obtaining the "go ahead" needed to establish, alter, or increase those functions which are in the interest of the executives, employees, and clientele of the particular agency. These objectives are always presented, however, as being in the public interest.

The civil bureaucracy differs from other power groups discussed to this point in that as employees of the government they are considered to be neutrals on political matters—and most members of the bureaucracy would likely be quick to agree to this position. Further, they do not recognize any ideological stand which would give some indication of how they, as a total, would lean on a specific issue. A recent study indicated that Federal employees do not vote as a "bloc," but are substantially divided among themselves and that there is a considerable degree of correspondence between the way Federal employees vote and the way society as a whole votes.[12]

[11] J. Leiper Freeman, "The Bureaucracy in Pressure Politics," *The Annals,* 319 (September, 1958), 11.

[12] Letter from Dalmas H. Nelson, San Fernando Valley State College, January 9, 1964.

Most members of the bureaucracy would probably be quick to oppose even the suggestion that an ideology could be attached to the bureaucracy. Most would likely assert that they are dedicated to executing the functions their agency has been authorized to perform, which are necessary for the public interest. What the members of the bureaucracy would probably not recognize is that as the members of the different agencies view their situation in the governmental process in this manner, a definite but somewhat hidden ideology is being established. The ideology rests like a blanket over the entire civil bureaucracy and has a marked effect on every segment of American society. It is the sum total of the attitudes of the members of each agency as to their own agency's role and its essentiality to the welfare of the public. It results from factors inherent in the system of bureaucracy and from agencies striving to prove the legitimacy of their existence.

The ideology will be discussed subsequently, but first an analysis will be made of the position of the bureaucracy in the governmental process of the United States. This position is a basic factor in understanding the bureaucracy's ideology as well as its effectiveness as a power community. Because of this strategic position the Federal agency is daily involved in a series of activities which are directed toward legitimatizing its existence. The success of these efforts has much to do with the vitality of the ideology.

STRATEGIC POSITION OF CIVIL BUREAUCRACIES

In this section it will be shown that the chief source of the bureaucracy's power is its position within the scheme of government. Of the factors that create and sustain the ideology of the bureaucracy, none is as significant as the strategic position of the agencies in the political process.

Relationship with Legislators

The relationship among individual legislators and the agencies is a continuing one. "Administrative agencies do not wait until a specific proposal is to be urged upon the legislature to cultivate harmonious relations with legislators. A continuous process of legislative liaison is maintained."[13] Agencies establish their closest ties with legislators who hold key positions in the committees with which the agency most frequently deals.

The strategic location of the agencies in Washington, D.C., close to Capitol Hill, facilitates liaison. Each major agency has a team whose job it is to maintain a close tie with congressmen. Within the State Department this function has achieved bureau status—the Bureau of Congressional Relations. These adept functionaries receive requests from congressmen and respond with courtesy and speed. In addition to yielding accurate and

[13] Freeman, 14.

vital information, administrative agencies can perform other favors to maintain friendly ties with congressmen.

Many private groups maintain substantial lobbying staffs in Washington, but they do not have quite the same access and privileges as administrative agencies. They cannot conduct congressmen on expense-free tours of Europe, provide free medical care, and make the life of congressmen more enjoyable in a number of other respects. Administrative agencies do this and for the most part questions are not raised. When private groups attempt similar activity, charges of "bribery" or worse are likely to be leveled.[14]

Agency employees working in the field frequently maintain a close connection with legislators from their area. Since these officials are close to and partially represent groups upon which the congressmen depend, the legislators are anxious to maintain this close association. For example, a senator at home during a brief Easter recess may obtain some of his best soundings of farm sentiment by talking to the regional director of the Farmers' Home Administration who, in approving farmers' loans, hears their comments and complaints continuously.

The liaison between congressmen and agencies of the Federal government often reaches its highest point between the career officials and the members of Congress with lengthy tenure. On this matter Marshall E. Dimock has said that "if the program involves legislation, the career officials may talk confidentially with members of the legislative branch with whom over a period of years they have developed a close relationship."[15]

Relationship among Agencies, Clientele Groups, and Congressional Committees

Some of the support agencies seek for their programs invariably comes from the agency's clientele groups—those groups whose activities are seriously affected by the agency and which, in turn, influence how the agency's programs are executed. The agency becomes the focal point of its sometimes diverse clientele groups.[16]

Because of the frequently close association between agencies and their clientele, the agencies often receive support resulting in considerable pressure on Congress. The groups which rally to the support of the different agencies are often among the most powerful, politically and economically. Any agency looks to its clientele groups as evidence of the legitimacy of its own existence. At the same time the groups look to the agency as their protector and spokesman.

The rule-making role of the administrative agencies is basic to the

[14] Peter Woll, *American Bureaucracy* (New York: W. W. Norton & Company, Inc., 1963), p. 135.

[15] Dimock, 203. [16] Woll, p. 54.

close linkage between many agencies and their constituency. Since most legislation affecting the power groups in America is skeletal, and since it devolves upon the administrative agency involved really to clothe the legislation, the formal power groups involved are anxious to have a healthy affiliation with the agency.[17] This helps explain why many groups devote as much effort to lobbying the executive as the legislative branch.

A study made of the relationship between government agencies and the public indicated that "in large part, the task of disseminating information about their programs was assigned to voluntary associations and economic groups—business, labor, and special interest."[18] Since government agencies are somewhat restricted in their informational activities, this support is very significant.

Because of the extent to which the administrative agencies are able to strengthen their position through their alliance with private groups, one writer has said that the wise administrator will make every effort to keep open the channels between his agency and groups concerned with its operation. "Indeed, next to maintaining an independent mind, the only question is whether these channels should be established on a formal basis or maintained as a matter of informal personal contact."[19]

The association of administrative agencies and the congressional committees is chiefly one of interdependence. Agency officials are consistently invited to testify at committee hearings. The origin of this need lies primarily in the technical quality of most of today's legislation. Administrative officials have, for the most part, become specialists in their fields. The legislative branch, through its committees, must turn to sources outside its own membership for advice and information on technical matters.

Private groups frequently do much to ensure a healthy relationship between the committees of Congress and the agency. If these groups are powerful and have high access to congressional committees, the agencies that gain their support will similarly enjoy conspicuous access.

Both the committees of Congress and clientele groups may look to the agency as a means of communicating with, supporting, and pressuring one another. What is sometimes overlooked is that the "go-between" often acquires more power in the process. When legislation is formulated by an agency, the committees of Congress and the private groups which may have sought the assistance of the agency on many occasions often support the agency with alacrity.

[17] L. Harmon Zeigler, *Interest Groups in American Society* (Englewood Cliffs, N.J.: Prentice-Hall, Inc., 1964), p. 278.

[18] Morris Janowitz, Deil Wright, and William Delany, "Public Administration and the Public," in Amitai Etzioni (ed.), *Complex Organizations: A Sociological Reader* (New York: Holt, Rinehart and Winston, Inc., 1961), p. 283.

[19] Avery Leiserson, "Interest Groups in Administration," in Fritz Morstein-Marx, *Elements of Public Administration* (Englewood Cliffs, N.J.: Prentice-Hall, Inc., 1959), p. 296.

David Truman has observed this close relationship:

The relations of interest groups with the Congress, and especially with its standing committees are . . . a good deal more extensive than a casual acquaintance with Washington affairs would indicate. Over a large number of comparatively routine and non-controversial matters one will normally find on closer examination a quiet collaboration among groups, Congressional committees, and executive agencies.[20]

John A. Vieg has asserted that "today we see most national policies . . . worked out in three-fold collaboration, with participation by congressional committees, by administrative officials, and by representatives of private interest groups."[21]

Quite basic to these relationships is the fact that many members of congressional committees closely align themselves with formal power groups and administrative agencies because of their constituent pressures or personal interests. The greater part of the businessmen, lawyers, and farmers sitting in Congress continue their occupational pursuits. A significant number of congressmen serve as officials of power groups which seek to obtain legislative measures.[22]

Support from the Chief Executive and Other High Administrative Officials

The strategic position of the Federal agencies is perhaps no more obvious at any point in the governmental process than when the Chief Executive or other high administrative officials act to support an agency in its efforts to obtain the passage of its proposals. "If . . . the bureau chief and department officials seeking the legislation can secure from the Chief Executive a statement to the legislative committee, or a comment to the press, or a paragraph in a speech favorable to their proposal, they may very well enhance its possibilities of adoption."[23]

In recent years, scholars have been quick to refer to the President as the "Chief Legislator" or "Lawmaker."[24] Although many reasons can be presented to justify this title, perhaps none is more significant than that the legislature looks to the President for leadership. At the same time that

[20] David B. Truman, "Organized Interest Groups in American National Politics," in Alfred J. Junz (ed.), *Present Trends in American National Government* (New York: Frederick A. Praeger, Inc., 1961), p. 132.

[21] John A. Vieg, "The Growth of Public Administration," in Morstein-Marx, p. 79.

[22] Bertram M. Gross, *The Legislative Struggle: A Study in Social Combat* (New York: McGraw-Hill Book Company, 1953), p. 93.

[23] Freeman, 15–16.

[24] See Clinton Rossiter, *The American Presidency* (New York: Harcourt, Brace & World, Inc., 1960), pp. 28–30; and Claudius O. Johnson, *American National Government* (New York: Thomas Y. Crowell Company, 1960), pp. 497–513.

the legislature seeks this leadership, the administrative agencies strive to use the President's popularity and power as a means of rallying legislative support for their proposals. Since most of the agencies are headed by men appointed by the President and since many of the high career officials have obtained his deep respect, the agency is in an enviable position for obtaining his support. Many are the cases where the support of the President has helped an agency win its battle for legislative proposals on which the Congress was reluctant to act.

Agencies may find considerable support for their proposals through Cabinet members and other high administrative officials who testify in committee hearings and otherwise influence the Congress. These officials are often anxious to assist in the procurement of the agency's proposals. The prestige of their position can make them potent at congressional hearings and with individual congressmen.

All this is not to suggest that the Federal agencies can coast along unchecked. The President and his appointees sometimes differ with the aspirations of their career subordinates. Furthermore, the power of the bureaucracy is hemmed in by the possibility of congressional investigations designed to expose civil servants who overstep the bounds of their legal authority.

Support from the Agencies' Employees

"One of the great reservoirs of political strength available to agency leaders in certain kinds of legislative activities lies in their organization's employees."[25] The support which government executives can expect from employees depends partly on the ease with which the employees can be informed and mobilized. This appears to be easiest when formal organization is strong and cohesive. The proposals must also benefit employees, or at least appeal to their ideological conceptions to win maximum support.

Since most Federal employees are scattered throughout the United States, some agencies can rely on their employees to influence many congressmen directly, and indirectly through their contact with the public. No group of Federal employees has a closer association with the public than the postal workers. William C. Doherty, president of the National Association of Letter Carriers, has asserted:

The only weapon left to the letter carriers was (and still is) the fact that individually and as a group they are liked and admired by the American public at large and that they visit each home in America every day, six days a week. Since people talk to their letter carriers as old friends, and vice versa, this is a formidable point with Congress.[26]

[25] Freeman, 16.

[26] William C. Doherty, *Mailman, U.S.A.* (New York: David McKay Company, Inc.. 1960), pp. 26–27.

The effect that the association between Post Office employees and the public has on Congress is well emphasized in a Brookings Institution study.

At times the postal unions achieve such strength that they almost seem capable of dictating to Congress the terms of their employment. Their power is based on numbers and the fact that their members are located in every electoral district of the nation. No other group of federal employees is in such continuing contact with almost every citizen.[27]

The support which an agency can obtain from its employees when a high degree of employee organization exists was exemplified in the case of the controversial Postal Rate and Pay Increase Bill which was passed by the 85th Congress in 1958. In this case the objectives of the Post Office Department officials were an increase in postage rates and a modernization of the postal service. Combined with these goals was a pay increase proposal for Post Office Department employees. During legislative consideration, the postal employees' organizations engaged in extensive lobbying activities. The roll-call votes in both the Senate and House on the conference report of the bill were unanimously in the affirmative.[28]

The report of the President's Task Force on Employee-Management Relations in the Federal Service, completed in October, 1961, found that of the 2,277,604 Federal civilian employees, 762,372, or 33 per cent, claimed membership in an employee organization which had been formed to represent Federal employees in dealings with the management of the respective agencies on matters of working conditions.[29] However, the report points out that the figure 33 per cent cannot be considered representative of all Federal agencies.

The Post Office Department, with 600,000 employees, reports that 84 per cent of its employees are members of employee organizations. This figure, reflecting the most comprehensively organized agency in the government service, has such a decisive influence on the computation of the government-wide percentage as to distort the meaning of that percentage. Excluding the Post Office, 16 per cent of the employees of the remaining agencies are members of employee organizations.[30]

Agencies which have the highest percentage of their employees in employee organizations include the Tennessee Valley Authority, 82 per cent; the Treasury Department, 46 per cent; and the Office of Civil and Defense Mobilization, 38 per cent. There are seventeen agencies in which none, or

[27] Marver H. Bernstein, *The Job of the Federal Executive* (Washington, D.C.: The Brookings Institution, 1958), p. 96.

[28] *Congressional Quarterly,* 85th Congress, 2d Session, 14 (1958), 382, 433.

[29] President's Task Force on Employee-Management Relations in the Federal Service, *Employee-Management Relations Practices in the Federal Service* (October, 1961), p. 11.

[30] *Ibid.,* p. 9.

less than 10 per cent of the employees belong to employee organizations.[31]

The report also points out that two government employees unions are most widely encountered among the agencies, the American Federation of Government Employees (AFL-CIO) and the National Federation of Federal Employees (unaffiliated). Table 3 shows the size of these organizations. It should be noted that they are dwarfed by two Post Office unions, the National Association of letter carriers (AFL-CIO) and the United Federation of Postal Clerks (AFL-CIO). Some of these major unions have had both ups and downs in membership, but their net growth from 1951 to 1962 was 426,242 to 545,008.

TABLE 3. **Figures for Selected Unions with Major Portion of Their Membership in the Federal Service**

Union	1962
Letter carriers	150,114
Post office clerks	145,000
Government employees	106,042
Federal employees (ind.)	49,500
Letter carriers, rural (ind.)	39,852
Postal supervisors (ind.)	26,000
Post office mail handlers	14,000
Post office and general services (ind.)	8,000
Post office motor vehicle	5,000
Messengers, special delivery	1,500
Total	545,008

SOURCE: Bureau of Labor Statistics, Division of Industrial and Labor Relations, October, 1963.

The significance of an agency's officials being able to mobilize its employees cannot be passed over lightly. As the Federal agencies continue to expand in size and as more and more agencies spread themselves over all parts of the country, congressmen feel increasing pressures from the agencies not only in Washington but also in their states and districts.

President Kennedy's Executive Order of January 17, 1962, based upon the recommendations of the report of the Task Force on Employee-Management Relations in the Federal Service, recognized the right of Federal employees to join bona fide employee organizations and to enter collective negotiations with management officials on matters of working conditions and personnel policies. It established three forms of recognition—informal,

[31] *Ibid.*, pp. 10–11.

formal, and exclusive—each determined by the percentage of employees of an agency who hold membership in an employee organization. If less than 10 per cent of the employees belong to an organization, that organization shall be granted informal recognition. If between 10 and 50 per cent hold membership in an employee organization, it shall obtain formal recognition. If 50 per cent or more of the employees of an agency have selected an organization, it shall receive exclusive recognition as the representative for the employees.

When an employee organization has been informally recognized, it will be permitted "to present to appropriate officials its views on matters of concern to its members. The agency need not, however, consult with an employee organization so recognized in the formulation of personnel or other policies with respect to such matters." If an organization is accorded formal recognition, "the agency, through appropriate officials, shall consult with such organization from time to time in the formulation and implementation of personnel policies and practices, and matters affecting working conditions that are of concern to its members." When an employee organization is granted exclusive recognition "it shall be entitled to act for and to negotiate agreements covering all employees in the unit." It will be "represented at discussions between management and employees . . . concerning grievances, personnel policies and practices or other matters affecting general working conditions of employees in the unit."[32]

Since the privileges of representation become greater as the degree of recognition increases, employees feel some incentive to consolidate into large unions. The privileges under the "exclusive recognition" status are so much greater than those under the other two forms of recognition that the order appears to have been directed to encourage the creation of large unions.

As Federal employee unions increase in size more of them may join the most effective lobbies. The lobbying efforts of the postal unions have already been mentioned. An account of groups reporting lobbying expenditures of more than $50,000 annually in four or more of the years 1953 to 1958 inclusive listed the National Association of Letter Carriers and the National Federation of Post Office Clerks.[33] In 1962, seven of the more than 300 reporting lobby organizations revealed expenditures of over $100,000. One of these was the United Federation of Postal Clerks.[34]

Although the history of the Federal employee unions suggests that their main concern has been increases in wages and improvement of personnel

[32] Executive Order 10988, "Employee-Management Cooperation in the Federal Service," *Federal Register,* 27 (January 19, 1962), 551–556.

[33] Truman in Junz, 129.

[34] Charles L. Clapp, *The Congressman: His Work as He Sees It* (Washington, D.C.: The Brookings Institution, 1963), p. 163.

policies, it is not uncommon for the employees to join with management in policy objectives. Whenever management regards a policy as essential to its existence or expansion, it can look to its employees for support if it is willing to include among its proposals provisions which the employees will recognize as benefiting them.

It appears probable that employee unions will gradually include a higher percentage of Federal employees, and there will be some consolidation to obtain exclusive recognition. As this occurs, union management will be even more inclined to seek ways to mobilize employees in support of proposals before Congress, especially when Congress is reticent in acting favorably toward the agency.

IDEOLOGY OF THE CIVIL BUREAUCRACY

Power relationships are inherent in every administrative situation. The executive must be fully aware of their necessary implications and prepared to struggle openly for power and for survival lest, by false modesty, weakness or self-delusion, he lose or seriously restrict his jurisdiction and endanger his program.[35]

The formal power groups which participate in the making of public policy are constantly checked in the pursuit of their objectives by other pressure blocs—both the branches of government and private power groups. Much of this opposition is created as a result of clashing ideologies, based on diverse interests. The civil bureaucracy, however, is considered to be neutral and not the possessor of an ideology that opposes that of some other group. The legislator thinks of his relationship with the bureaucracy chiefly in terms of several agencies with which he deals because of his assignments on committees and the area he represents. He is not inclined to think of these agencies as part of the huge Federal bureaucracy, but rather as agencies performing, for the most part, essential functions. He often thinks of the agencies in terms of personal friends in Washington and in his district or state who are dedicated to the tasks of their agencies.

The status of the bureaucracy has enabled its ideology to develop to the point of being recognizable in the operations of all agencies, but because of its position in the process of government the ideology escapes the attention of nearly everyone, including the bureaucrat.

The ideology is based upon the manner in which each agency views its own role and position in society. Each agency sees its existence as a result of society's approval of its creation to meet certain needs. In fact, the agency was created because certain segments of the public expressed a need for

[35] Marshall E. Dimock, "Expanding Jurisdictions: A Case Study in Bureaucratic Conflict," in Robert K. Merton et al. (eds.), *Reader in Bureaucracy* (New York: The Free Press of Glencoe, 1952), p. 290.

the vital role that it would play in strengthening and improving life in America. To the staff this means the right of the agency to meet as many of the demands of society as can be construed to fall in some way within the agency's jurisdiction. The scope of the legislation which gives birth to some agencies gives considerable encouragement toward the expansion of functions.

. . . these were to be the final goals of TVA, as stated in Section 23 of the Act: 1. The maximum amount of flood control; 2. The maximum development of said Tennessee River for navigation purposes; 3. The maximum generation of electrical power consistent with flood control and navigability; 4. The proper use of marginal lands; 5. The proper method of reforestation of all lands in said drainage basin suitable for reforestation; and 6. The economic and social well-being of the people living in said river basin.[36]

If new functions can be proposed and society can be shown that the new work of the agency is vital to the betterment of social conditions, the legitimacy of the agency's existence is further expressed, and its permanence made more secure.

The ideology can be stated in these terms: The existence of the agency is the wish of the public and evidence of the democratic process in America. The agency is performing services that are essential to the public welfare, and its value is determined largely by the way it uses the superior knowledge of its experts to consider the problems of a complex society. Society will be further improved if the agency expands the functions it now performs so as to service a greater part of the public. There are needs which either are not being met, or are not being met as well as they should be, which the agency may be able to handle. The agency is concerned with the greatest amount of efficiency possible so as to reward society for entrusting it with the things it wants done by government.

Classical ideologies contest the justification for growth of government, as explained in Chapter 2. They would take an argument such as the growing complexity of our economic society and say that this proves the human impossibility of successful centralization and that it argues instead for decentralization, with an emphasis on energetic private groups.

The bureaucratic ideology gives ranging degrees of internal cohesion to each agency and promotes their interests with respect to all external groups. It *justifies each agency's present size and desire for future growth in terms of the needs of society, service, and efficiency.* It is directed toward security and autonomy, which are constant concerns of the agency, and justifies expansional efforts, which are made to guarantee the preservation of the agency. It is an ideology of progressivism.

[36] Mario Einaudi, *The Roosevelt Revolution* (New York: Harcourt, Brace & World, 1959), p. 165.

No one speaks for the entire civil bureaucracy. However, since the bureaucracy is comprised of many Federal agencies, if a person backs away from his observance of one or several agencies and takes a look at the civil bureaucracy as a whole, he sees a bureaucracy which has as its basic aims *a preservation of and an increase in the role it plays in society.*

Occasionally government employees may profess a conservative view of the proper role of government. Still they desire to see their own agency in the strongest position possible. Even if a majority of the bureaucrats held to conservative feelings, the net effect of the bureaucracies' defense of their own units' expansion would produce a progressive ideology. The employees of each agency are anxious to see the functions of their agency increased to give them greater security, prestige, and responsibility.

In 1935 the Rural Electrification Administration was created by an Executive Order.[37] In 1936 it received a statutory basis. Its function was to construct electric power lines. Its operations were financed by direct appropriations and on funds from the Reconstruction Finance Corporation. From the standpoint of the agency heads, the "close-knit operation of the agency resulted in speed of operation and dedication to public purpose."[38]

REA functioned as an independent agency until July 1, 1939, when it was transferred to the Department of Agriculture by an act of Congress. The consolidation resulted in disputes over organization and policy. REA was opposed to attempts by the Department to bring its staff into alignment with Department policies on salaries, appointments, and promotions. "This meant lower salaries for some and much slower advancement for all. As a consequence, REA lost some of the staff which it had built up since 1935."[39]

The ideology of each agency, and therefore the entire bureaucracy, is directed toward avoiding what happened to REA. The fear of a decrease in autonomy is ever present in agencies. Agency heads have come to revere the policy they administer and the position their agency holds. Bernstein has said that "each bureau or unit has developed its own historical traditions and customary administrative approaches; and each unit gradually developed a vested interest in its statutory powers and political prestige. Created in response to a particular need, each bureau holds firmly to its separatist ways."[40]

Some agencies have been able to show that they are very essential to the public's protection and security—strong ideological symbols. This has given them greater autonomy and is a significant aid in helping them to win

[37] See Winifred McCullock, "The Rural Electrification Administration Personnel Report," in Harold Stein, *Public Administration and Policy Development* (New York: Harcourt, Brace & World, Inc., 1952), pp. 621–632.

[38] *Ibid.*, p. 624.   [40] Bernstein, p. 84.

[39] *Ibid.*

their proposals. The Federal Bureau of Investigation is an example of this type of agency. The strength arising from its position is shown in the case of the FBI Retirement Bill of 1947.[41]

In this case a bill for special retirement privileges for FBI employees was devised in the Department of Justice and introduced in both houses of Congress. The legislation was objected to by the Civil Service Commission and the Department of the Treasury. The former felt that special retirement privileges should not be given to FBI employees above those of all other Federal government employees. The latter felt that since within the Treasury Department there are agencies with important investigative functions, such as the Secret Service, greater retirement benefits should not be given to FBI employees than to other Federal employees performing comparable duties. Even with this type of opposition to the proposed legislation the bill passed the Senate "without debate and without dissent." Nearly three months later S. 715 passed the House without a dissenting vote. An interesting device was used to obtain this enactment. Former FBI agents, many of whom had become prominent citizens, were utilized to write to their national legislators, giving reasons why the bill should be passed.

In considering the action taken on the bill, the reader must keep in mind that "the deep and wide-spread concern over the security of the United States and the correlative concern over the well-being of the FBI as an agency dedicated to the protection of our security" greatly influenced the outcome of the legislation.[42]

A better understanding of the ideology of the civil bureaucracy will be gained by an examination of some of the elements which are inherent in the organizational form of bureaucracy. Since the ideology of any group has an origin which is largely the result of historical developments and social trends, these factors may shed some light on the present ideology.

INHERENT CHARACTERISTICS OF BUREAUCRACY AND SOCIETY'S DEMAND FOR EFFICIENCY

Peter Blau asserts that the basic characteristics of bureaucratic organization are "specialization, a hierarchy of authority, a system of rules, and impersonality."[43] According to Max Weber "experience tends universally to show that the purely bureaucratic type of administrative organization . . .

---

[41] Joseph F. Marsh, Jr., "The FBI Retirement Bill," in Harold Stein, *Public Administration and Policy Development* (New York: Harcourt, Brace & World, Inc., 1952), pp. 649–660.

[42] *Ibid.*, p. 652.

[43] Peter Blau, *Bureaucracy in Modern Society* (New York: Random House, Inc., 1956), p. 19.

is, from a purely technical point of view, capable of attaining the highest degree of efficiency."[44] He has also asserted that "precision, speed, unambiguity, knowledge of the files, continuity, discretion, unity, strict subordination, reduction of friction and of material and personal costs—these are raised to the optimum point in the strictly bureaucratic administration."[45]

These statements indicate that the stress of bureaucracy is on form, order, and routinization so as to reach the maximum degree of efficiency. Indeed, bureaucracies come into existence when a complex society seeks means of a systematic performance of its functions. Today's government agencies are in a position to influence the public and the lawmakers to recognize that certain problems exist and should be met. At the same time they are able to show the capability of taking care of the problem with greater efficiency than could be done by any other group. Thus, the inherent characteristics of the bureaucracy of the agency combined with its strategic position give it a great advantage for being granted the authority it needs to expand its functions. With each increase in size and functions, its existence becomes more secure by the fact that society depends upon it more than before.

The public's demand for efficiency is constantly of concern to the members of the agency: "Suffice it to say that the commandment: 'Be efficient!' is a major organizational influence over the decisions of the members of any administrative agency; and a determination whether this commandment has been obeyed is a major function of the review process."[46] Because of the myriad of rules which today give some protection to those parts of the bureaucratic structure which may be a threat to the efficiency of an agency, there is a strong tendency to overcome these weaknesses by expanding the size of the bureaucratic machinery to reach the efficiency point desired.

One scholar has taken an interesting approach to the matter of claims of inefficiency in bureaucracy. He feels that in dealing with bureaucratic groups, individuals may feel helpless before the powerful bureaucracy, especially if the bureaucracy fails to see the exceptional circumstances of his case and treats it as one of a general category. The frustrated petitioner may seek to relieve his feelings in terms of calling attention to bureaucratic inefficiency.[47] The same author states that "colloquially, the term 'bureauc-

---

[44] Max Weber, *The Theory of Social and Economic Organization*, translated by A. M. Henderson and Talcott Parsons (New York: The Free Press of Glencoe, 1947), p. 337.

[45] Weber, "Technical Advantages of Bureaucratic Organization."

[46] Herbert A. Simon, "Decision-making and Administrative Organization," in Robert K. Merton et al. (eds.), *Reader in Bureaucracy* (New York: The Free Press of Glencoe, 1952), p. 192.

[47] Blau, pp. 102–103.

racy' has become an epithet which refers to inefficiency and red tape in the government."[48]

Classical ideologists, particularly, argue that government bureaucracies are inefficient because they do not have the pressure of competition as private firms do. In the struggle for markets the efficient companies win and the inefficient companies die. Thus profits become a starkly realistic measure of efficiency for which there is no substitute in government.

The general attachment of the image of inefficiency to the bureaucracy by the same society which demands efficiency stimulates each agency to improve its programs and methods and to demonstrate efficiency in quantifiable terms in publicity and at congressional hearings. Illustrative of this is the giving of awards to civil servants who make suggestions to improve efficiency. Civil Service Commission chairman John Macy often gave examples of these awards and the estimated dollars saved by each suggestion in his talks to civic and business clubs.

CHANGING VIEW OF THE ROLE OF GOVERNMENT

As was pointed out in the introduction to this chapter, at the beginning of the twentieth century the size and functions of the civil bureaucracy were very limited in comparison with the situation today. This condition was largely the result of the general concept of the role of government. The ruling doctrine up to this time had been *laissez faire,* a doctrine of governmental noninterference. The crises of the twentieth century have presented a challenge to this doctrine, out of which has emerged the creation of many new agencies of the Federal government. These were established "to perform functions and to exercise over the lives and businesses of the American people controls which previously had not been the concern of the Federal Government."[49]

These changes in the general view of the role of government have placed the "service state" label on the United States.

The most distinctive characteristic of the service state is the prominence of public administration. As government shifts from a relatively passive to an increasingly active role, it inevitably expands its machinery of action. This machinery assumes the character of a permanent establishment because government is compelled to take on continuing responsibilities which can be fulfilled only through continuity of operations.[50]

---

[48] *Ibid.,* p. 13.

[49] John J. Corson, *Executives for the Federal Service* (New York: Columbia University Press, 1952), p. 16.

[50] Fritz Morstein-Marx, "The Social Function of Public Administration," in *Elements of Public Administration* (Englewood Cliffs, N.J.: Prentice-Hall, Inc., 1959), p. 97.

Aside from our modern wars with their government-directed economies, the greatest influences for changing accepted concepts of the role of
government were the Great Depression and the New Deal. Until the beginning of the New Deal the role of government, with certain exceptions, was
nonintervention. With the introduction of the New Deal, many new administrative agencies were spawned. Among the new governmental bodies comprising the modern administrative state were the TVA, the Housing and
Home Finance Agency, the Civil Aeronautics Board, the Securities and
Exchange Commission, the National Labor Relations Board, the Federal
Deposit Insurance Corporation, the Atomic Energy Commission, the Farm
Credit Administration, the Export-Import Bank, the Foreign Operations
Administration, and the Federal Security Agency.[51]

Mario Einaudi makes this interesting observation on these new
agencies:

> Most of them gained powers of discretionary action, for no effective inter-
> pretation and execution of often intricate laws was possible without them. The
> new agencies acquired substantial quasi-legislative powers. In itself, this was of
> course not a new development, but its impact was all the more acutely felt in
> the years after 1933, for the new powers were then being applied to far more
> important and sensitive areas of human affairs. The new agencies obtained
> powers of investigation and of execution as well.[52]

These changes have had an impact on the American public, the extent
of which is difficult to grasp. The bureaucracy became essential to the
preservation of America's strength and security. Even the image of the
bureaucrat was changed. He was recognized as performing an essential role
in America's growth and development. The businessman did not have the
answer to all of America's ills. Indeed, "there was a marked general improvement in public attitudes toward the civil servant since 1930."[53]

Not only did the New Deal succeed in changing the role of the civil
bureaucracy, but it also created a huge bureaucracy which was filled with
people who recognized the agencies of the government as points from
which they could fulfill their desires to take action on existing problems.
Many of the nation's intellectuals, lawyers, and students looked to the New
Deal as an opportunity of participating in a "democratic experiment rooted
in American soil and conditioned by contemporary American realities.
Public service became the alternative to the frustrations and pessimism that
were determining the activities of sensitive men of high skills."[54] The influx
of these people into the new agencies gave each agency a progressive view
of its own role that constitutes one of the most significant factors in the
development of the present ideology.

[51] Einaudi, p. 137.
[52] *Ibid.*
[53] Janowitz et al. in Etzioni, p. 281.
[54] Einaudi, p. 135.

Concerning the characteristics of these New Deal employees and the general attitude toward their work Herman Miles Somers has written: "Theirs was a tradition of proposing and initiating new ideas, programs, reforms. Theirs was the task of 'educating' the Congress and even doing battle for policy advances."[55] The changing attitude was exemplified as the bureaucrats began to appear to an unprecedented degree before congressional committees to support the programs of their agencies.

With regard to bureaucracy during the Roosevelt and Truman administrations Woll has stated:

. . . the bureaucracy was generally imbued with the idea that it should be active in the regulation of the economic life of the country and positive in making legislative recommendations to Congress and the President. Both Roosevelt and Truman preferred a bureaucracy that seized initiative, even if this meant a certain amount of opposition to presidential desires from time to time, over a bureaucracy that was unresponsive and passive.[56]

The emphasis placed on a progressive bureaucracy during the two decades from 1933 to 1953 was somewhat in conflict with the policy of the Eisenhower administration, which called for the withdrawal of the Federal government from many areas it had participated in since 1933. At the time Eisenhower was to move into the White House and considerable changes in the administrative machinery were expected to take place, *Fortune* magazine made this comment:

When Mr. Eisenhower's brisk businessmen move into their Washington offices this month, they will not find themselves surrounded entirely by friends, or all the corridors ringing with camaraderie. There will be a lot of people around who view businessmen with a fishy eye. Such highly placed Fair Dealers as Oscar Chapman and Oscar Ewing will have departed, of course, but a legion of little Oscars will still be on or in the bureaucratic anthills, enjoying long-term appointive jobs or perched out of reach in civil service.

The problem is not competence. Many are very competent. The problem they present revolves around their ideology. They are in key positions. For no matter what is said about the nonpolitical nature of civil-service appointments, in twenty years of Roosevelt and Truman it has been the dedicated New and Fair Dealers who have floated to the top.[57]

Eisenhower's eight years in the White House do not seem to have significantly affected the ideology of the bureaucracy. The Republicans found that it is very difficult to reduce the functions or size of an agency after a clientele which depends on the agency and has contact with Congress has been mobilized.

[55] Herman Miles Somers, "The Federal Bureaucracy and Change in Administration," *American Political Science Review*, 48, 1 (March, 1954), 137.

[56] Woll, p. 152.

[57] "The Little Oscars and Civil Service," *Fortune*, 47 (January, 1953), 77.

The Civil Service

The foundation of a career civil service for the Federal government was laid with the passage of the Pendleton Act in 1883. The act formalized the belief that to an extent government positions should depend upon ability and fitness rather than upon party affiliation. Since the passage of the act, the patronage or "spoils" system has given way to the merit system more and more until today some 91 per cent of Federal employees are under the merit system.[58]

With the growth in the number of public employees covered by the merit system there has developed an increasingly greater sense of cohesion and continuity. Without fear of being replaced solely on the basis of political factors, most Federal employees are able to look to a career within their agencies. Thus, *esprit de corps* develops within the agency, and its members view it with a sense of honor and pride. The employees associate their own prestige with that of their agency, and they cherish the opportunity of pointing out to associates the advancement of the agency in terms of methods of doing work, functions performed, numbers of employees, and money being spent.

The Civil Service Commission does much to imbue the career employees with an *esprit de corps*. This was shown in 1961 when its chairman said the major goals of the Federal civil service included attracting the nation's best talent into the Federal service, developing talent within the career service, obtaining an adequate and equitable pay system, and raising the prestige of the Federal service.[59] The commission also brings greater cohesion into the agencies by informing Federal employees of legislation that will in any way affect the civil service. This is done through the "A Look at Legislation" page which appears in most copies of the *Civil Service Journal.*[60]

The merit system was used very effectively by Roosevelt and Truman to establish a bureaucracy dedicated to progressive programs. "By placing these new civil servants under the merit system Roosevelt was taking the very course of action necessary to protect the New Deal. . . . President Truman brought a considerable portion of the bureaucracy under the protection of the merit system before he faced the uncertainty of the 1948 election."[61]

---

[58] Utah State Public Employees Association, *Why a Merit System for State Employees* (Salt Lake City, Utah, n.d.), 3.

[59] "Six Major Goals of the Federal Civil Service," *Good Government*, 78, 10 (October, 1961), 3.

[60] See, for example, U.S. Civil Service Commission, "A Look at Legislation," *Civil Service Journal*, 3, 4 (April–June, 1963), 5.

[61] Woll, p. 151.

The merit system has enabled a sense of cohesion and continuity to exist in the civil bureaucracy, and its use has been a significant factor in the creation of the present ideology. The success of the merit system was shown when President Eisenhower attempted to reduce the number of civil servants generally. There arose a feeling of distrust among the bureaucracy toward him which resulted in relatively few changes being made.

New Agencies

As the role of government has changed the Federal government has undertaken more and more new programs. Wallace S. Sayre has emphasized the point that "new governmental programs requiring innovations have most often been entrusted to newly-created agencies staffed by newly-recruited personnel."[62] The newly formed agency immediately becomes concerned with establishing its legitimacy and becoming as autonomous as possible. It must prove its essentiality to society's welfare. It must show that it renders a significant service and does so with marked efficiency. This leads to efforts to increase and activate its clientele, which usually mean growth of functions and size. Efforts are made to obtain the closest relationship possible with the power blocs of the policy-making process, which when established makes growth more possible.

Since most of the employees, including the executives, of the new agency are new recruits into the government service, they have a fresh concern about the security and prestige of their own positions.

It is significant to note that in the creation of new agencies, as well as at the top levels of established ones, executives are drawn extensively from outside the ranks of the government. Many of these are business executives, academic leaders, and professional people.[63] These appointees leave their positions to enter government service for the most part because of an "opportunity for public service; opportunity to pursue political objectives; opportunities for more interesting and stimulating work; opportunity to improve career prospects outside of government with government experience; desire for prestige, esteem or deference; desire to be influential in public affairs and occupy a position of power."[64] Each of these points indicates why the executives will be anxious to see the agency increase in size and tasks. They are generally anxious to use their position in government to initiate new programs and to make important decisions with respect to challenging social and economic issues.

These new leaders do much to establish and perpetuate the basic ideology of their respective agencies, which in turn add to the progressive, expansional ideology of the bureaucracy as a whole.

[62] Sayre, p. 291.   [64] Bernstein, p. 139.
[63] Corson, pp. 16, 17, 21.

The Federal Executive

Inasmuch as the agency of government acts under the direction of its spokesmen, these Federal executives should be discussed, at least briefly, to determine in what way they, as individuals, influence the ideology of the bureaucracy.

ORIGIN OF THE EXECUTIVE.   The results of two recent studies show that Federal executives come predominantly from urban areas. A study by W. Lloyd Warner and others showed that "the big cities are represented by a ratio of 182 to every 100 that would be expected by chance."[65] Warner's investigation was made of 10,851 civilian Federal executives from cabinet level down to General Schedule grade 14 or the equivalent.[66]

A study by Dean E. Mann indicated that among political executives 90 per cent were living in metropolitan areas when appointed to the government service, although only 59 per cent of the total population lived in such areas in 1950. Mann suggests that this may be one reason for conflicts between executive-legislative viewpoints, since a recent study indicated that a majority of senators were born in rural areas.[67]

The results of these studies also suggest that the origin of Federal executives may be significant in understanding the progressive ideology of the bureaucracy. The metropolitan areas are predominantly liberal in their view of the role of government. An overwhelming majority of high Federal executives from urban areas undoubtedly affects the bureaucracy's ideology toward more sophisticated and progressive stands.

THE EDUCATIONAL LEVEL.   The educational level of the Federal executives also needs to be given some consideration. Warner's investigation showed that of the civilian executives studied, 9 out of 10 have at least some college training, 8 out of 10 are college graduates, 25 per cent have the M.A. degree, 10 per cent have the Ph.D. degree, and 10 per cent have the LL.B. degree.[68] Among such groups as the Foreign Service officers, the level of education was even higher: 88 per cent have college degrees, 33 per cent M.A. degrees, 13 per cent Ph.D. degrees, and 8 per cent degrees in law. These figures far surpass those for all adult males in the United

[65] W. Lloyd Warner et al., "Our Public Servants," *Carnegie Corporation of New York Quarterly*, 11, 3 (July, 1963), 2.

[66] W. Lloyd Warner, Paul P. Van Riper, Norman H. Martin, and Orvis F. Collins, "A New Look at the Career Civil Service Executive," *Public Administration Review*, 22, 4 (December, 1962), 188.

[67] Warner et al., "Our Public Servants," 2.

[68] W. Lloyd Warner et al., *The American Federal Executive* (New Haven: Yale University Press, 1963), p. 11.

States, of which only 13 per cent have gone to college. Among business executives it was found that 57 per cent have graduated from college.[69]

The high level of education of Federal executives indicates that many of the intellectuals of the United States fill, or helped educate those who do fill, the high positions of government. There is no reason to assume that they are any less liberal in their view of the role of government than intellectuals outside the government service. Indeed, it is evident that many of them are serving in governmental positions because they feel they are in a position to use their knowledge in making practical decisions of considerable importance. The ranks of the intellectuals become a major source for the executives of new agencies. The lateral entry programs in the government service have been created largely to draw the well-educated into government without having to start at the bottom.

The dean of the Maxwell Graduate School of Citizenship and Public Affairs recently reported that in 1962 he sent letters to 800 alumni of the Maxwell Graduate School who were working for government and asked each one to send a note about his career.[70] The report is filled with statements indicating that government service offered unparalleled opportunities for those wishing careers of excitement, creativity, and service—those factors which most seem to attract the intelligentsia.

The study points out why well-educated men who could earn higher wages elsewhere enter the government service. For the highly educated person who is willing to take a somewhat lower monetary reward for his efforts, there are great opportunities to acquire a governmental position which will permit participation in some of the most revolutionary and challenging programs in American history. One Federal executive said he left a high-paying job in industry because "I make more important decisions in a day in Washington than I made in a year in industry."[71]

THE CASE OF THE FOREIGN SERVICE ACT OF 1946[72]

This case was selected because it demonstrates the concern of an agency for its self-preservation and autonomy and shows how these desires give impetus to the ideology of its personnel. The aim of any bureaucracy is to

[69] *Ibid.*, pp. 15, 19.

[70] Stephen K. Bailey, "The Excitement of the Public Service," *Civil Service Journal*, 4, 1 (July–September, 1963), 5–9.

[71] *Ibid.*, 652.

[72] Case based upon Harold Stein, "The Foreign Service Act of 1946," in *Public Administration and Policy Development* (New York: Harcourt, Brace & World, Inc., 1952), pp. 661–737.

survive as an organization and to strengthen its position and influence. This case shows how these goals are pursued while the ideological symbols of service and efficiency are stressed. It gives a rare illustration of the manner in which the efforts of an agency contribute to its gaining new functions and growth. It also provides insight into why the ideology of the bureaucracy is related to its position within the governmental framework.

The case was not selected because the Foreign Service can be considered typical of the government service. The Foreign Service has its own "distinctive entrance and tenure procedures, its own salary system, its own traditions and group attitudes."[73] Other "guild" organizations exist in the government, and in a sense they represent the fulfillment of the ideological tendencies of other bureaucracies. It is rare that an agency is as directly and effectively involved in legislation affecting the agency as it was in this case. But here the case represents the epitome of what is sometimes simply a lesser involvement of other bureaucracies in the legislative process. This case also is helpful in showing the complexity of the legislative process, and the reason that the endurance with which bureaucracies are often well endowed is a key to legislative success.

The modern Foreign Service was created by the Rogers Act of 1924. The basic premise of the act was the establishment of a corps which would be safeguarded from political patronage. The Foreign Service was created from the former Consular Corps and Diplomatic Corps and included all other State Department employees located abroad. Thereafter, entrance into the corps was by special examination.

World War II found the Foreign Service unprepared to handle vital economic, information, and intelligence functions because of the almost exclusively political responsibilities which its members had been trained to carry out. By 1944 it was realized that the prewar isolationism of the United States was an impossible anachronism and that we had to establish a permanent bureaucratic mechanism to handle economic, military, and political demands in an interdependent world. Questions were even raised as to whether a separate elite Foreign Service could handle these varied responsibilities or whether they should be assigned to specialized agencies.

In 1945 a Foreign Service Planning Staff was created to prepare new legislation revising and codifying all the laws affecting the Foreign Service. The group had two objectives: to maintain and strengthen the corps, and to improve its general flexibility and efficiency.

The final draft of the legislation, which was completed nine months after the creation of the planning staff, illuminates the basic ideology of the Foreign Service and other Federal units. It is an ideology which justifies in terms of service the efforts of an agency to strengthen its position and influence.

[73] *Ibid.*, p. 664.

Illustrative of the design of protecting and reinforcing the autonomous strength of the Foreign Service was the recommendation that a Director General be appointed by the President rather than the Secretary of State. This type of appointment would tend to place the Director beyond the control of the Secretary of State. In addition, both the Director and Deputy Director were to be Foreign Service officers of either Class 1 or Career Minister Class, which would severely restrict political control over the Service.

Furthermore, the Board of Foreign Service Examiners, which organizes and administers the entrance examinations for the Service, would have its position solidified in statutory form. This would guarantee the continuation of distinctive entrance requirements to the Foreign Service.

The elite position of the hard core of Foreign Service officers was to be protected by the creation of a Reserve Officers Corps for temporary appointees. The Reserve was also designed to provide flexibility in hiring outside specialists, without which the Service would be severely handicapped in handling the new tasks of the postwar era. The old Foreign Service had been built on a foundation of generalists—men who were prepared to meet any situation which might arise in a United States embassy abroad, and yet not qualified to perform such administrative functions as allocating funds for economic aid, determining the proper military equipment or training for an allied nation, or promoting propaganda activities.

The creation of the Reserve Officers Corps meant that the Service could now efficiently meet the new challenges inherent in American world leadership and provide the new services required as well as assume new functions as problems arose in the future. With the expansion of functions came also an increase in the size of the Foreign Service, with the regular Foreign Service officers retaining leadership in the Service.

Finally, the draft bill included detailed provision for a Foreign Service Institute. Its head was to be appointed by the President, and he would be under the supervision of the Director General of the Service. The creation of a Foreign Service Institute would do much to enhance the prestige of the Foreign Service. Future officers would be subject to academic disciplines and policy interpretation orientations chosen by senior Foreign Service officers. The Institute would contribute to the *esprit de corps* of the entire Service.

Once the bill had been drafted and approved by the Foreign Service Planning Staff, it had to gain clearance from the Department of State. This was a monumental task, for within the Department were agencies whose very existence was threatened by the new Foreign Service legislation. The three chief focuses within the Department for the revision of the draft legislation were the economic offices, the information and cultural offices, and the intelligence offices. The economic offices, under Assistant Secretary

Clayton, were not engaged in a struggle for survival, but the other agencies were.

In an effort to restrict Foreign Service power and increase his own, Clayton proposed that a Foreign Service Board be created to replace the Board of Foreign Service Personnel, which had been given statutory basis in the draft legislation. He contended that the Foreign Service serves the entire government; therefore, the entire government should be represented on the policy-making staff of the Service. Clayton knew that representatives from other offices appointed to the policy-making staff of the Foreign Service would have more in common with his economists than with the Foreign Service officials. Hence, he was assured of support in the event of a divergence of opinion with the Director General of the Foreign Service.

To some officials it appeared that if the power of the Foreign Service were increased, and it were made possible for the Service to meet the newly created problems facing it, there would be a submergence of the particular authority and responsibility of the information and cultural offices. The head of these offices, Assistant Secretary Benton, concurred with the economic offices in the attempt to limit the power of the Foreign Service and to assure to his section or bureau a real voice in policy making and adequate prestige and opportunities for his own staff.

The situation in the intelligence offices was similar. Director McCormack was attempting to establish a central office for the intelligence work of the Department that would have on its staff all the specialists in this work. This idea was opposed by those who felt political reporting and analysis were among the main functions of the Foreign Service.

Here we have the phenomenon of one segment of the bureaucracy seeking to protect and augment its own power while others, even within the same department, become anxious about the effect of such increased prestige upon their own existence.

After many memorandums and conferences, compromises were reached which accorded the Foreign Service its basic objectives while at the same time assuring the other interests of the soundness of their existence and the security of their programs.[74] Assistant Secretary Benton, who had been so opposed to the initial objectives of the legislation "felt impelled to present a memorandum to the Secretary's Staff Committee correcting a 'misunderstanding' of his attitude."[75]

The next step in the clearance process was the Bureau of the Budget representing the President. What are the criteria usually applied by the Bureau when judging prospective legislation? The Bureau is concerned with

---

[74] For a comprehensive listing of the final departmental compromises, see *ibid* pp. 687–688.

[75] *Ibid.*, p. 688.

precedents and general principles of administration. A great many precedents in governmental reorganization supported vesting control in the Department head, in this case the Secretary of State. Each new law or Executive Order which might deviate from such a precedent would make it harder to maintain the principle in the future.

The Budget Bureau was in favor of placing the Director General under the authority of the Secretary of State. To satisfy the desires of the other departments such as Commerce, Agriculture, and Labor, the Bureau came to support a statutory interagency board with generalized advisory powers.

The review performed by the Bureau of the Budget was brought into question by a concurrent review conducted within the legislative branch of the government. In April, 1946, the House Committee on Foreign Affairs began considering a temporary measure to raise the salaries of ambassadors. At the same time, a number of congressmen were expressing the need of comprehensive Foreign Service legislation, and some had requested its preparation. This was a significant advantage for the Service and its proposed legislation. Mr. Vorys of Ohio, like some members of Congress, took the trouble to read the *American Foreign Service Journal*. He, as well as others, was well informed on the new legislation and its recent progress by an article in the February issue. Vorys reminded his colleagues that it would be embarrassing to pass the temporary measure and then have many of its provisions revised by another piece of legislation shortly thereafter.

The committee decided to call for the new legislation and examine it rather than to concentrate on the temporary measure. A subcommittee of the Committee on Foreign Affairs was appointed for this purpose, consisting of Judge Kee of West Virginia, chairman, Mr. Richards of South Carolina, and Mr. Vorys of Ohio.

Mr. Chapin, Director of the Foreign Service, had become convinced that strict observance of the normal procedures of Budget Bureau and interagency clearances would lead to interminable delays. At the same time, the subcommittee was becoming increasingly anxious to begin hearings on the legislation. Mr. Vorys advised Chapin that the passage of the bill was possible if action was taken quickly. He further assured Chapin that he himself would do all he could to push the measure's passage. Vorys and Chapin were on friendly terms, Vorys having stayed with Chapin for two weeks in Algiers during the war. Chapin concluded that the only way to get action on the prepared version of the bill before the adjournment of Congress was to pursue the tricky course of circumventing the entire clearance process within the executive branch and begin actively pushing the bill among members of Congress.

When the subcommittee hearings began, Chapin feared the subcommittee might have some views similar to the Budget Bureau which would complicate the passage of the bill. However, the Foreign Service representa-

tives were excited to learn that on all major issues the subcommittee supported their position and in some cases even went beyond it. What were the
intriguing factors and pressures which produced this support? The subcommittee was predisposed toward a bill containing detailed prescription
for the administration of the Foreign Service because of the congressiona
view that during the New Deal Congress had abdicated all too much legis
lative power to the executive. It was time for Congress to take the reins o
control back into its own hands.

All three committee members felt that political patronage should have
no place in the appointment or promotion of Foreign Service officers and
doubted that strict control by the Secretary of State would ensure such
immunity. The frequent changes in the Secretary of State also led them to
believe that the administrative provisions of the bill were necessary to
ensure continuity and consistency in the operation of the Service. Since
they were also worried about charges of Communist infiltration into the
Department of State, they wanted to preserve the characteristics of the
Foreign Service which had prevented such infiltration.

Other factors also played a part in the subcommittee acceptance o
the draft legislation. Judge Kee felt the measure deserved his suppor
because it was sponsored by a member of the President's Cabinet. To
Mr. Richards it was a favored project of two fellow South Carolinians, Mr
Byrnes, the Secretary of State, and Assistant Secretary of State Russell
Mr. Vorys's interest in the Foreign Service dated back to his work with
the Disarmament Conference in 1922. He felt that a higher level of competence and devotion was shown by the career diplomats than by his fellow
patronage appointees on the staff of the United States delegation.

During the course of the eight hearings in executive session before the
subcommittee, a spirit of camaraderie developed between the Foreign
Service representatives and the subcommittee members. "There was some
social intercourse between the Foreign Service officers, especially Chapin
and Harrington, and the Congressmen. As the bill became more and more
'their bill,' the Subcommittee members seem to have adopted a rather
paternal attitude toward the Foreign Service."[76] They began to think of it
as being somewhat of a constituent, whose rights and interests deserved
congressional protection. With the incorporation of only minor technical
changes proposed by the Budget Bureau, the bill passed the House by
unanimous consent. The subcommittee had turned down the basic Bureau
proposals, such as the elimination of the statutory boards and the statutory
office of the Director General.

The bill went immediately to the Senate where the only chance for
passage, because the congressional session was soon to end, lay with the

[76] *Ibid.,* p. 710.

Consent Calendar and the possibility of unanimity. On July 29 the clerk of the Senate called the calendar, and the successive bills were either unanimously approved or passed over. Finally he reached the calendar number of S. 2451, and to the dismay of the bill's supporters, including Chapin and other Foreign Service officers who were present, Senator Revercomb of West Virginia objected. He did not feel that S. 2451 was suitable for passage without debate, although he had nothing against the bill itself.

Senator Austin of Vermont promptly spoke up and said that the length of the bill was due to the fact that it was a codification of existing law. Senator Connally of Texas stated that although the Senate committee hearings had been brief, the House committee had held extensive hearings, and the bill was supported by the Secretary of State and his Assistant Secretary. Senator Revercomb still objected to the bill, and the clerk resumed the call of the calendar.

Chapin left the Senate chamber, all hope gone. But just as he was leaving the Capitol, he was told to return: Something was still in the wind. He did, and a few minutes later Senator Revercomb reappeared. He explained that while he still disliked the idea of passage without debate, several members of the Foreign Relations Committee had told him how important the bill was. He had, at their request, withdrawn his objection.

The phenomenon of a long and complex bill passing virtually without debate is an unusual one. The reasons in the present case include the pressure of time, the legislators' sense of obligation to legislate where legislation is needed, and above all, the effectiveness of one small energetic group within the Congress to sponsor a measure. The active sponsorship by the subcommittee would not have occurred if a real community of interest had not existed between its members and the formulators of the legislation.

The unusual short-circuiting alliance of the subcommittee members and the Foreign Service officers was not to go without question. It was brought to the attention of the President and almost resulted in his veto of the bill passed by Congress. After hearing the history of the bill, the Director of the Bureau of the Budget, Mr. James E. Webb, decided that the Foreign Service officers had not acted in good faith. He was worried about the insulation of the Foreign Service from direct control by the Secretary and thus had reached the tentative conclusion that the bill was a bad one and should be vetoed. It was in this frame of mind that he talked to President Truman, who indicated some measure of agreement with his views.

However, upon reconsideration, Webb realized that a veto would cause Secretary Byrnes acute embarrassment since he had urged congressional approval of the measure. It was not the time for any rupture in the

President's relations with his Secretary of State, for the Secretary was in the midst of delicate and difficult negotiations in Paris for which the preservation of his prestige was essential.

Webb decided that a favorable recommendation would be filed with a call for future improvements by amendment. The President, even with the favorable recommendation, stated that he was still inclined to veto the bill. The White House call requesting more information came on the afternoon of Friday, August 9. Director Chapin of the Foreign Service and Assistant Secretary Russell were both about to leave town for the weekend. They had assumed that the delay had been normal. The possibility of a veto had never occurred to them.

The news from the White House came as a stunning and unhappy surprise. Weekend plans were canceled, for time was running out. If the President remained unconvinced, his failure to sign would automatically result in a pocket veto. Russell, taking charge of the affair personally, issued a memorandum which was a masterpiece of persuasive debate, a product of impatience and anger, yet written with force and logic. But the final push for the bill came from Secretary Byrnes in Paris in a teletype conversation with the President. He based his appeal on the embarrassment he would suffer from a veto and again confirmed his belief that the bill was a good one.

On August 13, 1946, the President signed the bill. On August 15 he released a statement stressing the importance of the Foreign Service and the need for strengthening it. He also listed the major improvements that the act would bring.

CONCLUDING SUMMARY

America's population increase, its urban surge, and its position of world leadership put the civil bureaucracy in a very favorable position with respect to its ideology and role as a power group. The current international bipolar power system places many heretofore unknown pressures on the United States, one being to present a governmental system capable of meeting economic and social problems in a manner superior to Communist systems. These factors encourage a more progressive government, which in turn means a growing bureaucracy.

The changing attitude toward the function of the government has brought a significant change in attitude toward the public servant. He is recognized more and more as fulfilling a vital role in America. A survey by *Fortune* magazine in 1940 to determine the prestige of government employment as compared with employment in private business if wages and working conditions were equal showed that 50 per cent of those interviewed favored work with a private firm, 40 per cent favored work with the United States government, and 10 per cent had no preference.[77] This survey was made after the New Deal, which was a period of sizable improvement of public employment prestige.

In 1954 Morris Janowitz and Deil Wright made a study on the prestige of the public servant, from which they concluded that the "prestige of public employment has moved into a new phase and lost much of its 'second class citizen' status." They found that of the 764 members of the adult population in the Detroit metropolitan area they surveyed, 56 per cent would prefer to work for the United States government than for a private firm if wages were the same. Thirty per cent said they favored working for a private firm, and 14 per cent were indifferent or had no opinion.[78]

The prestige of government service is on the increase today and will likely continue to grow as long as people feel the need of turning to government as an answer to problems. The greater prestige of the bureaucrat suggests a greater willingness of society to entrust the bureaucracy with new tasks. This sentiment places the ideology of the civil bureaucracy in a most healthy position.

The bureaucracy is recognized more and more as the representative of the people. As the number and functions of agencies increase, more people affiliate themselves with these governmental groups in one way or another. Woll has observed that "the bureaucracy is a highly representative branch of our government, in many respects more representative than Congress; it should be added that the bureaucracy may be more representative in some ways than the President."[79] This is more clearly seen when it is recalled that private groups look to the agencies of government for representation, and few Americans fail to associate themselves in one way or another with one or more of these private groups. As this representative role increases, the bureaucracy's power also grows.

The role and ideology of the bureaucracy also receive support from such scholarly views as that expressed by Seymour Martin Lipset:

> Inherent in bureaucratic structures is a tendency to reduce conflicts from the political to the administrative arena. Constant emphasis on the need for objective criteria as the bases for settling conflicts enables bureaucratic institutions to play major mediating roles. Thus in many ways the pressures to extend bureaucratic norms and practices strengthen democratic consensus.[80]

Here is a striking example of the way in which the bureaucracy is presented as one of the safeguards of democracy, which as we have seen, is part of the ideology of the civil bureaucracy.

---

[77] Morris Janowitz and Deil Wright, "The Prestige of Public Employment: 1929 and 1954," *Public Administration Review*, 16, 1 (winter, 1956), 17.

[78] *Ibid.*, 16–17.

[79] Woll, p. 172.

[80] Seymour Martin Lipset, *Political Man: The Social Bases of Politics* (Garden City, N.Y.: Doubleday & Company, Inc., 1960), p. 37.

These developments do not suggest that the civil bureaucracy goe unchecked. Indeed, any agency must be prepared to make compromise and even to give up some of its proposals when it enters the political arena As the case of the Foreign Service Act showed, there are power blocs al along the policy-making process that present opposition to the agency' programs. An agency must also consider the possibility of such oppositio to its activities as may come from congressional investigations, from re views made by the judiciary, and at times from close observation by th President or a commission under his direction.

The history of the civil bureaucracy during the past three decade indicates, however, that its position enables it to turn quickly to supportin power blocs when its position is endangered or when the going gets tough The President or private power groups may give an agency support whe Congress is reluctant to act favorably. If the President fails to give hi support, the agency has other power points it can readily turn to unless it proposals are completely out of line with the current trends in the role o government.

Competition between agencies has often been presented as a check on the ease with which bureaucratic power is expressed. Even though thi competition does check the freedom of the use of power, it appears tha these contests result very frequently in an overlapping of functions rathe than a victory of one agency over another. Bernstein has made this illumi nating observation: "A single agency thus can do little without dippin into the affairs of other agencies. A federal executive can scarcely min his own business without minding someone else's as well."[81]

The power of the civil bureaucracy then stems from several sources First, its members are frequently the initiators of new public policy anc are generally able to "shape" legislative programs by making suggestion to the administration concerning the type and details of legislation tha should be proposed. As well, they testify and give advice to Congress. Fo instance where other pressure groups are not resourceful, the civil bureauc racy has almost a monopoly on information in its sphere of interest. By releasing or withholding data, it can have considerable influence. Thus the civil bureaucracy has definite power and effect upon the type of legis lation that is actually proposed. Once a law is passed, it is the bureaucracy that has to make interpretations of it, to write the rules which make specific the general provisions of the law and its usage. Congress usually only out lines laws in a somewhat general form; consequently from there on, the interpretation is done by the bureaucracy. This of course amounts, in fact, to the legislating of the specific points of the law by the bureaucracy.

When all factors are considered, it appears that the trend in public

81 Bernstein, p. 78.

attitude is toward a continuously greater justification of the civil bureaucracy as a power—time appears to be on the side of the bureaucracy. The checks on Federal agencies seldom leave them without power groups which will assist them in their own power roles. Thus, the civil bureaucracy is and will continue to be among the most significant participants in the creation of American public policy.

9
the military bureaucracy

INTRODUCTION

With the beginning of World War II at Pearl Harbor, the military bureaucracy began an era of power and influence never before known in American history. Neither World War II nor the Korean conflict brought peace or disarmament to the United States. The development of the country into a more or less perpetual warfare or defense state coupled with the concomitant change toward a welfare state is certainly a major force in our contemporary political society. Both these factors have brought about the growth and increasing power of the military and the civil bureaucracies. The warning about the development of a military-industrial complex, given by President Eisenhower in his final address to the nation, was the official recognition of a fear that had gradually been growing in some quarters. Along with this fear was the awareness that the country faced an apparently unending series of international military crises. As early as 1956, anti-militarists such as C. Wright Mills observed that a military ascendancy was developing and that "the warlords have been only uneasy, poor relations with the American elite; now they are first cousins; soon they may become elder brothers."[1] The Hebert Probe in mid-1959, when Representative F. E. Hebert, head of the House Armed Services Special Investigations Subcommittee, questioned seventy-five witnesses regarding the employment

[1] C. Wright Mills, *The Power Elite* (Fair Lawn, N.J.: Oxford University Press, 1956), p. 198.

258

of retired officers by defense industries, also showed congressional recognition that dangers existed in the relations between defense expenditures by the military and the awarding of such contracts to industry.

While the military have traditionally maintained that they are nonpolitical and that they take no sides in the political life of the country, this posture becomes increasingly difficult as the defense expenditures have become the biggest item in the national budget, accounting for over half the Federal government's annual expenditures. As mentioned earlier, the spending of billions of dollars in our economy for whatever purpose affects so many individuals, businesses, states, and congressmen that it is, regardless of intent, highly political. Thus money, power, and politics are inseparably connected. This has undoubtedly made the military bureaucracy uncomfortable. Yet at the same time it cannot be avoided, nor can the military give up influencing defense spending and the letting of military contracts without giving up much of its power. The conflicts between the military and civilian defense secretaries, McNamara and Wilson, over these very decisions are examples of this fact.[2] Therefore, the military bureaucracy, even more than the civil bureaucracy, relies upon the status of its members as experts and specialists for the source of its power in dealings with civilians and Congress. Mills argues that "for even if they [the military] are not desirous of political power, power essentially political in nature may be and has been thrust upon them by civilian default; they have been much used—willing or not—by civilians for political purposes."[3]

The prestige of the position and/or popularity of military leaders has been used at times by regular politicians to lift political policy above "politics." The use of men such as Gen. George C. Marshall, Gen. Mark Clark, Gen. Walter Bedell Smith, Gen. Lucius Clay, and Gen. J. Lawton Collins as diplomats, not to mention President Dwight D. Eisenhower, is a good example of members of the military bureaucracy who have moved into diplomatic and political positions. Furthermore, for a military man to gain rank and climb to the highest levels requires, of necessity, that he be politically adroit. This skill is evident in the success many of the above-named men have had in nonmilitary government assignments. Some argue further that

. . . as a coherent group of men the military is probably the most competent now concerned with national policy; no other group has had the training in coordinated economic, political and military affairs; no other group has had the continuous experience in the making of decisions; no other group so readily

[2] For analysis of the problem of civilian control, see D. W. Brogan, "The United States: Civilian and Military Power" in Michael Howard (ed.), *Soldiers and Governments* (Bloomington: Indiana University Press, 1959), pp. 167–185; and Samuel P. Huntington, "Civilian Control and the Constitution," *American Political Science Review*, 50 (September, 1956), 682.

[3] Mills, p. 200.

"internalizes" the skills of other groups nor so readily engages their skills on its own behalf; no other group has such steady access to world-wide information.[4]

Some observers have jokingly commented that the Defense Department has a better state department than the State Department itself.

The fact that the top military men are deeply involved in our international policy, and that our policy is highly influenced by them, makes such transitions perhaps more frequently a change of name than of actual function. For in a world facing military catastrophe, the military cannot help but play a significant role. They are specialists of defense, and politicians and parties dare not ignore their advice. Political parties especially fear being called appeasers or being accused of permitting unpreparedness. Although it disappeared soon after the elections, the cry of the "missile gap" was a potent political foil against the Republicans in 1960. Thus for good or evil, whether they like it or not, the military bureaucracy (at least at the top level) is deeply involved in both internal and international politics. Because of this very involvement, the making of public policy cannot be discussed without mentioning the role and function of the military bureaucracy as a power group.

To understand the position, power, opponents, and ideology of the military in America today it is necessary to look back briefly over our history. For two major conflicting military ideologies in this country have deep historical roots—as the following account shows. The question of the power and control of the military and the threat it poses to our democratic institutions is one that was posed by the original founders of our country.

The Founding Fathers, concerned about the recent display of British military power, contemplated the problem of providing for the common defense of the country. The humiliation of the Boston blockade was stenciled with vivid clarity upon their minds, and many of these men could themselves remember the military aggrandizement and domination in Europe. With these and other experiences in mind, the constitutional writers approached the dilemma of having, on one hand, to create a free society, and on the other, to provide for both external and internal security. Alexander Hamilton clearly stated the problem in *The Federalist*, No. 8:

Safety from external danger is the most powerful director of national conduct. Even the ardent love of liberty will after a time give way to its dictates. The violent destruction of life and property incident to war, the continual effort and alarm attendant on a state of continual danger, will compel nations the most attached to liberty to resort for repose and security to institutions which have a tendency to destroy their civil and political rights, to be more safe, they at length become willing to run the risk of being less free.[5]

[4] *Ibid.*, 199.

[5] *The Federalist on the Constitution Written in 1788* (Washington, D.C.: Hallowell, Masters, Smith & Co., 1857), p. 34.

For a solution to this problem, the early statesmen turned to the British model of military control. They observed from previous international relations that only a government capable of speedy action could be truly effective. Thus they gave almost complete control of the military to the national government, with the President being the "supreme commander" or executive. At the same time, they gave to the legislature the power to check and balance the executive in the area of domestic affairs. Another Federalist and proponent of the Constitution, John Jay, saw the necessity of this arrangement when he wrote: "Nations in general will make war whenever they have a prospect of getting anything by it."[6] The Founding Fathers thus established a solution to the problem of the proper role of the military by initiating a system parallel in construction to the British system. Instead of the Crown, the President was to become the center of military power.[7]

From this central concept of how to organize and control the military, a tradition grew. The tradition was based mainly on the twin ideas of civilian control, assumed through checks and balances, and the rule of keeping the military force small and ineffectual during peacetime. This concept of a small military force was also meant to serve as a check on the President's power. The Founding Fathers and other Americans were well aware of the lesson of history which had shown the danger of large standing armies in peacetime. The Virginia Declaration of Rights spoke out strongly on this subject.[8]

The constitutional checks on the President's power consisted, first, of the idea of making him subject to impeachment and responsible to the electorate every four years. Second, the President had to have senatorial ratification both for the treaties he made and for his selection of army officers. Third, the power of the purse was another important constitutional check, whereby Congress was to provide the funds for the armed services. The Constitution limited these appropriations to no more than two years, thus giving each Congress opportunity of reviewing the expenditures, though in essence this is done every year. As a final gesture, the writers provided that only Congress had power to declare war (though in practice this check has not proved to be operative).

In the young nation this concept was followed, but as the nation grew older, it found that it had to meet new problems. The Civil War helped to prove that the creation of strong militias as counterbalances to the national army was more of a hindrance to national security than a check on the

[6] *Ibid.*, p. 3.

[7] Walter Millis, *The Constitution and the Common Defense* (New York: Fund for the Republic, Inc., 1959), p. 8.

[8] For example, Hamilton Albert Long, *Your American Yardstick* (Philadelphia: Your Heritage Books, Inc., 1963), pp. 60–61.

national military. Today state militias are only vestiges of power. The demobilization of the United States Army at the end of World War II helped to give to the Communists an extra impetus in their subjugation of over 700 million people, even though we held at that time superior potential military power, backed by an atomic-bomb monopoly.

The nonmilitaristic tradition also received some jolts from strong presidential personalities. Theodore Roosevelt's foreign policy awoke real fears of the executive military power. Later "strong" Presidents such as Wilson and Franklin Delano Roosevelt also brought forth such fears.[9] The creation of the Army General Staff in 1904 and the public awareness of the huge sums being expended by the military after World War I can be viewed as further links in the changing concept and practice of the military power.

The Korean conflict stands out as a major turning point away from the original Federalist tradition. The era of the permanent peacetime standing military forces had arrived. A new military ideology had been growing, and now it had matured and was in a visible form. No longer could the checks and balances and the keeping of the military establishment small be wholly effective. These notions appeared only as shadows of power of days gone by. The concept of a subservient military no longer appeared to be such a stable reality.

In the early 1950s, many critics and writers began to feel uncomfortable with a strong national military in peacetime. They viewed the traditionalist ideology as being replaced with a new militaristic ideology. The new approach spoke in terms of "cold war," "arms control," and "deterrence." This new philosophy was much the same as that stated by John Jay when he expressed the opinion that the principal objective of nations is to try to dominate others. It meant that the best defense was an invincible offense.

With the emergence of a strong militaristic ideology there has also developed a counterideology designed to inhibit or curtail the growing militarism in America. President Eisenhower, who strangely mixed a pacifist family background as a Mennonite with a successful career in the United States Army, gave official recognition, in his final address to the nation, on January 17, 1960, of the fears which he held of growing American military power:

> The U.S. has been compelled to create a permanent armament industry of vast proportion and to maintain a defense establishment employing 3.5 million persons and spending huge sums. This conjunction of an immense military establishment and a large industry is new in the American experience. The total influence—economic, political, even spiritual—is felt in every city, every state house, every office of the federal government. We must recognize the imperative

[9] Millis, p. 19.

need for this development. Yet we must not fail to comprehend its grave implications.[10]

President Eisenhower's fears were that the country was being faced with an apparently unending series of international military crises coupled with the development of a military-industrial complex which was a potential threat to our personal freedom. Another counterideology group are the liberals who believe that social programs are being shunted aside by the demands of the military complex. David Riesman and Nathan Glazer have pointed out recently:

> The Strategic Air Command has considerably greater power than any single agency possessed in 1948. . . . In alliance with the AEC (Atomic Energy Commission), it forced the Oppenheimer hearings and temporarily silenced the opponents of Teller and the H-bomb foreign policy. In alliance with big and little contractors, their unions and workers, and their "Senators," it has made the war economy so central to our economy that the stock market rises when the summit breaks down.[11]

The pacifists are also representative of this counterideology against military power. They are desirous of developing a rapprochement with the Soviet Union. The American Friends Service Committee has expressed this viewpoint in a pamphlet saying: "We suggest that the more a nation focused on reconciling differences, the more creative would be the power and the life that would flow from it."[12]

The State Department as a group can also be placed within this counterideology approach. Throughout the publications and recent books about the State Department, the theme that the United States should seek rapprochement with the Communist countries is evident. An address given on disarmament by Secretary of State Rusk illustrates this attitude: "The United States and its free-world partners do, I believe, have a common interest with the Soviet Union, in that both sides desire to preserve their mutual security against the dangers of an arms race. I hope this common interest will become increasingly apparent in the period ahead."[13]

Also there are the people, in addition to former President Eisenhower, who fear the creation of a United States garrison state. They see money,

---

[10] See *Public Papers of Presidents of the United States, Dwight D. Eisenhower, 1960–1961* (Washington, D.C.: Government Printing Office), 1038.

[11] David Riesman and Nathan Glazer, "The Lonely Crowd: A Reconsideration in 1960," in Seymour M. Lipset and Leo Lowenthal (eds.), *Culture and Social Character* (New York: The Free Press of Glencoe, 1961), pp. 449–450.

[12] David S. McLellan, William C. Olson, and Fred A. Sondermann (eds.), "A Quaker Search for an Alternative to Violence," *The Theory and Practice of International Relations* (Englewood Cliffs, N.J.: Prentice-Hall, Inc., 1960), p. 372.

[13] Dean Rusk, "Disarmament and Arms Control," *The Department of State Bulletin* (July 2, 1962), 5.

power, and politics as inseparably connected and destined to lead to this evil consequence. This, in part, prompted S. E. Finer to remark, "Instead of asking why the military engage in politics, we ought surely ask why they ever do otherwise.[14]

Within the pages of this chapter on military bureaucracy the two ideologies will be represented. The pervasive and dominant voice of the military and those who adhere to the doctrine of a strong military will be evident, as well as the less powerful but more rapidly vocal antimilitarist ideology of those who want to see the power of the military circumscribed and that of the nonmilitaristic civilian agencies and administrators increased.

The question of the control of the military has taken on unprecedented dimensions and implications in this modern nuclear age. The question of whether there is a potential military threat to our democratic institution is important.[15]

THE GROWTH OF MILITARY POWER

If there is any one point upon which the opponents and proponents of a strong military state have consensus, it is on the fact of actual growth of the military. The area of contention is over what this growth really indicates in terms of present and potential use or abuse of power.

Despite the natural fluctuations of wartime and peacetime conditions, the number of those on active duty in the armed forces has steadily increased. Nearly 3.5 million men make up our present peacetime force. Besides these, we have over 1 million civilians on the Department of Defense payroll, which taken together represents nearly the total population of Norway. Furthermore, there are an additional 4 million workers in the United States arms industry—indirect employees of the military. In its amount of real estate alone, the military owns land equaling in extent the whole state of Tennessee.

In terms of fiscal expenditures, one author has said:

> The Defense Department . . . uses nearly 10 per cent of our gross national product. It spends more than the whole national product of Canada, Japan, India or Communist China, more than all state and local governments in the United States, including all public education for 40,000,000 people from kindergarten to state universities.[16]

[14] S. E. Finer, *The Man on Horseback: The Role of the Military in Politics* (New York: Frederick A. Praeger, Inc., 1962), p. 5.

[15] Harry L. Coles (ed.), *Total War and Cold War: Problems in Civilian Control of the Military* (Columbus: Ohio State University Press, 1962), p. vii.

[16] Harlan Cleveland, "Dinosaurs and Personal Freedom," *The Saturday Review* (February 28, 1959), 13.

As regards the comparison between the military and business world he says, quoting Jay Westcott:

Every other American institution or business is a dwarf by comparison with the Department of Defense. Defense assets are greater than the combined wealth of the 100 largest corporations in America. (Indeed, some of their wealth depends largely on their ability to get contracts from the Defense Department.) Some individual defense installations have a greater worth than does the Ford Motor Company. The annual purchases of the Air Force alone are larger in volume than the output of America's greatest industrial producer, General Motors. . . .[17]

In the area of state and local government, the impact of defense spending has been great. *The economies of at least twenty-two of the fifty states depend heavily upon military spending. In fourteen states military industries make up a significant percentage of total manufacturing employment.* In seven states (California, New Mexico, Utah, Arizona, Connecticut, and Washington) war industries account for more than 20 per cent of all manufacturing. Further, in Alaska, Hawaii, Virginia, and the District of Columbia, the military payrolls account for 10 to 26 per cent of all payroll income. Added to the raw figure of the military payroll is the multiplier factor, or the number of jobs dependent upon these defense positions. It is quite apparent that genuine peace or drastic disarmament, without adequate provisions, could be nearly disastrous for many state economies, not to mention individual military business suppliers. This was demonstrated by the cries of anguish raised by congressmen over President Johnson's plan to cut back military spending at various bases, a relatively minor cut in overall terms. Along with these facts a United States Arms Control and Disarmament Agency report, headed by Prof. Emile Benoit, concluded that "certain states are clearly subject to disproportionately heavy impacts because of the relatively heavy dependence of their manufacturing on major items of procurement."[18]

Political excitement and activity are caused when a defense project is dropped or cut back. Good examples of state, local, and business interests' pressure have been the Skybolt curtailment and Secretary McNamara's order in March, 1961, to close down fifty-two military installations in twenty-five states over a period of three years. Congressmen of these areas received a great amount of local pressure to preserve the *status quo* and to keep the military dollars pouring in.

The desire of local areas for a part of the military budget, regardless of the implication it might have, can be exemplified in the incident of the

[17] *Ibid.,* 13–14.
[18] Emile Benoit, *Economic Impacts of Disarmament,* U.S. Arms Control and Disarmament Agency, Publication no. 2 (Washington, D.C.: Government Printing Office, 1962), p. 4.

installation of a Titan missile base at Tucson, Arizona. The initial reception of the news of the installation of such a base in Tucson was at first greeted with excited anticipation. However, soon after the announcement, a group of scientists at the University of Arizona pointed out that if Tucson were ringed with missile sites the city would become a prime target for the enemy, and worst of all, that if Tucson avoided a direct hit the population would still be wiped out by fallout carried by the prevailing winds from the west. The university scientists proposed that the Air Force place the Titans east of the city in an unpopulated region. This proposal seemed so logical and evident to the citizenry that a great deal of public opinion was stirred up in favor of it. The City Council even passed a resolution expressing concern for civilian safety.

However, pressures from Senator Goldwater's office and from the Air Force caused the City Council to reverse itself and pass a resolution expressing confidence in any Air Force decision. In the end, the demands of the Air Force were met.[19] This example indicates that through the power of spending the military is strong and often gets its demands satisfied. In all the world only the Soviet Union approaches this type of military development and spending.

While there is general recognition of the need for military strength, the meaning of this growth is interpreted differently by various experts.

Dr. Kenneth E. Boulding, professor of economics at the University of Michigan, has expressed his fears concerning complexity and size of organization. He believes that efficient organizations are limited in size, much as organisms are, and once you go beyond certain limits you obtain diminishing returns. He says that "beyond a certain point, increase in the scale of organization results in a breakdown of communications, in a lack of flexibility, in bureaucratic stagnation and insensitivity."[20]

While Boulding equates the increase in organization (Pentagon) with breakdown in effectiveness, Fred Cook tends to view the military organization as becoming stronger and more powerful only as the military increases in size. "The twin theme of the Warfare State—more guns and bombers, yes: Better education, medical care, disarmament, decidedly no—found expression everywhere from the moment President Kennedy finished his Berlin Crisis speech on July 25, 1961."[21]

In addition, Cook recites the instance when Senator Ralph E. Flanders, Vermont Republican, on the floor of the Senate, in response to the growth of the military said, "It is not only that we are sacrificing to defense our

[19] Fred Cook, *The Warfare State* (New York: The Macmillan Company, 1962), pp. 198–201.
[20] Kenneth E. Boulding, "The Jungle of Hugeness: The Second Age of the Brontosaurus," *The Saturday Review* (March 1, 1958), 12.
[21] Cook, p. 19.

standard of living and the free independence of our economic life, we are sacrificing our freedom itself. We are being forced to shift the American way of life into the pattern of the garrison state."[22]

Another point of view on the relationship of size and control of policy in the United States is expressed by Harlan Cleveland in a reply to Dr. Boulding. Cleveland believes that men can achieve both freedom and security under the shadow of huge organizations. He says: "The Defense Department has never been a unit. The larger it gets the less likely it is to achieve effective unity. . . . It is the internal administrative tensions in a bureaucracy which keep it alive."[23]

The analysis of increased American military bureaucratic power is not complete without consideration of interservice growth and power relationships. The increase of interservice controversy has been one of the major changes in the military picture since World War II. Prior to this time the military services were mainly separate unities. When they had a problem or a program to pursue, they found that they were on their own. Each service had its independent battles. All services found that generally they were aided by a few interest groups and usually opposed by some very vociferous civilian pressure groups. The traditionalist concept of a weak military under civilian control was the dominant ideology of this pre-World War II era.[24]

The division of the military forces after World War II into groups opposing one another was looked upon with favor by many civilian administrators. This concept of military competition facilitated by keeping the military under civilian control can be traced back as far as the Founding Fathers' idea of having the state militias as a national army. Also the civilian administrators saw this rivalry as a means of keeping the Defense Department weak; and in some cases the military group could be used as a whipping boy to receive the blame for policy errors.[25]

Thus the traditionalists tend to look upon interservice controversy as a major link in maintaining civilian control in these modern times. They believe that the hostilities which could be created between the military and civilian administrations are better channeled into this interservice battle.

[22] *Ibid.*, p. 24.

[23] Cleveland, 14.

[24] This period of ideology is well represented in Edward Pendleton Herring, *The Impact of War* (New York: Farrar & Rinehart, Inc., 1941), chap. 8, and in Samuel P. Huntington, *The Soldier and the State* (Cambridge, Mass.: Harvard University Press, 1957), pp. 282–312.

[25] Samuel P. Huntington, "Interservice Competition and the Political Roles in the Armed Services," in Harry L. Coles (ed.), *Total War and Cold War: Problems in Civilian Control of the Military* (Columbus: Ohio State University Press, 1962), p. 185.

The holders of the military ideology have since 1945 been in favor of more unification of the services. One interesting study pointed out that within the services it was generally the officer's position in the military hierarchy rather than his service alignment which decided his viewpoint on unification. The higher the position an officer held, the more likely he was to subscribe to the idea of unification of the services.[26] Officers who were assigned to the Pentagon or on duty with the Joint Chiefs of Staff were most receptive to the "nonservice" approach. The Reorganization Act of 1958 has in fact been a result of the efforts of these military power groups to enhance their positions.

There is another group of people who take a more middle-ground approach. They believe that not only does the military need to be more unified in order to meet its modern challenges, but also civilian control and techniques need to be strengthened. Thus a counterbalancing effect could be achieved. Morris Janowitz believes that this balance is not being achieved because the civilian management has failed to produce the proper climate for a realistic unification of the services. He cites the lack of congressional control as another factor in causing imbalance. A third and most important reason, he says, is the factor of civilian control vested in the executive branch. This, he believes, causes a fierce competition between the services for access to this power group—the Chief Executive and also the National Security Council.[27]

When contemplating the increased power of the military and the factor of interservice rivalry as a weakening or strengthening influence, the position of the Air Force must be considered, perhaps because it has been the most aggressive of the service groups. From the time of Capt. Billy Mitchell until the full blooming of the modern Air Force as a separate service, the various divisions of the military placed little reliance on the scientific and technological phases of warfare. The Air Force has been able, to a high degree, to convince the holders of the purse that the Air Force concept of national security is the backbone of military defense and that it exclusively possesses the only effective system of attack. A classical example of this job of salesmanship was the Universal Military Training (UMT) issue in 1948. The Air Force by clever moves "has been able to convince the country that by a substantial increase in appropriations for Air, there would be no necessity for UMT."[28]

[26] Andrew F. Henry, John W. Masland, and Laurence F. Radway, "Armed Forces Unification and the Pentagon Officer," *Public Administration Review*, 15 (1955), 178–180.

[27] Morris Janowitz, *The Professional Soldier* (New York: The Free Press of Glencoe, 1960), pp. 349–350.

[28] James Forrestal, *The Forrestal Diaries*, Walter Millis (ed.) (New York: The Viking Press, Inc., 1951), p. 388.

Because of this increase in power by the Air Force there has been increased competition within the military services. Since the Air Force does get the biggest slice of the funds, it has been more open to attack from its sister services. Also, those who advocate a balanced budget have been quite critical toward the Air Force's ability to secure huge appropriations.[29]

As the unification principle is pushed more by the Defense Department and as the functions of defense become more technologically complex, it appears likely that the interservice rivalry, with the Air Force often in the center of controversy, will lessen in intensity. The realization that their total power is increased by their cooperation—or other attitudes than conflict—is somewhat parallel to the recognition of oligopolies in economic situations, that it is to their natural benefit to act, even if tacitly, like monopolists rather than to compete.[30]

It is impossible to analyze the growth of military power without recognizing the vast increase in scientific warfare and technology. These two factors have definitely added to the power of the military. "Since the war, military research has spread even more widely into our national life. It is now supported by $10 billion per year from the Defense Department. By 1960 one of our leading universities accepted more than $40 million of defense funds."[31]

It is not only the increase in money which had added to the military power but also the complexity factor. No longer is Congress able to check on appropriations closely because of their magnitude and the inability of congressmen to understand their content. The problem as one writer sees it is that "the Congress must pass upon huge budgets for research and other complex scientific issues, yet within their ranks there is not a single scientist. Also very few committees have men with scientific knowledge."[32]

What then is the real meaning of the power of the military bureaucracy? Undoubtedly there are few people who do not agree that the military has grown in size and in power. The difference between the advocates and the critics of a rising military strength is how best it should be channeled and utilized. The military power in America today represents, then, either a power for achievement or a power for destruction. It is evident that the scales have not as yet been tipped in either direction, but are hanging in the balance. Which way they will fall may become clear within the next decade or two.

[29] Edgar S. Furniss, Jr., *American Military Policy* (New York: Holt, Rinehart and Winston, Inc., 1959), pp. 41–43.

[30] See William John Fellner, *Competition among the Few: Oligopoly and Similar Market Structures* (New York: Alfred A. Knopf, Inc., 1949).

[31] Ralph E. Lapp, *Kill and Overkill: The Strategy of Annihilation* (New York: Basic Books, Inc., Publishers, 1962), p. 17.

[32] *Ibid.*, pp. 18–19.

THE MILITARY'S USE OF ORGANIZATIONS, PUBLIC RELATIONS, AND POLITICS

The Organizations

The military bureaucracy uses to a great extent external organizations, public relations, and politics to represent and promote its interests. The military's use of external groups came into being mainly because the individual service leaders felt a need to express service interests. Their restricted position produced a need for external spokesmen. They saw that the Chief of Staff was a spokesman not only for his service but also for the administration and the Department of Defense. For them, the service association spoke only for the service.

At the conclusion of World War II, rivalry among the services became a permanent factor in military relations.[33] With this sudden increase in competition, the use of backstop organization mushroomed overnight. The change in technology from the airplane to the intercontinental missile age was a major factor in this growth cycle. The services were now in a struggle to see who could acquire the biggest and most contracts. The Department of Defense was instrumental in encouraging the formation of many of these associations.[34]

Prior to the post-World War II period, the external—or professional—organizations were mainly used to encourage professionalism within the service and as an outlet for publishing military articles of scientific and professional interest. The oldest service "backstop" organization is the Navy League, which was organized in 1902 by a group of civilians who wanted to overcome some of the adverse public feeling against the Navy because of its part in the Spanish-American War.[35] The Air Force Association (AFA) was organized in 1946 and has since then become the largest and most influential of these semiofficial service groups. The Army was the last of the major services to develop such a group when in 1957–1958 it converted its Combat Forces Association into the Army Association.[36]

The old external service groups changed their roles. They no longer had the primary function of encouraging professionalism within the ranks but became advocates of their particular service's point of view to the public. The services had found that they could influence legislative and executive decisions by getting public opinion behind them. A good example

[33] Coles, p. 182.

[34] L. Harmon Zeigler, *Interest Groups in American Society* (Englewood Cliffs, N.J.: Prentice-Hall Inc., 1964), p. 102.

[35] Samuel P. Huntington, *The Common Defense: Strategic Programs in National Politics* (New York: Columbia University Press, 1961), p. 394.

[36] Janowitz, pp. 383–384.

of this was the techniques used by the Air Force Association in getting Congress, in March, 1948, to bypass the Universal Military Training Bill by convincing them that more air power was the answer to the present national defense problems.

Table 4 gives some indication of the size and power which these semi-official service and private organizations possess. Included within the chart are "backstop" organizations which belong to related groups interested in promoting the interest of the armed services.[37]

These organizations are private in form and thus are not under the direct control of the military organizations of government. They all insist that their prime function is to inform and educate. Of them all, only Aero-space Industries Association has registered under the lobby law, and even this organization said it registered only to be safe, not because it believes it is a true lobby group. Of the three direct service groups, the Navy League has made the greatest effort to represent itself as an independent civilian organization. Its monthly publication regularly contains a statement to the effect that its contents do not have the official sanction or approval of the Navy Department.[38]

On the other hand, the Air Force Association has been uninhibited by the concept of the professional organization which the other services have experienced. From the start it was conceived not to be an organization to promote professionalism but one to promote the overall interests of the Air Force. It is a semiofficial organization whose directors have generally been high-ranking Air Force officers.

The last major service group to be organized was the Army Association, which has had a large number of retired Army generals as directors. However, it has a wider civilian representation among its leaders than the other two service groups. This move to take in a wide spectrum of leaders with industrial and social backgrounds caused one public relations officer to remark when he first saw the list: "A colonel in the chief of staff's office must have read C. W. Mills' *The Power Elite,* and thought it a good idea to have one."[39]

Thus, the Air Force Association represents the most cohesive of the three, the Navy League is more of a pressure group in behavior, and the Army Association has the characteristics of being the most disunited.

The non-service-connected external organizations were in their initial relationship generally allied quite closely with a particular service. Companies such as Boeing would usually expend their effort on one service and would belong to an organization which represented this interest. They would at times put on a large campaign on behalf of a particular service to save a certain contract. However, since many of the major companies

[37] Information from *The 1961–62 Congressional Quarterly Guide to Current American Government* (Washington, D.C., 1961), 53.

[38] Janowitz, p. 386.   [39] *Ibid.,* p. 387.

TABLE 4. **Semiofficial Service Groups and Organizations**

Organization	No. of members	1958 income	Aims
Air Force Association	60,000, including 30,000 Air Force personnel	$1.2 million	To support the achievement of such air power as is necessary for national security
Army Association	63,000, including military personnel on active duty	$290,000	To foster public understanding and support of the Army
Navy League	38,000, including active duty personnel	$211,000	Considers itself the civilian arm of the Navy
American Ordnance Association (formerly Army Ordnance Association)	42,000	$474,000	Armament preparedness
Aerospace Industries Association (formerly Aircraft Industries Association)	79 member companies	$1.4 million	To promote the manufacture and sale of "aircraft and astronautical vehicles of every nature and description"
National Security Industrial Association (formerly Navy Industrial Association)	502 member companies	$238,000	To establish a close working relationship among industrial concerns

have been receiving more than one type of service contract, the distinctions have been less. Also, many companies have often joined more than one type of service-connected organization. At one time, Douglas Aircraft had major missile contracts with all three services.

A backstop group which is one of the hardest to understand and evaluate is the veterans. The four main veterans associations are the American Legion, Veterans of Foreign Wars, Disabled American Veterans, and the American Veterans of World War II (Amvets).

These groups are drawn together and organized because of two main stimuli. The initial and main objective is to acquire special material assistance for the veteran from the government. This has been referred to as the "pension objective." The secondary factor which draws a group like this together is the feeling of shared experiences which veterans carry with them into the civilian orbit.[40] The veterans have a sense of having been involved together in a huge enterprise and feel a degree of comradeship because of it.

The relationship of the veterans organization to the service itself is a hard one to trace. There is apparently no overt evidence that there is a formal link between them, as there is with the other semiofficial organizations previously mentioned. The link between them is an informal one. It is based on the concept of experience and association in the past which has a gravitating pull on future attitudes. It is comparable to the same feeling and attitude which many college graduates have toward their alma mater, a feeling of "that's where I spent some of the best years of my life."

Veterans organizations generally assume a position of being nonpolitical and thus avoid any partisan politics. A good example of this attitude is a portion of the American Legion constitution which says: "The American Legion shall not be used for dissemination of partisan principles."[41] This does not mean that many of the veterans groups will not speak out on national and international issues. When these groups have spoken, it has been usually with a conservative and nationalistic voice. They have been advocates of a strong national defense system. Their literature during the period of the 1960 presidential election was most vocal in expressing the dangers of what was conceived to be the "American missile gap."

The leadership within the veterans groups is typically a strong oligarchy. On most issues and policies, the leadership sets the pace for the membership to follow. It controls the conventions and usually can manage the important votes.

One important difference between the veterans and other external groups is that the former servicemen are able to elicit more sympathy for their cause, even though the cause is usually an attempt for a material benefit. The Disabled Veterans have been particularly successful because of their image as an especially deserving and needy group. Another important factor which accounts for the consistent success of some of these veterans groups is that there are no counterpressure groups working against

[40] V. O. Key, Jr., *Politics, Parties and Pressure Groups*, 4th ed. (New York: Thomas Y. Crowell Company, 1958), p. 118.

[41] *Ibid.*, p. 120.

them, as with the semiservice groups with their infighting for victory over one another.

What type of prestige do these veterans groups have? A study made in the early 1950s, based on the thesis that associations may vary in influence in correlation with the degree to which nonmembers look to them for leadership, placed the Veterans of Foreign Wars and the American Legion on the top of the list as high in prestige among both nonmembers and members.[42]

From the data available, it seems unlikely that the veterans groups would go so far as to give their support to a particular service group against another service group, or even to support a service group against a particular branch of government. Because of their interservice membership and their civilian status, they will likely remain a broad-spectrum group which will not go much further in defense pronouncements than advocating a strong military preparedness. Their basic aim will continue to be that of a self-interest economic pressure group.

These external organizations, both semiofficial and private, are viewed with mixed feelings. There are some people who believe that the increase in size and number of them is a manifestation of the truth that the military eventually is going to assume a ruling capacity. The critics of military external organizations believe that the groups are highly controlled by the particular ruling military oligarchy. As one critic says, he believes that the Air Force Association never seems to worry about military threats to the nation which would not enhance the Air Force's budget.[43]

Other viewpoints on the growth of military external organizations take a more moderate approach. They point out that these organizations do serve a useful function in educating and informing. They believe that one of the beneficial results of these groups is the counterbalancing effect they have on one another. They serve as a type of "veto" group.

One factor both critics and defenders agree on is that the groups have grown in size and power. It appears likely that these groups will continue to grow and become increasingly political power groups to be reckoned with.

Public Relations

Public relations and propaganda are natural by-products of these associations. A public relations action by one of the services has usually meant

[42] Howard E. Freeman and Morris Showel, "Differential Political Influence of Voluntary Associations," *Public Opinion Quarterly,* 15 (winter, 1951), 703–714.

[43] Raymond D. Senter, "Rebellion in the Air Force?" *The New Republic* (September 28, 1963), 19.

that the other services had to match it by comparable actions if they were going to maintain a *status quo*.

The early beginning concept of military public relations was based on the need to engender morale, both in the service and on the "home front." By 1915 the civil administration felt that things were getting a little out of hand, and President Woodrow Wilson issued his General Order No. 10-1915. This order stated that officers should not involve themselves in public relations. By 1948, however, conditions had changed. Gen. Douglas MacArthur alone had 135 military and civilian personnel on his Far East publicity staff. At the same time, the Chief of Staff had 44 military and 113 civilian personnel assigned to public relations, and the Commanding General of the European Theater had 107 military and 30 civilian personnel involved in correctly publicizing the military. Eventually, every base and headquarters, every general and admiral, had a public relations force.[44]

The Air Force launched a campaign of public relations after World War II which was aimed at gaining equal status with the Army and Navy. This program was so successful that the Air Force not only achieved equality but acquired superiority in some respects. Rapidly the other services began to emulate the Air Force. An interesting example of this interservice competition in public relations is reported by Douglas Cater. He writes that when the Air Force began a massive campaign to celebrate the tenth anniversary of the Strategic Air Command, the Navy reacted by almost immediately beginning a countercampaign to extol its own virtues.[45] The increased focus on public relations by the military is further exemplified by Gen. Matthew B. Ridgway's statement in 1959 when he called for "the creation of a public relations–conscious Army."[46]

The reasons for the increase and overall pervasiveness of public relations are many, but two stand out. First, the interservice competition for material advantage, along with the desire for prestige, has expanded the movement. This interservice competition has had the effect of weakening the overall military posture but has strengthened each of the services. The result has been an overall increase in military power in terms of material and policy goals. The individual services found themselves in the position of having to compete in the political arena much as the other interest groups were doing. The use of public relations was a natural tool.[47]

A second important reason for the increase in public relations in the services was the increase in technological change. Each service had to compete in various weapon areas. There was no longer a hard and fast line to separate weapons into service groups. The ship had always been a

[44] Mills, p. 220.

[45] "Government by Publicity," *The Reporter* (March 19, 1959), 15.

[46] Gen. M. B. Ridgway, "Army Troop and Public Relations," *Army Information Digest* (August, 1954), 5.

[47] Huntington, *The Common Defense*, pp. 384–385.

Navy weapon, but which service should have jurisdiction over the production of missiles? Do missiles belong to the Air Force exclusively?[48]

For convenience of analyzing public relations in the services, the subject can be divided into two broad areas: the internal public relations effort, mainly aimed at congressmen and public opinion leaders, and the external effort, having the objective of engendering public opinion favorable to the achievement of military goals.

Prior to World War II, the Army and Navy had public relations offices, but they were subordinate to the intelligence division. By 1947, all three services had offices of public relations under the service secretaries. At about the same time, the services began to maintain efficient liaison offices in Washington, whose purpose was to smooth relations with Congress.[49] By 1959 the Air Force had the largest number of officers involved in public relations legislative liaison work, with 160 full-time employees.[50] Though none of these legislative liaison officers are registered as lobbyists, they do exhibit many characteristic attitudes and actions of registered lobbyists. An address given by an Air Force legislative officer points this out:

> A member of Congress is very important, not only to the military, but to the operation of the entire government. . . . Just because you don't agree with him or approve his actions, don't sell him short. . . . It is our duty to understand him, how he thinks, how he feels about things, what his likes and dislikes are. In the Air Force we don't always know our Congressmen as we should. It will be good for the Air Force if we get to know them better.[51]

The techniques of these liaison groups are numerous and varied and frequently resemble those of other lobbying groups, most of whom go into elaborate rehearsals to prepare their representatives before hearings of Congress. Also, liaison officers always make it a point to cultivate members of Congress who saw duty in their own branches during World War II and who still hold reserve commissions. A good example of this is the interest the Air Force had in Senator Barry Goldwater, a reserve Air Force colonel. Most liaison officers conduct themselves on the basis that theirs is the job of informing Congress with truth when asked for it, but not of going out of their way to give uncalled-for information.

The role of the congressman is a dual one. He has the responsibility of representing the nation as a whole and is required to consider the mili-

[48] William S. Fairfield, "PR for the Services—In Uniform and in Mufti," *The Reporter* (May 15, 1958), 20.

[49] Furniss, p. 38.

[50] Fairfield.

[51] Maj.-Gen. Joe W. Kelly, USAF, "The Air Force and the Congress," An Address on the Military Legislative Relationship with Congress. Office of Secretary of Air Force, July 7, 1955.

tary bills and appropriations in light of actual need; he is also required to eliminate waste where he finds it. The second role he has is that of a representative of a district or state who is pressured by vested interests in the area. Oftentimes these roles conflict and the congressman is in a dilemma. The administration's decision to close an obsolete military installation within his district is an example of this dilemma.

Some groups and individuals look upon the increase in public relations activity by the services, and especially the legislative maneuvering, as a potential danger to our democratic system. This thought was expressed in an article which indicated that

> Congressmen see the problems of the Defense Department through the eyes of the military, whose testimony has more meaning for them than that of the high civilian Pentagon official who, they know, is only in town for something like a year and a half before his own business beckons him back home.[52]

Even within the Congress itself, fears are expressed of the increased activity by the military. Representative James L. Whetten (Mississippi), speaking about the pressure of the military-industrial complex, said in a House committee meeting, "We have reached the point where tenure of office of a Congressman or Senator in Washington to a great degree is controlled on how many defense contracts they may get in their own area."[53]

However, there are other individuals and groups who believe that the growing increase in public relations within the Congress is a healthy sign. They think that it will help to keep the services divided and competing with each other. This they believe will have the result of keeping the civilian control dominant and also will help Congress to receive balanced amounts of information, instead of having only one source of military wisdom.

A major approach of military public relations has been to appeal to the grass roots of American politics, but attempts by the services to reach this level have often met with difficulties. The main reason for their failures has been essentially that the services are national organizations, and the practice of getting public opinion behind a movement is best accomplished through local channels.

An Air Force bulletin called *Information Services Program* gives an indication of the increased emphasis the services are placing on getting public opinion on their side. "Facts must be convincing, demonstrated, living salesmen of the practical. These are the only kind of facts that mold

[52] Edward L. Katzenbach, Jr., "The Pentagon's Reorganization Muddle," *The Reporter* (May 15, 1958), 16.
[53] "Politics in the Arms Business?" *U.S. News & World Report* (May 13, 1963), 40.

opinions and channel vibrant tensions of public thinking; always deciding issues in the end, altering military policy as surely as defeat in war—they make public opinion the most powerful tool of all, even more powerful than war itself."[54]

The services, in order to reach the grass roots levels, have used the local reserve corps. Also, the services have called upon the National Guard to disseminate information to the local level. While the Guard has moved more successfully in applying pressure on Congress, because of its numbers and image as a representative of national opinion, its actions have not always been satisfactory to the services. The National Guard has not tended to accept service leadership, while the reserve units hew more to the line. Another group which the services attempt to use in a grass roots movement consists of the high-powered public relations staffs of defense contractors. They perform the dual function of spreading the information to the local level as well as gathering up the public opinion and giving it to Congress. These groups operate similarly to the Guard in the respect that the service control over them is tenuous.

The Army has made the greatest effort recently to reach the public. This is owing probably to its declining status, and because of the greater use of manpower, it believes it can influence the local areas more readily.[55]

In some six hundred communities, advisory committees have been established to promote the military view and to advise the military of unfavorable reactions. Liaison with important national and business organizations is developed, and conferences and field trips for leaders of key groups in business, educational, religious, and entertainment areas, usually at government expense, are arranged. Therefore, the news pertaining to the military that appears on the air and in print almost always has been screened, summarized, and analyzed by the staff before its release.

Evidence is not hard to come by to illustrate the use of propaganda techniques by the military to influence public opinion and legislation. The Harness report to the Committee on Expenditures in the Executive Department, July 24, 1947, reported that "the War Department is using government funds in an improper manner for propaganda activities supporting compulsory military training." It noted that the use of funds in such manner "for the purpose of influencing legislation before Congress is unlawful," and it recommended to the Attorney General that he "at once" start proceedings "to stop this unauthorized and illegal expenditure of public monies." Since the Truman administration was favoring UMT (Universal Military Training), the Attorney General did nothing, and the Army kept right on propagandizing, reportedly on an even larger scale.

One of the problem areas for the public relations officer in his role of

---

[54] Fairfield, 21.   [55] Coles, p. 202.

representative of the grass roots sector is the problem of handling complaints and inquiries from citizens. One liaison officer points out the problem with the following story.

You people know all about the Small Business Administration. We have had a lot of procurement business with it. We get lots of investigations in that field. We had one very recently of a contractor out in the Midwest who had a contract to provide dehydrated hamburgers for the Air Force. Those hamburgers were to be dehydrated exactly 30 per cent, and they were to be packed in cans horizontally instead of vertically. The contractor came up to the contracting office and said: "Unfortunately, when I dehydrate these hamburgers 30 per cent, they turn into little round rubber balls, just like handballs. And it doesn't make a bit of difference whether they are packed horizontally or vertically." The contracting office said: "Well, I am sorry. I appreciate your problem. But the contract says specifically, in writing, that they have to be packed horizontally. I am going to have to reject them," which he did. The contractor said, "What is my next step?" The reply was, "Why don't you write your Congressman?" He did. We are still answering that one.[56]

Neither critics nor supporters of the military deny that it has expanded its public relations function. Some believe that this is being done by means which are detrimental to our society. Fred Cook of the antimilitarist school believes that each of the services, by having its own association and publicity function, has put the cost of giving service information beyond reasonable terms. The bill for these functions, he believes, is being paid by the military-industrial complex, and in essence the ultimate payer is the public through the defense contracts.[57]

However, there are others who see this increase of publicity by the services as a healthy sign of the dissemination of ideas. They believe: "The advocates of the three services as well as the champions of greater unification have both the right and the obligation to continue the debate and to provide Congress, the public, and the press with what they consider relevant information."[58]

How much danger this increase in publicity and public relations holds can still be regarded as speculative. There appear to be benefits and problems on both sides of the question. Two ultimate dangers do need to be thought about when the increasing size and power of the military public relations are considered. There is always the danger that the service debates on national security and its military solutions could turn from looking at alternative solutions into a debate over ideological concepts, much the same as our foreign policy debates have in some cases. Another ultimate danger is that the public relations of the military could get so strong as to distort the international relations problem effectively in their favor. This would

[56] Kelly, pp. 7–8.   [58] Fairfield, 23.
[57] Cook, p. 8.

have the effect of creating rigid military approaches to these problems and the cutting off of civilian oversight.

Politics

In many countries, the military has traditionally been aligned with the reactionary and fascist groups. There is little reason to believe that such alliances typify the military in the United States, although it is generally seen as a basically conservative group. This is not to say that the military as an interest group in politics is not a danger, or a possible one. Its sheer size and inherent power makes the military a greater threat than the other groups. The military bureaucracy has greater potential power than any other interest group discussed in this book, and *if* it ever became united and dominant, there is no guarantee that any group could prevail against it. However, the position of the military man in politics is a new one, and one in which he does not feel comfortable. The traditional military approach to politics has been based on the doctrine that the military should be controlled by the civilian administration. Thus, the military leader in a political situation finds himself in a psychological dilemma. Though he accepts the civilian control concept, he finds himself forced into political activity because of the lack of civilian leadership in defense policy making. In many cases the civilian administrator has turned his functions over to what he considers the expertise of the military man.[59]

It does not appear that the military has "moved in" on the historical civilian position in politics as much as that it has been "sucked" into an area which lacked leadership and organization. The demobilization of controlling civilian groups after World War II left a vacuum in policy making for the military. This was coupled with the great increase in the technical aspects of modern warfare, causing Congress and the executive agencies to be overwhelmed.

President Eisenhower's 1953 cut in the Air Force budget of $5 billion stimulated the services to move faster than ever to put up a concerted fight for funds. This meant that they would have to become involved more than ever in politics. The *Congressional Quarterly Service* indicated in a 1955 issue that several members of Congress called up President Eisenhower and told him that they were changing their votes in response to pressure generated by the services.

Just what is the military man's attitude toward politics? An article in the *U.S. Naval Institute Proceedings,* entitled "Politics and the Naval Officer," gives a good straightforward approach to this problem.

[59] Gene M. Lyons, "The New Civil-Military Relations," *American Political Science Review,* 55 (March, 1961), 53.

The essence of politics has always been control of power. Therefore the relations between politicians and the military have always been strongly influenced by the fact that a considerable part of the national power has been entrusted to the officers who—to say it bluntly—may abuse it. . . . A combination of experienced politicians and well educated officers is the best safe guard against dangers of this kind.[60]

Most officers are not concerned with politics, and only as they ascend the ladder in the military hierarchy do they become more conscious of their political ideas. Once in the hierarchy, these top military leaders are often faced with the problem of whether to follow the Commander in Chief or to follow Congress when they differ on political matters. The military man involved in politics is also torn between his loyalty to the administration as opposed to the loyalty he might perceive he has toward the people of his country.

Thus, traditionally, the military has assumed a posture of avoiding politics. This avoidance of politics has given the military an image of conservatism, based on a desire to retain the *status quo*. This conservatism is also based on the belief in the imperfectibility of man. Since man is imperfect, then violence becomes the final move in any military situation. This move to violence is inevitable. Another set of circumstances which tended to make the military politically conservative was the great emphasis on the "honor code" and the concept of the military man as a professional public servant. Today there is a tendency, because of the change in military technology and the "cold war," for the military to abandon some of their old beliefs and to be less conservative in the new situations.

The military man's political beliefs are no longer centered within his organization, but are being expanded to include the larger society. They are becoming more evident, more explicit, and more ideological in content. A manifestation of this change can be found in the way the military person views the politician with much the same suspicion as does his civilian counterpart. Usually the military man has little patience with compromise in politics. Another attitude which the military has about politics is that the military man is able to give a positive contribution to the political jungle. The great increase of military advisers in administrative agencies is evidence of this changed attitude.[61]

The military, however, is not without its agitators in the political field. Some of the most adamant military spokesmen have aligned themselves with the "radical right." These men had oftentimes pressed home the theme of the need for a stronger military establishment. The civil administration and others have not let their activity go unnoticed. Secretary of Defense McNamara in 1961 issued a memorandum listing at least eleven meetings at

[60] *U.S. Naval Institute Proceedings* (January, 1962), 116.
[61] Janowitz, chap. 12.

which the military had joined hands with "extremely radical speakers" in condemning foreign and domestic policies of the administration in office. The final result of this memorandum was announced in the *New York Times,* July 21, 1961, when Secretary McNamara issued a directive "placing restraints on the freedom of military officers to advocate right-wing political theories in official public appearances." Another instance of the radical right influence in the military was the Reuther Memorandum, which suggested that the Attorney General "muzzle the military and stop the recall" to active duty of conservatives such as Gen. James Van Fleet.[62]

As to the actual importance or danger of the military in politics, the opinions of "experts" differ. Some believe that our political structure is harmed by such activity, that politics should be served only by politicians, and that there is a great danger that the military could dominate policy making.

Others believe that the politics of the military leaders in each administration are likely to follow the line of those in charge. Each administration will choose the military leaders much the same as Cabinet officers are chosen. This does not mean that they will all be chosen on party lines. The promotion system within the services tends to downgrade partisanship.[63] But the Joint Chiefs of Staff have become increasingly politically oriented and sensitive to the views of the administration.

Some feel that the actual involvement of the military in partisan politics has been so slight as not to be significant. They view the conflicting political interest of the services as a means to check the power of the military as a whole.

Undoubtedly, the military will become more involved in politics as long as the civilian administration does not take the initiative. It also is probably impossible, because of their expertise, to keep the military completely out of politics and policy-making decisions. The ultimate danger of the military in political affairs is that a situation is created whereby a very powerful organ of government is lobbying and manipulating politics for its own benefit. Because the military bureaucracy is so much bigger and more powerful than other interest groups, it would be very difficult to contain or stop them if they should get out of control.

CIVIL-MILITARY RELATIONS

The concept of civilian supremacy of the military establishment has been both a constitutional precept and a political dogma since the beginning of American government. Until World War II any militant threat to our basic

[62] Reuther Memorandum to the Attorney General of the United States, given to the Attorney General by Victor Reuther on December 19, 1961.

[63] *The New York Times* (April 15, 1956).

values was considered primarily an internal threat. This fear was reflected in the refusal to maintain large standing armies during peacetime or to make any advance military commitments. It is interesting to note that as recently as 1949 and 1953, the first Hoover Commission and the Rockefeller Committee on Defense Organization both warned of the danger militarism posed to our democratic institutions.[64]

World War II, the Korean conflict, and the cold war have drastically transformed the nature of civil-military relations in America. The external threat to American values and liberties demonstrated that crucial politico-military decisions have to be made far in advance of actual crises. The unprecedented burden of responsibility for free world defense was thrust on American leadership. Today "civilian opinion freely accepts the need for continuing high-level peacetime defense mobilization."[65]

What is needed is an understanding of military policy and strategy by responsible civilians and a like understanding on the part of military leadership of the art of politics and the values of a civilian society they are committed to defend.

It is difficult to pin down a precise distinction between civilian and military factors in national policy making. The concept of civilian-military relations has been described as "a distressingly wooly abstraction. It conceals important distinctions within each group of partners to the relationship . . ." and it also "conceals a distinction between two forms of relationships. One is vertical among officials of different levels of authority. The issue here is who shall rule and why. The other is essentially a horizontal relationship among officials with different types of expertise. The issue here is who is right and why."[66]

In order to have an adequate understanding of the civilian-military relations, there is a need to analyze their historical development. The real struggle between the civilian and military groups began in 1903 when Elihu Root, Secretary of War, and President Theodore Roosevelt initiated an Army Reorganization Plan. The Spanish-American War had clearly exhibited the inefficiencies of the War Department, which had bureaus that were headed by permanently assigned Army personnel who had developed into minor political figures controlled by Congress. In an attempt to restore central authority in the War Department, Root and Roosevelt met formi-

---

[64] Commission on Organization of the Executive Branch of Government, *The National Security Organization,* A Report to Congress, February, 1949, pp. 2–3; and *Report of the Rockefeller Committee on Department of Defense Organization,* Committee print, Senate Committee on Armed Services, 83d Congress, 1st Session (1953), p. 1.

[65] William T. R. Fox, "Representativeness and Efficiency: The Dual Problem of Civil-Military Relations," *Political Science Quarterly,* 76 (September, 1961), 361.

[66] Lawrence I. Radway, "Uniforms and Mufti: What Place in Policy?" *Public Administration Review,* 18 (summer, 1958), 180.

dable opposition from military hero Nelson A. Miles, Commanding General of the Army, who had strong connections in Congress. Root succeeded in establishing a general staff system and a Chief of Staff.[67]

A similar attempt to create a Chief of Naval Operations analogous to the Chief of Staff met violent opposition in 1915 from Secretary of the Navy Daniels, who considered it a threat to civilian control. The feeling in both the Army and Navy at that time was to consider the military instruments of national policy but not participants in its making, however contradictory and inconsistent civilian policies had plagued the Army leaders.[68]

From 1916 to 1920, Secretary of War Newton Baker viewed the conflict between bureau chiefs and centralized staff control as a contest between legislative and executive influence in the military departments.[69]

During the 1930s and up to the eve of America's entry into World War II, diplomatic actions of the State Department and military planning were treated as separate categories.[70] This separation was emphasized during the war as the Joint Chiefs of Staff, created by President Roosevelt, rose to eminence in creating war strategy. Internal tensions were created in the status of civilian secretaries as well. Secretary of the Navy Knox threatened to resign twice because he was too seldom included in high policy discussions between the President and the Joint Chiefs of Staff.[71]

At the war's end there was a lack of understanding by both statesman and soldiers of the importance of politics in war and peace, as well as inadequate governmental machinery for fusing political with military objectives.[72] However, the war, the rise of air power, and other factors generated a move for "unification" and a greater awareness of the political implications of military strategy.

The major problem to be faced in the reorganization of 1947 was to unify the military services, while at the same time correlating them with the rest of the government, and leaving the Joint Chiefs of Staff undisturbed as an institution. The result was the National Security Act of 1947, which established a Department of Defense. The Joint Chiefs of Staff were to provide strategic and logistic plans, the services under civilian secretaries would implement them through their own command organizations, and the National

[67] Paul Y. Hammond, *Organizing for Defense* (Princeton, N.J.: Princeton University Press), pp. 11–12.

[68] *Ibid.,* pp. 72–86.

[69] *Ibid.,* p. 47.

[70] Walter Millis, Harvey L. Mansfield, and Harold Stein, *Arms and the State* (New York: The Twentieth Century Fund, 1958), pp. 20–23, 28–30, 46–52.

[71] Paul Y. Hammond, "Effects of Structure on Policy," *Public Administration Review,* 18 (summer, 1958), 175.

[72] Harry Rowe Ransom, "Organizing for National Security Decisions," *Public Administration Review,* 19 (autumn, 1959), 262–263.

Security Council would provide overall coordination. The Secretary of Defense was a compromise figure between the Joint Chiefs of Staff and the National Security Council, who was not to be either the architect of defense policy or the chief administrator of the defense establishment.[73] "Civilian and military control had been intermingled all along the line . . . with neither in a position of clear responsibility for the results."[74]

The ambiguities of the 1947 legislation were quickly clarified by actual practice. The Secretary of Defense was nearly powerless, the National Security Council failed to generate policy, the Joint Chiefs of Staff remained aloof and independent, and the service secretaries could not administer their individual departments and still act as deputies in formation of overall policies.

Subsequent amendments and reorganizations in 1949, 1953, and 1958 all moved toward greater centralization in the Secretary of Defense and the Joint Chiefs of Staff, emphasizing civilian domination to supply the Joint Chiefs of Staff with political guidelines. The impact of technology and increased defense costs were important factors in this centralization.

What, then, are some possible solutions to the ever-increasing problem of maintaining civilian control over our defense establishment without weakening its effectiveness or failing to take adequate advantage of the expertise of military officials in the determination of national policy? It would be difficult to assert positively which branch of government, the executive or the legislative, is most able to guarantee civilian supremacy in policy and organization questions. In view of the complicated set of relationships existing between those officials and departments responsible for the making and implementing of our national defense policies, a brief analysis of their current roles and influence in this process may provide some useful answers.

There is some justification in Walter Millis's observation, "The legislature, on which the authors of the Constitution placed so much reliance as the final regulator of civil–military affairs, has in modern times proved unsuited to discharge the function."[75] On the one hand, Congress has often been little more than a "rubber stamp" for the executive branch, and on the other hand, it has sometimes severely undermined the effectiveness of the Secretary of Defense, the key to civilian control in the executive branch.

Since World War II, Congress has not vetoed directly a major strategic program, a force level recommendation, or a major weapons system proposed by the administration.[76] It is striking that Congress readily accepted the 1958 changes in the Joint Chiefs of Staff in view of the potential power

[73] Hammond, *Organizing for Defense,* pp. 223, 226, 231.

[74] Millis et al., *Arms and the State,* p. 181.

[75] *Ibid.,* pp. 347–348.

[76] Samuel P. Huntington, "Strategic Planning and the Political Process," *Foreign Affairs,* 38 (January, 1960), 287.

created by these changes.[77] Even though Congress risked political repudiation at that time to resist transfer to the President of its jealously guarded power over the functions and roles of the military services, it eventually accepted this diminution of authority.[78]

Lack of proper information and technical competence is often cited as the reason for congressional inability to act effectively on strategic programs. Although this is a contributory factor, according to Samuel P. Huntington, the primary failing is political in nature.

The initiation and elimination of programs and the apportionment of resources among them are highly political decisions involving conflicting interests and groups. . . . Congress cannot effectively determine strategic programs because interests which are primarily concerned with those programs are not adequately represented in any single congressional body. . . . Congressional bodies may become advocates of particular programs, but they lack sufficient political competence to determine an over-all program.[79]

It can be argued that the channels of communication, both formal and informal, which exist between Congress and various military officials or other subordinate elements in the Defense Department serve to encourage the flow of information from a variety of sources, thus enhancing intelligent decision making as well as checking the power of the Secretary of Defense. This may be true to a certain extent. But it is also true that these alliances between members of the defense establishment and congressional interests have often undermined the programs of the Secretary of Defense and the administration. Congressional sympathies for air power in 1949 consistently rendered ineffectual the efforts of Secretary Forrestal to create a common program between the services.[80]

The "power of the purse strings" has proved to be at best a limited means of exercising control with respect to military matters. Congress has generally appropriated the funds requested. Congress also has the function of legislative oversight. As one author puts it, "With the executive as decision-maker, Congress has become the lobbyist," and "Congressional groups engage in sustained campaigns of pressure and persuasion to produce the desired strategic decisions." Often the administration must give public justification of its defense policies, thus educating the public on strategic issues.[81] Congressional control over military matters, although somewhat limited, does provide a greater measure of civilian control than would unbridled executive power.

[77] Hammond, *Organizing for Defense,* pp. 381–382.

[78] Max M. Kampelman, "Congressional Control vs. Executive Flexibility," *Public Administration Review,* 18 (summer, 1958), 186–187.

[79] Huntington, "Strategic Planning and the Political Process," 286–287.

[80] Hammond, *Organizing for Defense,* p. 238.

[81] Huntington, "Strategic Planning and the Political Process," 287.

The military has long argued for a more militant anti-Communist foreign policy and has, therefore, at times been used by right-wing groups to give backing to their positions. The military has often been at direct odds with the State Department over foreign policy. Decisions that are made by the State Department, therefore, can affect and restrain military decisions. In this situation there is inherently a conflict situation between the two groups.

This frequent conflict over foreign policy becomes all the sharper since it can affect the military's budget requests and programs. In terms of patriotism, the military can and does justify a stronger America, an America in which, obliquely, it has greater status and control. The ideology and desire for "more" in all power groups are strong. In the military, however, the demand for dollars for increased defense is backed by the use of fear, fear lest the country actually be too weak. The cry of "missile gap," which Kennedy effectively used in winning the Presidency in 1960, exploited doubts on this matter. These doubts existed among both the general and the informed public. This is true since politicians do not dare get the reputation of being soft toward communism or of making the country vulnerable to attack. The military, more than any other group in the economy, is able to demand and to win "more." Fear of something as widely distressing as military catastrophe, when combined with congressional, political, and economic interests, is a most effective ideology for increasing a budget. Often Congress has actually appropriated more money for military expenditures than the President recommended. It is little wonder that by now the military budget is over half the entire Federal government budget.

It is the ability to use these two techniques that makes the military bureaucracy latently the most powerful in the country, particularly when combined with defense business interests. C. Wright Mills claimed, and quite possibly correctly, that the coincidence of economic, political, and military interest has provided the country with a military power elite new to United States history.

The President is responsible for the "whole" of national policy, while the military is responsible for only one of the means to the attainment of one of the objectives—national security. The increasing responsibility of the executive branch to make crucial decisions on strategic programs has undermined the ability of the President to lead. The more the President becomes the judge, the less he can advocate. That is, the process of decision within the executive branch is primarily a legislative one. Strategic programs, like other major policies, are representative of compromise between different groups with different interests and perspectives, all within the executive branch. The decisions hammered out are then approved by the President. Debate ends when the decision is reached, and the primary role of the administration, and thus the President, becomes one of saying yes or no. The policy then must be protected from the impact of outside interests and forces.

Huntington suggests that this defensive role of the administration and the tenuous character of its decisions could be modified by broadening the scope of discussion at an early stage in the policy process before key decisions are made, thus broadening the scope of policy consensus, and improving the quality of policy content. Public participation, focusing on proposals of an adequate legislative leadership within the executive branch, would enhance the President's actual power of decision rather than committing him to the defense of a decision already made before it reaches him.[82]

The main issue facing the Department of Defense is how to centralize the military operations without sacrificing the civilian control. Increased centralization of power in both the office of Secretary of Defense and the Joint Chiefs of Staff, together with a changing approach to service roles, has resulted in greater integration, but has not lessened the problem of achieving effective civilian control without jeopardizing the effectiveness of centralized military planning. These two "sides" of the Department of Defense have generally been the focal points around which revolve the major issues in civil-military conflict. In shaping final decisions, each has to balance the risks involved in alienating the other against the benefits gained in pressing for policies believed to be essential.

The search for an appropriate policy-making role for the Joint Chiefs of Staff has been a very difficult one. The failure to achieve independent position and a tendency to become involved in nonprofessional matters of high policy have been major problems.[83]

When the Department of Defense was organized in 1947, the Joint Chiefs of Staff was already a "going concern" with an effective staff, great prestige, and much power. The wartime relationship of direct contact with the President was difficult for the Joint Chiefs of Staff to give up. Similarly, the Korean conflict produced almost daily direct consultation between the State Department and the Joint Chiefs. These relationships were extremely difficult for the Secretary of Defense to penetrate, and he found that because he lacked a policy-oriented staff, he could not offer strong counterpressures.[84]

The closed staff features of the Joint Chiefs of Staff have been a constant problem in relationship with civilian leadership. The relatively free exchange of data and viewpoints which existed between the civilian secretariat and the general staff in the old War Department is critically missing

---

[82] *Ibid.*, 299.
[83] Hammond, "Effects of Structure on Policy," 179.
[84] *Ibid.*, 177–178.

between the Secretary of Defense and the Joint Chiefs of Staff.[85] Decisions have been reached by relatively unfettered and unobserved deliberations.

The 1958 reorganization made the role of the Joint Chiefs of Staff all the more vital. Its power was extended by making it responsible for the strategic direction of military operations. Hammond considers this equivalent to command authority, even though obscured by "the characteristic administrative fiction that the Joint Chiefs of Staff is only the advisor of the Secretary of Defense." He asserts that this change, along with the placing of the Joint Chiefs of Staff outside of the office of Secretary of Defense, thus supporting claims to greater independence, has significant implications for civilian responsibility. He also points out that presidential and congressional hope in the new role of the Joint Chiefs of Staff as a moderator of interservice disputes is not encouraging. Suppression of these rivalries will likely produce strengthening of the closed staff characteristic. The increased power of the chairman of the Joint Chiefs of Staff is even more important, as this power is very unclear and his responsibility even more so. He concludes that one major factor prevents the power of the Joint Chiefs of Staff from achieving preeminence, the divided loyalties of the three chiefs.[86] Huntington essentially agrees, and points out that this has also stimulated a less military attitude on the part of the Joint Chiefs of Staff in dealing with civilian leaders.[87]

The Secretary of Defense, as another factor in the civilian-military relationship, has become one of the most prominent members of both the President's Cabinet and his inner circle. By the reorganization of 1958 he was given responsibility for the unified commands and greater decision-making power. Posed against the potential growth of the Joint Chiefs of Staff is the Secretary of Defense's managerial controls, the most important of which is the budget procedures of the Comptroller's office.[88] The Secretary of Defense is still faced with the problem of how to utilize and deal with the semiautonomous Chief of Staff group. One solution to the problem has been that the assistant secretaries have provided the function of giving advice and information in order that the Secretary of Defense might have a greater choice of alternatives upon which to base his decisions. Hammond suggests, however, that in light of the failure of National Security Council staff methods to provide concrete programs, this arrangement has little hope. He proposes instead, as do other writers, the development of a cohesive personal staff for the Secretary that would be "entirely his own."[89]

[85] Hammond, *Organizing for Defense*, p. 385.

[86] *Ibid.*, pp. 377–380.

[87] Samuel P. Huntington, "Interservice Competitive and the Political Roles of the Armed Services," *American Political Science Review,* 55 (March, 1961), 42.

[88] Hammond, "Effects of Structure on Policy," 176–178.

[89] Hammond, *Organizing for Defense*, pp. 389–390.

Such a staff must function without power or responsibility, and is a necessity if the major defense policy decisions are to be made at the center of the defense establishment.

It is conceivable that such a staff might make the work of the Joint Chiefs of Staff more available to the Secretary of Defense and enhance his confidence in its product. On the other hand, the Secretary's staff might find itself simply a rival of the Joint Chiefs of Staff, unable to compete effectively with it.

Another possibility is an effort by the Secretary of Defense to get along better with the Joint Chiefs of Staff, if necessary by intruding upon them until they do as he wishes. Gates, Deputy Secretary of Defense, initiated the practice of being present with the Joint Chiefs of Staff in their meetings and deciding issues there promptly. He got impressive results, but this method is limited. In the first place it is a personal performance by the Secretary, and in the second place it opens the Joint Chiefs of Staff up to the Secretary alone.[90]

The capability to generate policy will determine the respective roles of the Joint Chiefs of Staff and Secretary of Defense. The Secretary must be able to balance the major forces of organization. Organization and administration devices themselves will not solve these problems. As Radway observes, they can be no more effective than the person they serve. "The first requirement is still a Secretary with the competence, tenure, and desire to discharge his total responsibilities."[91]

Secretary of Defense McNamara made his office an effective instrument for maintaining civilian control by use of the personal staff technique suggested above, as well as his own competent leadership ability. His RAND Corporation Ph.D. aides, dubbed the "whiz kids" or "McNamara and his band" by the military, provided an important alternative source of information and advice upon which to base policy decisions. This scientific approach put the military very definitely on the defensive in many areas where it had traditionally made decisions. The culmination of this trend is difficult to ascertain.

What are the current and future trends in basic civilian-military relationships? Obviously the nature of these relationships is in a significant state of evolution. As Gene M. Lyons suggests, a fundamental break with tradition is occurring as the civilians apparently are becoming "militarized" and the military "civilianized." This is due (1) to the strengthening of central organization in the Department of Defense, (2) to professionalization of civilian leaderships, and (3) to the broadening character of the military profession.[92]

---

[90] *Ibid.*, p. 389.
[91] Radway, 185.

[92] Lyons, 54, 63.

The need for government experience, expertise, and continuity in high Pentagon posts below the Secretary of Defense is now recognized as vital to the effectiveness of the Defense Department, and there is a marked emphasis on standards of competence and experience in making appointments.

Another trend is the increasing influence of career executives in the development of major policy decisions. Two other important influences on the professionalization process are innovations in administration, which have brought outside experts into government through a variety of institutional devices, and growing interest in military affairs among civilians outside of the government, particularly among writers, scientists, and scholars. The recent outpouring of material from scholarly sources has provided additional sources of advice and information outside of the military services which responsible civilian officials can utilize in their policy decisions. It seems safe to predict that these trends will continue to gain momentum, and their collective effect on the nature of civilian leadership in military affairs will in turn have important repercussions on the nature of civil-military relations.[93]

The biggest problem facing civilian leadership, compared with military leadership, is the training and education of future personnel. There is "no single, authoritative source of civilian insight into politico-military problems," a situation which should not exist in "our pluralistic society."[94]

As the prior analysis has indicated, under modern conditions of continuing high-level external threat, the public interest will not be served by viewing the civilian and military components of the national government as natural enemies. Disagreement between the two is not inherently evil, for it can clarify alternatives and pave the way for positive action.[95]

Three issues which will undoubtedly be debated far into the future are the questions of whether the making of defense policy reflects a proper consensus of political, economic, scientific, and military judgments; whether the Defense Department civilians should extend or diminish their influence both horizontally and vertically; and what the concept of civilian control should actually encompass.

MILITARY IDEOLOGY

In order to present the ideology of the United States military, it is necessary to analyze three important influences which have helped to determine its nature. First, there is the historical development of the American military;

[93] *Ibid.*, 56, 61.
[94] Fox, 355–356.

[95] *Ibid.*, 364.

second, the concept of an overall military ideology which is pushed and pulled by the ideologies of the separate services as well as by the administration; and third, the factor of increased strength.

For the purposes of this section, the "military ideology" will be the military as it represents itself to the public and as it perceives the problems which it faces.

The early colonial period in the military history of the United States in many ways represents the European model which was based upon patriotism, honor, and military professionalism. Particularly did the young country attempt to follow the pattern of British naval professionalism.[96]

By the nineteenth century, however, the American military had developed into something quite different from its British counterpart. Two factors stand out as causing this difference. The custom of keeping the army small while keeping the state militias strong helped to widen the disparity between the two. This had the effect of making the national military units well aware of their weakness and of putting them in the position of always trying to maintain at least a *status quo* position. The use of the military in domestic affairs such as Indian uprisings, strikes, and rebellions also helped to differentiate the role of the American military from that of its counterparts across the sea.[97]

Another factor which drove the two systems apart was the basic belief which the Founding Fathers had instilled into the American society—that the military was inherently a danger to civil society. This idea was prevalent in almost all the early governmental relations between the military and the civil bureaucracy. In response to this attitude, the American military began to express itself in the concept of specific "missions." This meant that they approached each military problem as though it had a separate identity and was not connected with an overall policy. The military, in a sense, felt very much like a parolee who is bound to explain his every action or be punished for not conforming.[98]

Thus, the United States military in this early period became rigid and dogmatic in its ideology. The prestige of the combat officer was very high. The services placed emphasis on past military traditions and were generally unwilling to adopt innovations, although some small effort was made to create new procedures. It was in terms of traditions that ideology was expressed.

World War I, however, changed traditions considerably. But it was not until World War II that the real impact of a changing weapons technology and a closer relationship between military services and foreign aid

---

[96] Norbert Elias, "Studies in the Genesis of the Naval Profession," *British Journal of Sociology* (1950), 291–309.

[97] Janowitz, p. 24.

[98] U.S. Department of Army, *The Role of the Army*, Pamphlet 21–70 (June 29, 1955), pp. 3–4.

and economic programs blew apart the old traditional foundations.[99] The military during World War II, and after, found that in most cases the old military professionalism and customs were in opposition to the new technological inventions. Innovations such as nuclear bombs, guided missiles, and atomic submarines forced them to take new approaches to old problems. No longer was the concept of the combat hero as the leader nearly so effective as it had been.[100] Military ideology based on the "specific mission" approach was failing to meet the problems, and the new type of martial situation called for an overall continuous planning function.

This change in environmental conditions has caused many problems. As with all sudden changes, there has developed a cultural-lag factor on the part of the military toward accepting the new technical advances. Part of this lag has been because the military has not known how to apply military policies to attain nonbellicose objectives. The American military has not, on the whole, been able to accept what the great eighteenth-century thinker Karl von Clausewitz said about war's being "nothing but a continuation of political intercourse with an admixture of other means."[101]

After 1945, the classical American approach began to develop some cracks, and the military had to make some reevaluations. The specter of a third world war being fought with atomic and hydrogen weapons caused rethinking about old traditions. The new technological advances have forced the military to acquire more expertise. All these factors have caused, to a high degree, a closing of the gap between the military and civilian approaches to the problems of war.

Military ideology cannot be understood without realizing that it does not represent a wholly united front but is pushed and pulled by many internal ideologies. Thus, though the thinking of the individual services may have an overall similarity, rivalry has caused each one to develop its own separate ideology. This represents a move, on the part of the services, to rationalize their own points of view so as to enhance their power and prestige.

The Air Force, because it was a new branch at the end of World War II, did not have a long line of traditional patterns. It was the first service to become concerned with a separate doctrinal approach. The Air Force became so successful in convincing both Congress and the public of the need for increased air power that the other services felt a need to counterattack. The Army and Navy both reevaluated their ideological stands and began extensive campaigns to enhance their positions. When the Air Force would

---

[99] U.S. Military Academy, "The National Security Policy of the United States," *Thirteenth Annual Student Conference on United States Affairs* (New York: West Point Press, 1961), 33.

[100] Lyons, 61.

[101] Karl von Clausewitz, *War, Politics and Power,* Edward M. Collins, Colonel, USAF (ed.) (Chicago: Henry Regnery Company, 1962), p. 255.

speak out on the concept that air power was the solution to national defense, the Army and Navy would issue counterstatements expressing their individual ideologies. A good example of this attack and counterattack is found in an Army publication which expresses this conflict.[102]

These separate ideologies have also helped to develop the tendency for the services to look more to the executive branch than to Congress as a leader in policy, for Congress is viewed mainly as a stumbling block to overcome. This change in concept developed during the two world wars, when it became accepted military practice for the highest commanders of the services to deal directly with the President. The services have pressed for a continuation of this practice. In 1947, the War Department expressed this idea when it said: "Direct access to the President is a mark of the highest status in the executive branch; it represents a large and quite legitimate aspiration of the military services."[103]

These units have come to feel the need not only of an ideology for their own groups but also of an ideology to give interservice solidarity. This need first impressed itself during the major war period when there was such an influx of civilian inductees. The earliest in-service planning was based on the "chain of command" concept, underpinned by a strong hierarchy system. This meant that the inductee or soldier was required to obey orders issued from above and not to question the reasons. The Korean conflict caused a shock wave to ripple through this in-service ideology. Many Americans and most of the military hierarchy were deeply concerned over the defections of American soldiers to the Communist Chinese. Some of the best civilian and military brains began to work on this chink in the military armor. A general consensus was reached which said that these defections took place because the "action" in Korea was not in line with the old American concept "that the United States fights a war to win a complete victory."[104]

A military interservice movement began to rectify this problem. The overall decision was made that what the service needed was a new "political injection," an injection of morality serum which would give it an ideological defense. The philosophy of this new approach is exemplified by the concept of the "American way of life."[105]

The military extensively overhauled its intraservice education system so as to reach all levels of the service with this new message of Americanism. The things taught were in absolutist terms, and the "American way of life" was shown to be diametrically opposed to the one absolute Communist

[102] U.S. Department of the Army, *A Guide to Army Philosophy*, Pamphlet 20–1 (January 22, 1958).

[103] Hammond, *Organizing for Defense*, p. 225.

[104] Janowitz, pp. 402–406.

[105] William H. Boyer, "Armed Forces Ideology: Our Mistaught G.I.'s.," *The Nation* (November 30, 1963), 362.

deology. An example of this absolutist approach can be seen in a pamphlet entitled *The Battle for Liberty,* which mentions men such as Russell Kirk, but neglects to mention those such as Dewey and Fromm who are at variance with the military social philosophy.[106]

The third important influence of military ideology is the factor of increased power of the military and its effect on the group thinking. There are few military experts who would not agree that the military has grown by leaps and bounds during the post-World War II period. The fact that over 60 per cent of our national budget goes for national security adequately attests this fact. This increased military has had to become more involved than ever in international relations. When it has been dealing with international communism, a tough-minded attitude has developed—that America should not give an inch when faced with the might of the Communist world. This attitude is apparent in many of the military conferences which are being held.[107]

Louis Horowitz sees a definite difference between the Department of State and the military bureaucracy on various international issues. He explains it in these terms:

> Here we see the difference between a position which takes into account an over-all political dimension to the present cold war, and one which discusses the matter of thermonuclear war abstractly and in narrow military terms only.[108]

The military also has a suspicion that civilian foreign policy agencies are more appeasement-oriented in their cold war philosophy. They look upon these agencies with a jaundiced eye and believe that their conciliatory positions are a threat to national security. A recent example of this suspicion has been the vocal protests which the military has expressed over the test ban treaty.[109] The military has been very skeptical about the ending of atomic tests. They believe that this type of curb on the military could endanger the United States security. They look upon this ban as a detriment to weapon development.

Also, the military in its expanded role has shown a definite preference for strong men as leaders in foreign countries, even though they may not perceive and help the development of popular aspirations. Chiang Kai-shek is an example of this support for a strong leader. Also, the United States military definitely backed President Rhee of Korea after World War II.

At present there may be a certain weakening of this attitude because of what took place in the latter part of 1963 in South Viet Nam. This case indicates that the military would be willing to withdraw support of these

---

106 *Ibid.*

107 U.S. Military Academy, *op. cit.* The major theme is the necessity of being ready and adequately prepared to meet the Communist challenge.

108 Irving Louis Horowitz, *The War Games* (New York: Ballantine Books, Inc., 1963), p. 31.

109 *Wall Street Journal* (July 26, 1963).

strong leaders if public opinion against them became too strong. Support can also be equated in terms of how strong the leader actually is.

Several other ideological trends are significant. In the area of economics, the military bureaucracy in the past had usually adopted an attitude of noninvolvement. They believed that the free enterprise system was adequate and the military should not interfere. This ideology has changed a great deal, until today the military bureaucracy has been pressing the point that since the 1933 Depression only during a war economy has the United States really been able to sustain a high level of employment. Of the three services, the Air Force has tended to be the least critical of government budgetary practices. This is because it has been the most successful in meeting its own wants. The military also believes now that a certain amount of government intervention in the economic sphere is necessary, but it would be against anything which approaches the concept of socialism, either civilian or military.[110]

Another ideological trend which is evident is based on the need the military feels to increase the degree of preparedness. The military looks back into the past with 20-20 hindsight and tells the public that in previous wars we have been caught militarily weak, and only because of our tremendous natural resources and industrial know-how have we been saved from annihilation by our enemies. The possibility of atomic war has cut the prewar preparation period down to nothing. The military bureaucracy says we cannot afford not to be ready. An Air Force policy statement points out this attitude.

The dangerous strategic concept of so-called minimum deterrence [which] is undermining the nation's defense effort—the shrinking margin of our deterrent posture, already thin enough to encourage Soviet ventures into nuclear rocket blackmail, must be widened with all speed at all costs.[111]

Another element in the change in military ideology has been the inclusion of a new group of civilians into the military establishment. This group has been called such things as the "new civilian militarists," "whiz kids," and "brain trusters." With the appointment of Robert S. McNamara as Secretary of Defense, the use of civilian intellectuals who have scientific and technological knowledge to assist in making military decisions became a significant factor. The initial resentment to this inclusion, by the "old guard" military men, was at first intense and unified. Also, the intellectuals came in for a lot of criticism from left-wing and pacifist groups, as well as from some of their own colleagues in the academic world.[112] Yet for all this initial opposition, this group of men in the military showed that they could get results. Although many of the senior officers still look at the "whiz kids"

110 Janowitz, p. 240.
111 Senter, 14. This was part of the AFA's policy statement, 1960.
112 *U.S. News & World Report* (March 4, 1963), 58.

with disdain, there appears to be an increasing number of younger officers who concur with this group on many of their decisions. These younger officers tend to elevate the importance of scientific and technological expertise over battlefield experience.

The academicians in the military look problems right in the eye. They believe that, though present-day weapons could destroy mankind, yet a thermonuclear war does not mean an unlimited one. Thus there is a need for preparedness. Disarmament policy, they believe, should be contingent upon national policy and security and not foreign policy; thus they favor arms control. They also believe that in a war the advantage does go to the aggressor. Some critics have seen this pronouncement as an advocation of a preemptive strike.[113]

Though it is difficult to discredit the efforts of the intellectuals, it should not be overlooked that there is always a danger of this group's making decisions outside the realm of military feasibility. The need appears to be one of reaching a balance between the contributions of the military brains and those of the civilian intellectuals. The results can then be put into realistic and effective solutions to problems.

There is a great deal of mixed opinion and feeling about the ideology of the military. Opponents believe that its present-day status is having the effect of transforming the military into a caste system which is becoming a potent and independent sector of the American political arena—that the military is becoming a decision-making body in its own right.[114] Also within this hostile group are those who see the increase of in-service and training-group indoctrination as a danger to the American educational system. They believe that the military ideology, saying that either our system or else the Communists will win, is a self-defeating one. They fear that once this type of thinking gets started it will permeate our whole educational system.[115]

However, there are other observers of the military scene who are more moderate in their evaluations. They view the military ideology as now changing into a period when old slogans are being replaced with a new approach to international relations. The military, they feel, is now making more accurate analysis of the strengths and weaknesses of American participation in world affairs. To them it appears that the military has begun to develop an ideology which will blend military and nonmilitary functions of foreign policy into a coherent and consistent strategy.

It is difficult to visualize what the future role of ideology in the military will be. One trend seems certain. Ideology and its propagation will increase and continue to increase as long as the military is called upon to take a greater part in foreign policy, as long as the cold war is a "war." There is

113 Horowitz, 14.
114 For this viewpoint see the works of C. Wright Mills and Louis Horowitz.
115 For this approach see Senter or Cook.

little likelihood that the American military bureaucracy will be able to come down from its ideological perch.

It is impossible to close this chapter without considering one of the newest theses on the trend of military ideology.[116] The basic thesis is that a change which is taking place in the character of civilian-military relationships is altering the ideology of both these groups. This change is one in which the civilians are becoming more militarized and the military is becoming more civilianized. The basic reason for the military's change is predicated upon its need for civilian-like skills in the increasing technological situations. Lyons points out that things such as centralized budgeting, programming, tax programs, and a wide range of complex programs of resources, allocations, and research and development have required skills which are civilian in nature. Not many officers in the past have had these; today they are being forced to acquire them.[117]

Military men are being used more and more in policy decision conferences in Washington. One outward manifestation of this "civilianizing" of the military is indicated by the experience of a graduate student serving in the State Department during the summer of 1963. During the first policy conferences he attended he was unaware of any military advisers present; but as he got to know the people attending, he learned that there was a high military adviser at each of these conferences but these advisers were in civilian dress.[118]

Morris Janowitz concludes this thesis by posing the question: "With the advent of continuous technological innovations, will the military and civilian establishments ultimately blend into one?" He does not believe so. He believes that the military will not lose its distinctive characteristic of the role he calls the "fighter spirit." The essential element which will keep a gap between the civilian and military, he believes, is the need civilians will have for some form of heroic leadership.[119]

THE CASE OF THE HEBERT PROBE[120]

The following case material on the Hebert Probe is presented to show how difficult it is to document military influence on congressional legislation and how the military restrict and censor unfavorable information.

[116] Morris Janowitz. This is the recurring theme throughout his book *The Professional Soldier*.

[117] Lyons, 54.

[118] Interview with Peter Prina, graduate student of Brigham Young University, January 20, 1964.

[119] Janowitz, chap. 2.

[120] This case was based upon material from the *Congressional Quarterly Guide to Current American Government*, the *Congressional Quarterly* (March 24, 1961), and *The New York Times*.

President Eisenhower's reference to an alert and knowledgeable citizenry was well founded. In mid-1959 a special congressional subcommittee had been established to investigate the "military-industrial complex" mentioned by Eisenhower. It was headed by Representative F. Edward Hebert (D, Louisiana) and hence came to be called the Hebert Probe, for it was literally to probe into the alleged conduct of some military men "who depart the ranks of defense for lush places on the payrolls of defense contractors." How many former military officers were employed by defense industries? What were their names? What kind of influence did they wield over their ex-colleagues in the granting of defense contracts? These were some of the questions the probe was to answer.

The atmosphere at the time of the probe was highly charged. The general problem was well known to the congressmen. They recognized that the defense industry, particularly the aircraft and missile industry, is and will continue to be a multibillion dollar business. Hundreds of thousands of people, entire towns and regions, and whole industries are dependent upon defense contracts.

The pressures generated in Washington by the billions of dollars expended annually for defense are enormous and have been growing. Local chambers of commerce, municipal and state officials, labor unions, industrial associations, industries concerned, and congressmen representing affected areas all combine to exert pressures in favor of their own areas.

The members of the subcommittee were convinced that they were on the trail of something hot. Chairman Hebert ended his opening speech with something like crusading zeal when he said, "The innocent have nothing to fear; but the guilty should tremble in their boots!" He hastily added, however, that "we do not intend to deprive the country of the brains of the retired military, but only to find out if there exists any influence peddling."

During the first session it was recognized that the investigators were dealing with the difficult field of "morality, ethics, and propriety." The question arose as to what constitutes "selling" as such. Is an officer who introduces his firm's selling agent to his former boss in the Pentagon actually involved in the selling process? It was at first thought that concrete breaches of the conflict-of-interest laws could be located by use of a questionnaire. These were to be sent out to all former high military officers, Cabinet officials, and members of Congress now associated with defense companies. Some of the questions asked were where these men were employed, what their present duties were, and what their compensation was. Any refusals to answer were to be met by court subpoenas. In addition, witnesses in key positions were to be called in person before the subcommittee. The first witness was Thomas S. Gates, Jr., Deputy Secretary of Defense. He stated, quite reasonably, that the retirement age in the service is low, both for economic reasons and to allow younger men to move up in the ranks. Often officers just become tired of military life and long to "get back in civilian clothes." There is a natural propensity for these men to seek jobs in firms with which they worked while in military service. Nothing could be more honest and more helpful to the defense industry than this influx of retired military men, Gates maintained.

Of course an ex-officer actually involved in a direct sale or a direct negotiation for a product would be using bad judgment, but the checks and balances in the procedure for buying would undoubtedly disclose this type of unethical behavior, Gates assured the subcommittee.

He did admit, however, that the present conflict-of-interest statutes were inadequate, especially when Chairman Hebert pointed out that "in all the years that these laws have been on the books, there has not been one single conviction!"

Gates was the only witness of the day, and the *New York Times* summarized the proceedings as "polite" but said that the investigation itself had got off to a slow start.

The next day, July 8, saw two members of Congress testifying before the investigating subcommittee. Senator Paul H. Douglas of Illinois, co-sponsor of the Javits bill, stated that three-fourths of defense business goes to companies having 769 retired high-ranking officers on their payrolls. These men he characterized as having very high salaries but sketchily described duties. Sometimes these men, Douglas claimed, would sit in the back of the room while negotiations were going on, or would actually negotiate with their fellow officers themselves. They would often be hired on the basis of the information obtained while working in military service, which was very helpful to the hiring company.

Representative Santangelo, Democrat from Manhattan, summarized his attitude briefly by saying that "this practice of hiring retired officers smells to high heavens."

July 9 began the much-heralded appearance of Admiral Rickover. "Yes, this spring some retired military officers did try to pressure me," he replied to a question of Representative Hebert. "However," he continued with a good deal of bravado, "there has never been one single incident where any influence or anyone visiting me has had the slightest impact or effect on my program." This statement was greeted with applause and laughter from the congressmen and the gallery.

Admiral Rickover concluded his statement by promising to furnish the names of those guilty officers; however, it would be "reluctantly." When, several months later, the specific names were announced by the Admiral, his evidence was surprisingly void of the guilty action which he had earlier charged. The committee was both confused and disappointed.

Admiral Radford testified on July 10 that "any sales pressures exerted by defense contractors are properly brought to bear; that there is most certainly nothing sinister about it," after which the subcommittee recessed until July 21. The *New York Times* reported that the four days of testimony had ended on an inconclusive note with Representative Hebert a bit defensive as to why the investigation had been undertaken in the first place.

An editorial published in the same paper on Sunday, July 12, summarized many participants' attitudes when it said, "What is obviously needed is a clear definition (not acrimonious accusations) of what can be held as good practice and what must be avoided. It is important that we make the best use of those skills that are available. But they must be used in such a way that the integrity of the individual and of government itself cannot be compromised. That is the real problem, and it should be solved."

During the next ten-day interlude, the General Accounting Office dropped a bombshell when it announced that it had some disturbing information to bring before the committee. The Navy, it reported, had been overcharged a total of $12 million during the last year on its defense contracts. Besides, it charged, the Defense Department had refused to furnish other statistics vital to the probe.

It was thus with an air of apology that Cecil P. Milne, Assistant Secretary of the Navy, took the witness stand when the sessions opened again on July 20. He admitted that some bad mistakes had been made, but that with $40 billion worth of contracts, "it was inevitable that occasional mistakes and oversights will occur."

Representative Gavin of Pennsylvania was far from content with the Assistant Secretary's answer. Anger showed in his voice as the retort came back, "Millions of dollars are involved here (of taxpayers' money) and I don't like to see it handled indifferently!"

Next on the stand was Mr. Trowbridge, General Council for the Navy. In answer to the charge that the Defense Department had willfully concealed information, he replied that most of the records were available but that certain data, considered part of the decision-making process, had been kept from public scrutiny.

This time, Representative Hebert showed his dissatisfaction by snapping back that such action was "nothing but censorship!"

The following day, July 21, brought the much honored General Bradley before the investigating committee. As he reviewed his retired career, it became clear to the subcommittee that similar experiences had been shared by numerous other officers. While continuing to draw his Army retirement pay of $20,543, he had accepted a post with the Bulova Company, which handles defense contracts, at a salary of $25,000 and had subsequently been named board chairman, receiving $50,000 a year for his services in that capacity.

He appeared to take the suspicions of the subcommittee with regard to the influence of retired officers rather lightly. He agreed with Admiral Radford that "retired officers have much less influence than one realizes."

He added, perhaps a bit ruefully, that "when you are retired you are really out of the picture." He confirmed that he himself had never been pressured, but added that if such a case came up it certainly should be punished.

On July 23, Lieutenant General Irvine (retired) testified that he had been virtually forced into taking a commercial job. He would have much preferred to stay in the government in a civilian capacity, but that according to conflict-of-interest statutes now operating, he would lose his $13,500 Army retirement pay. He stated that he was now receiving $55,000 a year from the Alvo Manufacturing Company, which also handles defense contracts, but that "I'm just not happy in my present post."

The next highlight of the investigation occurred on July 28 when Admiral Houser testified that all bans on the employment of retired officers should be repealed—"just as long as military men didn't use the information gained in the service to undue advantage."

Chairman Hebert's comment was tinged with mild contempt. "Aren't you being a bit naïve, sir? We are certainly not in a position to throw out all the laws, and live solely by the Ten Commandments and the Golden Rule!"

During the next three days, July 29 to 31, representatives of three organizations "engaged in promoting the mutual interests of the armed services and their contractors" were questioned extensively for signs of lobbyist activity.

Representative Hebert accused outright the Aero-Space Industries Association as being "a lobby paid for with taxpayers' dollars" and ordered it to "produce lists of cocktail party guests."

Orval R. Cook, representative of the denounced organization, protested vigorously against Hebert's terminology. He stated that although the organization had made several unsuccessful tries at influencing legislation, its main business was "technical in nature."

The interview with Peter J. Schenk the next day followed somewhat the same pattern of accusation and defense, but Frank Gard Jameson of the Navy League retorted more vigorously. "Former military officers," he claimed, "might have the influence of logic, but certainly not of personality, and a distinction had to be made between the two." He further testified that retired officers "serve as much-needed catalysts in industry. They show the ivory-towered scientists how to make complex new weapons practical under combat conditions."

At this point in the investigation, the question of advertisement of defense weapons was brought in. Shortly before the Hebert hearings began, a major controversy developed in and out of Congress over the respective merits of two competing antiaircraft missile systems—the Army's Nike-Hercules and the Air Force's Bomarc. While the issue was before Congress, advertisements extolling the virtues of the two weapons were placed in

Washington newspapers by their major contractors—Western Electric Company and Boeing Airplane Company, respectively.

Questioned by the Hebert subcommittee about the timing and purpose of the advertisements, spokesmen for the companies insisted that they were parts of long-term "information" programs. However, Boeing's Harold Mansfield acknowledged that his company was fighting against a "campaign of misinformation" about the Bomarc, while Western Electric's W. M. Reynolds said the Nike advertisements had been suggested to the company by the Army.

Both companies also acknowledged discussing proposed cutbacks in the Nike and Bomarc programs with members of Congress from areas where employment would be affected. Summarized, Mansfield said: "Many of the most important decisions in the defense of our country are not made by military technicians. They are made in the Congress of the United States. And the Bomarc-Nike decision is certainly one such decision."

On August 11, the executive vice-president of Westinghouse, Edwin V. Huggins, formerly Assistant Air Force Secretary, brought the subcommittee its first concrete admission that influence peddling does exist. He stated that while he had been in the Defense Department from 1952 to 1953, retired officers had been too evident "by their presence." "It was clear that they were too much around," admitted Huggins, "but I can tell you right now that they were resented by defense officials."

Chairman Hebert tried to conceal his triumph: "You, Sir, are the first witness in weeks to concede that influence exists. I congratulate you on your frankness." He added: "We know that this situation exists, but are having a hard time getting at it. Everyone else has thrown up his hands and said 'No'!"

On August 18, the subcommittee began to investigate Drew Pearson's accusation that the major reason for the United States' failure to beat the U.S.S.R. in launching the earth satellite was the illicit influence peddled by an employee of General Electric.

Pearson maintained that, because of influence waged by Dr. Richard Porter, acting in a dual capacity as adviser to the Defense Department and employee of General Electric, the satellite project switched to a GE rocket engine at a critical time, and thus sidetracked Von Braun and delayed completion of the project.

Seven days later the man in question, Dr. Richard Porter, came before the subcommittee. It was true that he had been manager of GE's guided missile department, but when the secret advisory commission began to consider the GE Vanguard missile, he had offered to resign. It was only at the insistence of the other members of the committee that he stayed on as an adviser. Besides, although he had voted for the Vanguard, his vote had not been decisive. A majority of the committee had been for the GE engine anyway. Thus Drew Pearson's account appeared to have been misleading.

The climax of the entire Hebert Probe finally came on August 13 when George M. Bunker of the Martin Air Craft Company testified in a secret hearing about his company's defense contracts. It was not until December 5, six months later, that the report of the meeting became public. At that time it hit the front pages of all the major newspapers in the country. It appears that the Martin Company had been in the habit of throwing swanky weekend parties for men in key positions in the Defense Department and in the services. The favorite rendezvous was at the Cotton Bay Golf Club on Eleuthera Island in the Bahamas. Gen. Nathan F. Twining, chairman of the Joint Chiefs of Staff, headed the list. Bunker maintained that the interludes were designed to get the military and contractors "better acquainted in a friendly atmosphere" to promote good working conditions. Bunker appeared to be shocked that the question of illicit influence had even been raised. "I cannot conceive that anyone could possibly believe that men of their character and responsibilities could be improperly influenced by playing golf with me on Eleuthera."

Chairman Hebert noted that the Martin Company itself had $800 million worth of defense contracts. "Ninety per cent of the American public," he declared, "would suspect some kind of influence on these contracts." The twenty-five men invited all had titles relating to the selling of defense contracts: chiefs of staff for planning and programs, research and development commander, director of procurement and production. These men came from such diverse military establishments as Wiesbaden, Germany, Waco, Texas, and Honolulu, Hawaii.

A *New York Times* editorial of the following day figured that an expenditure of $18,000 had been made in three years, which, by the way, the Martin Company had tried to list as tax-deductible.

The editorial continued in a balanced and thoughtful tone:

No one is accusing anybody of anything—what these officers needed was better judgment and a greater sense of dignity. Friendship between people who spend government money and people who receive it is not an evil thing. But if $800 million worth of contracts produce an average of $233 a year in free vacations for officers involved, the competition might get out of control.

Public employees have an obligation not merely to spend honestly but to keep all of their relationships above even the shadow of reproach.

In taking stock of the actual results of the Hebert Probe, we find that they appear rather inconclusive. It is true that seventy-five witnesses were questioned over the twenty-five-day period. More than fourteen hundred retired officers in the rank of major or higher were found to be employed by the top hundred defense contractors. But with little variation, retired officers asserted that they were "has-beens" without influence on the decisions of their former colleagues. Why many of them were hired, then, might be hard for a company to justify to its stockholders. As it turned out, the committee was able to find no conclusive evidence of misconduct.

In its report filed January 18, 1960, the Hebert subcommittee said it was "impressed by several obvious inconsistencies in testimony" relating to the influence enjoyed by retired officers in the employment of defense contractors. Said the report: "The better grade and more expensive influence is a very subtle thing when being successfully applied. . . . The 'coincidence' of contracts and personal contacts with firms represented by retired officers and retired civilian officials sometimes raises serious doubts as to the complete objectivity of some of these decisions." The subcommittee proposed, among other steps, a much tighter law regarding "sales" to the government by retired personnel; the House later passed a watered-down version of the proposal, but it died in the Senate Committee for Armed Services[121] (a committee strongly influenced by the military establishment). While the Hebert Probe, therefore, did not produce any enacted legislation, it produced evidence that influence and pressure do exist and are vigorously used, but are usually carried on in a manner very difficult to expose as illegal under present laws.

CONCLUDING SUMMARY

Today the power of the government bureaucracy has become a major and growing factor in the shaping of legislation and regulation. While both the civil and military bureaucracies are part of the governmental structure, they do have important differences. Nevertheless, the similarities are as important as the differences in outlining the nature and character of the two organizations.

The civil and military bureaucracies are similar in four important aspects. First, both groups attempt to rationalize and routinize decision making in order to increase efficiency and performance. Since profit making is not a meaningful criterion to either group, efficiency (though sometimes difficult to measure) generally replaces the profit criterion of business in the government bureaucracy. It is because of this lack of objective measures of profit and market growth that businessmen often doubt the efficiency of the bureaucracy.

Second, the organizations' major aim is to survive and grow. "Empire building" is the natural development of successful bureaucracies. It should be recognized that within these two empires there is a great deal of small empire building going on, i.e., the interservice rivalry. This factor, however,

[121] References to the legislative history are found in *Congressional Record*, 86th Congress, 2d Session, Index, 837.

has not had the result of stunting the growth of the overall bureaucracy, but has tended to push it to greater size and power.

Third, the basic ideology of both groups of bureaucrats is highly limited in scope. Their ideologies do not cover the broad range of issues found among the other main occupational groups previously discussed. Basically, their ideologies are limited to justifying the functioning and growth of their organizations and the increase of their position, status, and prerogatives.

Fourth, both groups tend to gain their goals and policy objectives in similar ways. Making recommendations to Congress, testifying before congressional committees as expert witnesses, lobbying with allied interest groups, and attempting to affect public opinion are all methods utilized by both groups. As indicated, both the civil and military bureaucracies work through external groups, and this brings us to the points of difference.

The first major difference is that civil bureaucracy does not use these informal groups in the same manner as does the military. In fact, the Congress would be quite hostile to the suggestion that any branch of the civil bureaucracy form a group like the semiservice groups in the military. The State Department, because of its inability to have such a group as a voice for its policy statements, feels itself at a disadvantage sometimes in its conflicts with the military.

The second difference is that the civilian bureaucracy, although not generally a partisan group, tends to be more sympathetic with the Democratic party than does the military. This is so mainly because it has been able to flourish more under recent Democratic administrations than under Republican administrations. The expansive welfare philosophy of the Democrats and the fact that a significant share of high-ranking civil servants were "New Deal," "Fair Deal," or "New Frontier" appointees have reinforced this tendency. The military has tended to gravitate more toward the Republican party because of its "harder" line against international communism and its greater identification with patriotic traditions.

Third, the military is generally more nationalistic, more "patriotic," less trustful of other nations, and more inclined to feel that both the civil bureaucracy (particularly the State Department) and the intellectuals as groups tend to be more willing to appease the Communists in their efforts to negotiate with and conciliate them. The civil bureaucracy tends to be concerned that the military may turn out to be warmongers if not checked. Specialized training and thinking of military versus generalist training of civil bureaucracy explain such variation in their positions.

Fourth, the civil bureaucracy ideology is based on the idea that it exists as the expression of the will of the people. They believe that every agency addition or expansion is a direct manifestation of public need. On the other hand, the military bases its existence not on what the people want but more on external considerations. The military exists to meet the challenge of international communism which is being forced upon the American people. This explains the need the military has to play up the danger of the external threat.

Finally, the civil bureaucracy has a wider spectrum of issue involvement than the military. The military tends to be rather highly specialized with its concern for the protection of the nation. The many other national issues are left largely to the separate groups within the civil bureaucracy. However, this greater specialization on one major policy issue by the military, because of the vast area it covers and the huge sums spent, gives them power in their area of interest generally unmatched by any group of civil bureaucrats. Thus, in the United States economy and society of today, the civil and military bureaucracies, in rather different ways, wield tremendous influence. The changing power structure of the country is seen nowhere more clearly than in the growth of these informal power groups and the effect they have upon the making of American public policy.

10

the dangers of success: consequences of fully implementing each ideology

What would happen if any one power group were to gain sufficient power to control the government and enact the legislation it desired? In a plural society such as ours this is somewhat of an extreme assumption. At various times in history, however, certain power groups have had great sway over public policy; for example, business in the last century and labor in the 1930s. This question will be discussed here *as a means of summarizing the goals of the major power groups and of pointing out the perils for American society if a single group should dominate the body politic.*

Although we recognize the improbability that any one power group will determine public policy without compromise with the other power groups, it is nonetheless interesting to contemplate the radical change in American institutions and economic relationships which could result from the policies of a single group. Because of factions within some economic groups, it is not enough to speculate on business, for example, as dominating society. Rather it requires identifying which power group and ideology within business acquires control to know what impact might develop upon the economy and society.

The classical ideology of business differs greatly from the managerial ideology on many issues. Those supporting the classical ideology of business would, according to their present position, eliminate many of the controls and regulations over business now administered by government. The power of government would be vastly decreased, deficit spending would be eliminated, the national debt might be scaled down, and countercyclical fiscal policy would be abandoned. Most economists believe that such policies, strictly carried out, would cause deflation and possibly a depression. The government would not be permitted to interfere with the adjustment of the market. The market rather than the political arena would be the dominant allocator of resources. Many of the Federal regulatory agencies, such as the ICC and the FCC, might be eliminated. For instance, the control over television stations regulating the number of commercials per hour might be dropped. State and local governments would assume many Federal tax sources and would be expected to handle their own problems without Federal aid or intervention.

In a sense, the classical ideology of business would favor restoring the respective roles of business, government, and labor of the last half of the nineteenth century when the classical ideology of business dominated public policy. Government was involved in fewer economic functions and labor was relatively impotent—but also our economic growth rate was higher than it has been recently. Certainly the elimination of high progressive taxes would be very enriching for successful businessmen. In other words, the distribution of income would shift back in favor of owners of property, reversing the trend of increasing the workers' share. While part of the business community may dream of returning to such an era, and their ideology reflects this, there is also the possibility that, actually given power, they would respond like the Conservative party in England which made only minor modifications on the legislation of the previous labor government. It is hard to turn back the clock and return to previous relationships and situations.

This is simply to indicate that, although the protest elements of the classical business creed cause it to assert goals that seem reminiscent of past periods, it may well be that, given the power to change society, they might not wish to go as far as their ideology suggests. There is little doubt, however, that business would want to curtail the power of labor and government interference in their decision making, thereby increasing business wealth, power, and social position. How much farther they would go is difficult to know.

While some writers, such as Robert S. Brady in *Business as a System of Power,* argue that business when given power tends toward fascism and not democracy, it is assumed here that the dominance of any one group would not radically change the political assumption of representative government for the country. Any group would likely modify the structure and processes of government, however, so as to enhance the maintenance of its power. For example, farm groups might increase rural overrepresentation. Furthermore, the dominance of any single group would tend to break down the pluralistic concept of group democracy as we now know it in the United States. It could be argued, therefore, that the assumption of a single group dominating the public policy-making machinery of the country as posited in this chapter would ultimately lead to dictatorship or totalitarianism. To be able to achieve all the major goals of any one group, in a short period at least, would require that the other competing groups be silenced or otherwise made ineffectual.

While admittedly unlikely, such a course is not impossible since the American system of group democracy has been in existence for less than two hundred years, and there were few flowerings of anything comparable to that system during previous recorded history. The course of the Roman Empire demonstrates how a country can evolve from a republic to a dictatorship. There are no automatic guarantees against totalitarianism arising within America even from the Constitution. For constitutions can be and are rewritten, changed by tradition, and disregarded. *The major safeguard for our pluralistic democracy is actually the competition for power among economic groups within our system—a competition including a sufficient number of groups that compromise—and consensus among several or all is required to create public policy.* Add to this a system of overlapping memberships when all groups are taken into account, which develops links of sympathy between members of key groups, and you have further protection against excess. The Balkanization of groups and the complete domination of a single one would present an open invitation for totalitarianism —regardless of whether the control was exercised by business, labor, or the bureaucracy.

Implementation of the managerial business ideology would produce fewer and far less drastic changes in our present economy than the classical business creed would. The basic changes the managerialists would make would be to check the prerogatives and power of labor, decrease taxes, particularly those which restrict investment, spur economic growth, eliminate subsidies and controls over agriculture, and prevent government from interfering with wage and price decisions of business. Overall, they would not produce a substantial cutback in government. Countercyclical spending with temporary deficits would not be eliminated, nor would most of government's present-day activities. Social welfare programs might be either pruned or restricted in their growth, however.

To a degree, the managerialists were in control during the Eisenhower administration. The basic difference between that administration and the Kennedy administration seems to have been the closer relationship between business and government and a more frugal and less welfare-oriented approach during the Eisenhower Presidency. In terms of most issues, with the exceptions noted above, the managerial creed reflects a business group that is not fundamentally hostile to present public policy. Although occupational ties ameliorate the divergence between the two basic groups of business, their ideologies are actually farther apart than the NAM and the Farm Bureau or the CED and the intellectuals.

The dominance of labor as the maker of public policy in this country would create significant changes in contemporary society. As a close reading of the labor ideology reveals, labor not only would lessen the power of business as a group within the society but would largely take over much of its decision making. This, of course, has already occurred to a degree in the past half century. But the conflict between business and labor is real and natural since they are continually opposed in bargaining situations. Further, labor supports many economic measures which are anathema to most business and professional people, such as greater equality of wealth in the country by increasing inheritance and gift taxes, government medical service, and generally greatly increased public welfare programs. Labor would not decrease government power and functions, except in relation to legal restrictions on labor operations and decision making and government involvement in wage setting. To the contrary, labor would enlarge the sphere of government activity to expand labor's economic benefits and social security.

Labor's full public policy control in the United States, while probably not resulting in government ownership of certain basic industries as occurred in England, would result in programs that had similar effects. In fact, the differences might be very small between a United States dominated by labor and England, Norway, or Sweden controlled by a Socialist Labor party. The actual nationalization of ownership in the United States would probably not occur—but the increasingly government-controlled industry would so restrict the prerogatives and rights of private ownership as to make the owners relatively powerless. In this sense, the American non-socialist-oriented labor movement might reach a mere variation of the type of society which would be produced by the more socialist-oriented ones of Europe. The desire for greater economic and social status for workers could stimulate sufficiently strong motives to create a welfare state that would be socialist in all but name. It should be added that the gradual flow of legislation and public opinion in this country has been in this direction. Thus a more substantial welfare state may be achieved even without labor arriving at full public policy powers. The course of democracies is inevitably in the direction of greater economic and social equality, because the sizable majority who have less become politically activated and demand laws against the minority who have more.

Ideological techniques using such words as "socialism" which are laden with emotional overtones, combined with superior strategy, may delay, minimize, and on very rare occasions terminate or repeal social welfare legislation. But it would appear from our recent history that the usual pragmatic test of issues will continue to produce welfare legislation that labor favors—even if labor's power as a group diminishes. The reason is simply that in a democracy the majority which has less economically will eventually be utilized by the various power groups (particularly labor, the intellectuals, and occasionally agriculture and the bureaucracy) to pass social legislation. Thus, in this way, many of labor's policy aims will be achieved even without our assumption of labor controlling the policy-making powers of the nation.

Agriculture as a power group is even more splintered internally than business. The Farmers Union, the Grange, and the Farm Bureau suggest public policy for both agriculture and the economy in general that essentially reads from left to right. The position of the Farmers Union is little different on most issues from that described above for labor, while the Farm Bureau seems to differ very little in its policy goals from that of the NAM's classical business ideology. The Grange standing in between these two groups is harder to define—largely because its ideology tends to be middle of the road on most major issues.

As a group, agriculture probably saw the high point of its power during and right after World War II. It seems inevitable that the increasing rural to urban population shift and dramatic congressional redistricting will curtail the power and privileges of agriculture as a group.

The effect on the economy of any of the farm groups attaining power over public policy has been implied above. The policies of the Farmers Union (except for its emphasis on a greatly subsidized and controlled agriculture) would be essentially those already outlined for labor itself. The Farm Bureau, on the other hand, judging from its expressed ideology, would differ little in policies from those already described for the classical business group, except for its stronger demand for freer trade. The true nature of Grange policies, once given independence of the other two farm groups in policy making, is difficult to determine beyond a rather middle-of-the-road course on most issues. Even on policies for agriculture the three farm groups differ. Perhaps only on general issues that the farmers have come to accept as rightfully theirs—farm credit and the like—can a general consensus among farm groups be predicted. This divergency itself will undoubtedly make possible the erosion of much of agriculture's power as other groups find it to their own interest to contain the benefits and power presently belonging to agriculture as a power group.

The full attainment of the goals of the Negro power group (with the exception of the Black Muslims who desire a separate black nation) would be for full integration in all respects. Such integration would undoubtedly necessitate a good many laws making it illegal to discriminate against Negroes in employment, housing, education, etc. Further, preferential treatment over whites in hiring, scholarship, and government aid would also probably be sought. Such preferential treatment is based on the current argument that Negroes need special aid for them to gain equal income and status levels. Thus, the logical extreme to which the current Negro position can be pushed is a legal sanctioning of discrimination against whites in favor of Negroes. As the urban political power of the Negro continues to grow, so likewise will the pressure for the attainment of these goals. However, all indications are that stiffer opposition to the attainment of the Negro goals may also occur—in the North and West instead of just the South. Nonetheless the Negro power group, with the liberal trend of American history and their rapidly increasing population, will undoubtedly continue to make headway toward their basic goal of a freely integrated society.

The basic goals of the public school teachers are for a greater allocation of money for public education and greater control over educational policy by the teachers themselves. As the power of the teachers increases, through the probable use of greater militancy and collective bargaining, progress toward these goals will be made, particularly for: (1) higher salaries and fringe benefits; (2) improvement in educational facilities; (3) control of educational policy (not by the school boards but by the teachers organizations); (4) eventual Federal aid to education. The growth and centralization of power in teachers unions and organizations can be expected to occur just as in industrial unionism. However, progress toward these goals cannot be expected to occur easily or without (as in the Negro power movement) the use of strikes and public demonstrations. The teachers will also, in time, focus greater attention at the national level of public policy and attempt to gain Federal support for their goals. When the teachers organizations become more fully organized at national and local levels, they will be one of the strongest power groups in the nation. At that point, the attainment of the teachers' objectives, including Federal aid to education, can be expected to become legislation by some form of compromise with the opposing power groups (i.e., the classical business group).

The intellectuals as a power group reached their highest position of eminence in our modern history under the Kennedy administration. Yet the fulfillment of their policy desires is still some distance from being achieved. If the intellectuals should be given full policy-making powers, the tempo of social change in America would visibly quicken.

Certainly greater emphasis and spending (probably creating a continued annual deficit) on education and social welfare measures would be pushed. Federal aid to education, the arts, public health, urban renewal, and basic research would be a hallmark of their legislation. The Federal government would absorb a greater number of state and local functions. Economic planning might well be developed. There might be an attempt to change the values of the nation from economic- and business-oriented status symbols toward educational and intellectual ones. This would be an obvious move since the intellectuals have long felt undercast by the American status system, as contrasted, for example, with Europe. The intellectuals feel their values are superior to the predominantly economic ones of our culture. Rational government regulation and planning would probably be emphasized over greater reliance on the unregulated market as a mechanism for the allocation of resources between products and groups within the country.

All told, then, if the intellectuals as a group had full public policy power, most of President Kennedy's legislative proposals would have been passed—but probably on a larger and more far-reaching scale. It may well be that the informal power groups (the intellectuals and the civil and military bureaucracy) are entering an era in which they may become even more significant makers of public policy than business, labor, or agriculture. Whether this is true or not, it does appear that for the present at least, and probably into the future, the intellectual establishment is having a major effect over public opinion and public policy. Probably an increasing number of their ideological goals will be accomplished in public policy—even if in a somewhat diluted and compromised form due to the continuing influence of the other power groups. But there appears a strong coalition of interests at times between the managerialists, labor, the civil bureaucrats, and the intellectuals. Where this consensus does exist, it can usually determine most public policy issues.

The civil and military bureaucracy, despite certain similarities, are less of one mind than might be supposed on public policy issues. The civil bureaucracy is in many ways relatively closely allied on public policy measures with the intellectuals. The military bureaucracy, however, is often more closely allied with the business groups than any other. In fact, there is often direct conflict on foreign policy (which has not been the basic concern in this book) between the military and civil bureaucracy. The military frequently feel that the State Department, for example, is too "soft," and some civilian foreign policy makers correspondingly consider the military to verge on being warmongers. The military probably receives its greatest group support from the classical business group (and those in the managerial group connected with defense). The civil bureaucracy, of course, has certain alliances with all the groups—the Commerce Department with business, the Labor Department with labor, the Agriculture

Department with agriculture, the Health, Education, and Welfare Department with its beneficiary groups, as well as many others such as the State Department, the Council of Economic Advisers, etc., with the intellectuals. The fact that the State Department has little by way of a beneficiary group, for example, puts it at a disadvantage when it is in conflict with other departments, requiring that State operate with close support from the President. With the exception of some civilians in the Defense Department, the civil bureaucracy is generally closer on most public policy issues to the intellectuals as a group than to the military bureaucracy.

If the civil bureaucracy, therefore, were to attain full policy-making power, the results in some types of legislation would probably only be watered-down versions of those ascribed above to the intellectuals. It is doubtful that the civil bureaucrats would move as fast in pursuing social welfare measures as the intellectuals, and certain departments (Commerce and Agriculture) would continue to be spokesmen for their economic blocs. Thus in such areas legislation, which the intellectuals would pass, would not likely occur. Also, because of the resulting conflicts between various departments of the civil bureaucracy, compromise would force most policy measures to resemble, in many ways, the present results of legislation as passed by compromise among these interests in Congress. The civil bureaucrats, however, could be expected to expand and rationalize government services and functions and rely more on regulated and administered markets than free ones. As with the intellectuals, there would probably be more professional planning in both the economic and social areas.

The military bureaucracy, by and large, appears to hold considerable sympathy with the business groups. Yet the military would, if in power, increase military training and military spending; and it *might* create what has been called a garrison state (where business, certainly, would be subservient to military interests). While some elements within the military look favorably upon the superpatriotic groups of the far right, the military generally would not design a fascist system. It would more likely continue to maintain a democratic political system, but one whose economy would become even more defense-dominated than at present. With the economy under increased pressure to produce military goods, our present consumption levels would be difficult to maintain (i.e., as in the U.S.S.R.). Further, the social policies that might be put into effect with a dominant military would probably reflect those institutions accepted within the military itself. The examples of foreign military-business collusion in the Axis powers of Germany, Italy, and Japan were, of course, frightening. However, the closest approximation of a garrison state with a democracy is our own experience during World War II and the Korean conflict. Such examples may suggest what public policy in our society would be like, given military dominance. Obviously, there are many and direct conflicts between a military state and a democratic political system. Whether the latter would survive indefinitely under the former is doubtful. Roman history, among others, points to the disintegration of republican government under the impact of sustained military domination. Whether United States history could be different is not easy to foretell.

As a way of vividly summarizing the views of each major group the preceding pages presented a hypothetical world which might occur if each group alone had policy-making power and if each carried out its presently indicated goals. As is obvious from this discussion, some power groups would create a world far different from that existing today. A few, however, either are less ambitious or else have been sufficiently successful so as to hold up as ideological goals a world not too far different from the present. Even in this case, an essential characteristic is missing: that is, the fabric of our society as made up of minority groups. As is discussed in the next chapter, public policy in the United States today functions upon a system of minority consensus. The conflict and compromise between power groups is one of the major distinguishing features of our society and public policy. *To eliminate, as this chapter has assumed, compromise through group interaction and conflict would change American society fundamentally,* for we would face the dangers of majority rule without minority rights—a situation which could lead all too directly to an authoritarian state.

II

how american democracy really works

By way of summary, the potential effects of the implementation of the ideologies of the major power groups were outlined in the previous chapter. Often full effectuation of these ideologies would inflict grave damage on their opponents. Despite the recognition by such Founding Fathers as Madison that "the majority who rule . . . are the safest guardians both of the public good and private rights,"[1] he and others who framed the Constitution were also aware of the dangers of majority power being uncontrollably inflicted to the damage of minorities. In American thought there is an element which generally opposes drastic action toward minority groups. Most citizens like the idea of a government which corresponds to Teddy Roosevelt's slogan of a "square deal" for all citizens whether laborers, farmers, or professional people.

But people are motivated by their interests. What is to prevent minorities from being seriously damaged under a system of majority rule? This has been a crucial problem of American democracy. For as Thomas Nixon Carver observed in a rather extreme caricature: "There are few things more democratic than a lynching bee, where everybody is satisfied

[1] James Madison, "Vices of the Political System of the United States," April 1787, in *The Writings of James Madison,* Gaillard Hunt (ed.) (New York: G. P. Putnam's Sons, 1901), Vol. 2, p. 336.

except a small and insignificant minority of one."[2] Or as former Harvard President A. Lawrence Lowell pointed out, if two highwaymen steal a wallet from a belated traveler, it would be an abuse of terms to say that in that lonely assemblage public opinion favored a redistribution of property.[3]

The idea that there is something sacred about the figure 50 per cent plus one, and that this is the real source of policy making, is a myth. Lord Bryce observed that "government was always government by the few, whether in the name of the one, the few, or the many."[4] The truthfulness of this statement is borne out by the fact that the average turnout of eligible voters in presidential elections in the last forty years has been only 53.6 per cent; no President in this period has ever come close to receiving a majority of votes of the nation's citizens.[5] In a different way, this lack of political participation is even found among lobbyists themselves, 44 per cent having never been active in a political party.[6] Clearly, the central tendency and characteristic of American politics is not found in the will of the majority. To dramatize this point, Robert Dahl stated that "the eight largest states with 54 per cent of the voters have the same number of votes in the Senate as the eight smallest states with less than 3 per cent of the voters."[7] He further found that "a majority of votes in the Senate can be cast by Senators representing less than 15 per cent of the voters."[8] As further evidence on this point, one has only to see the massive compilation of polls in *Public Opinion, 1935–1946*,[9] by Hadley Cantril and Mildred Strunk, to note that, in retrospect, the majority opinions registered on public polls frequently did not correlate with public policy outcomes. In E. E. Schattschneider's words: "It is necessary only to look at the polls . . . to realize that public opinion about specific issues does not necessarily govern the course of public policy."[10] In a 1960 study of state legislators, Wahlke, Buchanan, Eulau, and Ferguson postulated that "public interest is never more than the harmonization of . . . partial and private interests and that

---

[2] A. A. Ekirch, Jr., *The Decline of American Liberalism* (New York: Longmans, Green & Co., Inc., 1955), p. 220.

[3] A. Lawrence Lowell, *Public Opinion and Popular Government* (New York: Longmans, Green & Co., Inc., 1913), pp. 2–3.

[4] Harold D. Lasswell, *Politics: Who Gets What When and How* (Gloucester, Mass.: Peter Smith Publisher, 1950), p. 235.

[5] John C. Livingston and Robert G. Thompson, *The Consent of the Governed* (New York: The Macmillan Company, 1963), p. 36.

[6] Lester Milbrath, "The Political Party Activity of Washington Lobbyists," *The Journal of Politics*, 20 (May, 1958), 339.

[7] Lewis A. Froman, Jr., *People and Politics: An Analysis of the American Political System* (Englewood Cliffs, N.J.: Prentice-Hall, Inc., 1962), pp. 83–84.

[8] *Ibid.*, p. 84.

[9] Princeton, N.J.: Princeton University Press, 1951.

[10] E. E. Schattschneider, *The Semisovereign People: A Realist's View of Democracy in America* (New York: Holt, Rinehart and Winston, 1960), pp. 132–133.

organized interest groups . . . play an indispensable part in defining and legislating in the public interest."[11]

"The American political system is less able to use the democratic device of majority rule than almost any other modern democracy. Nearly everyone makes obeisance to the majority, but the ideal of majority rule has not been well institutionalized, and never been fully legitimatized."[12] In fact Edward Hollett Carr has said:

> History points unmistakably to the fact that political democracy, in the forms in which it has hitherto been known, flourishes best where some of the people, but not all the people, are free and equal; and, since this conclusion is incompatible with the conditions of the new society and repugnant to the contemporary conscience, the task of saving democracy in our time is the task of reconciling it with the postulate of popular sovereignty and mass civilization.[13]

There is no particular logic in numbers that gives a majority the right to impose a decision on a minority, since intensity of feeling is not thereby measured or allowed nor is justice assured to the minority. Majority rule is not an obviously correct or true principle—particularly when it is based upon majority tyranny. Dahl contends that

> The likelihood of peaceful adjustment to a conflict is increased if there exist institutional arrangements that encourage consultation, negotiation, the exploration of beneficial solutions. Conversely, the prospects of deadlock and coercion are increased if institutional arrangements severely inhibit such activities.[14]

Majority rule, without safeguards, could lead to some rather absurd situations. For example, if 51 per cent rather mildly favor the confiscation of property of the other 49 per cent of the society, the logic of unrestrained majoritarianism would so dictate. Judge Learned Hand has said: "The Spirit of Liberty is the spirit which is not too sure that it is right."[15]

Dahl also found that Americans have always had voter lethargy. For example, in 1784 New Haven became a city. At that time about 250 people were excluded as voters either because they did not hold property or because they had been loyal to England. Of the 343 remaining eligible males, about one-fourth failed to take the oath, and therefore they could not vote in elections, and on the first election day only about 100 citizens of the

11 John C. Wahlke, William Buchanan, Heinz Eulau, and LeRoy Ferguson, "Toward Pressure Groups," in S. Sidney Ulmer (ed.), *Introductory Readings in Political Behavior* (Chicago: Rand McNally & Company, 1961), p. 390.

12 Schattschneider, p. 102.

13 Edward Hollett Carr, *The New Society* (Boston: Beacon Press, 1951), p. 61.

14 Robert A. Dahl, *Modern Political Analysis* (Englewood Cliffs, N.J.: Prentice-Hall, Inc., 1963), pp. 56–57.

15 John Fischer, "Unwritten Rules of American Politics," *Harper's Magazine* (November, 1948), 36.

261 eligible cast their votes.[16] This problem is not peculiar to America alone. Aristotle wrote in the fourth century B.C.:

> Payment for attendance at the assembly was, at first, a step which they [the restored democrats, once more in control after the perturbations at the end of the Peloponnesian War] refused to take. The citizens, however, failed to attend; and the presidents of the assembly were driven to one device after another in order to induce the populace to present themselves for the purpose of ratifying measures. In these circumstances Agyrrhius began by providing an obol a day for attendance: Heraclides . . . increased it to two obols; and Agyrrhius afterward advanced it to three.[17]

It is obvious that not all men are instinctively political animals. People do not always care what happens in politics. Nor do they know much about political events or share in making decisions. It is Dahl's contention that an individual is unlikely to get involved in politics unless he believes the outcome will be relatively unsatisfactory without his involvement. The percentage of voters rises sharply in depression years such as 1873 to 1878 or in a movement such as the Populist in 1893 to 1897.[18]

It is in the light of the above-mentioned facts that the appeal of majority rule for many Americans as well as its actual operation must be examined. Thomas Jefferson declared in his first inaugural address: "The will of the majority is in all cases to prevail."[19] How did the early Democrats such as Jefferson, as well as Thomas Paine, John Taylor, and Samuel Adams, handle the problem of potential tyranny of the majority? Jefferson had no illusion that the majority would always be right. He recognized that to be rightful the majority will had to be reasonable and that the minority possessed their equal rights, "which equal law must protect and to violate would be oppression."[20] Jefferson did, however, have the optimistic view that men were capable of making reasonable decisions. There is also an emphasis upon men's being able to make judgments within a framework of the public interest.[21] As the Puritan democrat John Wise asserted, "Man is not so wedded to his own interest, but that he can make the common good the mark of his aim."[22]

[16] Robert A. Dahl, *Who Governs? Democracy and Power in an American City* (New Haven: Yale University Press, 1961), p. 17.

[17] Aristotle, *On the Constitution of Athens* [Appendix IV, in Barker ed., 379–383], quoted in Dahl, *Modern Political Analysis*, pp. 56–57.

[18] Dahl, *Modern Political Analysis*, p. 63.

[19] John Vance Cheney (ed.), *Inaugural Addresses of the Presidents of the United States from Washington to Lincoln* (Chicago: The Lakeside Press, Christmas, 1906), p. 34.

[20] *Ibid.*

[21] Livingston and Thompson, pp. 48–49.

[22] John Wise, *A Vindication of the Government of New England Churches* (1717), reprinted in Alpheus Thomas Mason, *Free Government in the Making* (Fair Lawn, N.J.: Oxford University Press, 1956), p. 69.

The Jeffersonians also hoped to ward off majority tyranny through specific prohibitions against government's infringing on rights, particularly through the Bill of Rights.

A different view of man and the prevention of majority tyranny was taken by such Federalists as James Madison and John Adams. They believed people to be more emotional and less rational than did Jefferson.[23] Adams warned that "majoritarian democracy would lead to candidates pandering to every popular 'passion and prejudice' and exploiting every flattery, trick, bribe, feast, and threat possible."[24]

Many conservative theories of democracy have stemmed from similar views that human reason is too fallible, rare, and capricious to rely on. These theories call for traditions, religion, or a "delicately contrived equilibria of the forces struggling for power,"[25] to prevent tyranny of the majority.

Along these lines the objectives of the preponderance of the participants in the Constitutional Convention were to restrain and disperse power so as to minimize the danger of majoritarian tyranny. The main substance of constitutionalism is to balance liberty and authority between the powers of government and individual rights.[26] The rule of law and the separate powers given to the three main divisions of government were to stand "as a guarantee of individual liberty against the exercise of arbitrary governmental power."[27] As Andrew Hacker says "The rights of individuals—as distinct from groups—can only be protected if some department of the government intervenes and exercises power on their behalf."[28]

The Founding Fathers believed they could protect minorities through an ingenious constitutional system with three key devices.[29] The first was the written constitutional prohibitions upon certain government powers,

[23] Thrasymachus, Hobbes, Jeremy Bentham, and Marx all interpreted the search for power as rational and conscious pursuit of self-interest. But Freud showed that the desires, terrible in their untamed lawlessness, of which Socrates spoke, did more than drive human beings into conflict with one another as Hobbes argued. They also drive human beings into conflict with themselves. These inner conflicts, according to Freud, are fierce gales that often blow out the flickering light of reason.

Robert A. Dahl and Charles E. Lindbloom, *Politics, Economics and Welfare* (New York: Harper & Row, Publishers, Incorporated, 1953), p. 67.

[24] Livingston and Thompson, pp. 43–44.

[25] *Ibid.*, p. 57.

[26] Herman C. Pritchett, *The American Constitutional System* (New York: McGraw-Hill Book Company, 1963), p. 3.

[27] *Ibid.*

[28] Andrew Hacker, *The Study of Politics: The Western Tradition and American Origins* (New York: McGraw-Hill Book Company, 1963), p. 87.

[29] The historical changes in the key doctrines of restraint on government are summarized by Edward S. Corwin in "Introduction," *The Constitution of the United States of America: Analysis and Interpretation* (Washington: Government Printing Office, 1953).

such as the taking of private property without due process of law. The second was the detachment of most of the government from direct election, thereby giving them a cushion against the passing passions of popular majorities. Thus, senators were to be elected by state legislatures. The President was to be elected by the electoral college, and judges were to be appointed by the President with confirmation of the Senate. Only the House of Representatives was subject directly to the will of the people by popular election.

The third device was a dispersion of power both vertically between the state and Federal levels of government (federalism)[30] and horizontally between the executive, legislative, and judicial branches of government (separation of powers). Such functions were never "separate and distinct."[31] The design of such a checks-and-balances system was explained by Mr. Justice Brandeis: "The purpose was not to avoid friction, but, by means of the inevitable friction incident to the distribution of governmental powers among three departments, to save the people from autocracy."[32]

These structural principles of the constitutional architects have been greatly modified and diluted with the development of a complex, interdependent, technological society.

The pressures for stronger presidential leadership in a mass democracy to produce more uniform and efficient national programs of ever greater scope have ameliorated the originally conceived system of dispersed power. What possible alternatives exist to the now somewhat emaciated system of dispersion of power previously envisaged?

An alternative which has been recognized is the dispersion of power among highly organized, alert private groups with consequent checks and balances.

In terms of society, Madison said that "the social whole would be broken into so many parts, interests, and classes of citizens." No single part or interest or class would contain a majority of citizens: if a majority were formed on any issue, it would simply consist of a transient coalition of groups. For example,

[30] The Constitution provided for a national government largely independent of the federated government. It contemplated, of course, that the people of the states would control the national government. But it contemplated also that the control would be direct not through the agency of state governments . . . it did arrange things in such a way that state officials had to use the political party, not state government, to make their influence felt in Washington.

William H. Riker, "The Senate and American Federalism," *American Political Science Review*, 49 (June, 1955), 454.

[31] Morton Grodzins, "Centralization and Decentralization in the American Federal System," in Robert A. Goldwin (ed.), *A Nation of States: Essays on the American Federal System* (Chicago: Rand McNally & Company, 1963), p. 7.

[32] *Myers v. United States*, 272 U.S. 52 (1926), 293.

there is a Protestant majority in America, and it may be inquired why its representatives do not enact legislation penalizing the Catholic minority in the country. Madison's answer was not that the Protestants were notably tolerant nor was it that they believe in religious liberty for all. The answer was that the Protestant majority is itself a coalition of Baptists, Methodists, Episcopalians, Presbyterians, and Lutherans. Each of these denominations had had its own history of persecution when it was in the minority, and therefore all of them agree to tolerate other religions—including the Catholics—for fear that they may at some future time be subjected to majority oppression.[33]

These groups are all relatively large minorities in our total society. With their growth, in the course of history, a concomitant development has occurred. That is, as these groups have increased in size, they have developed bureaucracies. A rationalized organizational structure has developed with attempts to speak for the group within the national area, thereby making the group effective even though many of its members are passive.

J. K. Galbraith has called this development "countervailing power." While Galbraith, an economist, has focused on the central issue in explaining the manner in which policy is determined in this country, the theory of countervailing power lacks complete realism and consistency. Galbraith defines countervailing power most succinctly as "the neutralization of one position of power by another."[34] He calls it the "answering bargaining power" to check the power of sellers or buyers by the organizing of those subject to such power. "Private economic power begets the countervailing power of those who are subject to it."[35] The development of strong unions, in this argument, is viewed as an inevitable and automatic development to neutralize or balance the power of the large firms. One wonders, however, whether the present structure of strong unionism would have been achieved without the changed economic ideology and power congregation that developed during the Great Depression. Galbraith summarizes his theory by saying:

> Private economic power is held in check by the countervailing power of those who are subject to it. The first begets the second. The long trend toward concentration of industrial enterprise in the hands of a few firms has brought into existence not only strong sellers . . . but also strong buyers.[36]

Government's role under this theory is to assist in the development of countervailing power. Competition then, Galbraith argues, has been replaced as the autonomous regulator of economic activity by the self-generating forces of countervailing power.

[33] Hacker, p. 84.
[34] J. K. Galbraith, *American Capitalism, the Concept of Countervailing Power* (Boston: Houghton Mifflin Company, 1952), p. 1.
[35] *Ibid.*, p. 4. [36] *Ibid.*, p. 11.

Without going into an analysis of countervailing power in more detail, perhaps it can be most succinctly evaluated in the following manner. On the positive side, countervailing power does focus upon the crucial fact that it is the major economic groups in this country who hold power and make public policy. Furthermore it spotlights the natural impulse of a dominated group to seek devices to strengthen its bargaining position.

Galbraith's groups, however, are vague; the role of politics, politicians, and ideology are undeveloped, and historically the development of countervailing power groups has not occurred inevitably and automatically in response to other power groups. Further, since the theory is stated in equilibrium terms (that is, it describes society as in balance between opposing forces), it must maintain that the power of one group will automatically be offset by its opposition. There is nothing, however, to prevent government from becoming the dominating power or to prevent collusion from occurring between various power blocs to maintain an indefinite upper hand. Galbraith did not develop the theory sufficiently to handle these and other problems. Stigler, in his review, says: "Galbraith's notion of countervailing power is a dogma, not a theory. It lacks rational development and must be accepted or rejected without reference to its unstated logical antecedents."[37]

It is interesting that the Founding Fathers (with perhaps the exception of Madison) failed to see the potential benefits of groups or factions. On the contrary, they felt that factionalism was fraught with danger and evil. Even political parties were not anticipated. The parties emerged out of the necessity of organizing power to gain control of government once the differences between the Federalists and Democrats became clear. In fact, one writer suggests that "political parties exist, not because there are two sides to every issue, but because there are two sides to every office—an inside and an outside."[38]

Actually the majoritarianists who hoped men would be rational and pursue the public good, and the conservative Federalists who believed that majorities would be created by the pursuit of economic gain and emotional causes, both had considerable insight. Both beliefs contribute to an understanding of the fact that America, with certain exceptions, has not generally had flagrant oppression by the majority or a minority, but has developed a system of minorities rule.[39] For example:

[37] D. George Stigler, "The Economist Plays with Blocs," *American Economic Review*, 44 (May, 1954), 10.

[38] Max M. Kampelman, "The Legislative Bureaucracy: Its Response to Political Change," *The Journal of Politics*, 16 (August, 1954), 539.

[39] See, for example, Robert A. Dahl, *A Preface to Democratic Theory* (Chicago: The University of Chicago Press, 1956), p. 132.

To take some . . . recent decisions, how many people indicated their preferences in a politically relevant way when governmental leaders: decided to contract with large corporations for operating the atomic energy installations? legislated against imports of European cheese and other agricultural products? refused for the umpteenth time to approve the St. Lawrence Seaway project? passed legislation setting up the council of economic advisors? agreed on the Pick-Slan plan for the Missouri Valley? Each of these decisions was a product of a tiny minority.[40]

The term "minorities rule" describes the situation in which "public policies are the result of opinions and interests of neither a majority nor a minority, but rather arise through compromises of the interests of various organized and vocal minorities. This model differs fundamentally from the traditional descriptions of democratic politics."[41]

Thus Madison's principal anxiety about faction, that a self-seeking majority in the lower classes would vitiate the property rights of the minority in the upper classes, has never been realized. Had Madison's apprehensions been realized, something very close to economic equality could have resulted. Yet, even though many of the traditional structural supports of freedom have been eroded, nothing approaching income equality has yet been obtained or demanded by the poorer majority. The relative position of the wealthy has not been radically lowered in modern times.

The distribution of personal income does not shift violently from year to year. Rising total and average money income changes the relative proportions among the income size brackets: in 1945 fewer than 10% of the spending units received as much as $5,000, by 1950, 20% received as much as that or more. . . . However, while the proportion of spending units in, and personal income received by, the $5,000 and over class was increasing by more than 100% and almost 90% respectively, the share of the top 10% of the income receivers increased from 29% in 1945 to 33% in 1947 and then returned to 29% in 1950. The bottom half of the income receivers had 22%, 21% and 23% in the corresponding years.[42]

In 1956 the top 1 per cent of adults owned 26 per cent of the wealth in the United States. This share of wealth was smaller, but not substantially smaller than the 31.6 per cent owned by the top 1 per cent in 1922, before the impact of progressive income taxes.[43]

To illustrate the small change which has taken place in the lower

[40] Dahl and Lindbloom, *Politics, Economics and Welfare,* p. 44.
[41] Livingston and Thompson, p. 37.
[42] Alan T. Peacock, *Income Redistribution and Social Policy* (London: Johnathan Cape, Ltd., 1954), pp. 185–186.
[43] Robert J. Lampman, *The Share of Top Wealth Holders in National Wealth: 1922–1956* (Princeton, N.J.: Princeton University Press, 1962), p. 24.

income groups, the percentage of national personal income before taxes, received by the poorer half of the United States, was evidently 27 per cent in 1910, which dropped to 23 per cent by 1959.[44]

It was reported by the Federal Income Tax Bureau that those reporting an income in excess of $1 million was higher in 1962 than in any year since 1929. Thus, in spite of the considerable talk about the confiscation of wealth due to the steeply progressive income tax (and there have been a few individuals who actually paid 91 per cent of a part of their income), most wealthy people avoid or minimize such high rates by income splitting with a spouse, by delaying part of their income through certain types of pension plans, by arranging to earn a high share of their income through stock options and capital gains, which are taxed at a maximum of only 25 per cent, and by investing in municipal bonds which are exempt from Federal taxes. Furthermore, many other taxes, such as sales and gasoline taxes, are regressive—that is, they take a higher percentage of the income of the poor than of the rich. Thus when the total tax system is analyzed, one study concludes, there is only mild progressiveness in the middle- and lower-income portions of the structure.[45] A more recent conservative tax authority concluded that the structure displayed almost no progressiveness and was actually regressive, if social security is included, until people earn almost $15,000 a year, and it is steeply progressive only for a small percentage of people with high incomes.[46]

In spite of the fact that the tax structure does not appear to be progressive except at the high income levels there is still some redistribution of wealth through government, both state and local as well as national, because poor people benefit from government expenditures more in relation to their tax payments than do rich people.[47]

The point is that in spite of the ideology of labor unions, for example, in calling for elimination of tax loopholes, and for steeper inheritance taxes, they have not as yet moved our society any significant distance toward a

---

[44] Gabriel Kolko, *Wealth and Power in America: An Analysis of Social Class and Income Distribution* (New York: Frederick A. Praeger, Inc., 1962), p. 15.

[45] Peacock, p. 198.

[46] This analysis concludes that there is only a 2 per cent variation between the lowest and highest percentage of income which goes into all United States taxes from income groups up to $15,000. The range is from 20.4 to 21.6 per cent for 1958. The percentage of income paid in taxes for those earning $15,000 and above, however, was 34.4 per cent. If social security taxes were included, the percentages of income going to taxes varied from 23.9 for the $8,000 to $9,999 income class to 28.3 for the under $2,000 class. The $15,000 and over group averages 35.9 per cent of income going to all taxes. Tax Foundation, Inc., *Allocation of the Tax Burden by Income Class* (New York: Tax Foundation, Inc., 1960). See also Table A4 in Appendix.

[47] Jacob Cohen and Morton Grodzins, "How Much Economic Sharing in American Federalism?" *American Political Science Review*, 57 (March, 1963), 16–19.

"dead level" equality, feared by the wealthy. "The most common and durable source of factions has been the various and unequal distribution of property." Had Madison's fears been realized, it would have been easy for labor unions to form a majority coalition of the less well off and rewrite the tax laws accordingly.

Why has this not been done? To answer this question, further elaboration of the operation of minorities rule is necessary, especially as it involves Jefferson's hope that men would seek the public good.

Calhoun's desire, that a concurrent majority of all the regions in the country be required to prevent the ganging up on a minority region for legislation, was never adopted. Yet something approaching a concurrent majority among the major power groups has become a *modus operandi*. This does not mean that a minority can veto any action, as John Fischer apparently believed.[48] In the statutes enacted in the legislative arena there are real winners and losers, as seen in the Wagner Act and Taft-Hartley Act and in the inability of the bankers to "veto" Franklin D. Roosevelt's currency reforms.

What all this means is that beyond the point of moderation, a group often can veto damaging enactments. Why is this? First, the threat of truly serious damage to a group would normally produce an extraordinary intensity of political activity on the part of the minority affected. This could vastly multiply its political influence because of the widespread apathy which generally characterizes citizenry. This apathy is illustrated by the fact that only 7 per cent of the adults contributed money to a party or candidate during a four-year period.

Second, American society involves overlapping memberships. There are very few Balkanized groups such as the Arabs and the Jews in the Middle East. This American system of overlapping memberships allows a threatened minority to multiply its influence through its members' using their other affiliations to gain the sympathy of segments of other groups.

Third, in most battles there are numerous groups which do not become deeply involved but prefer to remain on the sidelines. Many members of a group can be activated if they perceive that another group's power is being fundamentally and unfairly damaged. Thus the response of business to the Wagner Act was to work toward a new coalition which later won the battles of the Taft-Hartley and Landrum-Griffin bills. Many groups which sometimes cooperate with labor did not rush to labor's defense during these struggles because they viewed the reforms as being valid in the public interest (and the reforms did not circumscribe any group but labor).

Suppose, however, that the proposals had gone much farther than these laws. For example, suppose that the proposals included a national

48 Fischer, 27–36, 30 particularly.

right-to-work law and the disassembling of labor unions under the antitrust laws. Some minorities would have become activated in labor's behalf, fearing that such a blow might serve as a precedent against them. Some otherwise neutral groups on labor issues, such as the intellectuals and the bureaucracy, would likely have come to labor's rescue, because they would have felt it was not in the public interest to weaken a basic group that much. Just as Great Britain traditionally gave its support to the weaker nations in order to maintain a balance of power in Europe, many groups would give their support to labor if necessary to maintain a political balance of power. In fact, it was perhaps the widespread feeling that labor had attained excessive power that put many groups, at least tacitly, on the side of business.

Madison was correct when he contended that "factions" would use politics for economic gain. Jefferson was also correct in hoping people could take into account the public interest. As William Fulbright pointed out, citizens are not "incapable of reason."[49] This reason can attempt to calculate public interest as well as to fulfill personal interests. It is the examination of apparent public interest, particularly by groups which have little at stake and which are not tied by overriding obligations to one of the contending groups in a particular battle, which helps produce a compromise which is not excessively harsh on the losing group.[50] Similarly, in Congress the solons who do not have one-sided constituency pressures and who are not tied by obligation to fellow legislators on either side of an issue are freer to be "statesmen," giving primary weight to the public interest as they perceive it. This operation of both the early American conservative and liberal conceptions of man in the actual functioning of the system of minorities rule has been little recognized.

Even though the groups which are the legislative combatants are more highly organized and politically sophisticated now than earlier, the style of negotiation and compromise has long been fundamental to the Western political tradition. American democracy suffered a grave threat during the Civil War and the Reconstruction when these tenets were largely deserted. Desertion of this style of politics again could result in renewed civil war, strife, riots, oppression of minorities, or totalitarianism.

In developing nations, minorities of one type or another—whether

[49] J. William Fulbright, *The Elite and the Electorate* (New York: The Fund for the Republic, Inc., 1963), p. 4.

[50] It should be kept in mind that there are exceptions to this tendency. These exceptions, such as the relocation into a type of concentration camp of American citizens of Japanese descent early in World War II, usually take place when emotional waves roll through the country silencing most opponents of the groups instigating drastic action. See Morton Grodzins, *Americans Betrayed: Politics and the Japanese Evacuation* (Chicago: The University of Chicago Press, 1949).

they be Communist, militarist, traditionalist, or nationalist—attempt to take over by force and often refuse to negotiate a compromise with the other groups in the society. Democracy, as we know it, has no chance unless there is a general tacit agreement that disputes are to be settled by non-violent negotiation and compromise among the interested parties. Peter Odegard has said that he would "like to see political scientists exerting more of their energies in defense of reason in politics."[51] This basic consensus or reasonable approach to the solving of community problems is not rooted in most of the older traditional societies where elites of one form or another have always ruled by force. It requires an entirely new educational process to bring about a basic unity within a society so that its decisions are reached by peaceful bargaining means between the various groups in the society rather than by the domination or force of one group (even if a majority) over the whole society.

THE SOCIAL FUNCTION OF GROUPS AND IDEOLOGIES

It is apparent that for man to have influence as well as fulfillment in a modern society he must be a joiner. He must be represented by one or more of the major power groups if he is to feel any identification with society or public policy. In present American society it is membership in these groups that gives meaning to individual lives by providing common goals and values which are expressed by the groups in ideological form. Ideologies, therefore, are necessary enunciations for the group to use in order to hold its membership together. Just as in past generations religion served much this same function, so today in America membership in a major power group provides common purposes and shared emotional meanings as well as patterns of relatively definite role and status. Ideologies of the power groups serve today as the theology of the present mass man. Disputes today are less between Catholics and Protestants over the merits of their respective theologies than between the various power groups where ideological discussion and debate replace the theological disputes of previous eras. The fact, however, that individuals are members of a number of other groups such as PTA, churches, political parties, social and regional organizations (though seldom of more than one of the major occupational power groups discussed here), leads to a certain moral relativism. A conflict in goals and values occurs among these groups (both large and small), and individuals tend to pick and choose in their allegiance between con-

---

[51] Peter H. Odegard, "A Group Basis of Politics: A New Name for an Ancient Myth," *Western Political Quarterly* (September, 1958), 699.

flicting points. When a man "belongs to several groups whose political views are different, he must choose among them, compromise or withdraw from the field."[52]

The older order of a religion-structured society where all other groups and problems fit within it is, for the majority of Americans, a bygone era. Rather, religion today is frequently used more as a club or social outlet or from time to time as a spiritual tonic.[53] The present tendency for a broad merging of religious views, and frequently religious organizations as well, is indicative of the fact that it is no longer either good taste or expected behavior to foster religious contention or even religious differentiation. Social and economic issues (e.g., segregation or distribution of income) and foreign policy issues, such as disarmament or the spread of communism in Latin America, seem to be the burning moral issues of present American society.

Also in this same way, consumption and mass styles are determined by the affiliation with business, labor, agriculture, intellectual, or bureaucratic groups, tempered by climate and geography.

Each of these groups tends to have its own characteristic rules on correct style of dress, neighborhood, leisure-time activities, and in some cases, even cars. For instance, it is not considered good taste for an intellectual to drive a Cadillac. It is membership in essentially one of the occupational power groups (with which this book has dealt) with its own particular style of living that sets individuals' consumption patterns and dictates general opinions and taste.

The fact that the major groups discussed in this book represent sociological as well as economic and political groups has not been taken up here at length. Since our emphasis has been upon how public policy is made and the particular role and effect that various groups play in this process, their sociological nature has, of necessity, not been a focal point. Nonetheless, the evidence that these groups do serve their members by providing common emotional meanings to contemporary society and by providing common purposes, values, and roles does enhance the power of these groups over their membership. The tendency of members of these groups to observe similar styles of living is merely an external evidence of a degree of inner conformity among the members of each group. The adherence to a common group ideology even though each group has deviant minorities is further indication that vast numbers of individuals in a mass society find

---

[52] Robert E. Lane, "Political Personality and Electoral Choice," *American Political Science Review,* 69 (March, 1955), 175.

[53] The reputed increase in church membership in this country is argued here to be more of a social commitment generally than necessarily a powerfully spiritual or theological one. There are of course, many exceptions to this trend, particularly among converts to the small evangelical churches.

a certain meaning to their lives by accepting the norms of the major group to which they belong. Since, in America today, occupation is perhaps the most powerful economic thread that binds men together, the major occupational power groups discussed here and their ideologies have widely replaced religion with its theology as the major sociological institution in modern man's life. When the power of economics and politics is combined with the above-mentioned sociological forces, the power of these groups becomes all the more understandable.

POLITICIANS AND PARTIES

The role of the politician and the political party in our mass democracy is to act as a broker of interests. The politician today finds the most successful way to win office is simply to represent the major interests of his constituency rather than to become involved in issues that might alienate one of the primary power groups within his district. Wilder Crane in 1957 had an opportunity to study whether or not Wisconsin legislators represented the majority interest of their constituency. In February, 1957, Wisconsin legislators were considering a bill which would establish daylight saving time. The bill, after being considered by the legislature, was subject to the approval of the voters in a referendum conducted in April of the same year. The bill itself would establish daylight time, but would require the approval of the majority of voters to become operative.

A larger study of the 1957 Wisconsin assembly, the lower house of the Wisconsin legislature, enabled the author to determine something about the extent to which assemblymen represented their constituents on this issue and to determine how assemblymen perceived their roles on a question which was void of partisan or ideological considerations.

The Wisconsin assembly passed the daylight time bill by a vote of 72 to 27 on February 19. It was supported by 46 Republicans and 26 Democrats and opposed by 20 Republicans and 7 Democrats. All 47 urban representatives voted for the bill, while rural representatives voted 27 to 25 against it.

In April the majority of voters approved daylight time by a vote of 578,661 to 480,656. Comparison of the votes cast by the assemblymen with the majority vote in their respective districts indicates that 85 per cent of the assemblymen voted in February consistently with the way majorities in their districts voted in April.[54]

When conflicts arise between constituents, the politician essentially

[54] Wilder W. Crane, Jr., "Do Representatives Represent," *The Journal of Politics,* 22 (May, 1962), 296–297.

plays the role of a neutral broker attempting to work out the conflict in a mutually acceptable compromise. Political parties serve a similar role. For, as John C. Livingston and Robert G. Thompson have observed:

In the politics of mass society, interest groups become stronger than political parties. Parties become, in effect, loose coalitions of interest groups. Since both parties seek, above all, to win elections, each seeks to put together a package that will appeal to all organized groups. The differences between the parties are thereby minimized, reflecting only differences in judgment about what combination will be a winning one . . . Parties, in short, seldom operate to organize the debate of public policy alternatives. They no longer stand above group interests; they serve, rather as clearinghouses and brokers for the interests.[55]

In contrast to the above, Senator Fulbright has said that a congressman's "constituents, must recognize that he has a duty to his office as well as to them and that their duty in turn is to fill the office but not to run it."[56]

As far back as 1913, Harvard President A. Lawrence Lowell foresaw that a mass democracy would produce an age of brokers and an age of advertisement. By brokerage, he meant the negotiating process of resolving conflict of interests in mass democracy; by advertisement, he meant the techniques of organizing and engineering consent in the electoral process.

It should be remembered that party rather than class plays a major part in American voting behavior perceptions. Heinz Eulau found that people giving reasons for their perceptions, regardless of whether they were working-class or middle-class, received their notion from a party-related frame of reference. (See Table A3.) He further found:

Those seeing their class as voting Democratic tend to give 'interest-oriented' reasons for their perceptions while those seeing it going Republican tend to give reasons which are not interest-oriented. In conclusion, there does not seem to exist at present a syndrome of class identification, class awareness, and interest orientation which might warrant the label 'class awareness.'[57]

What are the loose coalitions of interests which comprise the two parties in America? (See Table A1.) The Democrats include substantial majorities of the following groups: union members; unemployed; Farmers Union; the South; minorities such as Catholics, Negroes, Jews, Italians, Irish; grade school and high school educated; urban dwellers; descendants of recent immigrants; those who earn less than $5,000 per year; and an intellectual elite. The Republican coalition draws heavily from the following groups: business and professional; Farm Bureau; English, Scotch, Scandinavian, and German descendants; Protestants; suburban and rural

[55] Livingston and Thompson, p. 37.
[56] Fulbright, p. 4.
[57] Heinz Eulau, "Class Identification and Projection in Voting Behavior," *Western Political Quarterly*, 8, 4 (December, 1955), 452.

dwellers; those who earn more than $7,500 per year; and the college educated. When an individual is a member of several groups which tend to belong to one party, his political preference finds reinforcement. For example, the probability that an unemployed urban Catholic Negro union member would vote a Republican ticket would be almost zero. (See Table A2.)

One of the methods by which a party serves as a broker in broadening a coalition is to nominate a candidate who can attract away a segment of the opposing parties' coalition without alienating the components of one's own coalition. For example, the amazing majorities of as high as almost a million votes won by Senator Jacob Javits of New York[58] were due partly to the fact that being Jewish and liberal he added many normally Democratic Jewish votes to the Republican column for his race, at least.

Sometimes for a historic reason (e.g., the Civil War) almost complete ideological disagreement characterizes components of the same party, such as the conservative Southerners and the Northern urban liberals in the Democratic party. On the other hand, ideologies can be a handicap in bringing new groups into a coalition. Consider the problem of the Republican party.

One possible method of rebuilding a Republican alliance to become a majority coalition would be to concentrate on bringing as many members of a specific target group into the coalition as possible. For example, the incomes of many union members now place them well into the middle classes financially, and many have shown themselves willing to switch parties for Eisenhower and Rockefeller types. But the ideology of the Republican leadership of most states represents the same hostility to unions as the business and Farm Bureau segments. Some of these elements believe it would be a selling of principle to make concessions in order to win union members. This ideology inhibits potential efforts to attract union membership.

To take another example, teachers share the higher educational background which characterizes other key groups in the Republican coalition. If the Republicans would drive for superior public education, there would be the possibility of bringing many teachers, with all their influence, into the Republican coalition. Many teachers are unattracted by either businessmen as a group or laborers as a group. If educators' interests and the public good, as they saw it, were satisfied through a coalition with business, many teachers would probably just as soon be allied with business and professional people as continue what amounts to an alliance with the working classes and less well-educated groups who are significant components of the Democratic party membership.

However, the Republican ideology of curbing public expenditures,

---

[58] *The New York Times* (November 7, 1962).

reflecting those elements of the party which are anxious to save taxes, frequently inhibits a type of policy which could attract such groups as the teachers. The restraining influence of ideology is even more conspicuous when it comes to Federal aid to education. Here the typical Republican ideology against the growth of Federal power and encroachment on states rights and responsibilities is evident. Thus the fact that most teachers favor Federal aid to education, while most GOP leaders oppose it, inhibits the grafting of a major segment of this articulate group into the party. The effect of group and party ideologies is particularly significant here in that frequently in local bond or tax elections for the public schools the wealthier Republican sections of the cities vote much more in favor of tax hikes for public schools than do the poorer Democratic areas. This suggests that there may well be a greater basis for a natural alliance between the teachers and the more well-to-do and better-educated population elements than ideologies of these elements on organized bases permit to exist.

Thus while parties and politicians have perhaps become "nothing but the brokerage of minority interests,"[59] the *ideologies of these minority interests often guide and restrain the brokerage process.* The pattern of the strength of minorities and the intensity of their ideological commitments vary from region to region, which makes the challenge to the politician in forging a majority coalition differ tremendously from one area to another. In this regard President Lyndon B. Johnson is an example of a remarkably successful politician, having proved his effectiveness as a political broker in such varied situations as Texas politics, the United States Senate, and presidential coalition building.

CODA

Thus today, the theory of minorities rule has become a major theory of American mass democracy.[60] Without mass society in which the individual found it necessary to find satisfaction in the impersonality of large cities, large corporations, and giant public institutions by identifying with those in similar occupations to find some type of identity and meaningful values and goals, the development of democratic minorities rule could not have occurred as it has. Further, it could not have occurred without a strong democratic tradition, a tradition that combined the varying ideals of liberty and popular sovereignty with a pragmatic recognition of the need for compromise. The measure of workability as against dogmatism was induced

[59] Livingston and Thompson, p. 149.

[60] Similarly in the judiciary, our law and courts can be thought of as another level of compromise under a minorities rule. In this case, the courts merely perform, with different techniques, the function of a broker between various interest groups.

partly by the practical problems of conquering the frontier land. This contrasts, for example, with the rigid doctrinal emphasis among French politicians, which stemmed from the continuing philosophical disputes arising out of the French Revolution. The uncompromising position of the various French parties produced the frequent turnover of governments unable to win majorities in parliament on specific issues prior to the advent of General De Gaulle. The search for workable compromises among American politicians blends the pursuit of economic interest with a recognition that the public interest is not served by excessively harsh treatment of a defeated minority.

Our modern political system of the brokerage of interests among minorities (wherein a consensus of minorities—or a majority of minorities— determines public policy after negotiation and compromise) represents a highly effective and generally quite equitable way of settling disputes in a diversified society. This system has achieved, pragmatically, a means of allowing minority groups to be heard—and even more important, it provides a means for intensity of feeling on specific issues to be registered by minority groups. Thus, in a sense, American democracy today has achieved a political system which political philosophers have long dreamed of, but never effectively worked out in theory. The making of public policy in America by minorities rule through a political brokerage system of negotiation and compromise, though imperfect, represents the most effective democratic system yet devised for a large bureaucratic society comprising rival economic interests.

appendix

TABLE A1. **The Voting of Major American Social Groups: Survey Research Center Findings in 1948, 1956, and 1960 Elections**

Group characteristic	Vote Republican	Vote Democratic	Other	Not voting
Education				
1948				
Grade school	16	35	4	45
High school	29	34	4	33
College	54	17	8	21
1956				
Grade school	35	24	1	40
High school	41	34	1	26
College	62	28		10
1960				
Grade school	29	37	1	33
High school	38	42	1	19
College	57	32	1	10
Occupation of head of family				
1948				
Professional and managerial	58	14	3	25
Other white-collar	38	38	5	19
Skilled and semiskilled	15	52	4	29
Unskilled	12	33	5	50
Farm operators	13	25	4	58
1956				
Professional and managerial	57	27	1	15
Other white-collar	48	30	1	21
Skilled and semiskilled	39	32	1	28
Unskilled	24	29	..	47
Farm operators	40	34	..	26
1960				
Professional and managerial	46	39	3	12
Other white-collar	46	37	1	16
Skilled and semiskilled	31	44	3	22
Farm operators	50	25	2	23
Unskilled	27	41	..	32
Trade union affiliation of head of family				
1948				
Member	13	55	5	27
Nonmember	32	26	4	38
1956				
Member	36	39	2	23
Nonmember	46	25	1	28

Group characteristic	Vote Republican	Vote Democratic	Other	Not voting
1960				
Member	27	48	2	23
Nonmember	44	35	1	20
Type of community				
1948				
Metropolitan areas	32	46	5	17
Towns and cities	30	28	5	37
Rural areas	12	25	4	59
1956				
Metropolitan areas	43	35	1	21
Towns and cities	46	25	1	28
Rural areas	38	29	1	32
1960				
Metropolitan areas	34	46	2	18
Towns and cities	41	36	1	22
Rural areas	40	35	2	23
Religion				
1948				
Protestant	28	25	5	42
Catholic	25	49	5	21
1956				
Protestant	44	25	1	30
Catholic	43	36	1	20
1960				
Protestant	47	28	1	24
Catholic	16	68	1	15
Race				
1948				
White	29	33	4	34
Negro	10	18	8	64
1956				
White	46	29	1	24
Negro	12	23	1	64
1960				
White	42	38	1	19
Negro	15	36	3	46

SOURCE: Fred I. Greenstein, *The American Party System and the American People* (Englewood Cliffs, N.J.: Prentice-Hall, Inc., 1963), p. 24.

TABLE A2.
Social Class and the 1952 Presidential Vote

	Upper middle	Lower middle	Upper lower	Lower lower	Farmers	Total
Eisenhower	65.0%	51.8%	32.7%	24.9%	43.3%	42.5%
Stevenson	23.9	28.7	43.3	29.7	24.4	30.6
Nonvoters	10.3	18.6	23.3	44.7	31.1	26.0
Other	0.8	0.9	0.7	0.7	1.2	0.9
Number	263	327	420	273	196	1,614

Ethnic-Religious Groupings and the 1952 Presidential Vote

	Negroes	Jews	Catholics	Nominal Protestants	Churchgoing Protestants	Total
Eisenhower	6.4%	25%	41.2%	47.5%	56.8%	42.5%
Stevenson	26.1	65.5	43.5	26.5	23.4	30.6
Nonvoters	66.9	7.7	14.4	25.4	19.8	26.0
Other	0.6	1.8	0.9	0.6	0.0	0.9
Number	(157)	52	338	677	337	1,614

SOURCE: Morris Janowitz and Dwaine Marvick, "Competitive Pressure and Democratic Consent," *Public Opinion Quarterly*, 19 (winter, 1955–1956), 384–385.

TABLE A3. **Class Identification and Perception
of Working-class Vote**

Working class will vote	Working		Middle	
	Working N = 482	Middle N = 169	Working N = 117	Middle N = 212
Democratic	65%	53%	64%	57%
Republican	9	10	11	14
Evenly split	26	37	25	29
	100%	100%	100%	100%

SOURCE: Heinz Eulau, "Class Identification and Projection in Voting Behavior," *Western Political Quarterly*, 8, 4 (December, 1955), 452.

TABLE A4. **Taxes as a Percentage of Total Income by Source and Income Class**

Calendar Year 1958

Source	Family personal income class							Total
	Under $2,000	$2,000– 3,999	$4,000– 5,999	$6,000– 7,999	$8,000– 9,999	$10,000– 14,999	$15,000 and over	
Total taxes, excluding social insurance	21.0%	20.4%	20.6%	21.6%	20.6%	21.6%	34.4%	23.7%
Total taxes, including social insurance	28.3	26.3	25.9	25.7	23.9	24.0	35.9	27.4
Federal taxes:								
Individual income	1.8	4.5	6.0	7.9	7.5	8.9	16.3	8.7
Corporation income	3.8	3.2	3.0	3.0	3.0	3.6	8.8	4.3
Excise and customs	4.0	3.3	3.1	3.0	2.9	2.7	1.8	2.8
Estate and gift	....	....	....	....	....	....	1.7	0.3
Total, excluding social insurance	9.6	11.0	12.1	13.9	13.4	15.1	28.6	16.1
Social insurance	6.1	4.9	4.3	3.3	2.7	2.0	1.2	3.1
Total, including social insurance	15.7	15.9	16.4	17.2	16.2	17.2	29.8	19.2
State and local taxes:								
Individual income	0.5	0.8	0.6	0.2	0.2	0.3	0.7	0.5
Corporation income	0.2	0.2	0.1	0.1	0.2	0.2	0.4	0.2
Excise and sales	4.8	3.9	3.7	3.6	3.5	3.2	2.1	3.3
Estate and gift	....	....	....	....	....	....	0.5	0.1
Property	5.9	4.6	4.1	3.7	3.4	2.8	2.1	3.5
Total, excluding social insurance	11.3	9.4	8.5	7.7	7.2	6.5	5.9	7.5
Social insurance	1.3	1.0	0.9	0.8	0.6	0.4	0.2	0.7
Total, including social insurance	12.6	10.4	9.5	8.5	7.8	6.9	6.1	8.2

SOURCE: Tax Foundation, Inc., *Allocation of the Tax Burden by Income Class* (New York: Tax Foundation, Inc., 1960), Table 10, p. 17.

index

Adams, John, 321
Adams, Samuel, 320
Aerospace Industries Association, 272
Age of brokers, 332
Agrarian spirit, 44
Agriculture, 96–132
   classical creed, 32
   Committee for Economic Development, 100
   cost, 96
   economist's position, 97, 98
   Farmers Union, 103
   ideological differences among groups, 128
   labor ideology, 86
   National Wheat Referendum, 122
   National Wool Growers Association, 127
   percentage of farm families, 100
   surpluses, 99
   technology, 97
Agriculture Department, 125, 226
Air Force, 268
Air Force Association, 272, 274
Alcorn, Meade, 211, 212, 215
Alexander, Holmes, 208
Almond, Gabriel A., 3
Alsop, Stewart, 146
Alvo Manufacturing Company, 302
American Bar Association, 136

American Economics Association, 203
American Enterprise Association, 26
American Federation of Government Employees, 234
American Federation of Labor–Congress of Industrial Organizations, 6, 64–95
   membership, 71
   political activity, 72
American Federation of Teachers, 154–157
   administrators and employees, 170
   affiliate of AFL–CIO, 154
   areas, of agreement, 161
    of ideological disagreement, 169
   ideology, 160
   labor, 170
   "professionalism," 156
   salaries, 167
   school reforms, 176
   share in decision making, 164
   size, 154
   teacher's welfare, 155
American Legion, 13, 273
American Medical Association, 6, 18, 38–43
American Medical Political Action Committee (AMPAC), 38, 41
American National Association of Junior Colleges, 13

American Ordnance Association, 272
American Political Science Association, 197, 199, 215
American Veterans of World War II, 273
Americans for Constitutional Action, 26
Analytical pluralists, 3
Annis, Dr. Edward R., 39
Aristotle, 2, 320
Armour and Company, 126
Army Association, 272
Army Reorganization Plan, 283
Aron, Raymond, 20
Associations, peak, 4
Atomic Energy Commission, 242

Babbidge, Homer D., 184
Bach, George Leland, 99
Bagwell, Paul, 215
Bailey, Stephen K., 247
Baker, Newton, 284
Baker v. Carr, 100
Balanced budget, classical creed, 32–34
  Farm Bureau, 117
  Farmers Union, 106
  Grange, 111–112
  intellectuals, 197
  labor, 75–76
  managerial, 51
Baldwin, James, 135, 138
Bardon, Graham A., 91
Barnett, Ross, 203
Bauer, Raymond, 62
Baumer, W. H., 25
Beck, Dave, 88
Bennett, Wallace, 42, 48
Benson, Ezra Taft, 123–124, 127–128
Bentley, Arthur, 2
Bernstein, Marver H., 9, 233
Black Muslims, 135, 140, 145
Blackmon, Robert E., 183
Blau, Peter, 239
Blough, Roger, 50, 199
Boeing Airplane Company, 303
Boulding, Kenneth E., 266
Bradley, Mark Edward, 301
Brady, Robert S., 309
Brickman, William W., 171
Brogan, D. W., 259
Brookings Institution, 24, 233

Brown, Burton, 162
Brown v. the Board of Education, 133
Bryce, James, 11
Buckley, William F., 180, 208
Budget (*see* Balanced budget)
Bulova Company, 301
Bunche, Ralph J., 185, 189
Bundy, McGeorge, 196
Bunker, George M., 304
Bunzel, John H., 27, 43, 45
Bureau of Budget, Director of, 253
Bureaucracy, 222–307
  criteria of, 240
  efficiency of, 239
  ideology, 237
  military (*see* Military bureaucracy)
  stress, 240
Burke, Edmund, 2, 4
Burns, Arthur F., 203
Burns, James MacGregor, 12
Burton, Laurence J., 216
Business, 24–63
  Farm Bureau, 117
  Farmers Union, 106
  Grange, 112
  national groups, 24
  political assets, 61
  political weaknesses, 61
  small business, 43–46
  National Federation of Independent Business, 27, 44
Butler, Paul, 211
Byrd, Harry, 62
Byrnes, James F., 253

Caldwell, Gaylon L., 140
Calhoun, John C., 327
Calkins, Robert D., 184
Canada, 124
Cannon, Mark W., 8
Cantril, Hadley, 318
Carey, James, 91
Carleton, W. G., 2
Carr, Edward Hollett, 319
Carver, Nixon, 317
Cater, Douglass, 188, 275
Catholics, 2, 8
Cattlemen's Association of Utah, 127
Celler, Emanuel, 128

Celler-O'Mahoney-Kefauver Act, 44
Center for the Study of Democratic Institutions, 66
Chamberlain, John, 152
Chapin, Seldon, 254
Cheney, John Vance, 320
Cherington, P. W., 24
Cherry, Howard L., 153
Chiang Kai-shek, 295
Civil Aeronautics Board, 242
Civil bureaucracy, 227, 314
  background, 222
  basic aim, 238
  case of the Federal Service Act of 1946, 247
  chief executive, 231
  civil service, 244
  Eisenhower, effect of, 243
  Federal employees, 235
  Federal employees unions, 235
  Federal executive, 246
  government, role of, 241–247
  ideology, 236–239
    opposition to, 228
  National Federation, of Federal Employees, 234
    of Postal Clerks, 235
  new agencies, 245
  New Deal, 243
  power of, 225, 256
  relationship, among agencies, clientele groups, and congressional committees, 229
    with legislators, 228
  rule-making role, 229
  size, 222
  strategic position of, 228
  support from agencies' employees, 232
  unions, 235
    right to join, 234
Civil rights, intellectuals, 202
  Negroes, 139–140
Civil service, National Civil Service League, 224
  Pendleton Act, 244
Civil War, 328
Clapp, Charles L., 235
Clark, Mark, 259
Classical business ideology, 26, 28–38
  government bureaucracies, 240
  growth of government, 237

Clay, Lucius, 259
Clayton Act, 44
Clements, Earle, 5
Cleveland, Harlan, 266
Cochrane, Willard W., 121–122
Cogen, Charles, 165, 170
Cohen, Jacob, 326
Collins, J. Lawton, 259
Colter, Neil, 217
Commerce Department, 226
Committee, for Constitutional Government, 26
  for Economic Development, 25, 46–56, 100, 311
  on Political Education, 72
Competition, 30
  agriculture, 50
  and bigness, managerial ideology, 48
Competitor, government, 49
  labor, 48
Compromise, 328
Conant, James Bryant, 162
Condon-Wadlin Act, 173
Conference of American Small Business Organizations, 45
Congress of Racial Equality, 134
  background, 144
Consensus, 335
Conservative movement, 66
Cook, Fred, 266
Cook, Orval R., 302
Cooley, Harold, 126
Cooperatives, Farm Bureau, 117
  Farmers Union, 105
  National Grange, 111
Corson, John J., 241
Council of Economic Advisers, 203
  labor, 77
Cowley, Malcolm, 177
Crane, Wilder W., 331
Cunningham, Robert M., 40

Dahl, Robert, 19, 318–319, 325
Dahlgren, Harold E., 3
Davies, Aled, 126
Defense Department, 226, 288
  Office of Civil and Defense Mobilization, 233
Deficits (*see* Balanced budget)

Democratic Party, 181, 209, 324, 332
    intellectual preference, 181–183, 186, 193
Derthic, Lawrence G., 217
de Toqueville, Alexis, 2, 6
Deutsch, Karl W., 7
Dimock, Marshall E., 223, 236
Dirkson, Everett, 211
Disabled American Veterans, 273
Distribution of personal income, 325
Dixon, Henry Aldous, 127, 216
Dobriansky, Lev, 212
Doherty, William C., 232
Dominick, Peter, 42
Douglas, Paul H., 88, 300
Douglas Aircraft, 272
DuBois, W. E. B., 141
Dunlop, John T., 32

Eastman, Max, 10, 11
Economic growth, ideology, classical business, 37
    intellectual, 205
    labor, 86
    managerial, 53
Education, de facto segregation, 139
    Farm Bureau, 119
    Federal aid, 151, 199
    Grange, 119
    intellectuals, 200
    Negroes, 138
    state aid, 151
Efficiency, public demand for, 240
Einaudi, Mario, 237, 242
Eisenhower, Dwight D., 47, 62, 190, 258, 259
    effect on civil and bureaucracy, 243
Eisenhower, Milton, 217
Eisenhower administration, 47
Electoral college, 12
Elias, Norbert, 292
Elites, 17, 18
Elliot Bill, 90
Employment (*see* Unemployment)
Equality, espousal of, 192
Estes, Billie Sol, 216
Eulau, Heinz, 332
Evening New York City School Teachers, 172
Executive, Federal, 246
Export-Import Bank, 242

Factions, 328
Fainsod, Merle, 97
Fair Trade Act, 127
Farley, James, 5
Farm, family, 103
    Farmers Union, 104
    Grange, 110
Farm Bureau, 50, 114–121, 311, 312
    age, 114
    balanced budget, 117
    business, 117
    cooperatives, 117
    county agents, 114
    education, 119
    farm policy, 115
    fiscal and monetary policies, 117
    free market, 115
    free trade, 119
    government's role, 115
    ideology, 115–120
    inflation, 117
    international affairs, 119
    international trade, 119
    labor, 118
    size, 114
    social legislation, 118
    tariffs, 119
    taxation, 117
    unemployment, 118
    Utah State, 127
    wages, 118
Farm Credit Administration, 242
Farm Credit Association, 111
Farm policy, Farm Bureau, 115
    Farmers Union, 103
    future, 121
    Grange, 110
Farmer, James, 134
Farmers Union, 87, 98, 102–108, 312
    age, 102
    agriculture, 103
    aims, 102
    balanced budget, 106
    business, 106
    cooperatives, 105
    family farm, 104
    farm policy, 103
    fiscal and monetary policies, 105
    free market, 103
    government's role, 104
    ideology, 103–108

Farmers Union, inflation, 105–106
  international affairs, 108
  international trade, 107
  labor, 107
  size, 102
  social legislation, 107
  tariffs, 107–108
  taxation, 105–107
  unemployment, 107
  wages, 107
Fast, Howard, 180
Federal Bureau of Investigation, 239
Federal Corrupt Practices Act, 42
Federal Deposit Insurance Corporation, 242
Federal Executive, educational level, 246
Federal Security Agency, 242
Federal Trade Commission, 125
Federalist, 96, 260
Federalists, 321, 324
Fellner, William, 269
Fels, Rendigs, 97
Finer, S. E., 264
Fiscal and monetary policies, classical business, 33–34
  Farm Bureau, 117
  Farmers Union, 105
  Grange, 111
  intellectuals, 197, 198, 204
  labor, 76
  managerial, 51
Fischer, John, 319
Flanders, Ralph E., 266
Flemming, D. F., 208
Fong, Hiram L., 70
Food Fair, 125
Ford, Henry, 62
Foreign aid (*see* International trade)
Foreign Operations Administration, 242
Foreign Service, 248
Foreign Service Act of 1946, 247
Forman, James, 134
Forrestal, James, 268
Fortune magazine, 48, 52, 68
Foundation for Economic Education, 26
Fox, William T. R., 283
Free market, classical business, 28
  Farm Bureau, 115
  Farmers Union, 103
  Grange, 111
  managerial ideology, 47

Free trade, classical creed, 38
  Farm Bureau, 119
  (*See also* International trade)
Freeman, Howard E., 274
Freeman, J. Leiper, 227
Freeman, Orville, 123
Freeman, The, 36, 37
Friedrich, Carl J., 199
Frischnecht, Reed, 127
Froman, Lewis A., Jr., 4
Fromm, Erich, 208
Fulbright, William, 328
Fuller, S. B., 136
Fund raising, 42
Furniss, Edgar S., 269

Galbraith, John Kenneth, 23, 97, 196, 197, 215
  "countervailing power," 323
Gates, Thomas S., 299
Gavin, Leon H., 301
General Electric, 303
Gibb, Cecil A., 19
Gillman, Richard, 178
Glaser, William, 39
Glazer, Nathan, 263
Goldwater, Barry, 31, 62, 96, 218, 266, 276
Gompers, Samuel, 69
Gottfried, Alex, 182
Government, role of, civil bureaucracy, 241–247
  civil service, 244
  classical business, 28
  Farm Bureau, 115
  Farmers Union, 104
  Federal Executive, 246
  Grange, 110
  growing, 7
  intellectuals, 185, 195
  labor, 311
  managerial, 46, 47, 49
  new agencies, 245
Government bureaucracy, summary, 305–307
Government spending (*see* Balanced budget)
Grange, 108–113, 312
  age, 108
  balanced budget, 111–112

Grange, business, 112
  cooperatives, 111
  education, 119
  family farm, 110
  farm policy, 110
  fiscal and monetary policies, 111
  free market, 111
  government's role, 110
  ideology, 110–113
  international affairs, 113
  international trade, 113
  labor, 112
  political activities, 109
  size, 108
  social function, 109
  social legislation, 113
  tariffs, 113
  taxation, 111
  unemployment, 111
  wages, 112, 113
Great Depression, 242
Grodzins, Morton, 322
Gross, Bertram, 10, 231
Groups, controlled by minorities, 17, 18
  definition, 5, 6
  political role of, 2
  social function, 329
Gunderson, Gunnar, 41

Hacker, Andrew, 19, 321
Hall, Leonard, 5
Halleck, Charles, 211
Hamberg, Daniel, 98
Hamilton, Alexander, 96, 260
Hammond, Paul Y., 284, 285, 289
Hannah, John, 217
Harder, C. W., 44
Harriman, Averill, 10
Harris, Lou, 180
Harris, Seymour, 197, 198
Hartz, Louis, 8
Hatch Act, 42
Hauge, Gabriel, 212
Hayes, A. J., 87
Hays, Brooks, 5
Health, Education, and Welfare Department, 226
Hebert, F. Edward, 258, 299–305
Hebert Probe, 258, 298–305
Hechinger, Fred M., 161, 175
Henry, Andrew F., 268

Herring, Pendleton, 3, 189
Higher Education Facilities Act, 151
Hildebrand, George H., 66
Hoffa, James, 69, 88
Hoffer, Eric, 30
Hofstadter, Richard, 177
Horowitz, Louis, 295
House Labor Committee, 60
Houser, Harold Alexander, 302
Housing, Negroes, 138
Housing and Community Development, intellectuals, 202
Housing and Home Finance Agency, 242
Huckshorn, Robert J., 217
Huggins, Edwin V., 303
Humphrey, George M., 25
Humphrey, Hubert, 14, 89
Hunter, Floyd, 17
Huntington, Samuel P., 275, 285, 286, 288–289
Hyde, David R., 40

Ideology, 19
  American Federation of Teachers, 160-171
  American Medical Association, 38–43
  civil bureaucracy, 236–239, 243
    opposition to ideology, 228
  classical business, 26, 28–38
  Farm Bureau, 115–120
  Farmers Union, 103–108
  Grange, 110–113
  intellectuals, 194–208
  managerial, 46–56
  military, 263, 279, 291–298
  National Education Association, 160–171
  Negroes, 135
  small business, 43
  social function, 329
Income, distribution of, classical business, 35
  intellectuals, 191–192
  labor, 85–86
  managerial, 52
  personal income, 325
  public school teachers, 151, 167–168
  total, taxes as percentage of, 341
Individual businesses, 24
Individualism, 8

Industrialization, 7
Inflation, classical business, 35
  Farm Bureau, 117
  Farmers Union, 105–106
  intellectuals, 198
  managerial, 52
  price stability, labor ideology, 77
Intellectuals, 177, 226, 311, 313
  anti-, 190–191, 214
  anti-Nixon, 183
  appointees, 188, 189
  budget and fiscal policy, 197
  case of the Republicans courting, 208
  causes of left-of-center ideology, 191
  civil rights, 202
  consensus, 178, 180, 184
  definition of, 177, 178
  education, 200
  effort to woo, 212
  fiscal policy, 204
  ideology of, 194–208
  influence, 184, 218
  international trade, 206
  journalists, 188
  left-of-center position, 180, 184
  Medicare, 201
  monetary policy, 198
  orientation toward Democratic party,
    182
  pro-New Deal, 181
  role of, 194
    in government, 185, 195
  social legislation, 199
  social scientists, 217
  summary of ideology, 221
  tariffs, 206–208
  taxation, 205
  unemployment, 203
  wages, 199
Interior Department, 226
International affairs, Farm Bureau, 119
  Farmers Union, 108
  Grange, 113
International trade, classical business, 37
  Farm Bureau, 119
  Farmers Union, 107
  Grange, 113
  intellectuals, 206
  labor, 87
  managerial, 54
Irvine, Clarence, 302
Ives, Irving M., 88

Jameson, Frank Gard, 302
Janowitz, Morris, 230, 255, 268, 292,
  298
Javits, Jacob, 197, 217, 333
Jefferson, Thomas, 320
John Birch Society, 193
Johnson, Gerald W., 195
Johnson, Lyndon B., 62, 80, 196, 211,
  334
Joint Chiefs of Staff, 282
*Journal of the American Medical Asso-
  ciation*, 42
Justice Department, 226

Kampelman, Max M., 286, 324
Katzenbach, Edward L., 277
Keezer, Dexter M., 191
Kempton, Murray, 180
Kennedy, John F., 7, 10, 50, 69, 88, 91,
  182, 195, 311
Kennedy administration, farm proposal,
  122
  intellectual consensus, 194
Kessel, John, 217
Key, V. O., 4, 68, 71, 273
Keynes, J. M., 28, 62
Keynesian economics, 47
Keyserling, Leon, 203
Khrushchev, Nikita, 94
Kile, Orville Merton, 102
Killian, James R., 217
King, Martin Luther, Jr., 134, 142, 148
Kingsley, J. Donald, 223
Kirk, Russell, 180, 187
Kirstein, George, 83
Kissinger, Henry A., 178, 189
Kistiakowsky, George B., 217
Klein, Herbert, 183
Kolko, Gabriel, 326
Korean conflict, 262
Kornhauser, Arthur, 70, 181
Kraft, Joseph, 189, 195
Kruglac, Theodore E., 183
Kuchel, Tom, 71

Labor, American Federation of Teachers, 170
  automation, 67
  balanced budget, 75–76
  classical business, 31

Labor, Department of, 226
  distribution of income, 85–86
  Farm Bureau, 118
  Farmers Union, 107
  fiscal and monetary policy, 76
  government role in, 311
  Grange, 112
  international trade, 87
  lobbyists, 72
    campaign organizer, 72
    contact man, 72
    testifier-expert, 72
  National Labor Relations Board, 242
  policies for full employment, 84
  political role, traditional, 69
  power of, 64
  pragmatic ideology of, 94
  price controls, 76–78
  profits, 81, 85, 86
  public relations, 72–73, 87–93
  strength of, 74
  unemployment, 83
  unions, European, 94
    problems, 93
  wages, 80
Labor-Management Relations Act of
  1947 (*see* Taft-Hartley Act)
Lampman, Robert J., 325
Landrum-Griffin Act, 49, 87
Landsberg, Hans, 121
Lane, Robert E., 56, 330
Lapp, Ralph E., 269
Laski, Harold J., 223
Latham, Earl, 2, 3
Lazarsfeld, P. F., 181, 193
Leiserson, Avery, 9, 230
Lewis, John, 134
Lichtheim, George, 177
Lieberman, Myron, 170
Liljenquist, Blaine, 127
Lippmann, Walter, 188
Lipsen, Charles, 71
Lipset, Seymour Martin, 43, 178, 192,
  255
Little Rock, Arkansas, 138
Livingston, John C., 325, 332
Lobbying, 15
  expenditures, 9
  Legislative Department lobbying sec-
    tion, 72

Lobbyist, 16
  Washington representatives, 24, 63
Locke, John, 8
Lomax, Louis, 134
Long, Hamilton Albert, 261
Lowell, A. Lawrence, 318, 332
Lubell, Samuel, 187
Lyons, Gene M., 280, 290

MacArthur, Douglas, 275
McCaffree, Floyd, 214
McCarthy, Joseph, 14
McCarthyism, 193
McClellan, John L., 88
McCloskey, Gordon, 163
McClosky, Herbert, 3
McConnell, Campbell R., 97
McCullock, Winifred, 238
McElroy, Neil, 224
McFarland, Ernest, 5
Machiavelli, 2
MacKenzie, W. J. M., 5
McLellan, David S., 263
McMurrin, Sterling, 153
McNamara, Robert S., 91, 281, 290, 296
Macy, John, 241
Madison, James, 2, 317, 321
Majoritarianists, 324
Majority rule, 317
Malcolm X, 145
Managerial ideology, 46
  development, 62
  economic growth, 53
  free market, 47
Managerialists, 310
The Mandate, 44
Mann, David E., 246
Mannheim, Karl, 19
Mansfield, Harold, 303
Marsh, Joseph F., 239
Marshall, George C., 259
Martin, Harry W., 40
Martin Air Craft Company, 304
Marx, 2
Marxists, 10
Mason, Edward S., 203
Masons, 8
Mass democracy, 332
Matthews, Donald, 32, 140
Meany, George, 78, 87

Medicare, 65, 80
  intellectuals, 201
Megel, Carl, 155, 169
Melville, Keith, 61
Menez, Joseph F., 3
Merit pay for teachers, 169
Merton, Robert K., 236
Milbrath, Lester, 15
Miles, Nelson A., 284
Military bureaucracy, 258–307, 314
  background, 258
  business-politics, 265, 277
  business relations, 298
  centralization, problems, 288
  civil-military relations, 282–291
    current and future trends, 290
    Secretary of Defense, 289
  civilian control, problems of, 285–291
  control, 261
  counterideology against military
    power, 263
  economic impact, 265
  Federalist tradition, 262
  future of, 298
  growth of, 264
  Hebert Probe, 298, 305
  interservice growth and power rela-
    tionship, 267
  organizations, 270
  President Eisenhower, final address,
    262
  political position, 287
  politics, 270, 280, 298
  public relations, 270
  state department, 263
  and veterans organizations, 273
Military ideology, 291–298
  anti-, 279
  background, 292
  classical traditions, 293
  new approach, 293
  unification of the services, 268
Miller, William E., 42, 217
Millis, Walter, 261, 284, 285
Mills, C. Wright, 17, 258
Milne, Cecil P., 301
Minorities, 317
Minority rule, 325
  theory of, 334
Moley, Raymond, 153, 157

Monetary policies (*see* Fiscal and mone-
  tary policies)
Monsen, R. Joseph, 20
Montesquieu, 2
Monypenny, Philip, 5
Moos, Malcolm, 212
Mormons, 8
Morse, Wayne, 4, 91
Morstein-Marx, Fritz, 241
Morton, Thruston, 215
Muhammad, Elijah, 135, 145
Muhammad, Farrad, 145

National Association, for Advancement
  of Colored People, 134
  age, 141
  size, 141
  of Letter Carriers, 232, 234–235
  of Manufacturers, 18, 25, 26, 56, 311
National Commission on Teacher Education and Professional Standards,
  162
National Council for Accreditation of
  Teacher Education, 162
National Education Association, 157–
  160
  accreditation, 162
  administrators and employees, 170
  areas of agreement, 161
  collective bargaining, 157
  composed of, 157
  consensus, 158
  ideology, 160
  obligatory mediation, 160
  professional negotiations, 176
  professional sanctions, 158, 176
  "professionalism," 158
  salaries, 167
  school reforms, 176
  share in decision making, 164
  size, 154
  Utah resolution, 154, 157
National Education Association resolution on professional negotiations,
  158
National Farmers Union (*see* Farmers
  Union)
National Federation, of Federal Employees, 234
  of Independent Business, 27, 44

National Federation, of Postal Clerks, 235
National Grange (*see* Grange)
National Guard, 278
National Labor Relations Board, 242
National Merit Scholars, liberalization, 186
National Security Council, 268
National Security Industrial Association, 272
National Urban League, 134
  age, 143
  background, 143
National Wheat Referendum, 122
National Wool Grower's Association, 127
Navy League, 272
Neal, Warner, 208
Negotiation, 328
Negroes, 133–149
  background, 133
  central ideology, 148
  civil rights, 139–140
  education, 138
  housing, 138
  ideology, 135
  march on Washington, 147
  as power group, 313
  social legislation, 138–139, 148
  unemployment, 137–138
  unions, 137
  urban shift, 134
  voting rights, 139
  wages, 137
  white reaction, 146
Nehring, Earl, 217
Nelson, Dalmas, 227
Neustad, Richard, 196
New Deal, 242
  civil bureaucracy, 243
Newcomb, Theodore M., 85
Nigro, Felix A., 166
Nixon, Richard M., 69, 89, 182, 213
Northam, Harry E., 41
Novak, Michael, 191
Nowak, Stefan, 192

Occupation, 2, 329–331, 334
Odegard, Peter, 5, 329
O'Mahoney, Joseph C., 128

Overrepresentation, 12, 100
Oxford, Mississippi, 138

Pacifists, 263
Packers and Stockyards Act Amendment of 1958, 125
Paine, Thomas, 320
Pasnick, Raymond W., 162
Patterson, Samuel C., 73, 93
Patton, James G., 106
Peacock, Alan T., 325
Percy, Charles, 211, 212
Peterson, Arthur, 217
Phillips, Wendell, 3
Planned economy, labor ideology, 76
Plant, Walter T., 185
Plato, 2
Pluralism, 310, 325
  analytical pluralists, 3
  power groups, 335
Political access, 12, 13
Political activity, 42
Political campaigns, 15
Political parties, 9, 331
Political role of labor, traditional, 69
Political stethoscope, 41
Politicians, 331
Politics, shift in opinions, 185, 186
  sun-moon pattern, 208
Poole, Elijah, 145
Porter, Richard, 303
Post Office Department, 226, 233
Pound, Roscoe, 92
Power, defined, 10
  groups, 24
    brokerage of interests, 335
    dangers of success, 308–316
    defined, 6
  leadership, 11
  membership, 11
President, chief executive, 268
  civil bureaucracy, 231
Price controls, 34
  labor, 76–78
Price stability, 77
Productivity, agriculture, 122–125
  labor ideology, 81
Profits, business, 53
  labor, 81, 85, 86
  (*See also* Taxation)

Public relations, business, 24–26, 56–60
labor, 72–73, 87–93
propaganda, military bureaucracy, 274
Public school teachers, 150–176, 313
case of strike, 171
distribution of income, 151, 167–168
local school boards, 152
merit pay, 169
National Commission on Teacher Education and Professional Standards, 162
National Council for Accreditation of Teacher Education, 162
power struggle on three levels, 150
sanctions, 153
social legislation, 151
strikes, 153
transformation into power groups, 151
wages, 151, 167–168
(*See also* American Federation of Teachers; National Education Association)
Pusey, Nathan M., 178

Quayle, Oliver, 146

Radford, Arthur William, 300
Radway, Lawrence I., 283
Rand, Ayn, 180
Rand Corporation, 290
Randolph, A. Phillip, 147
Randolph, Bayard, 148
Randolph, Jennings, 91
Ransom, Harry Rowe, 284
Rayburn, Sam, 89, 211
Reciprocal Trade Agreement Act, 108
Redistricting, 12, 100
Reisel, Victor, 155, 164
Reisman, David, 6, 263
Religion, 2, 8, 329
Republican party, 181, 209, 332
Arts and Science Division, 217
ideology, 333
Reuther, Walter, 154, 219
Reynolds, Lloyd G., 97
Reynolds, W. M., 303
Rhee, Syngman, 295
Richards, Richard, 70
Rickover, Hyman George, 300

Ridgway, Matthew, 275
Riker, William H., 322
Ringel, William, 143
Robinson, Joan, 20
Rockefeller, Nelson, 62, 82
Rogers Act, 248
Romney, George, 62
Roosevelt, Eleanor, 211
Roosevelt, Franklin Delano, 56, 166, 195, 262, 327
Roosevelt, Theodore, 262, 283
Root, Elihu, 283
Rossiter, Clinton, 9, 181, 231
Rostow, W. W., 207
Rovere, Richard H., 180
Ruml, Beardsley, 209
Rural Electrification Administration, 238
Rusk, Dean, 263
Russia, 124
Rustin, Bayard, 147

Salinger, Pierre, 183
Samuelson, Paul A., 98, 197
Sanford, Nevitt, 185
Santangelo, Alfred Edward, 300
Sayre, Wallace S., 225, 245
Scanlon, John, 158, 160, 164
Scatterfield, John C., 136
Schattschneider, E. E., 3, 71, 318
Schenk, Peter J., 302
Schlesinger, Arthur M., Jr., 21, 195, 196, 209
School boards, collective pressure technique, 159
consensus, 160
distrust of, 163
obligatory mediation, 160
threat to authority, 166
Schriftgiesser, Karl L., 27, 47
Schultz, Theodore W., 203
Schumpeter, Joseph A., 180
Scoville, John, 60
Scranton, William, 62
Secretary of Defense, 289
Securities and Exchange Commission, 242
Senate, United States, 14
Seniority system, 13
Senter, Raymond D., 274
Shannon, Fred A., 102

Shelley, John, 90
Shelley Bill, 90
Sherman Antitrust Act, 48
Shuman, Charles, 122
Simon, Herbert A., 240
Slichter, Sumner H., 68
Small business, 43–46
    committee, 43
    ideology, 26
Smith, Adam, 3, 8, 28
Smith, Walter Bedell, 259
Smith v. Allwright, 140
Smith-Lever Act, 114
Snow, Charles, 184
Social legislation, classical business, 31
    Farm Bureau, 118
    Farmers Union, 107
    Grange, 113
    intellectuals, 199
    labor ideology, 79
    managerial, 47
    Negroes, 138–139, 148
    public school teachers, 151
Social lobby, 13
Sorenson, Ted, 196
Southern Christian Leadership Conference, 134
    age, 142
    size, 142
Spero, Sterling D., 153, 156
Sputnik I, 151
Stanton, Frank, 219
Stein, Harold, 247
Stender, John, 211
Stevenson, Adlai, 69, 183, 190
Stigler, George, 324
Stinnett, T. M., 158
Stringfellow, Douglas, 216
Student Non-Violent Coordinating Committee, 134
    background, 144
Supreme Court, 133
Sutton, Francis X, 28
Swados, Harvey, 147
Swigert, J. Mack, 74

Taft, Phillip, 69
Taft-Hartley Act, 49, 56, 60
Tariffs, 87
    classical business, 37–38

Tariffs, Farm Bureau, 119
    Farmers Union, 107–108
    Grange, 113
    intellectuals, 206–208
    managerial, 54, 55
    (*See also* International trade)
Taxation, 326
    classical business, 34
    Farm Bureau, 117
    Farmers Union, 105–107
    Grange, 111
    intellectuals, 205
    labor ideology, 85
    managerial, 50–51
Taylor, John, 320
Teacher evaluation, 168
Teachers (*see* Public school teachers)
Tennessee Valley Authority, 118, 233, 242
Theobald, John J., 173
Thompson, Robert G., 332
Thurmond, Strom, 183
Tillett, Paul, 178
Trade (*see* International trade)
Trade associations, 24
Treasury Department, 226, 233
Trowbridge, Frederick Newell, 301
Truman, David B., 3, 5, 12, 109, 114, 231
Truman, Harry, 60, 253
Tucson, Arizona, 266
Turner, Henry A., 181
Twain, Mark, 3
Twining, Nathan F., 304

Unemployment, classical business, 36
    Farm Bureau, 118
    Farmers Union, 107
    Grange, 111
    intellectuals, 203
    labor, 83
    managerial, 53
    military, 265
    Negroes, 137–138
Unions, 70
    Federal employees, 234–236
    hierarchies, 68
    members, 66
    Negroes, 137
    strategies, 94
    (*See also* Labor)

United Federation of Postal Clerks, 234, 235
United States (*see* specific government organizations, i.e., Agriculture Dept., F.B.I., Justice Dept.)
US News and World Report, 66
United States Steel, 50
Universal Military Training, 268
Utah Cattlemen's Association, 127
Utah resolution, NEA, 154, 157
Utah State Farm Bureau, 127

Veterans Associations, 273
Veterans of Foreign Wars, 273
Veterans organizations and the military bureaucracy, 273
Vieg, John A., 231
von Clausewitz, Karl, 293

Wages, classical business, 34
    Farm Bureau, 118
    Farmers Unions, 107
    Grange, 112, 113
    intellectuals, 199
    labor, 80
    managerial, 48, 49
    Negroes, 137
    public school teachers, 151, 167–168
Wagner, Robert, 153, 173
Wagner Act, 56
Wahlke, John C., 318–319
Wakefield, Dan, 83
Walker, Wyatt, 142
Wallace, George, 203
Wallace, Henry, 183

Warner, W. Lloyd, 6, 246
Warters, Jane, 11
Washington representatives, 24, 63
Watkins, A. V., 126
Wealth (*see* Income distribution)
Webb, James, E., 253
Weber, Max, 222, 239, 240
Webster, Harold, 186
Weinstein, Leo, 3
Welby, Lord, 223
Welch, Robert, 193
Welfare measures (*see* Social legislation)
Westcott, Jay, 265
Western Electric Company, 303
Western States Meat Packers Association, 127
Whetten, James L., 277
White, Helen C., 191
White, William S., 14
Wilkins, Roy, 134, 135, 139
Wilkinson, Ernest L., 213
Wilson, Charles E., 190
Wilson, Francis G., 7
Wilson, Woodrow, 262, 275
Witte, Edwin E., 190
Woll, Peter, 229, 243
Working conditions, labor ideology, 80
Workweek, labor ideology, 82
Wright, Deil, 255
Wuerthner, J. J., 26

Yee, Robert, 182
Young, Whitney, 134, 143

Zeigler, L. Harmon, 45, 109, 230